The Writer's Response

A READING-BASED APPROACH TO WRITING

SIXTH EDITION

Stephen McDonald
Palomar College

William Salomone
Palomar College

Sonia Gutiérrez
Palomar College

Martin Japtok
Palomar College

D1736698

CENGAGE
Learning®

Australia • Brazil • Mexico • Singapore • United Kingdom • United States

CENGAGE
Learning®

The Writer's Response A Reading-Based Approach to Writing, Sixth edition
Stephen McDonald, William Salomone, Sonia Gutiérrez, and Martin Japtok

Product Director: Nicole Lloyd

Product Manager: Andrew Rawson

Content Developer: Brittany Miller

Associate Content Developer: Jacob Schott

Marketing Manager: Necco McKinley

IP Analyst: Ann Hoffman

IP Project Manager: Sarah Shainwald

Manufacturing Planner: Betsy Donaghey

Art and Design Direction, Production Management, and Composition: Cenveo® Publisher Services

Cover Image: ©Robert Cock/Getty Images

For product information and technology assistance, contact us at
Cengage Learning Customer & Sales Support, 1-800-354-9706.

For permission to use material from this text or product, submit all requests online at **www.cengage.com/permissions.**
Further permissions questions can be e-mailed to
permissionrequest@cengage.com.

Library of Congress Control Number: 2015946510

Student Edition:
ISBN: 978-1-305-10025-1

Loose-Leaf Edition:
ISBN: 978-1-305-96048-0

Cengage Learning
20 Channel Center Street
Boston, MA 02210
USA

Cengage Learning is a leading provider of customized learning solutions with employees residing in nearly 40 different countries and sales in more than 125 countries around the world. Find your local representative at **www.cengage.com.**

Cengage Learning products are represented in Canada by Nelson Education, Ltd.

To learn more about Cengage Learning Solutions, visit **www.cengage.com.**

Purchase any of our products at your local college store or at our preferred online store **www.cengagebrain.com.**

Printed in the United States of America

Print Number: 01   Print Year: 2015

Contents

Readings Listed by Rhetorical Mode

Articles that illustrate several modes may appear more than once.

Narration

Without Emotion, G. Gordon Liddy

Jailbreak Marriage, Gail Sheehy

In Defense of Voluntary Euthanasia, Sidney Hook

Anonymous Sources, Tina Dirmann

The Neglected Suicide Epidemic, Emily Greenhouse

Comparison-Contrast

Not-So-Social Media: Why People Have Stopped Talking on Phones, Alan Greenblatt

What American Has Gained, What America Has Lost, George Packer

Public Universities Should Be Free, Aaron Bady

Online Dating and Relationships, Aaron Smith and Maeve Duggan

Overwhelmed and Creeped Out, Ann Friedman

Is Internet Addiction a Real Thing? Maria Konnikoa

Searching Online May Make You Think You're Smarter Than You Are, Poncie Rutsch

Definition

Jailbreak Marriage, Gail Sheehy

It's None of Your Business: The Challenges of Getting Public Information for the Public, Kathleen Carroll

What American Has Gained, What America Has Lost, George Packer

Uncle Sam Doesn't Always Want You, Mark Arax

Public Universities Should Be Free, Aaron Bady

For Better, For Worse: Marriage Means Something Different Now, Stephanie Coontz

Is Internet Addiction a Real Thing? Maria Konnikoa

Dream Machines, Will Wright

Are You Living Mindlessly? Michael Ryan

Why Competition? Alfie Kohn

Division and Classification

Three Passions I Have Lived For, Bertrand Russell

How to Stay Alive, Art Hoppe

Killing Women: A Pop-Music Tradition, John Hamerlinck

Let Them Eat Dog, Jonathan Safran Foer

Online Dating and Relationships, Aaron Smith and Maeve Duggan

Overwhelmed and Creeped Out, Ann Friedman

Are You Living Mindlessly? Michael Ryan

It's Good Enough for Me: The Renaissance in Children's Programming, Emily Nussbaum

Illustration

Anonymous Sources, Tina Dirmann

How to Stay Alive, Art Hoppe

Printed Noise, George Will

Ordinary People Produce Extraordinary Results, Paul Rogat Loeb

Not-So-Social Media: Why People Have Stopped Talking on Phones, Alan Greenblatt

Killing Women: A Pop-Music Tradition, John Hamerlinck

Male Fixations, Dave Barry

Dropping the "T": Trans Rights in the Marriage Era, Emily Greenhouse

The Neglected Suicide Epidemic, Emily Greenhouse

It's None of Your Business: The Challenges of Getting Public Information for the Public, Kathleen Carroll

Preface

The premise of *The Writer's Response* is that it is nearly impossible to write well without also reading well, that college courses today demand not only that students write clearly and read accurately but also that they write effectively *about* what they have read. *The Writer's Response* is designed as an introductory text to academic writing, the type of writing based on the careful, deliberate reading and the clear, critical thinking demanded of students throughout their college careers.

THE REASON FOR THIS TEXT

WRITING IN RESPONSE TO READING

College courses outside of our English departments rarely ask students to write personal experience essays, nor do they ask students to write papers on topics *similar* to those they have read in some textbook. Rather, such classes more often ask that students write papers and essays in direct response to ideas they have encountered in assigned reading. Such writing assignments demand careful reading and clear summary. They demand that students be able to recognize and respond to specific points in the material they have read, to synthesize ideas from several reading selections, and to evaluate and to argue about the ideas they have found in their reading material. *The Writer's Response* introduces students to these and other skills they will need to write successful college-level papers.

USING PERSONAL EXPERIENCE

Although *The Writer's Response* introduces students to academic writing, it does not at all ignore the importance of their personal experiences, nor does it fail to recognize that writing about themselves is often the best way for writers to find their own voices and to discover that they do indeed have something to say. For this reason, the assignments throughout *The Writer's Response* ask students to use personal experience to respond to the material they have read in the text when it is appropriate to do so. Chapters 1–4 in particular emphasize personal responses. Then, when the students are writing more directly *about* what they have read in Chapters 5–8, optional assignments allow instructors to assign personal experience responses when they want to do so.

ABOUT THE TEXT

The Writer's Response integrates reading, writing, sentence combining, and editing. Its writing instruction is kept simple and clear, and its reading selections consist of over sixty short articles, most of which are both recent and timely in their subject matter.

ORGANIZATION

Part One: The Reading-Writing Conversation

Part One, consisting of the first four chapters, introduces students to the reading and writing processes and to the concepts of unity, coherence, and development. Each of these chapters contains a variety of reading selections to illustrate the points being made and to provide material that students can respond to using their own personal experience. In these first four chapters we want students to become comfortable with the writing process and familiar with the elements of well-written paragraphs and essays. At the same time, we want students to become careful readers and to recognize that accurate reading is an integral part of clear thinking and good writing.

Part Two: Writing about Reading

Part Two consists of four chapters that introduce students to ways of writing about what they have read. We start Part Two with a chapter on how to write brief summaries, extended summaries, and summary-response essays because so often students have trouble doing much more than identifying the central idea of what they have read. Writing the summary gives them practice in recognizing and expressing both the central idea and the supporting points of a reading selection. We then move to a chapter on evaluating the effectiveness of material they read. In this chapter students must read accurately as well as explain why they have or have not found a selection convincing, persuasive, or effective. In the next chapter, students synthesize the issues involved in several reading selections. Here, students must not only summarize what they have read but also recognize connections among reading selections and explain those connections in their papers. The final chapter of Part Two asks students to argue from several reading selections, using material from a number of brief articles to support their positions.

Part Three: Editing Skills

Part Three of *The Writer's Response* is meant to act as a supplement to the primary instruction provided in Parts One and Two. It serves as a brief handbook for those students who need help with grammar, punctuation, or usage problems, and it allows the instructor to cover such material as needed. We have arranged it as a separate part of the text rather than spreading its material throughout each chapter so that the student can quickly and conveniently use it as an aid in the editing process.

Part Four: Additional Readings for Writing

Part Four includes ten reading selections for the instructor to use in addition to those in the body of the text. These reading selections offer groups of related articles that can be used as multiple sources for synthesis or argument papers or that can be read and responded to individually. All of the reading selections reflect the criteria discussed below.

Appendix: Writing the Research Paper

The Appendix covers the writing of a research paper for those instructors who prefer to assign a full research paper at this level. We discuss choosing a topic, developing a thesis, doing the research using library services (including the Internet and library online subscription services), integrating research into the paper, and using MLA documentation methods. The Appendix also includes a sample student research paper.

FEATURES

The Reading Selections

In choosing the reading selections for *The Writer's Response*, we have kept several criteria in mind. First, we wanted most of the selections to be relatively brief since this text is, after all, an introduction to academic writing. For that reason, the majority of the selections are only a few pages in length. However, we also wanted our students to have to "stretch" their mental muscles at times, so we have included some longer, more complex articles for instructors to use as they see fit. Second, we wanted the reading selections to be both timely and interesting, appealing to as wide a range of students as possible. To achieve this end, we have chosen articles that challenge the students to think about who they are as well as about how they fit into our complex world. Titles ranging from "Are You Living Mindlessly?" to "How Racist Is Online Dating" to "Why You Should Think Twice before Shaming Anyone on Social Media" to "Education Is Not a Luxury" reflect the variety of topics to be found in this text. Finally, to allow for the kind of synthesis and argument that *The Writer's Response* is meant to encourage, we have included several articles grouped around common topics, such as "Online Worlds: Friend or Foe?," "Should Drugs Be Legalized?," "Should the Minimum Legal Drinking Age Be Lowered?," "Physician-Assisted Suicide," and "Online Dating."

Evaluating Sample Student Papers

In addition to writing instruction and brief reading selections, each of the chapters in Parts One and Two includes a section on evaluating sample student papers. This section has two purposes. First, it is designed to provide students with "models" of successful papers that can be used to discuss what is expected of well-written paragraphs or essays. Second, it is meant to teach students to distinguish between successful and less successful papers so that they can better evaluate the effectiveness of their own writing.

Sentence Combining

Each chapter in Parts One and Two includes a section on sentence combining. Since so many student writers rely primarily upon compound and relatively brief complex sentences, the sentence combining sections are designed to give students practice in writing sentences that move beyond the patterns they are most comfortable with. Beginning with simple exercises in recognizing when modifiers in one sentence can easily be "embedded" within another sentence, these sections gradually introduce more difficult sentence structures involving the use of coordination, parallelism, subordination, participial phrases, appositives, and sentence variety.

Group Work

Throughout the text, exercises and writing assignments encourage students to work together, discussing the reading selections, comparing their responses to those selections, and helping each other develop their papers. While individual instructors will, of course, use such group work as they see fit, we have found it to be an invaluable teaching device, helping students clarify their own thinking as they work with those around them.

NEW TO THIS EDITION

In this sixth edition of *The Writer's Response*, we have made the following improvements:

- We have added eighteen new reading selections, covering topics ranging from the marginalization of transgender people ("Dropping the "T": Trans Rights in the Marriage Era," Chapter 3) to an argument that public universities should not charge tuition ("Public Universities Should Be Free," Chapter 6), to an examination of the world of online dating ("Overwhelmed and Creeped Out," Chapter 7).
- We have updated the Appendix, "Writing the Research Paper," to reflect the latest changes in the *MLA Style Manual*. This Appendix covers how to choose topics; how to do the research, including making full use of the Internet; how to evaluate researched material; how to integrate researched paraphrases and quotations; and how to use MLA documentation within the text as well as on a Works Cited page. The Appendix also includes a sample student research paper.
- We have replaced 50 percent of the exercises in "Part Three: Editing Skills."
- We have replaced 50 percent of the sentence-combining exercises in Parts One and Two of the text.
- As in all previous editions, cultural diversity and reactions to it are emphasized in articles throughout the text.

INSTRUCTOR'S MANUAL

The Instructor's Manual for *The Writer's Response* provides suggestions for teaching the course on a chapter-by-chapter basis and offers comments about the reading selections. It also includes answers to all exercises in the text.

ACKNOWLEDGMENTS

We want to thank our friends and colleagues at Palomar College for their encouragement and support as we have revised this text. We particularly wish to acknowledge the many English instructors at Palomar College who have taken the time to suggest ideas or respond to our questions about the text.

We also wish to extend our gratitude to the many professionals at Cengage who have worked with us on this text, especially Andrew Rawson and Brittany Miller, who have assisted us in many ways as we navigated the revisions challenges of the text, and Margaret Bridges, who expertly coordinated the book's production.

We are especially grateful to the following students, who graciously allowed us to use their work as models for evaluation: Nancy Kwan, Rosemarie Tejidor, Amy Duran, Gabriel Borges, Sherrie Kolb, Brian Schmitz, Alicia Sanchez, Rosendo Orozco, Luis David Maciel, Jung Yun Park, Araceli Bautista-Meza, Scott Tyler, Desiree Gharakanian, Jeannie Atwood, Jeannine Welch, Dylan Greening, Yasunari Hatanaka, Nathan Jeffries, Xiomara Salazar, Danielle Colon, Elizabeth Harding, Tracy Thornton, Lisa Brand, Alison Martin, Rourke Stockel, Ray Serrato, Junior Monta, Justin John, and Ryan Roleson.

Finally, we are grateful to the following professors who took their time to provide valuable input for this text.

Sixth Edition Reviewers:

Annmarie Chiarini, *Community College of Baltimore County-Essex*
Tom Leal, *Diablo Valley College*
Annette Mewborn, *Tidewater Community College*
Lee Ritscher, *Hartnell College*
Mauricio Rodriguez, *El Paso Community College*
Victoria Sansome, *San Jose State University*
Lisa Schulze, *Lone Star College-North Harris*
Sarah Vallejo, *Los Medanos College*

Stephen McDonald
William Salomone
Sonia Gutierrez
Martin Japtok

DEDICATION

With love to George and Joan McDonald,
Kathryn and Michelle Salomone,
Nagadya Japtok,
and Estela and Francisco Gutiérrez

Part One

The Reading-Writing Conversation

Have you ever talked to someone who wouldn't listen or listened to someone who just rambled on and on without making a clear point? Probably you tried not to have many more conversations with that person. After all, in a conversation, both listening well and speaking clearly are important, and a poor listener or a confusing speaker is not a very enjoyable person to talk to.

Writing and reading are very much like speaking and listening. When you read, you listen to what someone else has to say; when you write, you speak your own ideas. Together, reading and writing make a conversation between the reader and the writer, and a poor reader or a poor writer can pretty much spoil that conversation.

As students in college classes, you will be asked to participate in this reading-writing conversation by writing in response to what you read. Depending on the instructor or the class, you might be asked to summarize the ideas you have found in textbooks, to analyze topics after reading about them, to evaluate opinions expressed by a writer, to define concepts discussed in several articles, or to respond in any number of other ways to what you have read.

Obviously, to write clearly and accurately in response to what you have read, you need to read clearly and accurately too. Part One of this text will help you work on both activities at the same time—clear and accurate reading and writing.

Writing with a Central Idea

THE WRITING PROCESS

Writing is a messy business. It is full of stops and starts and sudden turns and reversals. In fact, writing an essay can sometimes be one of the most confusing, frustrating experiences a college student will encounter. Fortunately, writing does not have to be a horrible experience. Like almost anything in life, writing becomes much easier as you become familiar with the "process" that makes up the act of writing.

Writing is often called a *recursive process*. This means that the many steps to writing an effective paper do not necessarily follow neatly one after the other. In fact, often you will find yourself repeating the same step a number of different times, in a number of different places, as you write a paper. For example, you might jot down notes on scratch paper before you start writing your first draft, but at any time while you write, you might stop to jot down more notes or to rethink what you are writing. To help yourself understand this writing process, think of it as being divided roughly into three stages: **prewriting**, **writing**, and **rewriting**.

PREWRITING

Prewriting involves anything you do to help yourself decide what your central idea is or what details, examples, reasons, or content you will include. Freewriting, brainstorming, and clustering (discussed later) are types of prewriting. Thinking, talking to other people, reading related material, outlining or organizing ideas—all are forms of prewriting. Obviously, you can prewrite at *any* time in the writing process. Whenever you want to think up new material, simply stop what you are doing and start using one of the techniques you will study in this chapter.

WRITING

The writing stage of the process involves the actual writing out of a draft. Unfortunately, many people try to start their writing here, without sufficient prewriting. As you may know from firsthand experience, trying to start out this way usually leads directly to a good case of writer's block. During this stage of the writing process, you should be ready to do more prewriting whenever you hit a snag or cannot think of what to write next.

REWRITING

Rewriting consists of revising and editing. You should plan to revise every paper you write. When you *revise*, you examine the entire draft to change what needs to be changed and to add what needs to be added. Perhaps parts of your paper will need to be reorganized, reworded, or thoroughly rewritten to express your ideas clearly. Perhaps your paper will need more examples or clearer explanations. Unfortunately, people pressed for time often skip this stage, and the result is a poorly written paper. Finally, after you have revised your work, you must edit it. When you *edit*, you correct spelling, grammar, and punctuation errors. A word of warning: do not confuse editing with revising. Merely correcting the spelling, grammar, and punctuation of a poorly written paper will not make much difference in the overall quality of the paper.

PREWRITING: FROM WRITER'S BLOCK TO WRITING

Have you ever had a writing assignment that absolutely stumped you? Have you ever found yourself *stuck*, staring at a blank sheet of paper for fifteen minutes (or thirty? or sixty?), wondering what in the world you could write to meet the assignment?

If you have not had this experience, you are a lucky person. Certainly almost everyone knows the frustrated, sinking feeling that comes as minute after minute passes and nothing seems to get written. In fact, for many writers, *getting started* is the most agonizing part of the entire writing process.

What we're talking about here is **writer's block**, a problem as common to professional writers as it is to student writers. Because it is so common, you need to learn how to get past it quickly and painlessly so that you can get on with your assignment. Here are a few prewriting techniques to help you.

FREEWRITING

Because writer's block means that you aren't writing, one of the quickest ways to get around it is to write anything at all, a technique called *freewriting*. You can write whatever you are thinking, feeling, wondering about, or trying to get out of your mind—just start writing.

Look at the *Zits* cartoon that opens this chapter. Jeremy, like many online writers, uses a form of freewriting as he writes his blog. (A *blog*, short for *weblog*, is a form of online journal.) He does not sit down wondering what to write. Instead, he writes about whatever is on his mind—in this case, his conversation with his mother.

When freewriting, don't stop to correct spelling, grammar, punctuation, or other elements of the writing. Set a time limit for yourself—five or ten minutes—and just keep writing. Here is how some freewriting might look from a person who was asked to write a paper explaining how a significant event affected his or her life:

> An event that affected my life. What event could I choose? There haven't been a lot of things that have really affected me. The death of Heidi did, I guess. My marriage, of course. Having a child. What else? How about when I was a child? I don't remember much that really affected me from then. No big traumatic events or anything. Nothing particularly wonderful either. How about in elementary or high school? Well—Heidi's death, like I said. My mom's alcoholism. That's a big event. I wonder how it affected me. I wasn't really home all that much then. I wonder if it counts as an "event." Something major. I'm trying to think of something major. How about moving to Boulder? That was big event for me. I'd never been away from home for so long. Yes. I like that one.

As you can see, freewriting is very informal. Notice that the above freewriting moves from questions ("What event could I choose?") to answers that the writer might be able to use in a paper ("The death of Heidi," "My marriage," "My mom's alcoholism," "Moving to Boulder"). This movement—from searching for ideas that you might use to focusing on possible topics—is very common in freewriting.

BRAINSTORMING

Brainstorming is similar to freewriting in that you write down whatever ideas come to mind. Don't censor or correct them. However, in this case, write the ideas in **list** form. Don't be surprised if you find one technique—brainstorming or freewriting—working better than the other. Use the one you find most productive. Here's an example, again responding to an assignment to explain how a significant event affected your life:

Heidi's death
- depressed me
- made me feel guilty
- made me love my life more
- helped me realize how short life can be
- made me reevaluate how I was living my life

Mom's alcoholism
- I was angry at her
- I avoided her
- I wouldn't talk to her when she was drinking
- I avoided going home
- I was embarrassed to be out with her

Moving to Boulder
- extreme loneliness
- didn't talk to anyone for days
- had to learn how to meet people
- had to learn to organize my time
- learned to balance play time with class time
- rethought my religious beliefs
- learned to value my friends more
- became stronger and more independent
- discovered what I wanted to major in
- saw the effects of drug and alcohol abuse
- helped me define myself
- learned to love nature even more

As you can see, brainstorming might help you discover which topic will provide the most ideas and details. The writer of the above lists can see that he has quite a few thoughts about his experiences in Boulder, so he chose that topic for his paper.

CLUSTERING

A third technique to help you generate ideas is called *clustering*. It differs from brainstorming and freewriting in that what you write is almost like an informal map. To cluster your ideas, start with a topic or question and draw a circle around it. Then connect related ideas to that circle and continue in that way. Look at the following example of clustering using the topic "How Moving to Boulder Affected Me." As you can see, clustering provides a mental picture of the ideas you generate. As a result, it can help you organize your material as you think of it.

Freewriting, brainstorming, and clustering are only three of many techniques to help you get past writer's block. When you use them, you should feel free to move from one to the other at any time. And, of course, your instructor may suggest other ways to help you get started. Whatever technique you use, the point is to start writing. Do your thinking on paper (or at a computer), not while you are staring out the window. Here's something to remember whenever you have a writing assignment due: **Think in ink.**

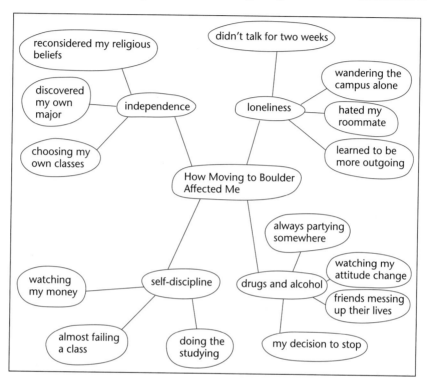

READINGS

Read the following articles. Then practice your prewriting techniques by responding to the questions at the end of each article.

Live Each Moment for What It's Worth   ERMA BOMBECK

Until her death, Erma Bombeck was one of the most popular newspaper columnists in the United States. Her humorous stories about the everyday events of her life were often full of wisdom and insight. In this brief essay, she reminds us all of an important life lesson.

BEFORE YOU READ

1. Look up the expression *carpe diem* in a dictionary. What does it mean? What do you think about that expression as an approach to life?

2. Where would you like to go, what would you like to do, or whom would you like to see if you had the time or were not as busy as

you are? What prevents you from going to those places, doing those things, or seeing those people?

I have a friend who lives by a three-word philosophy, "Seize the moment." Just possibly, she might be the wisest woman on this planet. Too many people put off something that brings them joy just because they haven't thought about it, don't have it on their schedule, didn't know it was coming, or are too rigid to depart from the routine.   1

I got to thinking one day about all those women on the *Titanic* who passed up dessert at dinner that fateful night in an effort to "cut back." From then on, I've tried to be a little more flexible.   2

How many women out there will eat at home because their husband suggested they go out to dinner AFTER something had been thawed? Does the word *refrigerator* have no meaning for you?   3

How often have your kids dropped in to talk and sat there in silence while you watched *Jeopardy*?   4

I cannot count the times I called my sister and said, "How about going to lunch in half an hour?" She would gasp and stammer, "I can't." Check one: "I have clothes on the line." "My hair is dirty." "I wish I had known yesterday." "I had a late breakfast." "It looks like rain." And my personal favorite, "It's Monday." She died a few years ago. *We never did have lunch.*   5

Because Americans cram so much into our lives, we tend to schedule our headaches. We live on a sparse diet of promises we make to ourselves when all the conditions are perfect. We'll go back and visit the grandparents ... when we get Stevie toilet-trained. We'll entertain ... when we replace *the carpet in the living room.* We'll go on a second honeymoon ... when we get two more kids out of college.   6

Life has a way of accelerating as we get older. The days get shorter and the list of promises to ourselves gets longer. One morning we awaken and all we have to show for our lives is a litany of "I'm going to," "I plan on," and "Someday when things are settled down a bit."   7

When anyone calls my "seize the moment" friend, she is open to *adventure, available for trips and keeps an open mind* on new ideas. Her enthusiasm for life is contagious. *You can talk to her for five minutes* and you're ready to trade your bad feet for a pair of roller blades and skip an elevator for a *bungi* cord.   8

My lips have not touched ice cream in 10 years. I love ice cream. It's just that I might as well apply it directly to my hips with a spatula and eliminate the digestive process.   9

The other day I stopped the car and bought a triple-decker.   10
If my car hit an iceberg on the way home, *I'd have* died happy.

PREWRITING PRACTICE

1. Freewrite for five minutes (or for a time specified by your instructor) to react to Bombeck's article in any way that you want. Write whatever comes to your mind.

2. Discuss your freewriting with other members of your class. Did they have similar responses?

3. Respond to one of the following questions by using the prewriting techniques of freewriting, brainstorming, and/or clustering:

   a. What does Erma Bombeck mean by "seize the moment"? Do you live by that philosophy, or do you avoid doing things that are spontaneous or unscheduled? Give some examples to illustrate your response.

   b. Think about your friends, relatives, and acquaintances. Do any of them "seize the moment"? Do any of them carefully avoid living in a spontaneous way? Describe people you know who do or do not "seize the moment."

4. Discuss your responses to the above questions with other members of your class. Explain to them why you or people you know do or do not "seize the moment."

Without Emotion
                                                            G. GORDON LIDDY

The following selection, drawn from G. Gordon Liddy's autobiography, narrates an experience from his childhood. As you read it, consider your reactions to the events he describes. Do they offend you? Do you find them understandable given the circumstances of the times?

BEFORE YOU READ

1. What do you make of the title "Without Emotion"? What does it make you expect to find in the reading selection?

2. Who is G. Gordon Liddy? If you don't know, ask other members of your class or your instructor. Does his background affect how you read this selection?

Squirrel hunting was a popular sport in West Caldwell in the   1
1940s. I loaded my homemade rifle, cocked the spring, and waited
on the steps of the porch. A squirrel was in the top of the pear
tree. I raised the rifle. The movement startled the squirrel and
he jumped to the oak tree and froze as I stepped off the porch. I
sighted along the side of the barrel, aimed for the squirrel's head,
and fired.

I missed the squirrel's head and gut-shot him. Bravely, he clung   2
to the tree as long as he could, then started to come down,
clutching piteously at branches as he fell, wounded mortally.

I didn't know it, but the shot alerted my mother. She watched   3
the furry creature's descent until it fell to the ground and I shot it
again, this time through the head at point-blank range, to put it out
of its suffering, then cut off its tail to tie to the handlebars of my
bicycle as an ornament.

When I came into the house my mother told me reproach-   4
fully that she had seen from the kitchen window the suffering I had
caused. I went off and wept. The dying squirrel haunted me. I kept
seeing it fall, clutching and clawing from what must have been a
terribly painful wound. I was furious with myself—not because I'd
caused the pain, though I regretted that, but because I hadn't been
able to kill without emotion. How could I expect to be a soldier in
the war? I had to do something to free myself from this disabling
emotionalism.

I cast about for an idea and found it across the street. Bill Jaco-   5
bus's father, to help combat the wartime food shortage and to
supplement rationing, had built a chicken coop in his backyard. He
and his son used to butcher the chickens, then drain, scald, pluck,
and clean them for sale.

I asked young Bill if I could help kill the chickens. He was glad   6
to have the help. He showed me how to grasp the bird in such
a way as to have control of both wings and feet, lay its neck on
an upended stump, and then decapitate it with one chop of an
ax held in the other hand. Bill explained that the shock made the
corpse convulse and, if I let go, the body would run about, wings
flapping, and bruise the meat. I'd need to control the corpse until
the shock wore off and the limp body could be hung up by the
feet to drain the remaining blood. I should wear my old clothes.

Using the ax tentatively rather than making a bold stroke, I   7
made a mess of my first chicken kill; it took me a number of chops
to get the head off. The bird slipped out of my grasp and half
flew, half jumped about, blood spurting from its neck all over me
and everything else in range. Bill was good about it and gave me
another chance.

I got better at it, and over a period of time I killed and killed   8
and killed, getting less and less bloody, swifter and swifter, surer
with my ax stroke until, finally, I could kill efficiently and without
emotion or thought. I was satisfied: when it came my turn to go to
war, I would be ready. I could kill as I could run—like a machine.

PREWRITING PRACTICE

1. Freewrite for five minutes (or for a time specified by your instructor) to react to Liddy's article in any way that you want. Write whatever comes to your mind.

2. Discuss your freewriting with other members of your class. Did they have similar responses?

3. Respond to one of the following questions by using the prewriting techniques of freewriting, brainstorming, and/or clustering:

   a. Did your feelings or thoughts change as you moved from the start of this article to the end of it? If so, what parts of the article caused them to change?

   b. Have you ever had to act "without emotion"? Describe any time you can remember when you had to repress or ignore your emotions.

4. Discuss your responses to the above questions with other members of your class. Did they develop ideas that had not occurred to you?

Anonymous Sources

TINA DIRMANN

Tina Dirmann is a Pulitzer Prize finalist in the breaking news category. She is a feature writer and regular contributor to the Los Angeles Times, Orange Coast *magazine, and* USA Today. *Dirmann is the author of two crime books,* Vanished at Sea *and* Such Good Boys.

BEFORE YOU READ

1. What do you believe "anonymous sources" refers to?

2. If you had $870,000 to donate, how would you effectively distribute your money?

Yazmin Adams never thought homelessness was something she'd have to worry about. But there she was, at just 18, pushed from the only home she'd ever known. And scared to death. [1]

Her family struggled after her mother lost a battle with lupus. Alone, her dad's paychecks barely covered rent on their small apartment in the Adams district of Los Angeles. A steep rent hike and an eviction followed. A relative took in her dad and little brother, but Adams spent evenings sleeping on the couches, and sometimes floors, of friends until the welcomes wore out. "I was embarrassed, you know?" she recalls. "And I was scared to ask anyone for help." Then came her saving grace: a $2,000 check, enough to cover two months' rent on a new apartment in Riverside, where the living was cheaper, and to buy a bed, linens, a few dishes and a shower curtain. [2]

Her benefactor? Two complete strangers. "I couldn't believe it," 3
Adams says of her gift. "They didn't even know me, and yet they
did so much for me."

And that's the point of the Pass It Along program, launched 4
eight years ago by two wealthy businessmen who, motivated
by nothing more than a gratefulness at their own success in life,
wanted to give back by helping people teetering on the brink. The
two donors put their money where their hearts were and gave
$870,000 to the California Community Foundation, leaving it to
the organization to find people most in need.

CCF, which was founded by L.A. civic icon Joseph Sartori in 5
1915, specializes in administering funds for a full range of charities
supporting educational opportunities, health-care needs, neighborhood revitalization projects and artistic development. Last year,
the CCF, led by president and CEO Antonia Hernández (who ran
MALDEF—the Mexican American Legal Defense and Educational
Fund—for 25 years), granted charities $228.4 million, largely col-
lected from wealthy individuals and companies. But rarely are
those funds available directly to individuals in crisis. In other words,
checks had always gone to the homeless shelters, not to the person about to become homeless.

Mindful of that gap in the charitable community, the donors 6
directed CCF to set up a system for doling out money straight
to a person in dire straits. The grant winner must, however, be
referred to CCF through one of hundreds of charities the foundation has worked with through the years.

Unlike most donors, the Pass It Along benefactors wanted 7
their names left off all public paperwork—no awards, no accolades,
no words of thanks. They didn't even try to explain what moved
them to such generosity. Nearly a decade later, they have chosen
to remain anonymous.

By any name, the concept hits home. "Some believe the high- 8
est form of giving is someone who gives anonymously, who doesn't
want to be thanked or who gives with no strings," says Amy Fack-
elmann, senior philanthropic adviser for CCF.

Adams herself still wonders about all the mystery. "I'm so curi- 9
ous to know why they didn't want to be known. I'm sure they have
their reasons, and I respect that. But I wish I could meet them and
just say, 'Thank you for everything.'"

The Pass It Along grants aren't exactly without strings. In fact, each 10
award winner has to agree to pay back the generosity. But not with
cash. Just with kindness. "These are people who are barely hanging on

in life," says Gregory Shepard, CCF's donor fund operations specialist. "We know that. So we don't ask for the money back. We ask the recipient to return the favor by doing something nice for someone else—cook for an elderly neighbor, go grocery shopping for someone housebound, befriend someone lonely. Just pay it forward."

Adams, who was nominated through the California Conservation Corps, a job-training program, even had to sign a certificate when she received her check, promising to live up to her end of the bargain. And she did, waking up at 5 every morning to commute from Riverside to Los Angeles for job training at the corps, then donating the last two hours of her workdays to a preschool. She enjoyed the volunteer work so much that on weekends she began tutoring at the elementary school her little brother attends. 11

All that was just over a year ago. Today, Adams still volunteers at her brother's school; that experience landed her a paying job at a preschool, and on the side, she attends Los Angeles Trade Tech College, where she is working toward her AA in child development. "I had no problem giving back, because someone gave to me," she says, tearing up at the thought of where she would have been if that small financial gift hadn't been there to pull her through. 12

A clinical social worker at the Venice Family Clinic, the largest free clinic in the United States, Steve Artiga has referred several of his clients to the program and seen firsthand how Pass It Along can change a life: "So frequently, people don't need major government help. They just need this boost in life, something to keep them from going under. Their needs may be so small, but the payoff is so big." 13

William Linartes, a onetime hardened gang member, still gets emotional when he recalls the day Artiga told him he was an award recipient. Linartes, 29, received funds to buy a computer and a printer—tools he needed so he could quit gang life for good and return to school. He was tired of a life spent in and out of jail—and, before that, juvenile hall—on an assortment of robbery, assault and counterfeiting convictions. 14

On top of that, at age six, Linartes learned he suffered from neurofibromatosis, more crudely known as Elephant Man disease, a nod to the story about a tragically disfigured man afflicted with an illness that causes tumors to develop throughout the body. Linartes is one of the lucky ones: Of the hundreds of tumors that have developed in his body since childhood, just one—in his pelvis—has been cancerous. That was nine years ago. He's cancer free today, which is a dual triumph. It means he has already lived a year longer than his mother, who died at 28 of the same disease. 15

After beating the cancer, Linartes vowed he'd do more with   16
the life he almost lost. He faltered a few times in the beginning,
once landing back in jail. But eventually, his social worker convinced
him to go back to school and apply for the $1,500 Pass It Along
grant that covered the cost of his computer equipment. "I just realized someone made an investment in me even I wasn't willing to
make," he says. "That never happened before. But because they did,
I won't let them down. Nothing can hold me back now." Today, Linartes carries a 3.5 GPA at Santa Monica Community College. In his
free time, he volunteers as a delivery driver for Meals on Wheels.

Such dramatic life turnarounds do sound a little too good to   17
be true. There are plenty who renege on their promise to pay it
forward. After all, the entire program runs on nothing more than
the honor system. But remarkably, most do not shirk their responsibility. And that, according to CCF officials, goes to show what a
little tender loving care can do when extended to those not used
to receiving such random acts of kindness.

Today, after eight years and 392 grants totaling $844,000, the   18
program that has meant so much to so many may be on the verge
of disappearing for good. With less than $30,000 left in the Pass It
Along account, administrators of the program expected it to run
out by early 2009. Then in January of this year, the original donor
contributed another $100,000 to keep the fund going. The second
donor has moved on, now working in other charitable capacities.
They are aware of all the lives they've helped turn around and are
hopeful others will pick up the baton and contribute funds to keep
the concept going. Even with the influx of new money, the fund is
still in jeopardy of extinction.

For now, all CCF administrators can do is cling to that same   19
kind of faith, hoping a new donor will step in as soon as possible to
breathe new life into a program that has inspired so much goodness. "We need someone with a philanthropic heart," Shepard says.
"Someone who can see we are helping not only the neediest of
the needy but people who really want to help themselves. Then
once they are stable, they turn around and help someone else.
And that's pretty special."

PREWRITING PRACTICE

1. Freewrite for five minutes (or for a time specified by your instructor)
   to react to Dirmann's article in any way that you want. Write whatever
   comes to your mind.
2. Discuss your freewriting with other members of your class. Did they
   have similar responses?

3. Respond to one of the following questions by using the prewriting techniques of freewriting, brainstorming, and/or clustering:

   a. Tina Dirmann begins, "Yasmin Adams never thought homelessness was something she'd have to worry about. But there she was, at just 18, pushed from the only home she'd ever known. And scared to death." With no money and no place to go, what would you do if you were stripped from the place you called home?

   b. In the middle of her article, Dirmann writes, "William Linartes, a onetime hardened gang member, still gets emotional when he recalls the day Artiga told him he was an award recipient. Linartes, 29, received funds to buy a computer and a printer—tools he needed so he could quit gang life for good and return to school." With a $1,500 Pass It Along grant, what would you buy? Or whom would you give that money to?

   c. Consider the following passage from Dirmann's article: "The Pass It Along grants aren't exactly without strings. In fact, each award winner has to agree to pay back the generosity. But not with cash. Just with kindness." What do you think of the Pass It Along repayment plan?

4. Discuss your responses to the above questions with other members of your class. Explain to them why you responded as you did. Respond sensitively to their ideas.

PREWRITING: CHOOSING A PRELIMINARY TOPIC SENTENCE OR THESIS STATEMENT

Once you have developed some ideas by using the prewriting techniques discussed so far, you are ready to decide on the topic and central idea of your paper and to focus those two elements into a *topic sentence* (for a single paragraph) or a *thesis statement* (for an entire essay). Your ability to write clear topic sentences or thesis statements can determine whether or not your readers will understand and be able to follow the points you want to make in the papers you write. In college classes, that ability can make the difference between a successful paper and one that is barely passing (or not passing at all).

FINDING THE TOPIC

In academic writing, deciding upon the topic of your paper is often not very difficult because it is assigned by your instructor. You may be asked to write about child abuse or a piece of literature or a particular political issue—but rarely (if ever) will your assignment simply be to "write about something." Of course, many times you may be asked to choose your own topic, but even then you will know which topics are appropriate and which are not. (For example, in a class studying the history of the Arab-Jewish tension in the Middle East, you probably would not choose state lotteries as the topic of your paper, right?)

FINDING THE CENTRAL IDEA

This is where many student writers get stuck. The problem is not "What is my topic?" but "What should I be *saying* about my topic?" For example, if you were asked to write a paragraph or essay explaining how an event in your life affected you, you might decide on an event easily enough, but you might not have any idea *how* it affected you. To put it another way, you wouldn't know what your *central idea* is, so how could you possibly write a topic sentence or a thesis statement? How do you decide what your central idea is? Here are two suggestions:

1. *Read your prewriting to find a central idea.*   As you examine your prewriting, watch for recurring ideas or for any idea that sparks your interest. For example, in the prewriting on pages 5, 6, and 7, you might notice that the writer listed a variety of ways his move to Boulder affected him. A preliminary central idea might be expressed this way:

central idea

> My move to Boulder, Colorado, to go to school <u>affected me in many ways</u>.

2. *Start writing your first draft to find a central idea.*   You may have been taught in the past that you should not even *start* writing until you have focused your central idea into a topic sentence or thesis statement—and you might have found that such advice led you right back to a good case of writer's block. Certainly, it would be convenient if you could simply sit down, think up a perfect topic sentence or thesis statement, and start writing, but the process of writing is just not that neat and orderly. So if you are not sure what your central idea is but do have details or ideas you want to write about, just start writing about them. Many times your precise, central idea will develop while you write.

FORMING THE PRELIMINARY TOPIC SENTENCE OR THESIS STATEMENT

Once you are somewhat sure what your topic and central idea will be, write them as a single sentence. If your assignment is to write one paragraph, this sentence will serve as its topic sentence. If you are writing an essay, this sentence will serve as its thesis statement. In either case, it will state the topic and central idea of the assignment. As you prepare this sentence, keep these points in mind:

1. *Make a statement that demands explanation. Do not merely state a fact.*   Because a central idea demands some explanation, argument, or development, a simple statement of fact will not work as a topic sentence or thesis statement. Note the difference between the following two statements:

FACT	Several years ago I moved to Boulder, Colorado, to go to school.
DEMANDS EXPLANATION	My move to Boulder, Colorado, to go to school changed the way I think about my parents.

2. *Make a limited statement that can be reasonably supported with facts or examples. Do not be too general, vague, or broad.*   Very general topic sentences and thesis statements result in very general papers. When you choose a topic and a central idea, *limit* your choice to something that can be covered in detail.

          broad topic   **vague central idea**

INEFFECTIVE   Many events have affected my life.

The sentence above commits the writer to discussing *many* events from his or her life (a very broad topic), and its central idea could refer to any changes at all—from insignificant to life-changing.

          limited topic   **vague central idea**

INEFFECTIVE   My move to Boulder, Colorado, to go to school was very
              interesting.

In the above sentence, the topic "My move to Boulder, Colorado, to go to school" is limited well enough, but the central idea—that the move was "interesting"—is much too vague.

          limited topic

EFFECTIVE   My move to Boulder, Colorado, to go to school caused me

          limited central idea
       to change in ways that would affect the rest of my life.

The statement above would work as a topic sentence for an extended paragraph or a thesis statement for an essay because it is focused on a limited topic (*My move to Boulder, Colorado, to go to school*) and because its central idea (*caused me to change in ways that would affect the rest of my life*) could be fully explained in one assignment.

EXERCISE 1.1

Examine each of the following sentences. If the sentence would be an effective topic sentence or thesis statement, underline its topic once and its central idea twice. If the sentence would not be an effective topic sentence or thesis statement, explain why not.

EXAMPLES

Many children today own cell phones and iPads.
   Not effective because it merely states a fact.

This paper will be about children watching too many hours of TV.
   Not effective because its topic and central idea are too general.

<u>Spending too much time in front of a TV, computer, or tablet</u> <u>can negatively affect a child's physical health.</u>
   Effective because the topic is quite limited, and the central idea demands explanation and support.

1. Smoking causes cancer.
2. Public schools should require school uniforms.
3. This paper will be about rape culture.
4. John and Paco went to the NSA rally.
5. Eminem and Rihanna's "Love the Way You Lie" presents misogynistic lyrics.
6. Misogynistic lyrics promote violent behavior in American society.
7. Several of my friends are dangerously distracted by smartphones and other handheld devices when they drive a car.
8. *NCIS*, a spinoff from *JAG*, premiered on September 23, 2003, on CBS.
9. Several recent studies attempt to prove that saturated fat is actually good for you.
10. Environmental actions will help improve our society.

EXERCISE 1.2

Look at the writing assignments on pages 26–27. With them in mind, reread the prewriting you did in response to the prewriting questions at the end of "Live Each Moment for What It's Worth," "Without Emotion," or "Anonymous Sources." Write a sentence that you could use either as a preliminary topic sentence for a paragraph or as a preliminary thesis statement for an essay. Compare your results with those of other members of your class to determine which sentences contain specific topics and clear central ideas.

PLACING THE TOPIC SENTENCE OR THESIS STATEMENT

As we mentioned above, the primary difference between a topic sentence and a thesis statement is that the topic sentence identifies the central idea of a paragraph and the thesis statement does the same for an essay. As you will see in Chapter 2, topic sentences and thesis statements can appear in many places, depending on the purpose of a particular piece of writing. However, in college classes you will be writing academic papers, and in almost all academic writing the topic sentences and thesis statements must be placed carefully.

1. *Place the topic sentence at the start of the paragraph.* Although there are exceptions, the first sentence of most academic paragraphs should be the topic sentence. The body of the paragraph should explain and support that topic sentence. (See Chapter 3 for a discussion of support within a paragraph.)

topic sentence | **One serious problem for many newly arrived immigrants is that they do not speak English well, if they speak it at all.** For example, when my parents left Hong Kong in 1972 and came to America, they couldn't understand what people were saying, so they didn't know how to respond to them. Not knowing how to speak English was a horrible experience for them. Because everything was in English, they couldn't even watch TV, go to the store, or read the newspaper. The only thing they could do at that time was to stay home. One of the most terrible experiences that my mom had happened when she got lost while trying to pick me up at school. Because she didn't speak English, she couldn't even ask for directions, so she just drove around in circles for hours. Although people in the neighborhood tried to help her, my mom just couldn't understand what they were saying. One group of people just pointed and laughed as my mom drove by. After that experience she said, "If I don't learn to speak English soon, people will take advantage of me all the time."

Nancy Kwan, student writer

2. *Place the thesis statement at the end of the introductory paragraph* . Again, there are many exceptions, as you will see in Chapter 2, but the thesis statement in most academic essays appears as the last sentence of the introductory paragraph. (See Chapter 3 for a discussion of writing introductory paragraphs.)

Does "happily ever after" really exist? For years, love books, love movies and love stories have made us believe that someday we will find a true love—one special person to spend the rest of our lives with. In "For Better, For Worse, Marriage Means Something Different Now," Stephanie Coontz claims that marriage today is not treated as seriously as it once was. Many people tend to get married on an impulse; as a result, most marriages do not seem to last. However, there are still those select few people who follow traditional customs of marriage. **To have a successful marriage, couples might consider keeping up with some elements that may make their marital relation strong and stable such as happiness, trust, and respect.**

thesis statement

Xiomara Salazar, student writer

PREWRITING: PREPARING A ROUGH OUTLINE

If you have ever been required to turn in a complete outline of a paper before the final paper was due, you know how difficult—even impossible, sometimes—it is to predict exactly what you will include in a paper, much less what *order* it will follow. So rest easy—although preparing a *rough outline* is part of the prewriting process, it is not at all the same as writing a complete, perfect, formal outline. Instead, it involves looking at what you have written so far in your prewriting, deciding what ideas you *may* use, and listing those ideas in the order in which you will *probably* use them. Essentially, you are trying to give yourself some direction before you start writing the first draft.

GROUPING RELATED POINTS

Let's continue to use the topic of "How My Move to Boulder, Colorado, Affected Me" as an example of how to write the rough outline. The first step is to look at the prewriting on pages 5–7 and group any details that seem related. (You might notice, by the way, that the clustering example has already grouped some of them.) They could be organized this way:

Group A	Group B	Group C	Group D
chose my own classes	didn't talk for two weeks	alcohol and drug use	learning to study watching my own money
discovered my own major	wandered the campus alone	watched my attitude change	almost failing a class
reconsidered my religious beliefs	hated my roommate	went to lots of parties	
	learned to be more outgoing	friends messed up their lives	
		decided to stop	

IDENTIFYING GROUP TOPICS

Once you have grouped the details you want to include, you need to identify the topic that each group seems to focus on. This step is particularly important if you are writing an essay rather than a paragraph. Because each group will most likely be developed into a separate paragraph, the topic of each group will help form its topic sentence.

Group Topics	
Group A:	Learning to think for myself
Group B:	Learning how to deal with loneliness
Group C:	Learning how to deal with drugs and alcohol
Group D:	Learning self-discipline

CHOOSING A TENTATIVE ORGANIZATION

After grouping the details and identifying their topics, you need to decide in what order you will discuss them. Here are three common ways to organize your material.

Emphatic Order

If you think some of your details should receive more emphasis than others because they are more important, complex, colorful, or memorable, arrange them so that they move from the least important to the most important. This type of organization will leave your readers with a strong impression of your most effective details.

For example, when organizing the above material about moving to Colorado, the writer might decide to save Group A for last because the idea of learning to think for himself is most important to him. On the other hand, another writer might choose to save Group C for last because learning not to abuse alcohol or drugs was a powerful, life-changing lesson.

Chronological Order

Chronological order presents details in the order they actually occurred. Whatever occurred first is discussed first, whatever occurred second is discussed second, and so on. This type of organization is effective when you want to describe an event or explain how something happened. If the first major change that affected the writer who moved to Boulder, Colorado, was the sense of loneliness he experienced, then he would present Group B first.

Spatial Order

Spatial order consists of describing a place or an object in such a way that a reader can clearly picture the various details and their relationship to one another. One way to do so is to describe the larger elements of a scene first, identifying where they are in relation to other elements, and then moving to a description of the smaller details. The writer of the paper about moving to Boulder, Colorado, would not use spatial order because he is not describing a place or an object.

EXERCISE **1.3**

Using the prewriting you did for "Live Each Moment for What It's Worth," "Without Emotion," or "Anonymous Sources," group the ideas or examples that you have developed so far into a rough outline, identify the topic of each group, and decide on a tentative organization. If you need to, do more prewriting to develop more details.

WRITING: THE FIRST DRAFT

If you have a preliminary topic sentence or thesis statement and have prepared a rough outline, you have everything you need to write your paper. So now is the time to sit and write. However, now is still *not* the time to worry about whether everything is spelled exactly right or worded perfectly. If you try to write your first draft and avoid all errors at the same time, you will end up right back where you probably started—stuck. Of course, you can correct some errors as they occur, but don't make revising or editing your primary concern at this point. What you want to do *now* is to write out your ideas. You can "fix" them later.

THE SINGLE PARAGRAPH: A FIRST DRAFT

If your assignment is to write one paragraph, open the paragraph with your *preliminary topic sentence*. Then use the details from your rough outline to explain and support the central idea of your topic sentence. Here is the first draft of a paragraph about the effects of moving to Boulder, Colorado, to go to school.

preliminary topic
sentence

> **My move to Boulder, Colorado, to go to school affected me in several ways.** First, when I arrived, I was very lonely, so I had to learn to deal with that. I wandered around the campus for weeks without speaking to anyone. After a while I learned to be more outgoing by talking to people in the lobby of my dorm. I also had to learn to be more disciplined about my study habits as well as my spending habits. Because there was no one to tell me to do my homework, I almost failed my physics class, and I spent the money that was supposed to last for a month in the first two weeks I was there. My parents were not very happy when I had to phone home for more money so soon. As the year away from home went by, I began to feel more and more independent. I realized that I had chosen engineering as a major to please my dad, not because I was interested in it. My new independent attitude helped me find the major I really loved, which was journalism. I even found myself rethinking the religious beliefs I was raised with. Some of them I kept, but others I left behind. As I look back over my year in Colorado, I think what it really taught me was to take responsibility for my own life.

EXERCISE 1.4

Respond to the following questions:

1. What is the central idea of the paragraph? Where is it stated?
2. Which of the organizational patterns from pages 20–21 is the writer using?
3. What details that appear in the rough outline on page 20 has the writer left out?
4. What idea in the final sentence could be used to improve the central idea of the preliminary topic sentence?
5. What advice would you give this writer to improve his paragraph?

THE BRIEF ESSAY: A FIRST DRAFT

If you are writing an essay, open your draft with an introductory paragraph that ends with a *preliminary thesis statement*. Then start each body paragraph with a *preliminary topic sentence* that supports or explains the central idea of the thesis statement.

preliminary thesis
statement

preliminary topic
sentence

preliminary topic
sentence

> A few years ago I had the opportunity to go to school in Boulder, Colorado. I had always lived in San Diego, California, so this move was a big change for me. **As I look back on it today, I realize that moving to Boulder to go to school affected me in several ways.**
>
> First, when I arrived, I was very lonely, so I had to learn to deal with that. **I wandered around the campus for weeks without speaking to anyone. After a while I learned to be more outgoing by talking to people in the lobby of my dorm.**
>
> I also had to learn to be more disciplined about my study habits as well as my spending habits. **Because there was no one to tell me to do my homework,**

I almost failed my physics class, and I spent the money that was supposed to last for a month in the first two weeks I was there. My parents were not very happy when I had to phone home for more money so soon.

preliminary topic sentence

As the year away from home went by, I began to feel more and more independent. I realized that I had chosen engineering as a major to please my dad, not because I was interested in it. My new independent attitude helped me find the major I really loved, which was journalism. I even found myself rethinking the religious beliefs I was raised with. Some of them I kept, but others I left behind.

As I look back over my time in Colorado, I think what it really taught me was to take responsibility for my own life.

EXERCISE 1.5

Respond to the following questions:

1. What is the central idea of the essay? Where is it stated?
2. What is the central idea of each preliminary topic sentence?
3. What would you add to each body paragraph to expand and develop it?

REWRITING: REVISING AND EDITING

REVISING

As we mentioned at the start of the chapter, rewriting consists of two stages: revising and editing. Unfortunately, many people—especially if they are pressed for time—omit the revising stage and move directly to editing, often with disastrous results.

The problem is that editing will correct grammar, spelling, and punctuation errors *without* improving either the content or the organization of your paper, and these larger areas do need to be addressed before you submit your work. Now is the time to *read* what you have written, *think* about it, and *decide* what changes you should make. Here are some suggestions.

1. *Refine your topic sentence or thesis statement.*   Usually, writing the first draft of a paper will help you become more specific about what your central idea really is. In fact, if you look at the concluding sentences of your first draft, you will often find a statement that sums up your central idea better than your preliminary topic sentence or thesis statement did.

When the writer of the first draft about the move to Colorado read the last sentence of the draft, he realized that *taking responsibility for my own life* was the central idea that tied all three points together. When you read the revised draft below, note how he refined the central idea.

2. *Reorganize your material.*   The writer of the above first draft reorganized the groups of details (A, B, C, D) listed on page 20 so that they appear in the

order B, D, A (leaving out Group C). This reorganization allowed the writer to follow a chronological pattern.

3. *Add details.*   One of the most effective ways to improve a paper is to add more specific and descriptive details to illustrate the points you are making. Note how the writer has added details to the draft below.

4. *Reword sentences.*   Many times you will find that your original wording of sentences can be improved. Note the changes made in the middle of the revised draft below.

THE SINGLE PARAGRAPH: REVISED DRAFT

Here is a revised version of the paragraph on page 22. Changes are shown in boldface.

<table>
<tr>
<td>refined topic sentence</td>
<td rowspan="6">My move to Boulder, Colorado, to go to school taught me to take responsibility for my own life. My first lesson occurred soon after I arrived. I didn't know a soul, so I wandered from my classrooms to the cafeteria to the library for weeks without speaking to anyone. When I realized that no one was going to introduce himself to me, I took responsibility for my own life and introduced myself to a guy reading a magazine in the lobby of my dorm. I also had to take responsibility for my own study and spending habits. Because there was no one to tell me to do my homework, I kept putting it off to go to parties. As a result, I almost failed my physics class. To make things worse, I spent the money that was supposed to last for a month in the first two weeks I was there. My parents were not very happy when I had to phone home for more money so soon. Finally, as the first year away from home went by, I learned to take responsibility for my own interests and values. I realized that I had chosen engineering as a major to please my dad, not because I was interested in it. My new attitude helped me find the major I really loved, which was journalism. I even found myself rethinking the religious beliefs I was raised with. Some of them I kept, but others I left behind. As I look back over my time in Colorado, I can say for sure that is where I learned to take responsibility for myself.</td>
</tr>
<tr>
<td>reworded sentences and added details</td>
</tr>
<tr>
<td>added details</td>
</tr>
<tr>
<td>reworded sentences</td>
</tr>
</table>

EXERCISE 1.6

Identify the central idea in the topic sentence. Then point out words throughout the paragraph that emphasize that central idea.

THE BRIEF ESSAY: REVISED DRAFT

Here is a revised version of the brief essay on page 22. Changes are shown in boldface.

expanded introduction	A few years ago I had the opportunity to go to school in Boulder, Colorado. None of my friends from my home in San Diego were going with me. I would be living in a dorm with people I had never met before, so I knew I was in for some big adjustments. **As I look back on it today, I realize that moving to Boulder to go to school was my first step in learning to take responsibility for my own life.**
refined thesis statement refined topic sentence	**My first lesson occurred soon after I arrived.** I didn't know a soul except for my roommate, and I really disliked him. So I wandered from my classrooms to the cafeteria to the library for weeks without speaking to anyone. When I realized that no one was going to introduce himself to me, I took responsibility for my own life and introduced myself to Marty, a guy reading a magazine in the lobby of my dorm. He ended up becoming one of my closest friends.
added details	
refined topic sentence added details	**I also had to take responsibility for my own study and spending habits.** Because there was no one to tell me to do my homework, I kept putting it off to go to parties with Marty. (He was from Denver, so he knew a lot of people at our school in Boulder.) As a result, I almost failed my physics class. To make things worse, I spent the money that was supposed to last for a month in the first two weeks I was there. My parents were not very happy when I had to phone home for more money so soon.
refined topic sentence	**Finally, as the first year away from home went by, I learned to take responsibility for my own interests and values.** I realized that I had chosen engineering as a major to please my dad, not because I was interested in it. My new attitude helped me find the major I really loved, which was journalism. I even found myself rethinking the religious beliefs I was raised with. Some of them I kept, but others I left behind.
expanded conclusion	As I look back over my time in Colorado, I can say for sure that is where I learned to take responsibility for myself. Some of my learning experiences were painful, but they all helped me to grow and become the person I am today.

EXERCISE 1.7

Identify the central idea in the thesis statement. Then point out words in the topic sentences of the body paragraphs and in the details of each paragraph that emphasize the central idea.

Editing

Now for the final step. You need to edit your draft before submitting your final copy. Read over your draft carefully, looking for spelling, grammar, and punctuation errors. Use your spell checker, but don't rely on it to catch every error. Many words used incorrectly (such as *there* instead of *their*) will not be highlighted by a spell checker. When you are satisfied with your draft, print it—and then do what every professional writer does: *Read the hard copy with a pen in hand, looking closely for errors you might have missed.*

Once you have corrected any errors and are satisfied with the final product, prepare a clean copy (double-spaced) and submit it to your instructor.

WRITING ASSIGNMENTS

WRITING WITH A CENTRAL IDEA

Write a paragraph or a short essay, whichever your instructor assigns, in response to one of the following assignments. If you write a paragraph, be sure to include a topic sentence. If you write an essay, include a thesis statement.

1. After reading "Live Each Moment for What It's Worth," write a paper in response to one of the following suggestions:

    a. Explain whether you do or do not live by the "seize the moment" philosophy. As you give examples to illustrate the type of person you are, be sure to make clear what you think about your approach to life.

    b. What do you think about Bombeck's idea that we should "seize the moment" more often? Give examples from your own life or from the lives of friends, relatives, and acquaintances to illustrate and explain your reaction.

    c. Discuss this article with your classmates or with people you know outside of class. Have any of them "seized the moment" in ways that you particularly admire? Describe one or more of those people, making it clear how they have lived by Bombeck's philosophy.

2. After reading "Without Emotion," write a paper in response to one of the following suggestions:

    a. If your reactions to G. Gordon Liddy or to the events in the article changed as you read it, explain which parts of the article caused your reactions to change.

    b. If you have found that at times you have had to repress or ignore your emotions, write a paper in which you describe specific situations that have caused you to do so.

    c. Interview other members of your class about this article. How did they react to it? Write a paper in which you explain the different types of reactions you discovered.

3. After reading "Anonymous Sources," write a paper in response to one of the following suggestions:

    a. Has giving been an important part of your life? Have you ever donated your time, money, or clothing to an organization? If you have, choose one particular incident that you remember vividly. Briefly describe it and then explain why or how you were affected. Give examples to illustrate your points.

    b. Choose a random act of kindness that affected you deeply; that somehow changed how you think or feel; that helped you become a different person. Briefly describe the event and then explain in what ways you were changed by it. Give examples to illustrate your points.

    c. Choose a meaningful quotation from the article. Explain what the quotation means to you, and then illustrate its truth with examples from your own life or the lives of people you know.

   4. Write a paper in response to one of the articles in Part Four, as assigned by your instructor.

EVALUATING SAMPLE PAPERS

At one time or another, most students have had the experience of turning in a paper they were *sure* they had done a good job on, only to have it returned a few class meetings later with a grade much lower than they expected. Even professional writers have had the disappointing experience of having their manuscripts returned by editors with less-than-favorable responses. Perhaps you can *never* be 100% sure that your writing is perfect, but you can *greatly* improve the odds of submitting a successful paper if you learn how to judge the quality of what you have written.

One way to become a good judge of your own writing is to practice judging what others have written. You can get such practice by evaluating sample papers. In this text, each chapter will provide you with several student paragraphs and essays. Practice your judging skills by using the following checklist (or a format provided by your instructor) to determine which paper is the most effective. If your instructor asks you to, use the same checklist to evaluate the papers of some of your fellow students.

STUDENT MODEL CHECKLIST

   1. Thesis statement or topic sentence:

     a. If you are reading an essay, underline the thesis statement and circle its central idea. If you are reading a single paragraph, underline the topic sentence and circle its central idea.

     b. Can the thesis statement or topic sentence be more exact or specific? Is it too broad? Should the thesis statement or topic sentence be revised to incorporate a term used in the last few sentences of the paper?

     c. Rank the overall effectiveness of the thesis statement or topic sentence:

1	2	3	4	5	6
ineffective					excellent

   2. Support:

Look at the examples used. Do they refer to specific personal experiences and exact details, or are they general and vague? Rank the overall effectiveness of the examples:

1	2	3	4	5	6
general and vague			specific and detailed		

3. Organization:

Can you tell where one idea or example ends and another begins? Rank the clarity of the organization:

1   2   3   4   5   6

unclear, confusing   clear

4. Spelling, punctuation, grammar:

Underline or circle any spelling, punctuation, or grammar errors that you find. Rank the effectiveness of the spelling, punctuation, and grammar:

1   2   3   4   5   6

ineffective   excellent

5. Rank the overall effectiveness of the paper:

1   2   3   4   5   6

ineffective   excellent

SAMPLE STUDENT PAPERS

The following paragraphs and essays were submitted as first drafts that would later be revised. To evaluate these papers, follow these steps:

1. Read the *entire* paper through before making any judgments about it.
2. Reread the paper to identify its topic sentence or thesis statement.
3. Identify the major sections of the paper.
4. Respond to the items on the student model checklist or to questions provided by your instructor.

PARAGRAPHS

The students who wrote the following papers were asked to write a 250- to 300-word paragraph responding to one of the writing assignments on pages 26–27.

Student Paragraph 1

My interpretation of Erma Bombeck's "seize the moment" is that one should live his or her life to the fullest. If some opportunity crosses your pathway you need to jump on it. A "just go for it" type of attitude is necessary. In my own life, I see this being needed in three areas. The first area is being able to have the "just go for it" attitude no matter what the cost. Who knows if I will have the chance to ever go to that place or do that something ever again. I tend to have too much to do to be able to drop everything and seize the moment. Also, now everything tends to cost so much money and I don't have the resources to pay the expenses. The second problem I have is the lack of ability to stand up for and tell people what I believe in.

That is the perfect time to seize the moment, express your feelings and tell people your personal views. You might help other people to understand, learn, and grow. So, it's important to stand up strong and speak out whenever you are given the opportunity. For me, I struggle when I tell people about how God has changed my life. The last problem I have deals with grabbing job opportunities to move up in the working world. My employer demands a lot from me, and I should be able to stand up for my rights and demand things as well. I also need to jump on any opportunity to move up or to take on different responsibilities. So, these are the three problems I have with the quote "seize the moment." However, I do believe people need to seize the moment whenever given the opportunity. Never let it slip by, because once its gone who knows if you will ever have the opportunity again.

Student Paragraph 2

The article "Without Emotion" stirred up a few unpleasant feelings inside of me that I certainly was not expecting. When I first started this article and read about how the author went outside, lifted his rifle, and shot a small defenseless squirrel, I felt very horrified and sad. Still, I was able to make it okay in my head because he was only a boy and all kids do mean things. Then he went on and wrote, that after his mother had told him it was wrong to kill things it made him cry. This made me feel very relieved to know that he didn't really enjoy causing pain to another creature. It was certainly a shock to me when I read that he wasn't crying because of the pain he had inflicted, but because he couldn't shoot the squirrel without feelings. I felt sick to my stomach at this point and I actually did not want to continue reading. My curiosity lead me to the next surprise which was him wanting to kill chickens so that he wouldn't feel anything. By this time the author could have said just about anything and it still wouldn't have shocked me. However, I did become a little scared and I was even more frightened when I read that he was able to kill and not feel bad. I wasn't only afraid of him doing the killing, but mainly of him wanting to do the killing. At the end of this horrible article I felt shivers inside of me and kept thinking of this person being out in the world with me. This article certainly did arouse quite a few negative feelings inside of me. It amazes me that such a short article could bother me so much.

Student Paragraph 3

After reading "Anonymous Sources," I was reminded of a humbling experience I had when I ran out of money in Tijuana. That weekend my father had given me money to get my hair and nails done for my graduation party. Once in Tijuana, everything went great—I got purple streaks in my hair, a cool haircut, and a manicure. Once I was done, I headed back to San Ysidro to get my car. As I walked back to the U.S., I felt like a goddess with my stylish purple locks until I reached the parking lot. That is when I realized I didn't have any money left to pay for my parking fee. I had used all my gift money and had forgotten about my car! So I did what I had never imagined I would ever have to do. Beg for money. When I approached a family, the woman ignored me and turned away. I was so embarrassed and could not believe I had gotten myself into this humiliating mess. I held back my tears and understood for the first time in my life what panhandlers must feel. After begging for money, finally, someone listened to me—a young man empathized with me and gave me $20, which was enough money to cover the parking fee. Even though I don't know the young man's name, I will never forget his act of kindness. When I am out on the street, I make sure I return that favor. Twice I have allowed strangers to use my cell phone, and I see the same brightened facial expression I must had that day I stood penniless at the San Ysidro Parking Lot.

BRIEF ESSAYS

The students who wrote the following papers were asked to write a brief essay responding to one of the writing assignments on pages 26–27.

Student Essay 1

I have always been the kind of person who likes to take all opportunities. Erma Bombeck's "Live Each Moment for What It's Worth" could have been written about me. From an adventurous trip to a tropical country to hang gliding, mountain climbing, and bungee jumping. I've done them all.

I try to do everything possible to enjoy my life, and seize all moments, making the best out of them. My friend Alan is also like me. Last summer we went to Rio de Janeiro, and all we did was meet women and play volleyball. I'm happy for being a spontaneous person, it makes life less boring.

However, nothing beats the fear and adrenalin rush of a high altitude sport. I remember as if it was yesterday when my cousin asked me if I wanted to go hang gliding. I didn't think twice and I said yes. Hang gliding was a lot of fun and I'll never regret that day.

My cousin also took me mountain climbing. Although I didn't quite like being two thousand feet up on a mountain with a little rope tied around my waist and a heavy bag on my back, it was an experience I'll never forget.

The last of my crazy high altitude adventures was bungee jumping. Until last year I was eager to feel the wind going against my face and the adrenaline rush on a hundred mile per hour vertical dive. However, on November 25, about 3:30 P.M., I bungee jumped and turned into a human yo-yo.

As I finished reading the article "Live Each Moment for What It's Worth," I realized how important it is to take chances and seize the moment. There are opportunities that only come up once in a lifetime. People should take their chances because they might not get another one.

Student Essay 2

When I first read Liddy's "Without Emotion," I was horrified by his desire to kill without feeling anything. However, the more I thought about it, the more I realized that there have been times in my own life when I needed to act without feeling too. In fact, many times I have had to repress my personal feelings just to make it through an unpleasant experience.

For instance, in 1984 I had to face the realization that a divorce was in order. I had no emotional or financial support, and I had an eleven-month-old son to take care of. It was a time when emotions had to be shelved, temporarily, and all of my attention directed toward how I would handle the more pressing issues. Those issues being: food, shelter, clothing, and a job. I struggled through the transition from marriage to solo living by remaining unemotional and methodical. There would be time enough to process feelings once the necessary tasks were taken care of.

A few years later, after the divorce was final and I was well settled into the daily living as a single parent, I was laid off from a typesetting position with a local newspaper. This time, also, I did not allow myself the luxury of feeling frightened, not even for a minute. I immediately busied myself with the task of finding a job. I didn't take time to feel sad or to feel sorry for myself; I just proceeded with what needed to be done, never once allowing myself to give in to everyone's barrage of "What if's?"

I think Liddy was trying to get to a point where he could kill without feeling emotion if he had to. He was aware of the "kill or be killed" probability that faced him as a soldier. For me, it was either conquer the challenges that had befallen me or be conquered by them.

Student Essay 3

This essay was written in response to an assignment asking students to explain how an important life event affected them.

When my parents separated, it was a very difficult and tough time for not only myself but my whole family. It changed my life forever. Everything was going great, and then my parents began to fight. It seemed to be no big deal, but after weeks and weeks of fighting, I started to get scared. One morning my mom told my brother and me that she was going to move into our other house so my dad and her could have some time apart. Since that time about two years ago, my parents are still not the best of friends, and I still cry at night when I think about the situation. This whole event caused me a lot of pain, but I have learned to bring a lot of positive things out of the whole situation.

I've learned to not take things for granted and to cherish every single day and everyone I love. This event has made me realize that one day I may have everything I need but the next day it all could be lost. That was how I felt when my parents separated. The whole time I was growing up I thought I had the perfect family and I was the luckiest kid. The family trips together to Utah and Canada were the greatest, and I thought it would always be that way. This event made me change the way I felt. I felt I had lost everything I had loved. Now everyday I live that day as if the next may take some bad turn. I don't want to look back and wonder, "What if?"

Now if I have a problem or I see that someone else needs some help, I'm always the first to ask for help and the first to give. Two weeks ago one of my good friends was having some girl trouble, so I decided to ask him what was wrong. He told me that they had got into a fight, so I sat down and had a nice talk with him. I helped them solve their differences. Before this event happened, I felt afraid to talk about my problems or others' problems. Today, I am more open as a person. I really enjoy helping others during their troubled times.

This event made me feel like I can do more things on my own and not be dependent on everyone else all the time. I used to go places with others and have them help me with stuff I could have done on my own. Last week I went to a movie by myself where before this event I would have been afraid to go by myself. This event made me realize that everyone else won't always be there for me but that I should always be there for myself as well as for others.

At the beginning this was a very tough time for me, and it is still very hard to handle. It is a tough subject, but it has taught me a lot of great lessons that would have been hard for me to figure out. Don't get me wrong, I would give anything to have my family back the way it used to be, but I know that's never going to happen. So I'm really glad I was able to learn such a valuable lesson at an early age and take something out of my parents' separation other than anger and pain. Some people never have a chance to learn these valuable lessons. They can change the way you look at life.

SENTENCE COMBINING: EMBEDDING ADJECTIVES, ADVERBS, AND PREPOSITIONAL PHRASES

As you have worked through the writing process presented in this chapter, we hope you have discovered that good writing develops as you write. Many times, for instance, you will not know exactly what your central idea is until you have done a substantial amount of prewriting, and sometimes you may not know exactly how your ideas or paragraphs should be organized until you have tried one or two different organizations to see which works best. This willingness to make changes and to rethink material as you discover new ideas is at the heart of all good writing—and it works at the level of individual sentences as well as at the larger levels related to the central idea or the organization of a paper.

As you write the initial drafts of your papers, you will express your ideas in sentence structures that are comfortable to you because they reflect your personal style of writing. (You *do* have a personal style, even if you write very rarely.) However, as you become more and more proficient in using the writing process, you will find that you can improve your personal style. At the level of sentence structure, this improvement can include, among other things, recognizing when separate sentences contain related ideas that should be expressed in one sentence and learning how to use different types of sentence structures to express different ideas.

EXERCISE 1.8

To illustrate what we mean, let's compare the following versions of a passage drawn from an article by Lois Sweet titled "What's in a Name?

Quite a Lot." One passage is just as Lois Sweet wrote it. The other is written as a beginning writer might have written it. Which is which? How can you tell?

> 1 Over the years, a lot of my friends have changed their names. 2 A number of them began to take an interest in their cultural backgrounds. 3 Their parents had wanted to deny cultural differences. 4 As a result, their parents had anglicized their names. 5 My friends were horrified. 6 They had been pushed into the great bland melting pot. 7 They felt more like they were being drowned than saved. 8 For them, their culture was a source of pride. 9 They demanded recognition for their "ethnic" names.

> 1 Over the years, a lot of my friends have changed their names. 2 A number of them began to take an interest in their cultural backgrounds and became horrified that their parents had anglicized their names in an effort to deny cultural differences. 3 To my friends, being pushed into the great bland melting pot felt more like being drowned than saved. 4 Their culture was a source of pride and they demanded recognition for their "ethnic" names.

As you can see, these two versions are quite different from each other, although they both express the same ideas. The first version uses nine sentences and eighty-two words. The second version uses nearly the same number of words (seventy-five) but only four sentences.

The second version is Lois Sweet's original. In it, you can see a professional writer's ability to combine related ideas into sentences that are longer and more varied than those written by an inexperienced writer. In her version, Sweet has written in a single sentence (sentence 2) what it took three sentences (sentences 2, 3, and 4) for the first writer to express. And Sweet has written in two sentences (sentences 3 and 4) what the first writer expressed in four sentences (sentences 6, 7, 8, and 9). Of course, combining related ideas is a skill all writers have to some degree, no matter how experienced or inexperienced they may be. For example, when you see that two or more ideas are related, you probably combine them without thinking much about it. Would you write this?

> My brother is an auto mechanic. I asked my brother to fix my car. My car had not run properly for weeks.

Probably not. But you might express yourself in any one of these ways:

> My brother is an auto mechanic, so I asked him to fix my car because it had not run properly for weeks.

> I asked my brother, who is an auto mechanic, to fix my car because it had not run properly for weeks.

> Because my car had not run properly for weeks, I asked my brother, an auto mechanic, to fix it.

> I asked my brother to fix my car, which had not run properly for weeks, because he is an auto mechanic.

My car had not run properly for weeks, so I asked my brother to fix it because he is an auto mechanic.

Which sounds better to you? Each of the above sentences might work in your speech or in your writing, depending on the situation. The point is that you already can and do combine related ideas in many different ways. And with practice, you will become even better at what you already do.

EXERCISE 1.9

To see what we mean when we say you already know how to combine related ideas, rewrite the sentences below. Join those ideas that seem obviously related into sentences that make sense to you. Don't worry about getting the "right" answer—just combine the ideas that seem as if they should go together.

> The man drove to the lake. He drove impatiently. He finally arrived at the lake. He marveled at the lake. The lake was a greenish blue. The man walked toward the lake with his fishing gear. He walked quietly. He placed his fishing gear on a rock. The rock was enormous. He was consumed by the sounds. He heard birds. The birds were chirping. He saw a duck. The duck quacked. The duck waddled off. The man kneeled down on one knee. He touched the surface of the water with his fingers. The water was cool. The water was refreshing.

THE EMBEDDING PROCESS

One of the most common ways to combine ideas is to use adjectives and adverbs to modify other words. For instance, in the exercise above, if you described the man as "quietly" walking, you used *quietly* as an adverb. If you described the rock as an "enormous" rock, you used *enormous* as an adjective.

What's the difference? It is that adjectives modify nouns and pronouns while adverbs modify verbs, adjectives, and other adverbs. However, knowing these definitions is not as important here as recognizing when a word in one sentence is related to a word in another sentence.

In sentence combining, the act of placing words or phrases from one sentence into another is called *embedding*. Look at the following examples. Note how the underlined adjective or adverb in the second sentence can be embedded within the first sentence.

EXAMPLES

He touched the water with his fingers.

The water was <u>cool</u> and <u>refreshing.</u> (adjectives)
    He touched the <u>cool, refreshing</u> water with his fingers.

The duck waddled off.

It left <u>abruptly</u>. (adverb)
    The duck waddled off <u>abruptly</u>.

Prepositional phrases also modify words, so in a sense they are adjectives and adverbs too. You use them all of the time in your speech and in your writing. You use prepositional phrases when you write that you are from Costa Rica or at a concert or around the corner or across the lake.

Each prepositional phrase starts with a preposition and ends with a noun (or a pronoun), called the *object* of the preposition. Between the preposition and its object you may find modifiers. For example, in the prepositional phrase "from the tired old man," *from* is the preposition, *man* is the object, and the words between the two are modifiers.

preposition	modifiers	object of the preposition
from	the tired old	man

Here is a list of common prepositions:

above	before	for	on	under
across	behind	from	onto	until
after	below	in	over	up
among	beside	into	past	upon
around	between	in spite of	through	with
as	by	like	till	without
at	during	near	to	
because of	except	of	toward	

Prepositional phrases should be embedded in sentences they are related to, just as adjectives and adverbs should be. Look at the following examples:

EXAMPLES

The boy was happy.

The boy was at the lake. (prep. phrase)
   The boy at the lake was happy.

Edgar Allan Poe wrote a poem.

The poem is about a lake. (prep. phrase)

He wrote the poem in 1837. (prep. phrase)
   In 1837, Edgar Allan Poe wrote a poem about a lake.

EXERCISE 1.10

Rewrite each of the following groups of sentences into one sentence by embedding the underlined adjective, adverb, or prepositional phrase into the first sentence of the group.

EXAMPLE

We told stories.
We told stories around the campfire.

We told them <u>enthusiastically.</u>
The stories were <u>mythical.</u>
   We <u>enthusiastically</u> told <u>mythical</u> stories <u>around the campfire.</u>

1. Frida Kahlo painted self-portraits.
   Her paintings are <u>stunning.</u>
   She painted <u>obsessively.</u>
   She painted <u>in a blue house.</u>
   The house was <u>in Coyoacán, México.</u>

2. The photograph blew away.
   The photograph was <u>historic.</u>
   The photograph was <u>important.</u>
   It blew away <u>violently.</u>
   It blew <u>across a field.</u>

3. Diane Arbus photographed two sisters.
   Diane Arbus photographed them <u>artistically.</u>
   She photographed them <u>at a children's identical twin party.</u>
   She photographed them <u>in 1967.</u>
   The sisters are <u>eerie looking.</u>

4. Mark Twain was an author who wrote novels and stories.
   He was <u>witty.</u>
   He was <u>American.</u>
   He was <u>from Florida, Missouri.</u>
   His novels and stories were <u>about American life.</u>

5. The students wrote sentences.
   Their sentences were <u>descriptive.</u>
   Their sentences were <u>complete.</u>
   The students wrote <u>diligently.</u>
   The students wrote <u>before class.</u>

EXERCISE 1.11

Combine each of the following sets of sentences into one sentence by embedding adjectives, adverbs, and prepositional phrases.

1. Fanatics discuss episodes every Wednesday.
   They are fanatics of *Star Trek*.
   The episodes are their favorite.
   They discuss them at a coffee shop.
   The coffee shop is local.

2. They can tell you the name.
   They can tell you easily.
   It is the middle name.
   It is of James T. Kirk.

3. The Prime Directive is the principle.
   It is the guiding principle.
   It is the principle of Starfleet interactions.
   They are interactions with a species.
   The species is alien.

4. They greet each other.
   They greet with a sign.
   It is a hand sign.
   It is a strange sign.
   It is a V-shaped sign.
   They always greet each other.

5. The Klingons were the villains.
   The Klingons were warlike.
   The villains were evil.
   They were the villains in the series.
   It was the television series.
   It was the original series.

EXERCISE 1.12

Combine each of the following sets of sentences into one sentence by embedding adjectives, adverbs, and prepositional phrases.

1. Robert Rodriguez insisted he could produce a film.
   Rodriguez insisted he could produce a low-budget film.
   He insisted he could produce a blockbuster film.
   He insisted he could produce a film inexpensively.
   He insisted he could produce a film with $7 million.

2. Steven Spielberg educates his audience.
   He educates on themes of human rights and social justice.
   He educates with films.
   His films are enlightening.
   His films are cathartic.

3. Ava DuVernay undertakes *Selma*.
   Ava DuVernay undertakes the representation of Martin Luther King, Jr.
   It is a cinematographic representation.
   She undertakes it in *Selma*.
   It is the first cinematographic representation of Martin Luther King, Jr.

4. Andy Warhol produced the film *Sleep*.
   Warhol produced the film in 1963.
   The film is black-and-white.
   The film is experimental.

The film *Sleep* is about his friend sleeping.
His friend sleeps for five hours and twenty minutes.

5. Marjane Satrapi codirected her first film
   She codirected an evocative film.
   It was codirected brilliantly.
   She codirected the film with Vincent Paronnaud.
   It was codirected in 2007.

EXERCISE 1.13

Combine each group of sentences into one sentence. Use the first sentence as the base sentence. Adjectives, adverbs, and prepositional phrases that can be embedded into the base sentence are underlined in the first five groups. In each group, the original version of the sentence can be found in one of the reading selections in this chapter.

EXAMPLE

Hunting was a sport. Squirrel hunting was a popular one in West Caldwell. This was in the 1940s.
   Squirrel hunting was a popular sport in West Caldwell in the 1940s.

1. I loaded my rifle, cocked the spring, and waited. I was waiting on the steps of the porch, and it was my homemade rifle.
2. When I came in, my mother told me that she had seen the suffering I had caused. She told me this reproachfully. I came into the house. She said that she had seen me from the kitchen window.
3. Bill Jacobus's father, to help combat the shortage and to supplement rationing, had built a coop. It was the wartime food shortage he was combating. He built a chicken coop. It was in his backyard.
4. Just possibly, she might be the woman. She might be the wisest of all the women on this planet.
5. I got to thinking one day. I was thinking about all those women who passed up dessert. They were on the Titanic. The dessert was at dinner that fateful night. The women had passed it up in an effort to "cut back."
6. We live on a diet. It is a sparse diet. It is a diet of promises we make when all conditions are perfect. They are promises we make to ourselves.
7. It's just that I might as well apply it and eliminate the process. I would apply it directly. I would apply it to my hips. I would apply it with a spatula. The process is digestive.

8. Alone, her dad's paychecks covered rent. They barely covered it. The rent was on their apartment. Their apartment was small. It was in the Adams district of Los Angeles.

9. She enjoyed the work so much that she began tutoring. It was volunteer work. She was tutoring on weekends. She was at the school her little brother attends. It is an elementary school.

10. Linartes carries a 3.5 GPA. He carries it today. He is at Santa Monica Community College.

Hagar the Horrible, by Chris Browne. © King Features Syndicate.

Reading for the Central Idea

2

In Chapter 1, you read that part of the writing process consists of developing a clearly worded statement of your central idea. Such a statement—whether it is a topic sentence or a thesis statement—serves as a guide for your readers, identifying for them the point you are trying to make.

In the "writing-reading conversation," you are a reader as often as you are a writer, and your ability to identify a central idea as a reader is certainly as important as your ability to express a central idea as a writer. In fact, in many college situations you will find that your ability to write a clear central idea depends first upon your ability to identify central ideas in what you read.

In the cartoon on the facing page, Hagar the Horrible and his companion have apparently not identified the central idea of the signs they have just read. (And the writer of the signs has not yet learned how to use *lay* and *lie*.) Of course, the message that Hagar and his friend have overlooked is a fairly clear one. Unfortunately, however, the central ideas of many paragraphs and essays are not always as clear—not necessarily because the paragraph or essay is written poorly but because it is complex and demands close attention.

In this chapter, you will practice reading to identify and to summarize central ideas, and you will practice writing in response to those ideas.

PARAGRAPHS AND TOPIC SENTENCES

In a paragraph, the sentence that states the central idea is called the *topic sentence*. It is often the first sentence (or two) of the paragraph, although a paragraph often has its topic sentence in the middle or at the end. Look at the following paragraphs. Their topic sentences are in italics. Following each paragraph is an example of how you could state its central idea in your own words.

> *Football has replaced baseball as the favorite American spectator sport largely because of television.* A comparison between a telecast of a football game on one channel and a baseball game on another could reveal baseball as a game with people standing around seemingly with little to do but watch two men play catch. Football would appear as twenty-two men engaged in almost constant, frenzied action. To watch baseball requires identification with the home team; to watch football requires only a need for action or a week of few thrills and the need for a touch of vicarious excitement.
>
> —*Jeffery Schrank, "Sport and the American Dream"*

SUMMARY OF CENTRAL IDEA

Television has helped football replace baseball as the favorite American spectator sport.

In the next paragraph, the "topic sentence" actually consists of more than one sentence.

> *Some people say the business about the jolly fat person is a myth, that all of us chubbies are neurotic, sick, sad people. I disagree. Fat people may not be chortling all day long, but they're a hell of a lot* nicer *than the wizened and shriveled.* Thin people turn surly, mean, and hard at a young age because they never learn the value of a hot-fudge sundae for easing tension. Thin people don't like gooey soft things because they themselves are neither gooey nor soft. They are crunchy and dull, like carrots. They go straight to the heart of the matter while fat people let things stay all blurry and hazy and vague, the way things actually are. Thin people want to face the truth. Fat people know there is no truth. One of my thin friends is always staring at complex, unsolvable problems and saying, "The key thing is ... " Fat people never say that. They know there isn't any such thing as the key thing.
>
> —*Suzanne Britt, "That Lean and Hungry Look"*

SUMMARY OF CENTRAL IDEA

The writer of this paragraph thinks that fat people are more pleasant to be around than thin people.

PARAGRAPHS WITHOUT TOPIC SENTENCES

Some paragraphs that you read will not have topic sentences. In these paragraphs, the topic sentence is *implied* (that is, it is not stated), but you can tell what the central idea is without it. Here is an example:

> The loose bones of Lincoln were hard to fit with neat clothes; and, once on, they were hard to keep neat; trousers go baggy at the knees of a storyteller who has the habit, at the end of a story, where the main laugh comes in, of putting his arms around his knees, raising his knees to his chin, and rocking to and fro. Those who spoke of his looks often mentioned his trousers creeping to the ankles and higher; his rumpled hair, his wrinkled vest. When he wasn't away making speeches, electioneering or practicing law on the circuit, he cut kindling wood, tended to cordwood for the stoves in the house, milked the cow, gave her a few forks of hay, and changed her straw bedding every day.
>
> —*Carl Sandburg, "Abraham Lincoln: The Prairie Years"*

SUMMARY OF CENTRAL IDEA

> Abraham Lincoln was an ordinary man who was not concerned about his appearance and who was willing to do ordinary work.

Many paragraphs in newspapers also do not have topic sentences. The columns in newspapers are so narrow that every third or fourth sentence is indented—not because a new topic idea has started but because an article is easier to read that way. Look at the following three paragraphs from a newspaper, and notice how they all support the same topic sentence in the first paragraph:

> The economics of the minimum wage are complex enough, and the historical record inconclusive enough, that economists can make arguments either way. So they do.
>
> A controversial February report from the Congressional Budget Office (CBO) was widely publicized as estimating that the $10.10 minimum wage would kill 500,000 jobs. But the report actually said the net job loss could be anywhere from zero to 1 million—not exactly a helpful estimate. The CBO's conclusion wasn't even based on original research—it was "synthesized" from existing studies of state-level minimum-wage raises in the past. Some of those studies found there were negative effects on employment. Some didn't.
>
> While nearly all economists accept the general (but not always true) principle that increasing the price of something—in this case, labor—results in fewer people purchasing it, low-wage employers don't have that much payroll fat left to trim. In other words, staffs are already extremely lean, workers are laboring at higher capacities than ever, and someone will still have to flip burgers. "I think everybody who's

reasonable on the issue realizes that it doesn't really have all that much of an impact," Thornberg says. "I look at Australia, where the minimum wage is $19 an hour, and the economy is fine. They don't have high unemployment, widespread small-business loss, none of that."

*—Jason Toon, "What Will Happen to the
Economy If We Raise the Minimum Wage?"*

SUMMARY OF CENTRAL IDEA

A minimum wage increase will likely have no or a negligible impact on employment.

EXERCISE 2.1

Read each of the following paragraphs. Underline the topic sentence of each one. Then summarize its central idea in your own words. Remember that the topic sentence might be the first sentence, or it might occur later in the paragraph. It might consist of more than one sentence, or it might be implied.

1. Don't meddle with old unloaded firearms, they are the most deadly and unerring things that have ever been created by man, You don't have to take any pains at all with them; you don't have to have a rest, you don't have to have any sights on the gun, you don't have to take aim, even. No, you just pick out a relative and bang away, and you are sure to get him. A youth who can't hit a cathedral at thirty yards with a Gatling gun in three-quarters of an hour, can take up an old empty musket and bag his grandmother every time at a hundred.

—Mark Twain, "Advice to Youth"

2. We were never born to read. Human beings invented reading only a few thousand years ago. And with this invention, we rearranged the very organization of our brain, which in turn expanded the ways we were able to think, which altered the intellectual evolution of our species. Reading is one of the single most remarkable inventions in history; the ability to record history is one of its consequences. Our ancestors' invention could come about only because of the human brain's extraordinary ability to make new connections among its existing structures, a process made possible by the brain's ability to be shaped by experience. This plasticity at the heart of the brain's design forms the basis for much of who we are, and who we might become.

—Maryanne Wolf, Proust and the Squid:
The Story and Science of the Reading Brain

3. I was born in Palo Alto, California, into the lap of an Iranian diaspora community awash in nostalgia and longing for an Iran many thousands of miles away. As a girl, raised on the distorting myths of exile, I imagined myself a Persian princess, estranged from my homeland—a

place of light, poetry, and nightingales—by a dark, evil force called the Revolution. I borrowed the plot from *Star Wars*, convinced it told Iran's story. Ayatollah Khomeini was Darth Vader. Tromping about suburban California, I lived out this fantasy. There must be some supernatural explanation, I reasoned, for the space landing of thousands of Tehranis to a world of vegan smoothies and Volvos, charkas, and Tupac.

—*Azadeh Moaveni*, Lipstick Jihad

ESSAYS AND THESIS STATEMENTS

The central idea of a complete essay is called its *thesis statement*. Usually, it appears toward the start of the essay (in the introduction), although, like a topic sentence in a paragraph, it can appear in the middle or at the end of an essay, or it might not appear at all because it is implied.

Sometimes a thesis statement is quite straightforward and easy to see. For example, in the following brief essay the thesis (shown in italics) is clearly stated in the first paragraph:

Three Passions I Have Lived For   BERTRAND RUSSELL

Bertrand Russell was a British philosopher, mathematician, Nobel Prize winner, and political activist. He is recognized as one of the most productive writers and thinkers of the twentieth century. In the following selection, he identifies three passions that have influenced his life.

Three passions, simple but overwhelmingly strong, have governed   1
my life: the longing for love, the search for knowledge, and unbearable pity for the suffering of mankind. These passions, like great winds, have blown me hither and thither, in a wayward course over a deep ocean of anguish, reaching to the very verge of despair.

I have sought love, first, because it brings ecstasy—ecstasy so   2
great that I would often have sacrificed all the rest of my life for a few hours of this joy. I have sought it, next, because it relieves loneliness—that terrible loneliness in which one shivering consciousness looks over the rim of the world into the cold unfathomable lifeless abyss. I have sought it, finally, because in the union of love I have seen, in a mystic miniature, the prefiguring vision of the heaven that saints and poets have imagined. This is what I sought, and though it might seem too good for human life, this is what—at last—I have found.

With equal passion I have sought knowledge. I have wished   3
to understand the hearts of men. I have wished to know why the stars shine. ... A little of this, but not much, I have achieved.

Love and knowledge, so far as they were possible, led upward   4
toward the heavens. But always pity brought me back to earth.
Echoes of cries of pain reverberate in my heart. Children in famine,
victims tortured by oppressors, helpless old people a hated burden to their sons, and the whole world of loneliness, poverty, and
pain make a mockery of what human life should be. I long to alleviate the evil, but I cannot, and I too suffer.

This has been my life. I have found it worth living, and would   5
gladly live it again if the chance were offered me.

SUMMARY OF CENTRAL IDEA

Bertrand Russell states that his life has been governed by the
search for love and for knowledge and by a sense of pity for
those who suffer.

Unfortunately, not everything you read will have a thesis statement as clear as
the one above. Sometimes essays, articles, or chapters in texts will have their
thesis statements in the second or third paragraph—or even later in the work.
Sometimes the thesis statement will be most clearly worded in the conclusion.
And sometimes it will not be stated directly at all. The point is that you need to
read college material carefully and closely. Certainly one of the most important
reading skills you will need to develop in college classes is the ability to recognize the central idea of what you read, even when it is not directly stated.

READINGS

Read the two articles below. After you have read each one, write a sentence
that briefly summarizes its central idea. Underline sentences that seem to
state the thesis of the article.

Jailbreak Marriage   GAIL SHEEHY

Gail Sheehy's text Passages, *from which the following selection is taken, and her
many subsequent texts examine the stages of life that men and women pass through
as they grow. Sheehy is a seven-time recipient of the New York Newswomen's Club
Front Page Award for distinguished journalism.*

BEFORE YOU READ

1. Consider the title. In what sense might a marriage be called a
   "jailbreak"?
2. As you read this selection, watch for sentences that will express the
   author's central idea about "jailbreak" marriages.

Although the most commonplace reason women marry young
is to "complete" themselves, a good many spirited young women
gave another reason: "I did it to get away from my parents." Particularly for girls whose educations and privileges are limited, a *jailbreak marriage* is the usual thing. What might appear to be an act
of rebellion usually turns out to be a transfer of dependence.

A lifer: that is how it felt to be Simone at 17, how it often
feels for girls in authoritarian homes. The last of six children, she
was caught in the nest vacated by the others and expected to
"keep the family together." Simone was the last domain where her
mother could play out the maternal role and where her father
could exercise full control. That meant goodbye to the university
scholarship.

Although the family was not altogether poor, Simone had tried
to make a point of her independence by earning her own money
since the age of 14. Now she thrust out her bankbook. Would two
thousand dollars in savings buy her freedom?

"We want you home until you're 21."

Work, her father insisted. But the job she got was another
closed gate. It was in the knitting machine firm where her father
worked, an extension of his control. Simone knuckled under for a
year until she met Franz. A zero. An egocentric Hungarian of pointless aristocracy, a man for whom she had total disregard. Except
for one attraction. He asked her to marry him. Franz would be the
getaway vehicle in her jailbreak marriage scheme: "I decided the
best way to get out was to get married and divorce him a year
later. That was my whole program."

Anatomy, uncontrolled, sabotaged her program. Nine months
after the honeymoon, Simone was a mother. Resigning herself, she
was pregnant with her second child at 20.

One day, her husband called with the news, the marker event
to blast her out of the drift. His firm had offered him a job in New
York City.

"Then and there, I decided that before the month was out I
would have the baby, find a lawyer, and start divorce proceedings."
The next five years were like twenty. It took every particle of her
will and patience to defeat Franz, who wouldn't hear of a separation, and to ignore the ostracism of her family.

At the age of 25, on the seventh anniversary of her jailbreak
marriage (revealed too late as just another form of entrapment),
Simone finally escaped her parents. Describing the day of her
decree, the divorce sounds like so many women whose identity

was foreclosed by marriage: "It was like having ten tons of chains removed from my mind, my body—the most exhilarating day of my life."

How to Stay Alive

ART HOPPE

Art Hoppe, a graduate of Harvard University, wrote for the San Francisco Chronicle for over fifty years. His work as a political satirist and humorist is recognized as some of the best of its kind. In the following selection, he tells the story of Snadley Klabberhorn.

BEFORE YOU READ

1. Read the title. What does it suggest will be the topic of this reading selection? What might be the central idea?
2. Read the first four words of this selection. What do they suggest to you?

Once upon a time there was a man named Snadley Klabberhorn who was the healthiest man in the whole wide world.   1

Snadley wasn't always the healthiest man in the whole wide world.   2

When he was young, Snadley smoked what he wanted, drank what he wanted, ate what he wanted, and exercised only with young ladies in bed.   3

He thought he was happy. "Life is absolutely peachy," he was fond of saying. "Nothing beats being alive."   4

Then along came the Surgeon General's Report linking smoking to lung cancer, heart disease, emphysema and tertiary coreopsis.   5

Snadley read about The Great Tobacco Scare with a frown. "Life is so peachy," he said, "that there's no sense taking any risks." So he gave up smoking.   6

Like most people who went through the hell of giving up smoking, Snadley became more interested in his own health. In fact, he became fascinated. And when he read a WCTU tract which pointed out that alcohol caused liver damage, brain damage, and acute *weltanschauung,* he gave up alcohol and drank dietary colas instead.   7

At least he did until The Great Cyclamate Scare.   8

"There's no sense in taking any risks," he said. And he switched to sugar-sweetened colas, which made him fat and caused dental caries. On realizing this he renounced colas in favor of milk and took up jogging, which was an awful bore.   9

That was about the time of The Great Cholesterol Scare.   10

Snadley gave up milk. To avoid cholesterol, which caused ath- 11
erosclerosis, coronary infarcts and chronic chryselephantinism, he
also gave up meat, fats and dairy products, subsisting on a diet of
raw fish.

Then came The Great DDT Scare. 12

"The presence of large amounts of DDT in fish ... " Snadley 13
read with anguish. But fortunately that's when he met Ernestine. They were made for each other. Ernestine introduced him
to home ground wheat germ, macrobiotic yogurt and organic
succotash.

They were very happy eating this dish twice daily, watching six 14
hours of color television together and spending the rest of their
time in bed.

They were, that is, until The Great Color Television Scare. 15

"If color tee-vee does give off radiations," said Snadley, "there's 16
no sense taking risks. After all, we still have each other."

And that's about all they had. Until The Great Pill Scare. 17

On hearing that The Pill might cause carcinoma, thromboses 18
and lingering stichometry, Ernestine promptly gave up The Pill—
and Snadley. "There's no sense taking any risks," she said.

Snadley was left with jogging. He was, that is, until he read 19
somewhere that 1.3 percent of joggers are eventually run over by
a truck or bitten by rabid dogs.

He then retired to a bomb shelter in his back yard (to avoid 20
being hit by a meteor), installed an air purifier (after The Great
Smog Scare) and spent the next 63 years doing Royal Canadian
Air Force exercises and poring over back issues of *The Reader's
Digest*.

"Nothing's more important than being alive," he said proudly 21
on reaching 102. But he never did say anymore that life was absolutely peachy.

PARTICIPATING ACTIVELY IN THE
WRITER-READER DIALOGUE

What would you do if a friend showed up at your door with something
important to tell you? Would you tell her to go ahead and talk while you finished watching a television show? Probably not. If you believed what she had
to say was important, you'd invite her in, turn off the TV, and sit down to talk
to her. If her message was complicated, you might find yourself asking her to
repeat parts of it, or you might repeat to her what you thought she had said.

Perhaps you would nod your head as she spoke to show that you were listening to her and understood her.

The point is, when you think something is important, you listen to it *actively*. You ask questions; you look for clarification; you offer your own opinions. Above all, you *participate* in the conversation. As we said earlier, reading and listening are very similar. Sometimes we read very casually, just as sometimes we listen very casually. After all, not everything needs (or deserves) our rapt attention. But some reading, like some listening, *does* demand our attention. The reading that you will do in college classes will, of course, demand active participation from you; so will reading related to your job or to major decisions that you must make in your life. In each of these cases, you must read in a way that is quite different from the casual way you might read a newspaper in the morning.

So what is active reading? How does one go about it? Here are some steps that you should learn to apply to all the reading you do in your college classes.

STEPS FOR ACTIVE READING

1. *Establish your expectations.*   Before you read an article or chapter or book, look at its title. Does it give you an idea of what to expect? Does it sound as if it is announcing its central idea? Read any background information that comes with the reading material. Does it tell you what to expect?

2. *First reading: underline or mark main points.*   With a pen, pencil, or highlighter in hand, read the material from start to finish, slowly and carefully. During the first reading, you're trying to get an overall sense of the central idea of the selection. Don't try to take notes during this first reading. Instead, just underline or highlight sentences or ideas that seem significant to you as you read. Often these sentences will express the thesis of the reading selection or the topic ideas of individual paragraphs. In addition, mark any details or explanations that seem more important than others.

3. *Second reading: annotate.*   This step is of major importance if you intend to understand fully what you have read. *Reread* what you underlined. As you do, briefly summarize those points in the margin. If you think a point is especially important, make a note of it in the margin. If you have questions or disagree with something, note that in the margin.

4. *Summarize the reading.*   Briefly write out the central idea of the reading. In your own words, state the thesis of the entire essay and the supporting topic ideas of the paragraphs.

5. *Respond to the reading.*   Write out your own response to what you have read. Do you agree with the writer's idea? Did it remind you of anything that you have experienced? Did it give you a new insight into its topic? You might write this response in a journal or as an assignment to be used for class discussion. Your instructor will guide you here.

Should you go through these five steps every time you read? Absolutely not. Who would want to underline, annotate, and summarize when relaxing with a good novel on a Saturday afternoon? However, you should take these steps when what you are reading demands close attention—when you read material you must analyze for a report or a paper, for example.

Here is an example of an article that has been read by an active reader:

Printed Noise
GEORGE WILL

Most of us are used to the strange names that businesses use to draw attention to their products. In the following essay, George Will takes a second look at these names and suggests that they are a form of language pollution. Will is a former philosophy professor, a Pulitzer Prize–winning columnist for the Washington Post, and an analyst for Fox News.

The flavor list at the local Baskin-Robbins ice cream shop is an (anarchy) of names like "Peanut Butter 'N Chocolate" and "Strawberry Rhubarb Sherbet." These are not the names of things that reasonable people consider consuming, but the names are admirably businesslike, briskly descriptive.

cuteness in commerce

Unfortunately, my favorite delight (chocolate-coated vanilla flecked with nuts) bears the unutterable name "Hot Fudge Nutty Buddy," an example of the plague of cuteness in commerce. There are some things a gentleman simply will not do, and one is announce in public a desire for a "Nutty Buddy." So I usually settle for a plain vanilla cone.

a gentleman won't say "Nutty Buddy"!

example of man who wouldn't say "Yumbo"

I am not the only person suffering for immutable standards of (propriety) The May issue of *Atlantic* consists of absorbing tale of lonely heroism at a Burger King. A gentleman requested a ham and cheese sandwich that the Burger King calls a Yumbo. The girl taking orders was bewildered.

"Oh," she eventually exclaimed, "you mean a Yumbo."

Gentleman: "The ham and cheese. Yes."

Girl, nettled: "It's called a Yumbo. Now, do you want a Yumbo or not?"

Gentleman, teeth clenched: "Yes, thank you, the ham and cheese."

Girl: "Look, I've got to have an order here. You're holding up the line. You want a Yumbo, don't you? You want a Yumbo!"

= outdated, but the author likes him

Whereupon the gentleman chose the straight and narrow path of virtue. He walked out rather than call a ham and cheese a Yumbo. His principles are anachronisms but his prejudices are (impeccable) and he is on my short list of civilization's friends.

more examples

That list includes the Cambridge (don) who would not appear outdoors without a top hat, not even when routed by fire at 3 A.M., and who refused to read another line of Tennyson after he saw the poet put water in fine port. The list includes another don who, although devoutly (Tory,) voted Liberal during Gladstone's day because the duties of prime minister kept Gladstone too busy to declaim on Holy Scripture. And high on the list is the grammarian whose last words were: "I am about to—or I am going to—die: either expression is correct."

Hah! This is funny!

Gentle reader, can you imagine any of these magnificent persons asking a teenage girl for a "Yumbo"? Or uttering "Fishamagig" or "Egg McMuffin" or "Fribble" (that's a milk shake, sort of)?

At one point in the evolution of American taste, restaurants that were relentlessly fun, fun, fun were built to look like lemons or bananas. I am told that in Los Angeles there was the Toed Inn,

fun restaurants replaced by fun menus

a strange spelling for a strange place shaped like a giant toad. Customers entered through the mouth, like flies being swallowed.

But the mature nation has put away such childish things in favor of menus that are fun, fun, fun. Seafood is "From Neptune's Pantry" or "Denizens of the Briny Deep." And "Surf 'N Turf," which you might think is fish and horsemeat, actually is lobster and beef.

hamburger names

To be fair, there are practical considerations behind the asphyxiatingly cute names given hamburgers. Many hamburgers are made from portions of the cow that the cow had no reasons to boast about. So sellers invent distracting names to give hamburgers (cachet.) Hence "Whoppers" and "Heroburgers."

Howard Johnson's menu—no excuse

But there is no excuse for Howard Johnson's menu. In a just society it would be a flogging offense to speak of "steerburgers," clams "fried to order" (which probably means they don't fry clams for you unless you order fried clams), a "natural cut" (what is an "unnatural" cut?) of sirloin, "oven-baked" meat loaf, chicken pot pie with "flaky crust," "golden croquettes," "grilled-in-butter Frankforts [sic]," "liver with smothered onions" (smothered by onions?), and a "hearty" Reuben sandwich.

verbal litter = language becomes printed noise

American is marred by scores of Dew Drop Inns serving "crispy green" salad, "garden fresh" vegetables, "succulent" lamb, "savory" pork, "sizzling" steaks, and "creamy" or "tangy" coleslaw. I've nothing against Homeric adjectives ("wine-dark sea," "wing-footed Achilles") but isn't coleslaw just coleslaw? Americans hear the incessant roar of commerce without listening to it, and read the written roar without really noticing it. Who would notice if a menu proclaimed "creamy steaks" and "sizzling" coleslaw?

thesis ⟶ Such verbal litter is to language as Muzak is to music. As advertising blather becomes the nation's normal idiom, language becomes printed noise.

SUMMARY OF THE READING

George Will calls advertising language, especially the kind we see on menus, "printed noise." He gives examples of many silly or unnecessary names given to food (like the "Yumbo"), and he admires people who resist what he calls "verbal litter."

PERSONAL RESPONSE TO THE READING

I thought this article was really funny. I remember feeling stupid the first time I had to ask for an "Egg McMuffin." The name sounds like something on a kindergarten menu. But I don't really think about those names anymore. I guess I've just gotten used to them. The article reminded me how much they are all around us, even though I don't notice them. How about "Wienerdude"? That's the stupidest name I've ever heard. When I first heard it, I thought I'd never order one of those, just because the name is so insulting to any intelligent person. But maybe it's really a good hot dog—so I guess I really would order one. I suppose I agree with the article's point that after a while you don't even notice these things anymore. They are like "verbal litter."

READINGS

Read each of the following essays *actively*. That is, as you read each essay, *underline* or *highlight* its thesis statement, topic sentences, and any examples or ideas that seem important to you. Then reread the parts you have marked and *annotate* the essay. Finally, write a brief *summary* of the article and a brief *personal response paragraph*.

Ordinary People Produce Extraordinary Results PAUL ROGAT LOEB

Paul Rogat Loeb is the author of Soul of a Citizen: Living with Conviction in a Cynical Time, *from which the following selection is adapted. He is an associated scholar at Seattle's Center for Ethical Leadership, he comments on social issues for* The New York Times, The Washington Post, CNN, *and* NPR, *and he blogs for* The Huffington Post.

BEFORE YOU READ

1. What do you know about Rosa Parks? Where did you first hear about her?
2. Would you consider Rosa Parks to be an "ordinary" woman? Why or why not?

We learn much from how we present our heroes. A few years ago, 1 on Martin Luther King Day, I was interviewed on CNN. So was Rosa Parks, by phone from Los Angeles. "We're very honored to have her," the host said. "Rosa Parks was the woman who wouldn't go to the back of the bus. She wouldn't get up and give her seat in the white section to a white person. That set in motion the year-long bus boycott in Montgomery. It earned Rosa Parks the title of 'mother of the civil rights movement.'"

I was excited to be part of the same show. Then it occurred to 2 me that the host's familiar rendition of her story had stripped the Montgomery, Ala., boycott of its most important context. Before refusing to give up her bus seat, Parks had spent 12 years help-ing lead the local NAACP chapter. The summer before, Parks had attended a 10-day training session at Tennessee's labor and civil rights organizing school, the Highlander Center, where she'd met an older generation of civil rights activists and discussed the recent U.S. Supreme Court decision banning "separate but equal" schools.

In other words, Parks didn't come out of nowhere. She didn't 3 single-handedly give birth to the civil rights efforts. Instead, she was part of an existing movement for change at a time when success was far from certain.

This in no way diminishes the power and historical importance 4 of her refusal to give up her seat. Yet it does remind us that this tremendously consequential act might never have taken place without the humble and frustrating work that she and others did earlier on. It reminds us that her initial step of getting involved was just as courageous and critical as the fabled moment when she refused to move to the back of the bus.

People like Parks shape our models of social commitment. 5 Yet the conventional retelling of her story creates a standard so impossible to meet that it may actually make it harder for the rest of us to get involved. This portrayal suggests that social activists come out of nowhere to suddenly materialize to take dramatic stands. It implies that we act with the greatest impact when we act alone or when we act alone initially. It reinforces a notion that anyone who takes a committed public stand—or at least an effec-tive one—has to be a larger-than-life figure, someone with more time, energy, courage, vision or knowledge than any normal person could ever possess.

This belief pervades our society, in part because the media 6 rarely represent historical change as the work of ordinary human beings who learn to take extraordinary actions. And once we enshrine our heroes on pedestals, it becomes hard for mere mortals to measure up in our eyes. We go even further, dismissing most people's motives, knowledge and tactics as insufficiently grand or heroic, faulting them for not being in command of every fact and figure or not being able to answer every question put to them. We fault ourselves as well for not knowing every detail or for harboring uncertainties and doubts.

We find it hard to imagine that ordinary human beings with   7
ordinary hesitations and flaws might make a critical difference in worthy social causes. Yet those *who* act have their own imperfections and ample reasons to hold back.

"I think it does us all a disservice," a young African Ameri-   8
can activist from Atlanta said, "when people who work for social change are presented as saints, so much more noble than the rest of us. We get a false sense that from the moment they were born they were called to act, never had doubts, were bathed in a circle of light."

She added that she was much more inspired to learn how   9
people "succeeded despite their failings and uncertainties." That would mean that she, too, had a "shot at changing things."

Our culture's misreading of the Rosa Parks story speaks to a   10
more general collective amnesia by which we forget the examples that might most inspire our courage and conscience. Most of us know next to nothing of the grass-roots movements in which ordinary men and women fought to preserve freedom, expand the sphere of democracy and create a more just society: the abolitionists, the populists, the women's suffragists, the union activists who spurred the end of 80-hour work weeks at near-starvation wages.

These activists teach us how to shift public sentiment, challenge   11
entrenched institutional power and find the strength to persevere despite all odds. Yet their stories, like the real story of Parks, are erased in an Orwellian memory hole.

Parks' actual story conveys an empowering moral that is lost   12
in her public myth. She began modestly, by attending one meeting and then another. Hesitant at first, she gained confidence as she spoke out. She kept on despite a profoundly uncertain context as she and others acted as best they could to challenge deeply entrenched injustices with little certainty of results. Had she and others given up after their 10th or 11th year of commitment, we might never have heard of the Montgomery boycott.

Parks' journey suggests that social change is the product of   13
deliberate, incremental action whereby we join together to try to

shape a better world. Sometimes our struggles will fail, as did many earlier efforts of Parks, her peers and her predecessors. Other times, they may bear modest fruit.

And at times, they will trigger a miraculous outpouring of cour-   14 age and heart, as happened in the wake of Parks' arrest. For only when we act, despite all our uncertainties and doubts, do we have the chance to shape history.

SUGGESTIONS FOR SUMMARIZING

1. What does this article suggest is true about many of the people we usually consider to be "extraordinary"?
2. Write three or four more sentences to summarize the major supporting ideas that are presented in the article.

SUGGESTIONS FOR PERSONAL RESPONSES

1. Have you ever known someone whom others might call extraordinary? If you have, describe that person's ordinary qualities that somehow led him or her to be an extraordinary person.
2. Describe situations from your experiences or observations that illustrate Loeb's statement that "ordinary human beings with ordinary hesitations and flaws can make a critical difference."
3. Talk to other members of the class about the idea that all great actions start out with small steps, full of "uncertainty and doubt." For what areas of life might this statement hold true?

Not-So-Social Media: Why People Have Stopped Talking on Phones   ALAN GREENBLATT

Are smartphones really bringing us together? In the following article, Alan Green-blatt, a reporter for National Public Radio, examines the reasons why more and more of us do not make many phone calls and the effects of that technology-induced shift to texting and apps.

BEFORE YOU READ

1. Why do we call certain media "social"? What does being "social" mean?
2. Are you talking on the phone much? Do you know people who talk on the phone regularly? When you or other people talk on the phone, why do they do so?

Emma Wisniewski felt exposed. The New York–based actress had   1 moments where she had to open up in a way that made her feel particularly vulnerable. She had to talk on the phone. In front of people—her fellow actors and the audience. "I've done several plays now that required talking on landlines, and what always strikes me is the relatively public nature of it," she says.

The desire to communicate privately is one reason people   2
have largely abandoned talking on the phone as a social medium. What was once a major indoor sport, taking up hours of many people's days, is now not only more limited but may be going the way of mailed letters and express telegrams. "Now, calling on a phone is almost like a violation," says Scott Campbell, a professor of telecommunications at the University of Michigan. "It's very greedy for your social presence, and texting is not."

Hiding from Mom

Wisniewski played a 16-year-old girl this spring in a play called   1
Soups, Stews and Casseroles: 1976. As its title suggests, the play is set in America's bicentennial year, nearly 40 years ago. One detail that made it a period piece was Wisniewski grabbing the phone off the kitchen wall, dragging the long cord into another room. For audience members of a certain age, it was a tableau instantly familiar, yet completely distant. Those of us in our 40s can remember fighting with our siblings to spend hours on those pea green and lemon yellow landline phones.

As it happens, the play had its premiere in Webster Groves, a   2
suburb of St. Louis where back in 1944 *Life* magazine took a series of photos of a teenage girl talking on the phone as part of her "evening ritual." She keeps a wary eye out for her mother, who can be seen occasionally looking on with disapproval.

Hiding from Mom is one reason texting took off in the first   3
place, says Danah Boyd, the author of *It's Complicated: The Social Lives of Networked Teens.* Stretching the phone cord down the hall was no longer good enough to get away from hovering "helicopter" parents. "This prompted an entire generation to switch to text-based media, starting with instant messaging," Boyd says. "Texting is seen as even more private, because it's harder for Mom to look over your shoulder."

Don't Call US

Texting became the norm for teens and young adults, but has   1
been adopted by older folks as well. Boomers are still more apt to pick up the phone in professional contexts, but at work as well as home a ringing phone has come to be seen as an unwanted

intrusion. "I used to think the millennials were wrong about this, but it is an imposition to call someone and say put aside whatever you were doing and give me 30 minutes of your time," says Neil Howe, president of LifeCourse Associates, which consults with corporations about generational attitudes and behaviors. As Boyd points out, communication is a two-way street. Both parties in the pair have to agree to a plan. Fewer people are willing to engage in a phone conversation, which not only eats up more time than texting but has to be done in that very moment. "Even if it's someone I know well and love, I resent the intrusion," says Amy Pickworth, a friend of mine who works as an editor at the Rhode Island School of Design. "The phone is so pushy. It's just suddenly so *there*, demanding, 'Talk to me, say funny things,' or 'I'm sad, cheer me up,' or 'Holy cow, listen to this.'"

Can You Call Back Later?

By contrast, your friends don't need to be available right this very moment to talk via text. "Conversations can ebb and flow, and it's no big deal," says Boyd, who is a researcher at Microsoft Research and Harvard University. "You'll see teens spend 45 minutes crafting the perfect 'casual' text message to send to someone they have a crush on." Landline use is down, while mobile phone use is up, according to the Federal Communications Commission. But that includes all the things people do on phones—talking, texting, playing games.   1

The onslaught of information and time spent with screens is another reason why people are talking less, says Campbell, the Michigan professor. "You can get a little saturated," he says. "If I'm going to be keeping up in this new, digital world, something's gotta give."   2

Getting Constant Updates

Most of the people I interviewed for this piece—largely through email—said they do engage in extended phone conversations, often with family members. There's still an intimacy to a phone call that texting can't match. But those conversations have to compete with a lot of demands for people's time and concentration. When you're talking on the phone, you've got to be all in. We've probably all had the experience of talking to someone and knowing we've lost their interest when we can hear them start to type in the background. Or, maybe worse, we've tuned out ourselves, sounding a little drunk as we lose the thread of our own thought as we check out websites.   1

It's not just that people have grown used to multiple stimuli.   2
Much of what they're looking at is social in nature. We keep up
with family and friends via Facebook, Instagram and other social
media channels. Those we're closer with, we might interact with
almost constantly through group texts on WhatsApp or Kik. For
many people, there's no need to pick up the phone to catch up.
Your friends already know what you did last night. "You constantly
know what's going on," says Nick Politan, a student at Washington
University in St. Louis, "so there's no point in ever wanting to catch
up with somebody, unless they're really close to you."

SUGGESTIONS FOR SUMMARIZING

1. Does this article seem to *explain* why phones are now used more for texting than for calling, or does it *argue* a point? In summarizing the article's central idea, make it clear which of these two approaches the author takes.
2. After you state the central idea of the article, write one sentence of summary for each major supporting section of the article.

SUGGESTIONS FOR PERSONAL RESPONSES

1. In what ways do your own experiences with texting and phone calls correspond to those described in this article?
2. Do you think that we've lost something in not talking on the phone any longer? Or do you think the gains outweigh the losses?
3. Does it matter whether a person is physically present, or whether one can hear a person's voice? Or does communicating mostly through texting change how we relate to one another?
4. Talk to other members of the class or other people you know and discuss whether texting has made us more social or more self-centered, or whether texting is merely a reflection of the higher demands on our time.

Killing Women: A Pop-Music Tradition   John Hamerlinck

John Hamerlinck is a freelance writer in St. Cloud, Minnesota, who specializes in popular culture. The following selection was originally published in The Humanist *in 1995. As you read it, consider in what way its argument is still relevant today.*

BEFORE YOU READ

1. Consider the word *misogyny*. What does it mean? What thoughts and feelings do you associate with that word?
2. The title of the essay implies an idea. What is that idea, and what is your initial response to it?

If there has been anything positive about the flood of media cover-   1
age of the O.J. Simpson trial, it has been an increased public awareness of the disturbing incidence of violence against women in our
society. According to the Family Violence Prevention Fund, an act
of domestic violence occurs every nine seconds in the United
States. Even though the mainstream press seems to have only
recently recognized this horrible reality, the signs of our tolerance
toward domestic violence have long had a prominent profile in
popular culture. This tragic phenomenon has often been reflected
in novels and on film, but perhaps the most common occurrence
of depictions of violence against women comes in popular music.
Indeed, the often innocuous world of pop music has cultivated its
own genre of woman-killing songs.

Violent misogyny in popular song did not begin with recent con-   2
troversial offerings from acts like Guns 'N' Roses and 2 Live Crew.
There's an old, largely southern, folk genre known as the "murder
ballad." And as long as men have sung the blues, they have told stories of killing the women who have "done them wrong." In a common scenario, a man catches "his" woman with another man and
kills them both in a jealous rage. In the 1920s, Lonnie Johnson sang
a song called "Careless Love," in which he promises to shoot his
lover numerous times and then stand over her until she is finished
dying. In "Little Boy Blue," Robert Lockwood threatens to whip and
stab his lover; while Robert Nighthawk's "Murderin' Blues" suggests a
deliberate values judgment in the premeditation: the song says that
prison chains are better than having a woman cheat and lie to you.

In many of the songs in this genre, the music belies the homi-   3
cidal lyrics. A song like Little Walter's "Boom, Boom, Out Go the
Lights" (later turned into an arena-rock anthem by Pat Travers) features a smooth, catchy, danceable blues riff. Little Walter caresses
the song's famous hook so softly that one gets the feeling that
perhaps his bark is worse than his bite. There is, however, no doubt
that retribution for emotional pain is going to come in the form of
physical violence.

This theme is not limited to blues artists. The Beatles provide   4
harsh and frightening imagery in "Run for Your Life," a song which
features premeditation along with traditional blues lines. It also
incorporates stalking and threats sung directly to the target. The
stalking transcends the mind-game variety we find in a song like
the Police's "Every Breath You Take"; "Run for Your Life" is pure
terror. Charles Manson aside, this Beatles offering is considerably
more frightening than "Helter Skelter."

Another song in this vein is "Hey Joe," which was a minor hit   5
for a band called the Leaves in the 1960s and was later covered by
numerous artists, including an electrifying version by Jimi Hendrix.
Thanks to Hendrix, the song became a garage-band staple in the
sixties and seventies: many a young vocalist cut his rock-and-roll
teeth singing that musical question: "Hey, Joe/Where you goin' with
that gun in your hand?" (The same bands probably also played Neil
Young's contribution to the genre, "Down by the River.")

The woman-killing genre has also been embraced by the MTV   6
generation. One of the video age's most recent additions to the
catalog of murder songs comes from the "man in black," Johnny
Cash, who is only one of many country artists to record such
songs. Cash recently released a single called "Delia's Gone" from
his latest album, *American Recordings*. The stark and eerie video,
which features Cash digging a grave for his victim, even made its
way into an episode of MTV's "Beavis and Butt-Head."

Occasionally the genre attempts to even the odds by arm-   7
ing the victim: for example, in Robert Johnson's "32-20 Blues," the
heartbroken man gets his revenge despite the fact that the victim
had a "38 Special." And sometimes the gender tables are turned:
for example, Nancy Sinatra covered "Run for Your Life" shortly
after the Beatles recorded it, changing the prey from "little girl"
to "little boy." In real life, however, the victims are overwhelmingly
women, and their primary form of defense usually consists of a
mere piece of paper called a restraining order.

It should quickly be pointed out, however, that these songs do   8
not *cause* violence. Their singers are not wicked, evil people. The
perseverance of this genre, however, certainly reflects a disturbingly
casual level of acceptance in society when it comes to so-called
"crimes of passion." When we hear tales of real domestic abuse,
we are appalled. Often, however, we rationalize the perpetrator's
actions and say that we can understand how he was driven to
commit such a crime. Shoulders shrug and someone ubiquitously
adds, "Well, we live in a violent society." Just as metal detectors and
X-rays have become an unquestioned, accepted part of the airport
landscape, our culture comfortably places violence and terror in
pop music's love-song universe.

"I-loved-her-so-much-I-had-to-kill-her" songs are not about   9
love; they are about power and control. But if the beat is good and
the chorus has a catchy hook, we don't need to concern ourselves
with things like meaning, right? We can simply dance on and ignore
the violence around us.

SUGGESTIONS FOR SUMMARIZING

1. Does the article merely provide examples of a pop culture phenomenon or does it propose a course of action? As you summarize the article's central idea, write a sentence that reflects which approach the article is taking.
2. After you state the central idea of the article, write one sentence of summary for each major supporting section of the article.

SUGGESTIONS FOR PERSONAL RESPONSES

1. Can you think of examples of songs you have heard but that are not mentioned in the article that condone violence against women? Have you found yourself singing along to such songs?
2. When such songs are played in a club or in a bar, or when you've listened to such songs in the car or at home and you have found yourself singing along or dancing to such songs, have you ever felt strange or uncomfortable? Why or why not?
3. What, if anything, do you think can or should be done about song lyrics advocating or condoning violence against women?
4. The U.S. Constitution enshrines the right to free speech, and artistic expression especially is dependent on free speech. Can you reconcile the right to free speech with the advocacy of harm to some group of people?

WRITING ASSIGNMENTS

WRITING WITH A PERSONAL RESPONSE

1. Write a paper that responds to one of the following questions about "Ordinary People Produce Extraordinary Results."
   a. Paul Rogat Loeb says of Rosa Parks that "her initial step of getting involved was just as courageous and critical as the fabled moment when she refused to move to the back of the bus." Consider your own life. Have you found that the first step toward some event or accomplishment was sometimes the most difficult one? Write a paper in which you describe several different "first steps" that have led to significant changes or events in your life.
   b. Consider a person in your life whom you do or do not love, respect, or admire. What specific actions caused that person to gain or lose your love, respect, or admiration? Write a paper in which you explain the everyday, ordinary actions that eventually helped you form your opinion about that person.
   c. According to Loeb, "We find it hard to imagine that ordinary human beings with ordinary hesitations and flaws might make a critical

difference in worthy social causes." Have you ever participated in a social cause? Write a paper describing the cause you were part of, your role in it, and how you were affected by your participation in it.

2. Write a paper that responds to one of the following questions about "Not-So-Social Media: Why People Have Stopped Talking on Phones."

   a. Do you and people you know text more than phone? What are the reasons a person might choose one method of communication over the other? Write a paper that uses specific examples to illustrate why you and people you know might text in one situation and phone in another.

   b. Have you found that both texting and phoning have disadvantages as well as advantages? Write a paper in which you examine what the *disadvantages* are of each method of communication. Or, if you prefer, write a paper in which you examine what the *advantages* are of each method. Use specific examples to illustrate your points.

   c. In what ways do your own experiences with texting and phone calls correspond to those described in this article? Write a paper in which you use specific examples to illustrate your points.

3. Write a paper that responds to one of the following questions about "Printed Noise."

   a. George Will describes some of the ridiculous ways restaurants name or advertise their food. If you think his observations have merit, write a paper that gives examples of your own. If you would like to, use a different type of product, such as cigarettes, liquor, cars, or grocery items. If you think Will is overreacting or has missed the purpose of such advertising, write a paper that explains why, and illustrate your points with examples of actual products.

   b. George Will has focused on one specific change in our culture—the trend toward silly names of food items in restaurants. Are there other specific cultural changes that you object to? Think of the places you visit, the people you see, and the situations you encounter. Choose one particular change that you object to, and illustrate it with examples from your own experiences and observations. Explain what you find objectionable as you present each example.

4. Write a paper that responds to one of the following questions about "Killing Women: A Pop-Music Tradition."

   a. John Hamerlinck is careful not to claim that these "woman-killing songs" *cause* violence. Rather, he writes that they *reflect* "a disturbingly casual level of acceptance in society when it comes to so-called 'crimes of passion.'" Do the lyrics of popular music reflect other attitudes toward women as well? Write a paper in which you analyze any other attitudes that such music reflects, supporting your points with specific examples and clear explanations.

   b. Although Hamerlinck suggests that violent lyrics do not cause violence, most people might agree that they are affected one way or another when they listen to music, whether the effect comes from the lyrics or the music. Consider many types of pop music. Write a paper in which you analyze ways that different types of pop music and/or its lyrics might affect the attitudes of its listeners, supporting your points with specific examples and clear explanations.

c. Hamerlinck focuses on depictions of violence against women, but on a more general level his article suggests that we have developed a casual attitude toward many instances of violence in our society. What do you think of that idea? Write a paper in which you analyze different types of violence toward which people have developed casual attitudes, supporting your points with specific examples and clear explanations.

EVALUATING SAMPLE PAPERS

Using the Student Model Checklist on pages 27–28, evaluate the effectiveness of the following student essays:

Student Essay 1

Reading George Will's article made me realize that I am bothered by many changes in our culture. I don't like the way that people have changed the way they drive around ambulances. As a driver on the road I have seen ambulance drivers experience rudeness in the worst ways.

For example one day I heard sirens and immediately looked for the direction the ambulance was coming in so to be prepared. A car coming to the left of me seemed to do nothing to prepare, so the driver either did not hear the sirens or did not care. He continued to drive but at the last minute he panicked, for now the ambulance was directly behind him, and he didn't know where to go. The driver is entirely rude because it slows down the ambulance from getting to its destination.

Another time I witnessed a car that had to have seen the ambulance coming in the drivers' direction, but still kept on driving as he watched the ambulance speed by. What I had just witnessed left me in awe wondering if these kinds of drivers think they are excluded from the pull over and wait law! I see many drivers do this but have never seen anyone be cited. The law needs to be enforced to act as a reminder to those who are not just rude but endangering lives.

Finally the worst rudeness I have seen on the road is the drivers who think they can make it through an intersection before the ambulance, so they do not have to wait. I actually have witnessed this near miss myself. I saw a black pick-up in front of me and the driver looking to see where the sirens were coming from. The ambulance was speeding towards us from the right hand side of the road. I pulled over, but to my dismay the pick-up hit the gas and flew through the intersection just seconds before the ambulance. How the driver made it without causing an accident I still do not know.

These kinds of people also have no idea to the lives they are putting endanger. The endangerment is more than the life in question or the ambulance drivers but also the idiots who impose this potential hazard. This type of driving should not be tolerated and the drivers need to be reminded of the dangers involved when not following the rules of the road.

Student Essay 2

After I graduated from Vista High School, I really looked forward to the future that lay ahead. I was looking forward to my first semester in college because all my friends were going to the same school I was planning to attend. I had heard great things about Palomar College from friends and people I knew that had attended school there for at least a year, and had me anxious to start my first semester. When the time finally came and I attended my first semester, I was stunned by all the troubles and difficulties that I had to go through during my fist semester of school.

Having heard that Palomar had an online registration system, I thought it would be all too easy to enroll in my classes with the comfort of being at home. I soon found out that this was all but true. The online system Palomar College was using was experiencing technical difficulties and was down on a daily basis, making it really hard to add the classes I desired. Sometimes I would be in the process of registering when the whole system would shut down and leave me waiting to see when the system would be up again. Other times, the system was busy because there was an overload of requests from students that were also desperately trying to enroll in the classes they needed. Finally, when I had enrolled and thought that everything was ready to go, I received a letter from school that confirmed the classes I had chosen, and found out that the system had made a mistake in my schedule. At this point, I had no alternative but to go to the administration office and personally register because I knew that it was going to be an impossible task to register through the computer. When I was finally enrolled in my classes, I looked back at all the troubles and difficulties I had to go through, and could not believe how hard it was to register. I had commenced my first college semester on a bad note.

To make my first semester even worse, Palomar College was under construction. The campus was full of trenches that had been excavated with tractors, and there were dozens of dirt mountains all across the school. There were work trucks, tractors, lumber, bricks, and other equipment on the passageways students would use to walk to class. Many times I was forced to walk around one or two buildings to find a different path to class. I also had to find myself a way to get through the maze of fences that were temporarily put up while the construction workers worked. I found this to be a real hassle for myself and the rest of the students. I also had to put up with all the loud noises that the workers created while they worked the tractors and the trucks right next to the class. It was hard for the instructors to give a class and not be disrupted by all the noises. I remember times when the instructor had to pause and wait until the noises dimmed to continue with his lesson; other times he had to repeat himself so we could listen to what he had said. Because of the construction that was taking place, it was difficult for me to concentrate on the lectures and to keep focus on what was being taught; therefore, the construction added to the difficulties and troubles I faced my first semester in college.

I thought that Palomar College, a well-known school that has many students, would have sufficient parking and facilities for all of them. On my first day of school, it took me thirty minutes to find a parking lot that was a ten-minute walk to my first class. I could not believe that there was not enough parking for the students and that the parking lots were so far away from the classes. This fact caused me to be late many times, and had me waking up forty minutes earlier so I could find a parking space and not be late to class. I struggled constantly throughout my first semester of school to wake up earlier, which made it difficult for me to have enough time to properly prepare myself to go to school. Because I had to leave forty minutes earlier to get a parking space, I would miss breakfast and found myself going to school on an empty stomach, which affected me physically. I think that students have too many things to worry about as it is to have to worry about parking. Furthermore, I was also late to class on a few occasions because I could not find a place to park, and I personally think that it was rude and distracting to my instructors for me to walk in late. Even though the school was a little better with its facilities, I found that a few more restrooms could be added to the campus as well as more desks in the classrooms. I remember having to sit on the floor for a week in one of my classes until I brought in a desk from a different class. This also contributed to one of the many difficulties that I went through during my first semester in college.

Throughout the last ten years of school I have attended, I have never experienced what I did that first semester of college. The difficulties and troubles that I endured my first semester in college caused me to have some the worst memories of my first semester of school. For those who are going to college for the first time and are expecting great things in their first semester in school, don't get your hopes too high on how great it's going to be because you might find yourself in a world of troubles and difficulties.

Student Essay 3

Humans have the final say! Do I want to have my hands crossed and watch or take a stand? Paul Rogat Loeb's article, "Ordinary People Produce Extraordinary Results," demonstrates how the normal person can make a difference by standing and fighting in what he or she believes in. For example, when immigrants from other countries unite as one because they want to be accepted as Americans. Events like this change history for the greater good. The smallest contributions can sometimes be the biggest change. The average human can make a powerful difference in society when they face their fears, speak up for what they believe in, and unite with others for a cause.

All humans have hesitations and fears; however, those who accept it and conquer them are those who can make a bigger difference in society. Rosa Parks, "The Mother of the Civil Rights Movement," was a black woman who would not go to the back of the bus when a white bus rider told her. She would not give up her seat in the white section to a white person. This was very brave because she had to know that every African American must give up her seat to a white person. Rosa Parks, a very brave woman, chose to fight for her beliefs knowing the consequences.

Hesitation can be a form of fear and hold a person back from standing up for what is right. A few years before President Obama was elected, my sister Annie got into an argument with two white men because they said, "*There will never be a Black President.*" Annie confronted two grown men because they were discriminating against African Americans. She embarrassed both men because she put them on blast at a Starbucks. All the people that were there clapped for what she had said. Days like those can change a person's perspective. Parks also fought for what she believed to be correct and went to jail for it. Not many would do or ever even think of doing what she did. "Hesitant at first, she gained confidence as she spoke out. She kept on despite a profoundly uncertain context as she and other acted as best they could to challenge deep entrenched injustices with little certainty of results. Had she and others given up after her 10th or 11th year of commitment, we might never have heard of the Montgomery boycott," writes Loeb. Parks even had hesitation; however, she continued and let her voice be heard even if others do not agree with her. Fear is a big thing, but knowing how to use it can really make "ordinary people produce extraordinary results. Only those who choose to face their fear, confront that which is scariest to change views on others despite the obstacles. Annie and Parks make the smallest difference. They make their voice heard no matter how the others may think or react towards.

Why do most people refuse to fight for what they believe in? I observed in the documentary *Brown Eyes, Blue Eyes*, an experiment on children and adults was taken to see how they reacted to it. They discriminated the brown eyes group to the blue eyes group. In the documentary, Jane Elliott, an Iowa school teacher, talked horribly about the people who had brown eyes because she wanted to make a point about the discrimination that was going on. Elliott said, "brown-eyed people should not be allowed in the same room as the blue-eyed people." That was a little hard for me to hear. The sad part was that only one person stood up for the whole group. Everyone else just watched with there hands crossed. Elliott and the blue-eyed people finally stopped the discrimination and had everyone speak out. Hopefully in the end it made them realize that it can be painful and that next time they will stand for one another. I love when people put their differences a side and make a powerful difference in society with their fears and making a group unite for a cause worth fighting for.

Joining forces with an activist or group can create more powerful change. "Two heads are better than one." Groups think better and faster than an individual person. The social activists contributed with their dramatic stands as a group. When a person fights towards for beliefs with a majority of people, positive results can happen. Inspiration can be the start of change. Many more join and the number just keeps in getting bigger. Most of the time they succeed in getting a reaction. We get more inspired from people who don't take "NO" for an answer. They fight and inspire others. For example, when I was small and learning about Martin Luther King, I said, "I want to be like MLK when I grow up." I might not have made a big impact like MLK or Parks, but every now and then I take a stand for myself as well for others. We all have dreams. He was an ordinary man, but he had extraordinary results because he fought for what he believed in. Nothing is impossible. Anything can be accomplished. MLK, Rosa Parks, and the social activists are great examples of fighting for your personal and group beliefs.

In order to change history, social issues need more people and groups led by Rosa Parks, Martin Luther King, and social activists. They took a stand and fought for everyone else who could not. They had their fears and hesitations, but they did not let that stop them. These were "ordinary" people who had "extraordinary" results when they faced their fears to make an impact on social injustices.

SENTENCE COMBINING: COORDINATION

In Chapter 1, you practiced *embedding* simple modifiers (adjectives, adverbs, and prepositional phrases) next to the words they modify in a sentence. Such embedding may have seemed rather easy to you, for it is something we all learned to do quite automatically at an early age. (Almost everyone would automatically change "I wrote a letter. It was long." to "I wrote a long letter.") However, not all combining of related ideas is as easily performed. As writers become more and more proficient, they develop the ability to create quite sophisticated sentence structures as well as very simple ones—but they develop that ability gradually, after much practice.

In this section, you will practice *coordinating* ideas. Like embedding simple modifiers, the process of coordination can be natural and easy. However, effective coordination also has its complexities, which we will take up in this section.

USING COORDINATING CONJUNCTIONS

Coordination consists of joining ideas that are grammatically alike, usually by using one of the seven **coordinating conjunctions**: *and, but, or, nor, for, so,* and *yet.* You can easily memorize these seven conjunctions by learning the acronym BOYSFAN. (An acronym is a word made up from the first letters of other words.)

But Or Yet So For And Nor

Of course, when we talk, we use each of these seven words all of the time. They are so common to our language, in fact, that we rarely think about them. When we want to join two ideas, it takes practically no thought at all to stick an *and* or a *but* or some other coordinating conjunction into our speech and to go on.

Writing, however, is more precise than speech. When someone else reads what we have written, we are usually not there to clarify things that might be confusing, so a careful choice of words the first time through is much more important in writing than in speech. For instance, is there a difference between these two sentences?

> Huck Finn was very superstitious, and he knew he was in trouble when he spilled the salt.

> Huck Finn was very superstitious, so he knew he was in trouble when he spilled the salt.

Both sentences suggest a relationship between the ideas of Huck's being superstitious and of his spilling the salt, but only the second sentence is *precise* in stating the relationship clearly. By using the word *so,* the second sentence makes it clear that Huck's belief about spilling salt was a *result* of his being superstitious.

When you use the coordinating conjunctions, keep their *precise* meanings in mind:

And suggests *addition.* It is used to "add" one idea to a similar one.
> My grass needs to be mowed, <u>and</u> my garden needs to be weeded.

Nor also suggests *addition,* but it adds two negative ideas.
> I have not mowed my lawn in the past two weeks, <u>nor</u> have I weeded the garden.

But suggests a *contrast* or *opposition.*
> I should mow the lawn today, <u>but</u> I think I'll watch a movie instead.

Yet also suggests a *contrast* or *opposition.*
> I feel guilty about not mowing the lawn, <u>yet</u> I really don't want to work today.

Or suggests *alternatives*.
I will mow the lawn tomorrow, <u>or</u> perhaps I'll wait until next weekend.

For suggests a *cause*.
My yard is becoming the neighborhood eyesore, <u>for</u> I hate to do yard work.

So suggests a *result* relationship.
My neighbors have stopped talking to me, <u>so</u> maybe I should clean up my yard today.

EXERCISE 2.2

Combine the following sentences using the coordinating conjunctions that most accurately express the relationship between them.

EXAMPLE

The forecast was for rain with strong winds. I decided to cancel our picnic.
The forecast was for rain with strong winds, so I decided to cancel our picnic.

1. Many people do not know that foods they associate with a specific place did not originate from that place. They are not aware that Africa and America have exchanged many food items.
2. The yam is a West African staple crop that Africans were used to eating. European ships transporting people from Africa loaded yams for their journeys to the Americas.
3. Many people assume that rice came to the Americas from Asia. It actually came from West Africa.
4. Many people associate plantains and bananas with Africa. Originally, bananas and plantains were an Asian plant.
5. Some plants that are now key ingredients in African cuisine arrived in Africa from the Americas on Portuguese or Spanish ships. Portugal and Spain conducted much of the 16th century trade between the two continents.
6. Peanuts, an important part of West and East African cuisine, came from the Americas. Papayas also came from the Americas to Africa.
7. Today, Ivory Coast, or Côte d'Ivoire, is a major exporter of pineapples. Pineapples originally came to West Africa from the Americas.
8. The Portuguese planted lemon, lime, and orange trees along the African coast. They were able to use these fruits to prevent outbreaks of certain diseases among the people they transported to the Americas.
9. One might say that food traditions in places like South Carolina and Louisiana are African. The eating habits of much of the American South have been shaped by African cooking.
10. Gumbo and fried chicken illustrate such African influence. Greens, black-eyed peas, and spicier seasoning do so as well.

EXERCISE 2.3

Each of the following sentences uses *and* as a coordinating conjunction. Where needed, change the *and* to a more precise and accurate coordinating conjunction. Some of the sentences may not need to be changed.

EXAMPLE

Last year I spent $500 on a membership to a local gym, <u>and</u> I used the gym only two times all year long.

Last year I spent $500 on a membership to a local gym, but I used the gym only two times all year long.

1. In the early 1900s, Alfred Wegener noticed that the coasts of Africa and South America looked as if they could fit together, <u>and</u> he began to investigate that idea.

2. He proposed the theory that the two continents were once connected, <u>and</u> fossils discovered in Brazil were similar to those found in Africa.

3. He then suggested that all the continents were once one giant landmass, <u>and</u> he named that landmass Pangaea ("All Land").

4. He developed the idea of "continental drift" to explain the movement of the land, <u>and</u> his theory was largely dismissed for many years.

5. He could not explain what could propel such huge landmasses, <u>and</u> he could not find sufficient proof to convince other scientists.

6. In his lifetime his ideas were disregarded, <u>and</u> today they are supported by the almost universally accepted theory of global plate tectonics.

7. The Earth's continents are moving, <u>and</u> the Earth's crust is divided into mobile sections called *plates*.

8. These plates can be as large as a few thousand miles across, <u>and</u> they can be as small as a few hundred miles across.

9. They move over the Earth's superheated, molten core as much as a few inches each year, <u>and</u> they average thirty to fifty miles in thickness.

10. Earthquakes often occur on the west coast of the United States, <u>and</u> the Pacific plate is moving northwest while the North American plate is moving south.

In each of the above exercises and examples, a comma has been placed before the coordinating conjunction because the statements being combined could stand alone as separate sentences. However, when a coordinating conjunction joins two sentence parts that can *not* stand alone as separate sentences, do not use a comma before the conjunction. (For a further discussion of this comma rule, see Chapter 17.)

EXAMPLE

COMMA   Mario worked all night on the new computer program, and his brother worked with him.

NO COMMA   Mario worked all night on the new computer program and all the next day on his accounting work.

USING SEMICOLONS

So far, we have seen that using a comma and a coordinating conjunction is one way to combine related sentences. Another way to combine sentences is to use a *semicolon,* usually (but not always) with a conjunctive adverb. Following are some common **conjunctive adverbs:**

accordingly	however	otherwise	as a result
also	instead	similarly	for example
besides	meanwhile	still	for instance
consequently	moreover	then	in addition
finally	namely	therefore	in fact
further	nevertheless	thus	on the other hand
furthermore	next	undoubtedly	
hence	nonetheless		

EXAMPLES

Henry ate all of the potato chips; however, he was still hungry.

Tuan knew that he should buy a new car; on the other hand, he really wanted a motorcycle.

The movie was too violent for Sabrina; the concert was too dull for Rocky.

If you use a semicolon to combine related sentences, remember these points:

1. Most writers—professional and nonprofessional—use semicolons *much less frequently* than the other methods of combining sentences that are discussed in this and other sections.

2. Conjunctive adverbs *are not* coordinating conjunctions and should *not be used to combine sentences with commas.*

EXAMPLES

INCORRECT	Sylvia had always wanted to visit the Far East, however she never had enough money to do so.
CORRECT	Sylvia had always wanted to visit the Far East; however, she never had enough money to do so.

3. It is the *semicolons* that join sentences, not the conjunctive adverbs. As a result, conjunctive adverbs may appear *anywhere that makes sense* in the sentence.

EXAMPLES

It rained for fifteen straight days. <u>Nevertheless</u>, my father jogged every day.

It rained for fifteen straight days; my father, <u>nevertheless</u>, jogged every day.

It rained for fifteen straight days; my father jogged every day, <u>nevertheless</u>.

EXERCISE 2.4

Combine the following sentences, either by using a comma with a coordinating conjunction or by using a semicolon with or without a conjunctive adverb.

EXAMPLE

Hillary wanted to attend college full-time. She needed to work forty hours a week to support her family.

Hillary wanted to attend college full-time, but she needed to work forty hours a week to support her family.

or

Hillary wanted to attend college full-time; however, she needed to work forty hours a week to support her family.

1. In the 1920s, record labels started producing so-called race records. These records were produced for an African American audience and featured African American musicians.

2. Most aspects of American life were highly segregated then. Some of the race records and their performers began to appeal to white audiences.

3. Bessie Smith became one of the most famous performers of this era. She is sometimes referred to as "Queen of the Blues" or even as "Empress of the Blues."

4. The blues originated in the late 1800s in the Mississippi Delta as an African American folk music. By the 1920s, the blues had gained some national and international attention.

5. Bessie Smith was born on April 15, 1894, in Chattanooga, Tennessee. She began performing as a child in Tennessee after both her father and mother had died.

6. She later moved to Atlanta and then to Philadelphia, signing with Columbia Records. During the 1920s, she became the most well-paid African American musical performer.

7. In 1929, the stock market crashed, causing the economy as a whole to suffer, and the record industry and musicians especially so. Columbia Records went almost bankrupt, which caused Bessie Smith to lose her contract with the firm.

8. By 1933, Bessie Smith was making blues records again for the Okeh label. When she began to perform at the famous Apollo Theater in Harlem in1935, she initiated a change in musical style as Swing had become popular.

9. Victor Records was interested in making Swing records with her. Her tragic death in a car accident at night on September 26, 1937, ended her revitalized career.

10. The driver of her car did not see a larger truck before them and hit it at high speed. Although a doctor happened to stop shortly after, she had lost too much blood and died on the way to the hospital.

11. Thousands of people showed up at her funeral in Philadelphia. In 1970, rock singer Janis Joplin contributed to the costs of a stone for Bessie Smith's grave that says "The Greatest Blues Singer in the World Will Never Stop Singing."

COMBINING PARTS OF SENTENCES

So far, we have focused on using coordination to combine *separate sentences*. Another way to improve your writing is to use a coordinating conjunction to join *part* of one sentence to *part* of another sentence. This type of sentence combining is more difficult than the simple joining of entire sentences, but it usually results in more concise and direct writing. For instance, here are two sentences as they might have been written by Gail Sheehy in "Jail-break Marriage." The parts of each sentence that could be combined are underlined.

Simone was the last domain <u>where her mother could play out the maternal role</u>. She was also the last place <u>where her father could exercise complete control</u>.

Of course, Sheehy recognized that these two ideas could really be expressed as one sentence, so she wrote this:

Simone was the last domain <u>where her mother could play out the maternal role</u> and <u>where her father could exercise complete control</u>.

Here is another example, taken from "Ordinary People Produce Extraordinary Results." When discussing Rosa Parks and activists for social change, Loeb could have written three sentences. The parts of each sentence that could be combined are underlined.

These activists teach us <u>how to shift public sentiment. In addition, they show us ways to</u> challenge entrenched institutional power. <u>Finally, as we move forward, they help</u> us <u>find the strength to persevere despite all odds</u>.

Here is how Loeb actually wrote the sentence:

These activists teach us <u>how to shift public sentiment, challenge entrenched institutional power</u> and <u>find the strength to persevere despite all odds</u>.

Note

When joining three or more items, as has been done here, you need to use the coordinating conjunction only before the last item.

PARALLEL SENTENCE STRUCTURE

When you use coordination to join ideas, you should do your best to word those ideas similarly so that they are clear and easy to read. Coordinate ideas that are worded similarly are said to be *parallel* in structure. Notice the difference between the following two examples:

NONPARALLEL STRUCTURE

My favorite sports are <u>swimming</u> and <u>to jog</u>.

PARALLEL STRUCTURE

My favorite sports are <u>swimming</u> and <u>jogging</u>.

Do you see how much clearer the parallel sentence is? Now let's look once more at the examples from the articles by Gail Sheehy and Paul Rogat Loeb. Notice how the coordinate ideas have been written so that they are parallel in structure.

Simone was the last domain

<u>where her mother could play out the maternal role</u>
and   <u>where her father could exercise complete control</u>.

These activists teach us how to

<u>shift public sentiment</u>,
<u>challenge entrenched institutional power</u>,
and   <u>find the strength to persevere despite all odds</u>.

As you can see, recognizing related ideas and combining them in parallel structure can result in sentences that are more direct and less repetitious than the original sentences.

Note   For a more thorough discussion of parallel sentence structure, see Chapter 6.

EXERCISE 2.5

Combine each group of sentences into one sentence by using coordinating conjunctions to join related ideas. Wherever possible, use parallel sentence structure. Parallel ideas that can be combined are underlined in the first three groups.

EXAMPLE

People <u>who stereotype others</u> are often insensitive to the pain they cause. The same is true for people <u>who tell ethnic jokes</u>.
People <u>who stereotype others</u> or <u>who tell ethnic jokes</u> are often insensitive to the pain <u>they</u> cause.

1. According to legend, Calamity Jane was a <u>fierce Indian fighter</u>. She also was a <u>brave scout</u>. In addition, legend describes her as <u>a beautiful, vivacious tamer of the Old West</u>.

2. In reality, however, she often brought misfortune <u>into her own life</u>. She brought misfortune <u>into the lives of others</u>, too.

3. Although born in Princeton, Missouri, she spent most of her life in Deadwood, South Dakota, a town notorious for its collection of <u>miners</u> and <u>Civil War veterans</u>. It was also full of <u>gamblers</u> and <u>outlaws</u>, and it was the home of many <u>prostitutes</u>.

4. It is said that she drank as heavily as any mule skinner. In addition, she cursed as coarsely as the roughest of men.

5. Calamity's life was characterized by drunkenness. It was also full of lawlessness. It even included prostitution.

6. Dime-store novels helped spread her legend by describing her as a natural beauty. She was referred to as the sweetheart of Wild Bill Hickok.

7. Calamity Jane did know Wild Bill Hickok. She was part of his gang for a while, but there is no evidence that he romanced her. There is also no evidence that he even paid much attention to her.

8. Easterners viewed the westward movement as adventurous. To them, it was romantic. It was exciting, so they preferred stories that idealized the West. They also liked stories that made their heroes seem larger than life.

9. Calamity Jane may have received her nickname from her many hard-luck experiences. It may also have come from the problems she caused others. It may even have resulted from her willingness to help victims of smallpox during an epidemic in Deadwood.

10. In her last years, Calamity drifted from place to place, selling a poorly written leaflet about her life. She also could be found performing as a sharpshooter in Wild West shows. In addition, she performed as a wild driver of six-horse teams in these same shows.

Supporting the Central Idea

3

Poor Irving! He wants a nice, fuzzy, somewhat vague relationship, but Cathy wants specifics. She wants Irving to explain *why* he had a great time, to elaborate on *what* was great about it. We're often the same way, aren't we? If we ask a friend how he or she liked a movie, we're not usually satisfied with answers like "Great!" or "Yuck!" We want to know specifically *why* the person liked or disliked it. Was it the plot or the acting or the special effects or the quality of the popcorn that caused our friend to react in a certain way? The more specific our friend can be, the more he or she will help us decide whether we want to see the film too.

The same is true of responses to other media, such as novels and television, or to public issues, such as elections or gun control or capital punishment. The more specific information we have on these issues, the better informed our decisions will be.

In the same way, the more you can support your topic sentence or your thesis statement with specific information, the more convincing your writing will be. The most common types of support are brief or extended examples, statistics, and expert opinion or testimony.

BRIEF EXAMPLES

From Personal Experience or Direct Observation

One of the most interesting and convincing ways to support your ideas is by relating brief examples drawn from your own personal experiences or observations. When we are discussing issues casually with acquaintances, we just naturally share our own experiences. Note how several brief examples are used in the following paragraph to support its central idea:

> People, at least the ones in my town, seem to have become ruder as the population has increased. Twice yesterday drivers came up behind me and gestured rudely even though I was driving ten miles per hour over the speed limit. The other day, as my friend and I were sitting on the seawall watching the sunset and listening to the ocean waves, a rollerblader with a boom box going full blast sat down next to us. When we politely asked him to turn off his radio, he cursed at us and skated off. Every day I see perfectly healthy people parking in spaces reserved for individuals with disabilities, smokers lighting up in no-smoking areas and refusing to leave when asked, and people shoving their way into lines at movie theaters and grocery stores.

Personal examples are usually not enough to prove a point, but they do help illustrate your ideas and make your writing more specific and interesting. In fact, good writing is always moving from the general to the specific, with the emphasis on the specific, and the use of brief examples is one of the most effective ways of keeping your writing interesting, convincing, and informative. Notice how the lack of examples in the following paragraph results in uninteresting, lackluster writing:

> There are a lot of animals to be found in Carlsbad. They come in all sizes and shapes. There are all kinds of birds and other animals besides dogs and cats.

Now let's see if it can be improved with the addition of brief examples:

> The typical yard in Carlsbad is visited by a wide variety of animals. Birds, especially, are present in abundance. House finches and sparrows flit through the trees and search the ground for seeds. Mockingbirds sing day and night, claiming their territory. The feisty and mischievous scrub jays, with their blue plumage, raid the food set out for cats. The homely California towhee, whose call sounds like a squeaky wheel, rustles among the fallen leaves looking for insects. And the exotic and mysterious ruby-throated hummingbirds go from flower to flower, searching for nectar, or visit feeders hung out for them. At night the slow-witted possum rambles about, getting into garbage cans and dog dishes. The elegant and clever raccoons compete with the possums. Occasionally one can sense that a skunk has visited someone's yard. In some places, bands of escaped domestic rabbits can be seen frolicking

and raiding gardens. Lizards and snakes ply the underbrush, searching for insects and small rodents. If one is observant and lucky, one can experience a multitude of critters right in the backyard.

As you can see, the many brief, specific examples in this paragraph improve it immensely, giving it texture, color, and interest. They also make the writing believable. Any reader would easily be convinced that this writer knows what he is talking about and has taken the time to observe the animals in Carlsbad carefully and to report them accurately.

From Other Sources

Brief examples from other sources are quite similar to brief personal examples or anecdotes. They may come from places such as books, magazines, television, films, or lectures, or they may come from the experiences of people you know. Like personal examples, they make your abstract ideas and arguments concrete and therefore convincing.

Here are some brief examples from recent news broadcasts that were offered in support of a gun control bill:

> Larry and Sharon Ellingsen were driving home from their 29th wedding anniversary party in Oakland, California, when a passing driver on the freeway sent a bullet through their window, killing Mr. Ellingsen instantly.
>
> Mildred Stanfield, a 78-year-old church organist from quiet Broad Ripple, Indiana, was shot twice in the chest at a bus stop when she tried to stop a 15-year-old boy from stealing her purse.
>
> Cesar Sandoval, a 6-year-old kindergartener, was shot in the head while riding home on a county school bus in New Haven, Connecticut. He and six classmates were caught in drug-related crossfire among three teenagers.

EXTENDED EXAMPLES

From Personal Experience or Direct Observation

Extended examples from personal experiences or observations are longer, more detailed narratives of events that have involved you or people you know. Sometimes several brief examples won't have the emotional impact that an extended example will. Sometimes people need to hear the full story of something that happened to a real person to understand fully the point you are trying to make. Suppose, for instance, that you are writing about the senseless violence that seems to be occurring more and more frequently in today's society. You could illustrate that violence with several brief examples, or you could emphasize its heartlessness and brutality with an extended example such as the following:

> The senseless, brutal violence that we read about in the newspapers every day seems very distant from the average person, but it is really not far away at all. In fact, it can strike any of us without any warning—just

as it struck my uncle Silas last week. After having dinner with his wife and two children, Silas had driven to the Texaco gas station at the corner of Vista Way and San Marcos Drive, where he was working part-time to earn extra money for a down payment on a house. Some time around 11:00 P.M., two young men carrying Smith and Wesson .38s approached him and demanded money. Uncle Silas was a good, brave man, but he was also a realistic person. He knew when to cooperate, and that's just what he did. He opened the cash register and the safe, then handed the intruders the keys to his new truck. They shot him in the head anyway.

Wouldn't you agree that the above extended example carries an emotional impact that brief examples might not carry? This anecdote might be used in a pro–gun control essay or even in an anti–gun control essay (Uncle Silas should have had his own gun). Or it could be part of an essay on capital punishment. In any case, it would add dramatic interest to a piece of writing. As you can see, examples of personal experience can be brief, perhaps only one sentence long, or extended, taking up several paragraphs.

From Other Sources

Extended examples taken from magazines, newspapers, books, or newscasts can also provide dramatic and persuasive support for your papers. Professional writers know the effect that extended examples can have on the reader, so they use such examples frequently. Notice how Ellen Goodman, a nationally known writer, uses the following extended example in an article debating the right of people to commit suicide:

> It is certain that Peter Rosier wouldn't be on trial today if he hadn't   1
> been on television two years ago. If he hadn't told all of Fort Myers,
> Florida, that "I administered something to terminate her life."
>
> His wife Patricia, after all, a woman whose lung cancer had   2
> spread to her other organs, had told everyone that she intended
> to commit suicide. Indeed she planned her death as a final elabo-
> rate production.
>
> Perhaps it was a dramatic attempt to control, or shape, or   3
> choose the terms of her death. Perhaps it was an attempt to win
> some perverse victory over her cancer. Either way, Patricia Rosier,
> forty-three, picked the date, the time, even the wine for her last
> meal. She picked out the pills and she swallowed them.
>
> Death, however, didn't play the accommodating role that had   4
> been scripted for it. While the Rosier children slept in the next room,
> the deep coma induced by twenty Seconal pills began to lighten. Her
> husband, Peter, a pathologist, went desperately searching for mor-
> phine. And then, as he said a year later, he "administered something."

—*Ellen Goodman,* Making Sense *© 1989 by the Boston Globe Newspaper Co./Washington Post Writers Group. Reprinted by permission.*

The details of Patricia Rosier's death, particularly the descriptions of the cancer that had spread throughout her body and of her careful plans to take her own life, help the reader understand the complexity of the decision that Peter Rosier had to make. Is he guilty of murder? Should he have ignored his wife's desire to avoid a painful death by cancer? In the face of detailed, real experience, answering such questions is not easy.

EXERCISE **3.1**

Examine "Jailbreak Marriage" on pages 46–48 and "Printed Noise" on pages 51–53 (or examine other articles assigned by your instructor) to determine whether the authors are using brief or extended examples. Discuss the effectiveness (or ineffectiveness) of the types of examples used in each article.

EXERCISE **3.2**

Choose one of the following sentences, and support it with at least three brief examples. Then choose another of the sentences, and support it with one extended example.

1. Some of my friends idolize celebrities who lead lavish and/or self-destructive lives.
2. Young people have committed suicide because of bullying, whether in person or online.
3. I have some family members who do not give money to street beggars because, according to them, homeless people are leeching off society.
4. Many students on campus still openly make religious, gender, or sexually intolerant comments.
5. Every day I see people who ignore others because they are on a smart-phone, tablet, or some other technical device.

STATISTICS

Examples are very effective ways to support your ideas, but sometimes examples just aren't enough. Sometimes you need support that is more objective and measurable than an example. Sometimes you need support that covers more situations than one or even several examples could possibly cover. At times like these, statistics are the perfect support. In fact, if statistics are used fairly and correctly and are drawn from reliable sources, they are just about the most credible and effective type of support. We are impressed, perhaps overly impressed, when a writer can cite clear numbers to support an argument. Notice how the writer Emily Greenhouse uses statistics in her article about the increase in suicides worldwide.

A week after Benjamin was reunited with Laybourn, *Le Monde*, the leading newspaper on the other side of the English Channel, published the results of a medical study of French fifteen-year-olds, which revealed that almost twenty-one per cent of girls and nine per cent of boys reported attempting suicide in the past year. That's a shocking number, and it speaks to a global trend. In the United States, suicide rates have risen, particularly among middle-aged people: between 1999 and 2010, the number of Americans between the ages of thirty-five and sixty-four who took their own lives rose by almost thirty per cent. Among young people in the U.S., suicide is the third most common cause of death; among all Americans, suicide claims more lives than car accidents, which were previously the leading cause of injury-related death.

—*Emily Greenhouse, "The Neglected Suicide Epidemic"*

As the above paragraph illustrates, statistics can be quite impressive. It is startling to read that 20 percent of French fifteen-year-old girls and 9 percent of fifteen-year-old boys attempted suicide in a single year. And certainly it is shocking to discover that "between 1999 and 2010, the number of Americans between the ages of thirty-five and sixty-four who took their own lives rose by almost thirty per cent." Such statistics present a convincing argument that suicidal thoughts and feelings are a "neglected epidemic."

EXPERT OPINION OR TESTIMONY

Another kind of support that can be quite convincing is information from or statements by authorities on the subject about which you are writing. Let's suppose that you are trying to decide whether to have your child vaccinated against measles. You have heard other parents say that a measles vaccination can harm a child, but you have never really known any parents who said their own children were harmed. So what do you do? Probably you call your pediatrician and ask for an expert opinion. After all, he or she is the one who has studied the field and who has vaccinated hundreds, perhaps thousands, of children.

In the same way, if you are writing a paper about a constitutional issue—such as the relationship of the Second Amendment to the need for gun control—you might decide to consult the experts for their opinions. And who are they? Probably legal scholars, political scientists, and even Supreme Court justices. Of course, you won't call these people on the phone; instead, you'll use quotations that you have found in articles and books from your college library. Here is an example of one such use of expert testimony:

Parents must strive to find alternatives to the physical punishment of children. Almost every effect of corporal punishment is negative.

Dr. Bruno Bettelheim, famous psychologist and professor at the University of Chicago, writes, "Punishment is a traumatic experience not only in itself but also because it disappoints the child's wish to believe in the benevolence of the parent, on which his sense of security rests."

If you do use expert opinion or testimony, don't believe too easily everything you read. When choosing authorities, you should consider not only their expertise but also their reputations for such qualities as integrity, honesty, and credibility. Also, you should determine whether other experts in the same field disagree with the expert whose opinion you have cited. After all, if the experts don't agree, testimony from just one of them won't be very convincing. In fact, because experts often *do* disagree, it is a good idea to use expert testimony only *in combination with* the other types of support discussed in this chapter.

COMBINING TYPES OF SUPPORT

Combining the different types of support is a very effective way to develop your ideas. Rarely will you find professional writers relying only on examples or statistics or expert testimony to support what they have to say. Instead, the more convincing writers provide many different types of support to make their point. Usually, the better and wider the support you use, the better your chance of persuading your reader.

EXERCISE **3.3**

The following excerpt appeared in the article "Be Not Afraid" in *The Atlantic* in 2015. It argues that the perception that the world is growing more dangerous is inaccurate. Examine it for each type of support discussed in this chapter.

Perception is even more skewed where terrorism is concerned. 1
"Terrorism Worries Largely Unchanged," ran [a] Pew headline, also
in 2013. That year, 58 percent of the public was worried about
another terrorist attack in the United States, a rate not all that
much lower in October 2001, immediately after the 9/11 attacks,
when 71 percent of the public was worried. A few months ago,
perhaps influenced by ISIS's atrocities, a large plurality of respondents told NBC News/*Wall Street Journal* pollsters that the country
is less safe than it was before 9/11.

Reality, once again, tells us otherwise. State-sponsored inter- 2
national terrorism, writes the intelligence analyst Paul R. Pillar in
Cato's *A Dangerous World?*, "is today only a shadow of what it
was in the 1970s and 1980s." As for the risk posed by terrorism

inside the United States, to characterize it as trivial would be very generous. Americans are about four times as likely to drown in their bathtub as they are to die in a terrorist attack. John Mueller of Ohio State University and Mark G. Stewart of Australia's University of Newcastle estimate the odds of such deaths at one in 950,000 and one in 3.5 million, respectively.

Surely we can at least agree to worry about a nuclear Iran, or nuclear terrorism, or ISIS? All are indeed worrisome, but Mueller persuasively argues that none merits the alarm it begets. Since Nagasaki in 1945, the few countries that have obtained nuclear weapons—including dangerous rogue states like Mao's China, the Iran of its day—have consistently found them militarily and diplomatically useless, except as ego boosters and perhaps as defensive weapons to forestall attack. The odds of terrorists' obtaining and deploying nuclear weapons are much lower than most people appreciate, for a host of technical and political reasons. ISIS, meanwhile, is an unusually vicious and destabilizing actor in a region that is full of them, but its menace has been almost entirely local. 3

From Jonathan Rauch, "Be Not Afraid," The Atlantic, February 16, 2015

EXERCISE 3.4

Examine "Anonymous Sources" on pages 11–14 (or another article assigned by your instructor). Identify the types of support that have been discussed in this chapter.

EXPLAINING THE SIGNIFICANCE OF THE SUPPORT

Remember that better paragraphs and essays almost always move from the more general topic or thesis to the more specific example, statistic, or expert opinion. Specific, detailed support will give color and life to your papers, and it will help make your points clear and convincing.

However, once you have provided specific support, you are still not finished if you want your ideas to be as convincing as possible. Now is the time to *explain the significance* of your support. You might explain how your supporting details relate to the central idea of your paper, or you might emphasize the parts of your support that you consider the most significant. The point is that *your ideas* will become clearest when you elaborate on your support, using your own words to explain the significance of the details you have given.

In the following example, note how the student writer elaborates upon her support.

topic sentence

supporting
example

explaining the
significance

> Sometimes it is very difficult not to respond to rude people with more rude-ness of my own. For instance, one day last summer while I was working as a cashier at Rice King, a Chinese restaurant, an old lady came in and said "Give me the damn noodles." I could not believe what she said. I was very angry. When I gave her the food, she opened the box in front of me and started picking through the noodles with her fingers. Then she said, "There is not enough meat." I knew there was more than enough meat in the box, but I ended up giving her more anyway. I suppose what I really wanted to do was to tell her what a disgusting person she was, but I'm glad that I didn't. After all, I didn't know her or what kind of problems she might be having in her life. Was she rude and obnoxious? Yes. Did that give me the right to be mean or hurtful in return? I didn't think so.
>
> —*Jung Yun Park, student writer*

WRITING INTRODUCTIONS AND CONCLUSIONS

So far in this chapter, we have been discussing how to *support* your ideas. In many ways, however, how you *introduce* and *conclude* your paper is as impor-tant as how you support it. In the next few pages, we will discuss some strat-egies you can use to write effective introductions and conclusions.

THE INTRODUCTORY PARAGRAPH

As we all know, first impressions can be deceptive, but they can also be of great importance. The opening paragraph of a paper provides the first impres-sions of the essay and of the writer. Thus, it is one of the most important paragraphs of your essay. Your introductory paragraph serves a number of important purposes:

- It gains the attention of your reader in the lead-in.
- It informs your reader about such details as the background of your subject and the purpose of your essay.
- It gives the reader some idea of you, the writer, particularly through its tone.
- It presents the thesis statement and often the plan or organization of your essay.

THE LEAD-IN

The lead-in generally consists of the first several sentences of the introduction. It may take any number of forms.

A General Statement

One of the most common ways of developing the introduction is to begin with a general statement and then follow it with more particular or specific statements leading to your thesis statement. This introductory strategy is sometimes referred to as a *funnel introduction* because, like a funnel, it is broad at the opening and narrow at the bottom. The following brief introduction from a student essay follows the general-to-particular pattern:

general
statement

specific thesis

> When disaster strikes, American people respond with their good hearts and numerous organized systems to help families cope with the disaster and its effects. There is beauty in a neighbor's heartfelt response to a disaster. My children and I discovered just how much caring and assistance Americans will help families with when a disaster strikes.

Here is another general-to-particular introduction. Note that the thesis in this introduction presents two particular points on which the paper will focus:

general
statement

specific thesis

> Some time around the middle of November, about half the population seems to begin griping about the "secularization" of Christmas. They become nostalgic for some old, ideal, traditional Christmas that may never have existed. They fume about artificial trees and plastic creches. However, P. H. Terzian, in an article entitled "A Commercial Christmas Is Not So Crass," states that these grouches are wrongheaded, and I agree. Terzian and I feel that the Christmas spirit is alive and well for several reasons: Christmas has always been a healthy mixture of the sacred and profane, and it has always been about joyfully getting, giving, and receiving.

A Question

Many writers open their essays with a question that is meant to attract the interest of the reader. Sometimes writers use a *rhetorical question*—that is, a question for which no answer is expected because the intended answer is obvious. Here is a rhetorical question: "Should we allow child abuse to continue?" Obviously, the answer to this question is no. Even so, a writer might open an essay with such a question to make the reader wonder why she or he is asking it and to draw the reader into the essay. Other times a writer might open an essay with a question that requires an answer—and the need to hear the answer keeps the reader reading. Here is a student's introductory paragraph that begins with a question:

question

specific thesis

> Is Tipper Gore overreacting? In her article "Curbing the Sexploitation Industry," Gore emphasizes the dangers posed for our children by what she calls the sexploitation industry. She claims that entertainment producers do not take our children into consideration when they present violent material. She says we should be concerned about the mental health of our children and the dignity of women. I do not think she is overreacting at all. Our society is facing a serious threat from the sexploitation industry: TV networks show excessive sex scenes, movie producers make films with excessive graphic violence, and rock recordings contain explicit sexual lyrics.

An Anecdote or Brief Story

We all enjoy stories. For most of us, reading about real people in real situations is far more convincing and interesting than reading about general ideas.

For that reason, opening an essay with a short description of a person, place, or event can be an effective way of grabbing your reader's attention. The following introduction opens with a short anecdote:

anecdote

> I found a *Penthouse* magazine in my twelve year old's room last week, and I panicked. I recalled that Ted Bundy, who roamed the country mutilating, murdering, and raping, had said right before his execution that he had been influenced by pornography. Was my son on his way to a life of violent crime? Probably not. But a recent article, "Ted Bundy Shows Us the Crystallizing Effect of Pornography," raises some serious concerns. We need to be more vigilant about what our children (and our fellow citizens of all ages) are experiencing in all of the media, and

specific thesis

> we need to make our lawmakers aware of our concern. However, we need to accomplish these missions without weakening the First Amendment to the Constitution and without harming the world of art.

A Quotation

A quotation from someone connected with your topic, from an article you're writing about, or from an expert on your subject can be a good way of opening your introduction. Or you might look up a famous quotation on your subject in a book such as *Bartlett's Familiar Quotations*. Notice how the following student paragraph moves from a quotation to a specific thesis statement:

quotation

> Martin Luther King, Jr., once said, "I have a dream that my four little children will one day live in a nation where they will not be judged by the color of their skin, but by the content of their character." Dr. King would certainly be disappointed if he could read a recent article by Richard Cohen in *The Washington Post*, entitled "A Generation of Bigots Comes of Age." The author claims that we are seeing an increase in bigotry, especially from the generation just coming of age (those in their twenties). He cites a great deal of information and statistics from the

specific thesis

> Anti-Defamation League and from a Boston polling firm. I believe Mr. Cohen because lately I have experienced an increase in prejudice at work, at school, at shopping malls, and at many other places.

A Striking Statement or Fact

"Coming soon to your local cable system: VTV, violent television, 24 hours a day of carnage and mayhem." This quotation was the lead-in for a recent article on the amount of violence children see on television and the effects it may be having on them. Later in the article, the writer pointed out that one hundred acts of violence occur on television each hour. This fact could also be used as a striking lead-in to your essay. Once you have captured the attention of your reader through a strategy like this, he or she will tend to keep reading. Here is an introduction based on the above quotation:

striking
statement

> "Coming soon to your local cable system: VTV, violent television, 24 hours a day of carnage and mayhem." So writes Joseph Perkins

specific thesis

in his article "It's a Prime-Time Crime." Perkins cites the American Psychological Association and the quarterly journal *The Public Interest* to support his idea that the enormous amount of violence viewed by American children may be doing them irreparable harm. I find the overwhelming evidence that violence on TV is making children overly aggressive and is having a negative effect on their mental health quite convincing, especially because so many of my own observations confirm that evidence.

EXERCISE 3.5

Examine the introductions to "Live Each Moment for What It's Worth" (pages 7–9), "Anonymous Sources" (pages 11–14) "Jailbreak Marriage" (pages 46–48), "Ordinary People Produce Extraordinary Results" (pages 53–56), and "Killing Women: A Pop-Music Tradition" (pages 59–62). Pay particular attention to the type of lead-in used by each article. Be prepared to discuss which introductions you find to be most effective.

THE CONCLUDING PARAGRAPH

Final impressions are as important as initial ones, especially if you want to leave your reader with a sense of completeness and confidence in you. Although the content of your conclusion will depend on what you have argued or presented in your essay, here are some suggestions as to what you might include:

- A restatement of your thesis, presented in words and phrases different from those used in your introduction
- A restatement of your supporting points, presented in words and phrases different from those used in your body paragraphs
- Predictions or recommendations about your proposals or arguments
- Solutions to the problems you have raised
- A quotation or quotations that support your ideas
- A reference to an anecdote or story that appeared in your introduction

Following are some concluding paragraphs that use some of these strategies.

A Restatement of the Main Points, and a Prediction or Recommendation

The following is a concluding paragraph from an article on the effects of TV violence on children. The author summarizes his main points and also offers a recommendation.

Given the overwhelming evidence that violent TV has deleterious effects on children, that it increases the level of violence throughout American society, it hardly seems unreasonable that the government ask that [the] TV industry tone down its violent programming. Those who find that request objectionable should forfeit their privileged use of public airwaves.

—*Joseph Perkins, "It's a Prime-Time Crime"*

A Solution to a Problem That Has Been Raised

Here is a conclusion from a rather unusual essay. Its thesis is that laws allowing men but not women to go topless at the beach are discriminatory and reflect our male-dominated culture. It offers two possible solutions to the problem.

> It was not too long ago that the law also attempted to shield children from pregnant teachers. But the Supreme Court held pregnancy no grounds for a forced leave of absence. Another court has ruled that unmarried pregnant students cannot be excluded from public schools—not unless unmarried expectant fathers are also excluded. It is time for the same equality to be applied to bathing attire. Whether that is accomplished by allowing all people to go topless or by requiring men to wear tops, the end result will be the same: discarding one more premise of a male-defined society.

A Restatement of the Main Points, and a Quotation That Supports the Ideas

The following conclusion to a student essay sums up the writer's ideas on her subject and then presents an effective quotation from the author of the article to which she is responding.

> Diversity, in America, is supposed to be good. This country was formed for freedoms like religion, speech, and sexual preference. America was formed for all ethnic groups and all traditions. When a certain group thinks that they are above all, that is when the problems begin. It is important to educate others on your background and to celebrate your heritage, to a certain extent. It is also important to learn about other cultures so that we feel comfortable and not threatened by others. As Schoenberger says, "I would much prefer them to hate or distrust me because of something I've done, instead of hating me on the basis of prejudice."

A Restatement of the Main Points, a Reference to an Anecdote or Story from the Introduction, and a Solution to a Problem That Has Been Raised

This conclusion is drawn from the article "Getting to Know about You and Me." Its introduction tells the story of the author being invited to join the Diversity Committee at her high school, an invitation she declined. The conclusion refers again to that invitation.

> I'm now back at school, and I plan to apply for the Diversity Committee. I'm going to get up and tell the whole school about my religion and the tradition I'm proud of. I see now how important it is to celebrate your heritage and to educate others about it. I can no longer take for granted that everyone knows about my religion, or that I know about theirs. People who are suspicious when they find out I'm Jewish

usually don't know much about Judaism. I would much prefer them to hate or distrust me because of something I've done, instead of them hating me on the basis of prejudice.

EXERCISE **3.6**

Examine the conclusions to "Live Each Moment for What It's Worth" (pages 7–9), "Anonymous Sources" (pages 11–14), "Jailbreak Marriage" (pages 46–48), and "Ordinary People Produce Extraordinary Results" (pages 53–56). Be prepared to discuss which conclusions you find to be most effective.

READINGS

As you read each of the following selections, pay particular attention to the type of support each writer uses and to the introduction and conclusion of each article.

Male Fixations

DAVE BARRY

Dave Barry, one of the most popular humor columnists in the United States, writes for the Miami Herald *and is published in more than five hundred newspapers. According to his official Web site (www.davebarry.com), he also "plays lead guitar in a literary rock band called the Rock Bottom Remainders, whose other members include Stephen King, Amy Tan, Ridley Pearson, and Mitch Albom."*

BEFORE YOU READ

1. What could the title "Male Fixations" possibly refer to? What is a fixation?
2. What assumptions do you or people you know have about what a man should or should not know how to do?

Most guys believe that they're supposed to know how to fix things. This is a responsibility that guys have historically taken upon themselves to compensate for the fact that they never clean the bathroom. A guy can walk into a bathroom containing a colony of commode fungus so advanced that it is registered to vote, but the guy would never dream of cleaning it, because he has to keep himself rested in case a Mechanical Emergency breaks out. 1

For example, let's say that one day his wife informs him that the commode has started making a loud groaning noise, like it's about to have a baby commode. This is when the guy swings into action. 2

He strides in, removes the tank cover, peers down into the area that contains the mystery commode parts, and then, drawing on tens of thousands of years of guy mechanical understanding, announces that *there is nothing wrong with the commode.*

At least that's how I handle these things. I never actually fix   3
anything. I blame this on tonsillitis. I had tonsillitis in the ninth grade, and I missed some school, and apparently on one of the days I missed, they herded the guys into the auditorium and explained to them about things like carburetors, valves, splines, gaskets, ratchets, grommets, "dado joints," etc. Because some guys actually seem to understand this stuff. One time in college my roommate, Rob, went into his room all alone with a Volvo transmission, opened his toolbox, disassembled the transmission to the point where he appeared to be working on *individual transmission molecules,* then put it all back together, and it *worked.* Whereas I would still be fumbling with the latch on the toolbox.

So I'm intimidated by mechanical guys. When we got our boat   4
trailer, the salesman told me, one guy to another, that I should "re-pack" the "bearings" every so many miles. He said this as though all guys come out of the womb with this instinctive ability to re-pack a bearing. So I nodded my head knowingly, as if to suggest that, sure, I generally re-pack a couple dozen bearings every morning before breakfast just to keep my testosterone level from raging completely out of control. The truth is that I've never been 100 percent sure what a bearing is. But I wasn't about to admit this, for fear that the salesman would laugh at me and give me a noogie.

The main technique I use for disguising my mechanical tonsil-   5
litis is to deny that there's ever anything wrong with anything. We'll be driving somewhere, and my wife, Beth, who does not feel that mechanical problems represent a threat to her manhood, will say, "Do you hear that grinding sound in the engine?" I'll cock my head for a second and make a sincere-looking frowny face, then say no, I don't hear any grinding sound. I'll say this even if I have to shout so Beth can hear me over the grinding sound; even if a hole has appeared in the hood and a large, important-looking engine part is sticking out and waving a sign that says HELP.

"That's the grommet bearing," I'll say. "It's supposed to do that."   6

Or, at home, Beth will say, "I think there's something wrong   7
with the hall light switch." So I'll stride manfully into the hall, where volley-ball sized sparks are caroming off the bodies of recently electrocuted houseguests, and I'll say, "It seems to be working fine now!"

Actually, I think this goes beyond mechanics. I think guys have 8 a natural tendency to act as though they're in control of the situation even when they're not. I bet that, seconds before the Titanic slipped beneath the waves, there was some guy still in his cabin, patiently explaining to his wife that it was *perfectly normal* for all the furniture to be sliding up the walls. And I bet there was a guy on the *Hindenburg* telling his wife that, oh, sure, you're going to get a certain amount of flames in a dirigible. Our federal leadership is basically a group of guys telling us, hey, *no problem* with this budget deficit thing, because what's happening is the fixed-based long-term sliding-scale differential appropriation fore cast has this projected revenue growth equalization sprocket, see, which is connected via this Gramm-Rudman grommet oscillation module to . . .

AFTER YOU READ

Work with other students to develop responses to these questions or to compare responses that you have already prepared.

1. Now that you've read the article, explain the male fixation referred to in the title.
2. What is Barry's point about this male fixation?
3. What does Barry mean when he says that he has "mechanical tonsillitis"?
4. What is Barry's thesis idea? Identify any sentences that seem to express it.
5. What types of support does Barry use? Identify any brief or extended examples. Does he use any statistics or expert opinions?
6. Examine the introduction and conclusion to this article. How does each accomplish its purpose?

Fear of Heights: Teachers, Parents, and Students Are Wary of Achievement BOB CHASE

The following selection was originally published as a paid advertisement in The Washington Post. *In it, the president of the National Education Association claims that the educational values of the average American need an overhaul. Do you agree?*

BEFORE YOU READ

1. Bob Chase is president of the National Education Association. In light of his position and the title of this article, what point do you expect him to be making about a "fear of heights"?

2. Which person do you worry about more, the C student involved in many extracurricular activities or the A student who spends most of his time studying? Why?

Imagine you're a high school chemistry teacher. One of your stu-   1
dents is a shy, brilliant girl who routinely does "A" work. Another
constantly chats on her cell phone during lab time. She plays var-
sity soccer, chairs the homecoming committee, and earns unspec-
tacular grades.

Which student troubles you more?   2

Shockingly, a majority of teachers say they're more worried   3
about the star pupil than the "C" student. And their sentiments
mirror those of most parents. A recent survey by the research
group Public Agenda found that 70 percent of parents said they'd
be upset if their child received excellent grades but had a limited
extracurricular life. Only 16 percent wanted their children to get
"mostly A's."

Similarly, 53 percent of America's public school teachers   4
worried about "A" students with two or three friends, while only
29 percent worried about "C" students who were popular.

Why? According to the survey, a majority of the population   5
agrees that "People who are highly educated often turn out to
be book smart but lack the common sense and understanding of
regular folks." Unsurprisingly, this perception filters down to students. Research by Public Agenda also reveals that "most teens
view the academic side of school as little more than 'going through
the motions.'" Explained one Alabama boy, "My parents don't care
if I make a C."

In many communities, after-school activities are more sacro-   6
sanct than academics. High school football victories garner more
newspaper ink than math decathlons. School plays confer greater
status on their participants than spelling bees. In perhaps the most
bizarre example, in 1991 a mother in Channelview, Texas, hired a
man to murder the mother of her daughter's rival for a spot on
the cheerleading squad. The National Honor Society has never
generated such feverish (albeit insane) competition!

Historically, Americans have embraced a degree of anti-   7
intellectualism as a badge of our populist spirit. But as our economy becomes increasingly reliant on technology, scientific research,
and a highly skilled work force, this attitude undermines our best
interests.

Proof came earlier this year, in the form of the Third Interna-   8
tional Mathematics and Science Study (TIMSS). A comparison of

academic performance in 21 countries, TIMSS showed that U.S.
12th graders ranked at or near the bottom in math and science.

TIMSS underscores the need for more rigorous curricula,   9
higher academic standards, and better teacher training. But policy
changes alone will not improve students' performance. Our basic
values need an overhaul. As long as teachers, parents, and students
remain suspicious of intellectual excellence, we will function as a
tripod for mediocrity—supporting a system that celebrates "aver-
ageness" over achievement.

What changes are in order?   10

TIMSS offers some important clues. The test revealed that   11
American students spend less time doing homework and more
time at after-school jobs than do their international peers. Indeed,
says researcher Gerald Bracey, "The American vision of teenager-
dom includes dating, malls, cars, jobs, and extracurricular activities."
In the name of being "well rounded," many students are being
spread too thin. We need to set new priorities, with academics
enshrined as the centerpiece.

It's ironic that many teenagers are unenthusiastic about learn-   12
ing at a time in their lives when they're generally passionate about
everything else. If we're going to cultivate world-class students, we
adults may need some remedial lessons ourselves. Says Kay Armstrong, a public school librarian, "If children go into video arcades,
it means they can operate a computer. If they can recite rap songs,
they can quote Shakespeare. The problem is that we as educators
have not learned what motivates this generation."

Poet William Butler Yeats once wrote, "Education is not filling   13
up a pail but lighting a fire." Together, we must kindle the sparks
fearlessly—and encourage the flames to burn as high and as bright
as they can.

AFTER YOU READ

Work with other students to develop responses to these questions or to compare responses that you have already prepared.

1. Which person does Chase think we should worry about more, the C
   student with extracurricular activities or the A student with a limited
   extracurricular life? Explain his reasoning.

2. "In many communities, after-school activities are more sacrosanct than
   academics." Do your own experiences or observations confirm this
   statement? Explain why or why not.

3. How would you express the thesis of this article? Use your own words.
   Then find any sentences in the article that express that idea.

4. What types of support does Chase use?

5. Examine the introduction and conclusion to this article. Explain how each accomplishes its purpose.

Dropping the "T":
Trans Rights in the Marriage Era   EMILY GREENHOUSE

Emily Greenhouse has written for The New Yorker, The New York Review of Books, *and* Granta *magazine. She is the co-editor of* Granta 113: The Best of Young Spanish Language Novelists *(Grove Press, 2010). Greenhouse currently writes for* Bloomberg Politics, *where she covers human rights, culture, feminism, and social media. The following selection appeared in* The New Yorker *in April 2013.*

BEFORE YOU READ

1. What does the title suggest will be the focus of this article?

2. How much do you know about the LGBT movement? What are its objectives?

3. Why might someone feel uncomfortable around a person who does not have a traditional male or female gender identity?

Two weeks ago, Hillary Clinton announced her support for gay marriage. Placid and well-coiffed, she looked at the camera with Clintonian firmness, and said, "L.G.B.T. Americans are our colleagues, our teachers, our soldiers, our friends, our loved ones, and they are full and equal citizens and deserve the rights of citizenship. That includes marriage." 1

That Monday, she joined the ranks of prominent Democrats— and even a share of prominent Republicans—in the righteous chorus seeking to strike down the Defense of Marriage Act, which her husband signed in 1996. (Not known for his penitence, Bill Clinton published an op-ed asserting that the law "is itself discriminatory" and "should be overturned.") Whether the law is struck down now, as DOMA is challenged before the Supreme Court, or years later—when the seventy per cent of under-thirty voters who support marriage equality rise up in age and power—there is no doubt, as Jeffrey Toobin wrote last week in the magazine, that nothing now "can reverse the march toward equality." 2

There is a question, however, in the language Clinton used, the particular lip service she chose to pay. The United States moves inexorably toward granting equality to the L.G.B., but in the process— while still pronouncing that satisfying final consonant—we often, in practice, drop the "T." 3

In New York, where in 1969 the riots at the Stonewall Inn   4
launched the movement, the privileging of only L.G.B. rights is telling. In 2002, in order to get a hard-fought non-discrimination bill
passed, gay and lesbian activists in New York stopped fighting for
provisions related to their transgender allies. The bill, the Sexual
Orientation Non-Discrimination Act ("SONDA"), made it illegal
to discriminate against gays and lesbians in employment, housing,
public accommodations, education, credit, and the exercise of civil
rights. Meanwhile, State Senator Tom Duane, the leading sponsor
of the original draft, which had extended trans rights, decried the
"terrible, horrible discrimination" that transgender people face:
"They risk public exposure and loss of jobs, and sometimes violence, loss of homes." Over ten years later, a Gender Expression
Non-Discrimination Act ("GENDA") is still not law.

No federal law offers protection to transgender people from   5
discrimination in the workplace; the population sees double the
usual rate of unemployment, and ninety per cent of transgender
individuals report harassment, mistreatment, or discrimination at
work. The great majority of states do not assure access to public
accommodations, including hospitals, for transgender people. In
2011, the largest-ever study of transgender Americans showed
that nineteen per cent of transgender or gender-nonconforming
people had been denied health care. Similar rates have been
refused a home or apartment because of their gender identity.
Twenty-eight per cent of those in the study reported being subject
to harassment in medical settings, and a full forty-one per cent
reported attempting suicide (this compared to 1.6 per cent in the
general population). Seventy-eight per cent of transgender people
in kindergarten through twelfth grade are subject to harassment. In
a community with staggeringly high rates of H.I.V. infection and levels of homelessness approaching four times the national average,
health care is urgently needed.

Slowly, attitudes are changing. Margaret Talbot wrote for this   6
magazine on the complex issues faced by sensitive and open parents
who, as legal guardians, have to make decisions for their children
that will affect their biology, fertility, and identity. Members of the Phi
Alpha Tau fraternity at Boston's Emerson College launched a campaign in February to finance female-to-male top surgery for Donnie
Collins, a transgender sophomore and new brother in the fraternity.

But protections count most on the legislative level. When laws   7
like GENDA are introduced, uniformly conservative politicians and
religious-affiliated groups raise the "bathroom issue"—the menace

of sexual predators in restrooms and locker rooms. When a transgender-rights bill was introduced in Massachusetts in 2011, a radio spot paid for by the Massachusetts Family Institute ran in which one mother tells another that, if the "bathroom bill" passes, it won't be safe for her daughter to go to the bathroom by herself anymore. The same week that Hillary Clinton voiced her support for L.G.B.T. rights, Representative John Kavanagh, a Republican in the Arizona State Legislature, introduced a bill that would make it illegal for a transgender person to use a bathroom that does not match the sex on his or her birth certificate. Kavanagh dropped the measure—dubbed the "bathroom birther" bill—in the face of wide opposition, but not before defending it on Phoenix's 12 News, saying that it "raises the spectre of people who want to go into those opposite sex facilities not because they're transgender, but because they're weird."

At the same time, there have been concerns that the advance   8
of marriage equality might, however counterintuitively, mean a slackening of attention for full L.G.B.T. rights—particularly rights for the "T." After gay marriage became legal in New York, in 2011, the chair of the New York Association for Gender Rights Advocacy, Pauline Park, told the Huffington Post, "The more privileged gay white men who live in Manhattan are more likely to open up their checkbooks" for same-sex marriage than for transgender rights.

Last week, during the oral arguments in the two marriage   9
cases before the Supreme Court, the Human Rights Campaign stepped up a drive to get people to change their Facebook profile pictures and Twitter avatars to a red equality sign, or some matzo-infused (it was also Passover) or Sesame Street variation thereof. A few million—a fairly staggering number of Facebook users—seem to have done so. But, in the midst of the arguments, there were also what the H.R.C., in an apology, called "two unfortunate incidents" at the demonstration it helped organize in front of the Court: "In one case, a trans activist was asked to remove the trans pride flag from behind the podium, and in another, a queer undocumented speaker was asked to remove reference to his immigration status in his remarks." The statement went on to say that those involved had "personally" said they were sorry, and also that the group was apologizing "to those who were hurt by our actions. ... [W]e will strive to do better in the future. Through both our legislative and programmatic work, HRC remains committed to making transgender equality a reality."

The organization might need more than a statement to make   10
its commitment to "coalitional" politics clear; one reason the

incidents at the marriage rally resonated is the sense that H.R.C., going back to the nineties, has "a long history of throwing trans people under the bus." H.R.C.'s decision, for example, to present a "corporate equality" award to Goldman Sachs despite employees' support for conservative politicians has fed into a sense that the major gay-rights organizations might be more interested in corporate comfort than in fighting trans discrimination.

Facebook profile pictures sporting bold equal signs, it can be   11
assumed, will change back once DOMA is overturned (or if it's not), and the public will move on. L.G.B.T. people, in their and our full diversity, will still not have been afforded the full rights of citizenship. More marginal, more "at risk," and more controversial life styles still feel less salient, and less politically appealing.

AFTER YOU READ

Work with other students to develop responses to these questions or to compare responses that you have already prepared.

1. How would you express the thesis of this article? Use your own words. Then find a sentence or sentences in the article that express that idea.
2. What kind of support does Greenhouse use? Identify the different types of support that you see.
3. What point is Greenhouse making when she refers in paragraph 4 to "the privileging of only L.G.B. rights"?
4. Explain your understanding of what Greenhouse refers to as "the bathroom issue."
5. Where does the introduction end? In what way does it introduce the article? Which paragraphs make up the conclusion? Why is it an effective conclusion?

The Neglected Suicide Epidemic   EMILY GREENHOUSE

Emily Greenhouse, who is also the author of the previous reading selection, has written for The New Yorker, The New York Review of Books, *and* Granta *magazine. She is the co-editor of* Granta 113: The Best of Young Spanish Language Novelists *(Grove Press, 2010). Greenhouse currently writes for* Bloomberg Politics, *where she covers human rights, culture, feminism, and social media.*

BEFORE YOU READ

1. What does Greenhouse's title suggest will be the focus of her article?
2. Has any essay or book you have read addressed the topic of suicide?
3. What assumptions do people make about individuals who commit suicide?

On a January morning six years ago, Jonny Benjamin walked halfway across the Waterloo Bridge, in London, stepped to the edge, and prepared to jump. Benjamin, who was then twenty, had just been given a diagnosis of schizoaffective disorder; he felt that all the days ahead were doomed. As he was about to leap from the bridge's walkway, a stranger approached him, and began to talk. The man, who was about the same age, asked Benjamin to join him for a cup of coffee. "It'll get better, mate," the stranger said. "You will get better."   1

Benjamin didn't jump. As the years went on, he forgot the name of the man who had persuaded him to go on living. This January, to help raise awareness of mental-health issues, Benjamin—with the support of celebrities like Stephen Fry, Boy George, and David Cameron—launched a social-media campaign to find the man he had nicknamed Mike. "I didn't expect to find him," Benjamin told the *Guardian*. "It felt like looking for a needle in a haystack. I couldn't remember anything about him." But millions of people shared the story online; the hashtag "FindMike" was among Twitter's trending keywords in the United Kingdom and as far afield as South Africa, Australia, and Canada. The Good Samaritan's girlfriend saw the plea on Facebook and encouraged her boyfriend to go public. He did, and the two men met once again—this time with a hug.   2

Mike is Neil Laybourn, a thirty-one-year-old native of Surrey who works as a personal trainer. He still walks over the Waterloo Bridge on his commute, a daily reminder of that day, six years ago, when he saved a man's life simply by asking him to talk. The connection wasn't even so hard: it turns out that the two men grew up ten minutes away from each other. But it was Laybourn's basic sense of compassion, Benjamin said, that did the trick: "When he came along it burst the bubble of that world I was in. I felt faith, like I could talk to him."   3

A week after Benjamin was reunited with Laybourn, *Le Monde*, the leading newspaper on the other side of the English Channel, published the results of a medical study of French fifteen-year-olds, which revealed that almost twenty-one per cent of girls and nine per cent of boys reported attempting suicide in the past year. That's a shocking number, and it speaks to a global trend. In the United States, suicide rates have risen, particularly among middle-aged people: between 1999 and 2010, the number of Americans between the ages of thirty-five and sixty-four who took their own lives rose by almost thirty per cent. Among young people in the   4

U.S., suicide is the third most common cause of death; among all Americans, suicide claims more lives than car accidents, which were previously the leading cause of injury-related death.

Last May, citing the "substantial" rise in suicide among the   5 middle-aged, the Centers for Disease Control and Prevention described suicide as "an increasing public health concern." That realization has begun to spread: in the same month, *Newsweek* ran a cover article called "The Suicide Epidemic," noting that, around the world, self-harm takes "more lives than war, murder, and natural disasters combined." In America, these numbers—which many experts believe are lower than the actual figures, owing to underreporting—cannot simply be attributed to the toll of a long recession, or increasing gun ownership: clinical depression is also on the rise. Suicide rates declined in the nineteen-nineties, but since 1999 more Americans have killed themselves each year than in the one before.

Alan Berman, the executive director of the American Asso-   6 ciation of Suicidology and the president of the International Association of Suicide Prevention, has said that in the developed world ninety per cent of those who attempt suicide suffer from psychological ailments. "We have effective treatments for most of these," Berman said last year. "But the tragedy is, people die from temporary feelings of helplessness—things we can help with." The relentless intensity of those feelings has always been difficult to convey to those who have not experienced them: William Styron, in his powerful memoir, *Darkness Visible*, lamented the insufficiency of "depression" as a label for "the veritable howling tempest in the brain." Styron, who checked himself into the affective-illness unit at Yale-New Haven hospital, lived to write an account of his suffering, but many others lack the wherewithal, or the capacity, to seek such help. This is why Jonny Benjamin now works with a British nonprofit called Rethink Mental Illness, whose mission is to provide support to those contemplating suicide—to help them in the same way that Neil Laybourn helped Benjamin walk away from the edge of a bridge.

In 2003, Tad Friend wrote in this magazine about the "fatal   7 grandeur" of the Golden Gate Bridge, which had been identified as the "world's leading suicide location." The iconic status of the span, and its majestic view, seemed to draw jumpers to its walkway. "Several people have crossed the Bay Bridge to jump from the Golden Gate; there is no record of anyone traversing the Golden Gate to leap from its unlovely sister bridge," Friend wrote.

A local California doctor named Jerome Motto told Friend that   8
he has participated in several efforts to erect a suicide barrier on
the bridge, after one of his patients killed himself there in 1963.
But the jump that had most touched him took place the following
decade. "I went to this guy's apartment afterward with the assistant medical examiner," Motto recalled. "The guy was in his thirties,
lived alone, pretty bare apartment. He'd written a note and left it
on his bureau. It said, 'I'm going to walk to the bridge. If one person
smiles at me on the way, I will not jump.'"

This, of course, is what Neil Laybourn did for Jonny Benjamin.   9
Writing after their reunion, Benjamin said:

> I wanted to let people know that it's ok to have suicidal   10
> thoughts and feelings, and that in fact it is a very human experi-
> ence. I also hoped to show people that through talking about
> it, and by having someone else listen, it is possible to overcome
> the darkness that overwhelms a person when they feel help-
> less. This is something that I learned from my exchange with
> Neil on the bridge six years ago, and a message that I've been
> trying to pass on to others.

The feelings that drive people toward suicide can be treated—   11
in Jonny Benjamin's terms, the bubble of that bleak world can
be burst. But, despite the numbers and the losses, suicide is a
phenomenon we push away, we mystify, even—it must be said—
romanticize, as if science cannot begin to confront its cause. We
invoke the brilliance and torment of women like Virginia Woolf and
Sylvia Plath, in whose suicides we see mystical forces that speak of
the suffering of artists. We've diagnosed something similar in the
recent death of Philip Seymour Hoffman, from a drug overdose, in
order to make sense of, to celebrate, his art.

When the writer Primo Levi killed himself, in 1987, a great many   12
scholars of the period were concerned and confused. Alfred Kazin
found it difficult to reconcile "a will to blackness and self-destruction
in a writer so happy and full of new projects." Another identified "a
sudden uncontrollable impulse." In *The New Yorker*, Elizabeth Macklin
suggested that "the efficacy of all his words had somehow been
cancelled by his death—that his hope, or faith, was no longer usable
by the rest of us." But William Styron, who had not yet written
Darkness Visible, offered a different view in the *Times*:

> To those of us who have suffered severe depression—myself   13
> included—this general unawareness of how relentlessly the

disease can generate an urge to self-destruction seems wide-spread; the problem badly needs illumination. Suicide remains a tragic and dreadful act, but its prevention will continue to be hindered, and the age-old stigma against it will remain, unless we can begin to understand that the vast majority of those who do away with themselves—and of those who attempt to do so—do not do it because of any frailty, and rarely out of impulse, but because they are in the grip of an illness that causes almost unimaginable pain. It is important to try to grasp the nature of this pain.

Faced with the hardened refusal to understand Levi's death, and the will to explain it as exceptional, Styron remarked that "the overwhelming majority of camp survivors have chosen to live, and what is of ultimate importance to the victim of depression is not the cause but the treatment and the cure." The language here is essential: treatment and cure, because this is a disease that can be diagnosed and managed. This is broadly understood now, but still some part of us keeps alive the stigma and the romantic strange-ness, refusing to hear what Styron knew.   14

Styron wrote, "Depression's saving grace (perhaps its only one) is that the illness seems to be self-limiting: Time is the real healer." If you need someone to talk to, please call the National Suicide Prevention Lifeline, at 1-800-273-8255, which will connect you to a counselor at a nearby crisis center.   15

AFTER YOU READ

Work with other students to develop responses to these questions or to compare responses you have already prepared.

1. How would you express the thesis of this article? Use your own words. Then find any sentences in the article that express that idea.
2. What kind of support does Greenhouse use? Identify the different types of support that you see.
3. Analyze how Greenhouse transitions from one paragraph to another.
4. Greenhouse begins paragraph 6 with the following topic sentence: "Alan Berman, the executive director of the American Association of Suicidology and the president of the International Association of Suicide Prevention, has said that in the developed world ninety per cent of those who attempt suicide suffer from psychological ailments." Read the rest of paragraph 6, and explain the author's point.
5. Examine the introduction and conclusion to this article. Explain how each accomplishes its purpose.

WRITING ASSIGNMENTS

As you write a paper in response to one of the following assignments, pay particular attention to the support that you use as well as to the paper's introduction and conclusion.

1. Dave Barry's article "Male Fixations" takes a humorous look at the behavior of some males who act as if they can fix everything. Have you ever known such a person? Have you known more than one? Write a paper in which you use examples drawn from personal experiences or observations to illustrate and explain the consequences of one particular kind of behavior practiced by a person (or persons) you know.

2. In "Fear of Heights," Bob Chase suggests that we should worry less about the A student with two or three friends and more about the C student with an active extracurricular life. What do you think? Write a paper in which you use examples drawn from personal experiences or observations to illustrate and explain your response.

3. Chase writes that "teachers, parents, and students [are] suspicious of intellectual excellence ... supporting a system that celebrates 'average-ness' over achievement." Write a paper in which you use examples drawn from personal experiences or observations to support or contradict this statement.

4. What do you think of Chase's idea that the American teenager is "spread too thin" and that too much emphasis is placed on extracurricular activities over academics? Write a paper in which you use examples drawn from personal experiences or observations to illustrate and explain your response.

5. In "Dropping the 'T': Trans Rights in the Marriage Era," Emily Greenhouse discusses the discrimination experienced by transgender individuals. Compose an essay in which you use examples drawn from personal experiences or observations to explain the ways you and/or others have experienced intolerance, whether as victim or perpetrator. You may write about religion, race, gender, and/or sexual preference.

6. Greenhouse claims, "Seventy-eight per cent of transgender people in kindergarten through twelfth grade are subject to harrassment." Write a paper in which you explain what can be done to create safer school environments for transgender students and all students.

7. In "The Neglected Suicide Epidemic," Emily Greenhouse writes, "Among young people in the U.S., suicide is the third most common cause of death; among all Americans, suicide claims more lives than car accidents, which were previously the leading cause of injury-related death." Write a paper in which you use examples drawn from personal experience or observation that addresses the following question: What drives young people in the United States to commit suicide?

8. Greenhouse's article presents alarming suicide statistics: "Suicide rates declined in the nineteen-nineties, but since 1999 more Americans have

killed themselves each year than in the one before." Write a paper in which you present several solutions that you believe will help diminish suicides rates. Your paper may draw from personal experience and/or observation.

EVALUATING SAMPLE PAPERS

Use the following checklist to determine which of the student essays on the next few pages is most effective.

1. Thesis Statement

Underline the thesis statement of the essay. Does it express a clear and specific central idea?

1   2   3   4   5   6

2. Introduction

Does the introduction clearly introduce the central idea of the writer's paper? Does it end with a thesis statement?

1   2   3   4   5   6

3. Topic Sentences

Underline the topic sentence of each paragraph. Does each one clearly state the central idea of its paragraph?

1   2   3   4   5   6

4. Support

Examine the supporting details in each paragraph. Are they specific and clear? Should they be more detailed, or should more support be included?

1   2   3   4   5   6

5. Conclusion

Does the conclusion adequately bring the essay to a close?

1   2   3   4   5   6

6. Sentence Structure

Do the sentences combine ideas that are related, using coordination and subordination when appropriate? Are there too many brief, choppy main clauses? (See the *Sentence Combining* section later in this chapter for a discussion of subordination.)

1   2   3   4   5   6

7. Mechanics, Grammar, and Spelling

Does the paper contain a distracting number of these kinds of errors?

1   2   3   4   5   6

8. Overall Ranking of the Essay

1   2   3   4   5   6

Student Essay 1

The following essay was written in response to an article titled "Rethinking What's Really Important," by Wendy Priesnitz.

What does the phrase living the American Dream really mean? In the article, "Rethinking What's Really Important," Wendy Priesnitz, an editor of *Natural Life Magazine*, informs us about the misconception of the American Dream. Unfortunately, many have fallen in the trap of marketers, who mislead people into believing they "must have" certain items in order to be happy. In this sense, the American Dream has come to mean living a materialistic lifestyle. According to Priesnitz, because of this, people find themselves overworked in an attempt of getting out of debt. Americans would much rather work less in exchange for a healthier and happier, well rounded life. The real meaning of the American dream needs to be reevaluated; people should focus on working less, spending less money, and spending more time with family.

Americans currently overwork themselves in striving to achieve the American Dream, which causes stress and leads to unhappiness. People often claim they spend more time working than they do in their own homes, often times resulting in a stressful life. A countless amount of people would agree that life would be more fulfilling without excessive stress in their lives. I know my cousin, a single parent of four, works an exhausting number of hours to provide "the best" for her family. In other words, a large house with all the amenities, top of the line clothing, expensive technology, yet often absent from family. Missing the point entirely, the happiness of her family is being overlooked. It seems fair to conclude that the majority of such stress begins from overworking to make up for spending more than necessary. While this is true, many still struggle understanding the difference between necessities versus luxuries finding themselves facing economic difficulties. People desire to live the American Dream so much that spending what they do not have is not so bad. However, the New American Dream survey reported some improvements from consumers. According to Priesnitz, "Much of the change has come since September 11, 2001, with 40 percent of Americans having made conscious decisions to buy less." People are still unconsciously setting themselves up for a heavy routinely work load which causes a lack of family time.

Many Americans are finding themselves relentlessly pursuing or trying to maintain a high expense life style when they will be happier by spending less money. A lot of that comes from misguidance to believe that wealth is valued at a higher scale than your precious time. For instance, my friend who neglected to make the adequate adjustments after experiencing a decrease in income suffered major consequences. Refusing to live a more affordable life put her family into a debt crisis. It was mind boggling to hear the struggles of making the next mortgage payment yet still paying for a maid and a gardener. In order for things to improve, society must be conscious of consuming less and concentrate on investing more for financial stability. Priesnitz continues with results from the New American Dream survey, "Eighty-eight percent believe that our society is too materialistic with four or five saying that society is too focused on shopping and spending." A materialistic life style can be a cause of why several believe they do not have a chance of reaching the dream. Too often, Americans live beyond their means because their too focused on their appearance, how they will be perceived by society, than what really matters.

Balancing work and finances are a challenge to Americans creating a loss of what is really important—family. While it is necessity for adults to be employed in order to support their families, there is a need for balance. Sadly, that is not easy to come by, and many families are hugely affected and in some cases children become victims of neglect. For example, my aunt that works twelve hour shifts, five days of the week is missing out on the little things that matter the most. Helping her children with their school or serving a home cooked meal while enjoying that time with her family. People are living life at large but complain they would rather spend their valuable time with their families. The author adds, "More than eight out of ten survey respondents believe that society's priorities are 'out of whack' and 93 percent agree that people are too focused on working and making money and not enough on family and community" (Priesnitz). Society needs to do a better job at prioritizing for a more satisfying life. In many cases, after a tiresome job adults are too drained to spend time with their loved ones as they would desire. It defeats the purpose of living the American dream if one is constantly too busy working and making money if people miss out on a happy family life. For this reason, the American dream should be reevaluated to prioritize family after all it is the reason why we work so hard.

Overall, Americans need to reevaluate the American Dream; a great start would be to slow down and become informed. The overworking and overspending issues need to be resolved as they are the effects of a stressful life as well as less desirable time allotted. A better approach of the American Dream is targeting what is important, what really matters. It is understood that living the American dream should be a healthy well balanced life style that can be reachable with an educated mindset.

Student Essay 2

While reading Dave Barry's article "Male Fixations," I couldn't help but to think of my neighbors who have different types of fixations. The fixations that I see in some of my neighbors are similar to Barry's because they seem to be know-it-alls who refuse to admit that they really don't know as much as they claim, they will be embarrassed at their mistakes, and go into a state of denial when proven wrong.

Many of my neighbors seems to have a know-it-all attitude when it comes to certain things, only later to learn that they really don't know much about what they were talking about. For example, my neighbor Gabe seems to know everything about the O.J. Simpson trial because he is always telling me what the defense team is going to do everyday in court with the prosecution's witnesses, only later to find that he was only guessing and didn't really know that much about it to begin with. Another example of a know-it-all neighbor is Bob. I remember the time that I had bought my computer, and Bob came over to my house to help get it set up because he believed that he was a computer expert. He said that to set up a computer was a basic thing and that anyone with half a brain should be able to set it up without having to use the enclosed instructions. After an hour of watching him getting frustrated and calling the machine a few choice words, I told him that we could finish it the next day. When he left I referred to the instructions and got the job done in a timely manner, and the next day I just thanked him for his help and gave him lots of credit.

Some of my neighbors seem to get embarrassed when they are wrong about something simple. One morning I went outside to move my car off the street so I wouldn't get fined by the street sweeper. My neighbor Peg was outside, and she told me that the street sweeper wasn't coming by that day and that it would be crazy for me to move my car. I believed her and later found a ticket on my windshield from the street sweeper for not moving my car. Even though I told her that it was a simple mistake, she was extremely embarrassed about it for weeks to follow.

Finally, the best example of a neighbor going into a state of denial is a situation with Bob in which he just wouldn't accept his wrong verdict of a problem and wouldn't let himself be proved wrong. Even though my washer broke down really late one night, Bob was quick to be on the scene to give his opinion on the mechanics of my washer that wasn't draining. He quickly came to the conclusion that something was in the pipe blocking the drain hose. I took his advice to try to unplug it, but it had then occurred to me that there is a filter on the washer to prevent such a thing from happening. I suggested to him that the problem could be an electrical failure, but he thought that I was kidding around with him. After we unsuccessfully tried looking for the blockage, I broke down and called a repairman the next day. Although it turned out that there was a problem with a switch, Bob just does not accept the fact that he was wrong and goes on by saying that whatever was blocking the pipe had been cleared.

My neighbors are good hearted persons that are eager to please. I believe that they do have practical ideas on how to fix things, but sometimes they are not always correct. It seems that whenever something goes wrong at my house with anything mechanical, a neighbor is there to assist because it is the neighborly thing to do. I guess I just have to accept the fact that they may have an opinion about everything, be embarrassed at their mistakes, and not accept their wrong solutions to certain problems.

Student Essay 3

According to the article "Fear of Heights," Public Agenda conducted a survey which found that 53% of America's school teachers worried about "A" students with a couple of friends, while only 29% worried about "C" students who were popular. Most of the current high school students I have spoken to fit in one of these two categories. For example, Shelly Beeby, a senior attending Oceanside High, has a 4.0 GPA and no real social life to speak about. Shelly would like to be a computer engineer in the future. On the other hand, Drew Gillespie, a junior attending La Costa Canyon High, has a 2.4 GPA, plays field hockey and works. In the future she would like to be a social worker. Natalie DelFrancia, a junior attending Carlsbad High, has a 4.3 GPA, works, attends dance classes and plays soccer. Natalie would like to make a career out of teaching math at the college level. What these three girls have in common is that they are all individuals with different capacities. I believe that we need not worry about the "A" student with a minute social life nor the average student with an abundant one, nor should we deny that there are students who can handle both a successful academic life and an active social one.

Most of the "A" students with minute social lives that I have spoken with seem to be geared toward careers that don't have a great amount of emphasis on social skills. Shelly Beeby, future computer engineer, explained to me that she has always felt most comfortable working on her own. In Shelly's case becoming a computer engineer fits her perfectly. She has the smarts to do it, and she enjoys one-sided situations. In high school a boy named Tom, who sat behind me in U.S. history, was a straight "A" student with about two or three friends. Our teacher would give us the option to work in groups; however, Tom always choose to do the projects on his own. He always talked about being some kind of scientist. Tom is another example of a straight "A" student who likes doing things alone. I feel that we do not need to worry about these students. It has been my observation that they often pick careers that fit their intelligence as well as their personality.

Contrary to the "A" students with minute social lives, most average students with abundant social lives that I have come in contact with seem to be interested in careers that focus on social skills. For instance, Drew Gillespie wants to become a social worker. Drew possesses average intelligence, has a passion for people, and loves to be involved; therefore, I believe that one day she will make a fine social worker. My friend Raymond, who was an average high school student, worked, played football, and was a part of the Orange Police Department's Explorer program. Raymond's dream of being a police officer finally came true last March when he was hired to work for the Santa Ana police department. Not only is Raymond good at what he does, but he also enjoys it. I believe we should not worry about these students because they see themselves in positions that require average intelligence with a major focus on people.

What the article failed to mention are those students who can maintain both an academic and social life. These students seem to be drawn to intellectual and prestigious careers. Natalie DelFrancia wants to be a math teacher at the college level. She has everything going for her, a high amount of intelligence and a wide array of people skills. My cousin Mike, who would like to be an international lawyer, graduated this summer with a 3.8 GPA. During his high school years, Mike played football, ran track and worked. He now attends the University of Michigan and is working towards his Master's degree in international law. Again, Mike has the high academic and social skills needed to achieve his dreams. These students should not be left out, for they too play a vital role in America's education system.

All the students I have mentioned in this paper are individual and highly important people. I don't believe that we need to worry that certain percentages of students are smart with no friends or average with many. What we need to focus on are students as individuals with certain capacities. We need to "encourage the flames to burn as high and as bright as they can." After all, if everyone in this world operated on the same level, how could life possibly go on?

SENTENCE COMBINING: USING SUBORDINATION

In Chapter 2, you practiced using appropriate coordinating conjunctions in your sentences. When you use coordination, you are suggesting that the ideas in your sentences are all of equal importance. On the other hand, when you employ subordination, you indicate to your reader which ideas are more important than others. The subordinate ideas in a sentence are usually the ones of lesser importance. Look at the following pairs of simple statements:

> I awoke from my nap.
> A burglar was smashing the window in my back door.
>
> The snow was falling lightly on the mountain road.
> A huge truck barreled straight at us.
>
> The professor stomped toward me and began to yell.
> I would not stop talking.
>
> A very dear friend recently sent me a baby alligator.
> She lives in Pittsburgh.

As you can see, in each pair of sentences, one sentence contains much more important information than the other. In the first two pairs, the second sentences convey the more important ideas. In the last two pairs, the first sentences seem to be more important. (Admittedly, deciding which sentences are more "important" can be rather subjective, yet you must attempt to make such distinctions when you combine related ideas.)

SUBORDINATING CONJUNCTIONS AND RELATIVE PRONOUNS

One way to combine ideas is to write the less important information as a **subordinate clause**. Doing so will emphasize the relative importance of the ideas as well as clarify *how* the words are related. To write a subordinate clause, begin the clause with a **subordinator** (either a **subordinating conjunction** or a **relative pronoun**). Here is a list of subordinating conjunctions and relative pronouns that you can use to start subordinate clauses:

Subordinating Conjunctions			Relative Pronouns	
after	even though	until	that	whom(ever)
although	if	when	which	whose
as	since	whenever	who(ever)	
as if	so that	where		
as long as	than	wherever		
because	though	while		
before	unless			

You can combine the above four pairs of sentences by using subordinators. Here is how the sentences look when the less important sentences are written as subordinate clauses. Each subordinate clause is underlined.

> **When** <u>I awoke from my nap,</u> a burglar was smashing the window in my back door.
>
> **As** <u>the snow was falling lightly on the mountain road,</u> a huge truck barreled straight at us.

The professor stomped toward me and began to yell **because** I would not stop talking.

A very dear friend **who** lives in Pittsburgh recently sent me a baby alligator.

As you can see, each subordinate clause begins with a subordinator that expresses the relationship between the main clause and the subordinate clause. Notice also that the subordinate clause can appear at the start, at the end, or in the middle of the sentence. (See pages 328–331 for further discussion of subordinate clauses.)

EXERCISE 3.7

Each of the following sentences is drawn from one of the reading selections in this chapter. Underline each subordinate clause and circle its subordinator. Some sentences may contain more than one subordinate clause.

EXAMPLE

Because Nick learned to save money, he could afford a camping trip to the Grand Canyon.

1. One of your students is a shy, brilliant girl who routinely does "A" work.
2. If we're going to cultivate world-class students, we adults may need some remedial lessons ourselves.
3. In New York, where in 1969 the riots at the Stonewall Inn launched the movement, the privileging of only L.G.B. rights is telling.
4. Meanwhile, State Senator Tom Duane, the leading sponsor of the original draft, which had extended trans rights, decried the "terrible, horrible discrimination" that transgender people face.
5. The United States moves inexorably toward granting equality to the L.G.B., but in the process—while still pronouncing that satisfying final consonant—we often, in practice, drop the "T."
6. When the writer Primo Levi killed himself, in 1987, a great many scholars of the period were concerned and confused.
7. Benjamin, who was then twenty, had just been given a diagnosis of schizoaffective disorder; he felt that all the days ahead were doomed.
8. In 2003, Tad Friend wrote in this magazine about the "fatal grandeur" of the Golden Gate Bridge, which had been identified as the "world's leading suicide location."
9. As the years went on, he forgot the name of the man who had persuaded him to go on living.
10. If you need someone to talk to, please call the National Suicide Prevention Lifeline, at 1-800-273-8255, which will connect you to a counselor at a nearby crisis center.

PUNCTUATING SUBORDINATE CLAUSES

There are a few rules you need to know in order to punctuate sentences with subordinate clauses correctly.

1. Use a comma after a subordinate clause that precedes a main clause.
   <u>Because I have a meeting in the morning</u>, I will meet you in the afternoon.

2. In general, do not use a comma when the subordinate clause follows a main clause.
   I will meet you in the afternoon <u>because I have a meeting in the morning</u>.

3. Use commas to set off a subordinate clause beginning with *which, who, whom,* or *whose* if the information in the subordinate clause is not necessary to identify the word the clause modifies.
   Dave Barry, <u>who is a very funny man</u>, writes for the *Miami Herald*.

   (Because the information contained in the subordinate clause is not necessary to identify Dave Barry, it is set off with commas.)

4. On the other hand, do not use commas to set off a subordinate clause beginning with *which, who, whom,* or *whose* if the information in the subordinate clause is necessary to identify the word it modifies.
   The woman <u>who stepped on my toes in the theater</u> apologized profusely.

   (The clause "who stepped on my toes in the theater" is necessary to identify which "woman" you mean.)

5. No commas are used with subordinate clauses that begin with *that.*
   Subordinate clauses <u>that begin with *that*</u> are never enclosed in commas.

EXERCISE 3.8

Combine each of the following sets of sentences by changing at least one of the sentences in each set into a subordinate clause. Use commas where they are needed.

EXAMPLE

Juanita outlined her essay a week in advance. She did well on her in-class essay.

> Because Juanita outlined her essay a week in advance, she did well on her in-class essay.

or

> Juanita did well on her in-class essay because she outlined her essay a week in advance.

1. The fire engine arrived at the scene. The Persian cat clung to the Purple Smoke Tree.
2. Jimmy Santiago Baca moved to San Diego, California. He worked as a plumber. Jimmy would hang out at the beach.
3. Zora Neale Hurston wrote *Their Eyes Were Watching God* in seven weeks. She was forty-six years old.
4. The guerrilla group blew up Fernando Botero's sculpture *The Bird*. The sculpture stood in the plaza. The guerrilla argued the sculpture represented oppression.
5. The poet could not stop for death. He kindly stopped for her.
6. Sergio Vásquez paints alebrijes. Alebrijes are Mexican mythological creatures. The artist imagines a colorful place where all creatures can live in harmony.
7. Andrea found the newspaper clip in a shoe box. He learned the truth.
8. Lucas preferred reading books at the library rather than watching films at the movie theater. He refused to waste his money on a tub of butter and a pint of sugar.
9. Aida cringed. She heard the story of the mermaid. The mermaid was cut in half and fed to a fisherman's children.
10. Teresa found word problems difficult. She enjoyed the challenge.
11. Sabrina did not know how to make molcajete salsa. She inherited her grandmother's green salsa recipe.
12. Shirley had a difficult time greeting customers. Her boss asked her to wash dishes instead.
13. The caged love birds chirped in the morning. My neighbor's cat visited the front porch. He purred and salivated.
14. Joel wrote an essay about his grandfather. He missed him dearly.
15. The Henderson family drove through the Whipple Mountains. They stopped to take photographs of the giant Saguaro cacti. The Saguaros are native to Arizona, California, and Sonora.

EXERCISE 3.9

Combine each of the following groups of sentences into one sentence. Use subordination and coordination where appropriate. Embed adjectives, adverbs, and prepositional phrases. Use commas where they are needed.

1. The English word for the Mesoamerican indigenous dish is *tamale*.
   In Spanish, the word for tamale is *tamal*.
   The word *tamal* comes from the Nahuatl word *tamalli*.
   The word *tamalli* means "wrapped."

2. Tamale making is rooted in oral tradition.
   People memorize ingredients and distinct flavors.
   Elders, mothers, and fathers share their knowledge of tamale making with the next generation.

3. One person can make a large batch of tamales.

A community of people usually comes together to prepare tamales.
The tamale community is made up of family and friends.

4. Tamales may look easy to make.

Tamale making is a laborious process.
Corn, lard or shortening, and salt are ground to a fine paste.
The masa, maize dough, is spread on corn husks.

5. In Mexico, a celebration requires a popular dish.

Guests can be guaranteed tamales will be served at weddings, on Christmas, and on other holidays.
The tamales will be served steaming hot.
Tamales will be served with beans, rice, and/or salsa.

6. The tamale maker decides what type of tamales will be served on a special occasion.

He or she will need maize dough.
He or she will need corn husks.
They can be bought at a local tortilleria.
Tamales reflect people's distinct flavors and tastes.

7. California chile peppers are used to make red chicken or beef tamales.

Tomatillos and green peppers are used to prepare green chicken or beef tamales.
Fruits are used to make sweet tamales.

8. In Brazil, pamonha, similar to the tamale, is made out of sweet corn and milk.

Pamonha can be filled with cheese, sausage, meat, chicken, and pepper.
Pamonha are wrapped with corn husks.

9. Nacatamales are Nicaragua's and Costa Rica's version of the tamale.

Nacatamales are filled with mashed potatoes, rice, vegetables, pork, chicken, and/or bell peppers.
The nacatamale ingredients also include milk or chicken stock.
Nacatamales are large corncakes wrapped in banana leaf packages.

10. Filipinos also prepare a dish that is similar to tamales.

Filipinos use a blended paste made out of rice, coconut milk, and toasted peanuts.
The filling ingredients include ham and shrimp.
Filipinos use banana leaves to wrap the tamale in square shapes.

Peanuts: © United Feature Syndicate, Inc.

Unity and Coherence

4

UNITY

As you can see from the "Peanuts" cartoon on the facing page, Sally is having trouble staying focused on her topic. Her tendency to drift from the subject of her report ("this stupid leaf") to why Christmas is the saddest time of the year is called a break in **unity**.

Think about the word *unity* for a moment. It means "oneness" or "singleness of purpose." A *unified* paragraph or essay is one that stays focused on its central idea. It does not wander into areas that are unrelated to that central idea. To put it another way, all the details, facts, examples, explanations, and references to authorities with which you develop a unified paper should clearly relate to and develop the central idea of that paper. If they do not do so, the paper lacks unity.

A good time to check the unity of your writing is after you have written the first draft. Until that time, you are still prewriting, and during the prewriting stage you really should not worry too much about unrelated material that creeps into your writing. Remember, when you prewrite, you concentrate on getting as many ideas on paper as you can. When you write, you produce your draft. And when you revise, you improve that draft. Checking your paper for unity will usually occur as you revise—before you submit your paper to your instructor but after you have produced a first draft.

EXERCISE 4.1

Read the following paragraphs, and identify the topic sentence of each one. Then identify any sentences that break the unity of the paragraph.

A. 1 The names of the seven days of the week have some rather interesting origins. 2 The names *Sunday* and *Monday*, for example, come from Old English words that refer to the sun *(sunne)* and moon *(mona)*, respectively. 3 *Tuesday, Wednesday, Thursday*, and *Friday* all refer to gods in Germanic mythology. 4 Tiu (for Tuesday) was a god of war. 5 Most cultures have some kind of name for a war god. 6 The Roman name was Mars; the Greek name was Ares. 7 Woden (for Wednesday) was the chief Germanic god. 8 He is known to many people as Odin. 9 The corresponding chief god in Roman mythology is Jupiter, and in Greek mythology it is Zeus. 10 Thor (for Thursday) was the Germanic god of thunder; Freya (for Friday) was the goddess of love and beauty. 11 Interestingly, *Saturday* comes from the name of a Roman god, not a Germanic one. 12 Saturn was the Roman god of agriculture. 13 How agriculture is related to the huge planet we know as Saturn may be confusing to some people, but it obviously did not worry the Romans very much.

B. 1 Folk remedies, which are passed on from one generation to another, are sometimes quite effective and at other times absolutely worthless. 2 One example of effective folk wisdom is the advice to eat chicken soup when you have the flu. 3 Many people love the taste of chicken soup, especially during cold weather. 4 Several scientific studies have shown that chicken soup improves the functioning of the fibers in the upper respiratory tract that help people get rid of congestion. 5 Usually, people buy over-the-counter drugs to alleviate the symptoms of the flu, and today generic brands are much more popular than name brands. 6 Unfortunately, not all folk remedies are as effective as chicken soup. 7 Scientists say, for example, that slices of raw potato placed on the forehead will do nothing for a fever, although many people believe otherwise. 8 In fact, many people believe almost anything they are told. 9 A friend of mine once told some children that the world used to have only two colors—black and white—and that was why old movies looked that way. 10 And the children believed him! 11 Another bit of folk advice that scientists say is untrue is that taping a child's ears back at night will change the positions of ears that stick out too much. 12 Finally, scientists say that boiling skim milk for children with diarrhea is dangerous as well as ineffective.

C. 1 Cities became possible when humans invented agriculture. 2 Although we may never know exactly when agriculture was invented, many historians claim it may have been independently invented around 12,000 years ago in several different areas: the Middle East, West Africa, North Africa, India, and China. 3 Agriculture made it possible for humans to stay in one place and develop a reliable supply of food. 4 Nutrition is very important for humans. 5 Today, many people study the relationship between organic agriculture and good nutrition. 6 Once a reliable food supply could be grown, harvests and fields also had to be protected. 7 Larger numbers of people could offer better protection. 8 Large numbers of people in close proximity also make diseases spread faster. 9 Once larger numbers of people congregated, specialization became a necessity. 10 Not all people would devote all their time to growing food: some would serve as craftspeople, some as soldiers, some as administrators. 11 Only a stable supply of food and a surplus of food made these developments possible.

COHERENCE

Another way to improve the clarity of your writing is to work on its **coherence**, which involves clarifying the *relationships* between ideas. When ideas (or sentences) are *coherent*, they are understandable. And when they are understandable, one sentence makes sense in relation to the sentence before it. When ideas (or sentences) are *incoherent*, they do not make much sense because they are not clearly related to each other or to the central idea of the paper.

For example, imagine someone passing you a note that read "Snow! Last winter! Trees! Gone!" What in the world could such a person possibly be trying to tell you? That the snow that fell on the trees last winter is gone? That the trees that were snowed on last winter are gone? That last winter's snow killed the trees? What is missing here is coherence, the connections between the ideas.

Of course, a person's writing is rarely as incoherent as the above example, but all writers—from students who are taking their first writing classes to professionals who make their living by writing—must consistently work on the clarity of what they have written. Here is an example of a paragraph that needs more work in coherence:

> 1 Some television viewers claim that Donald Duck cartoons are immoral. 2 For fifty years, Donald has kept company with Daisy. 3 Donald's nephews—Huey, Dewey, and Louie—are apparently the children of a "Miss Duck," who was last seen in a comic book in 1937. 4 Donald is drawn without pants. 5 The opinions of these persons have been largely ignored by the general public.

The above paragraph lacks coherence because each sentence seems to jump from one unrelated detail to the next. A careful reader will probably be able to figure out that each sentence is meant to be an example of the "immorality" of Donald Duck cartoons, but the relationship of each sentence to that central idea and to the idea in the sentence before it needs to be made much clearer. Clarifying such relationships involves working on the coherence of the paper.

A number of techniques will help you improve the coherence of your writing.

IMPROVING COHERENCE

1. *Refer to the central idea.*   One of the most effective ways to improve coherence is to use words that refer to the central idea of your paper as you write your support. In the above paragraph about Donald Duck cartoons, the central idea is that some people think they are "immoral," but none of the supporting sentences clearly refer to that idea. The relationship between the supporting sentences and the central idea will be clearer—and the coherence improved—if the writer uses words that connect her support to the central idea of immorality.

> 1 Some television viewers claim that Donald Duck cartoons are immoral. 2 For fifty years, Donald has kept company with Daisy, a relationship that to some seems **suspicious and dishonorable**. 3 Donald's nephews—Huey, Dewey, and Louie—are apparently the **illegitimate** children of a "Miss Duck," who was last seen in a comic book in 1937. 4 It seems **improper and indecent** to these critics that Donald is drawn without pants. 5 Donald's dressing habits **clearly upset** these particular television viewers. 6 The opinions of these persons have been largely ignored by the general public.

Now the relationship of each supporting idea to the central idea of the paragraph has become much clearer. Notice how the boldfaced words keep the emphasis of the paragraph on the "immorality" of Donald Duck cartoons.

2. *Use common transitional words and phrases.*   Transitions tell you what direction a sentence is about to take. When a sentence starts with *However*, you know that it is about to present a contrast; when it starts with *For example*, you know that it is about to move from a general statement to a specific illustration of that statement. Clear transitions will improve the coherence of your paper because they will signal to your readers how the sentence that they are about to read is related to the sentence that they have just finished reading.

Many transitions are so common that they are worded the same way no matter who is doing the writing. They are like road signs *(Stop, Yield, School Zone)* that all drivers are expected to recognize and respond to. These common transitions can improve your paper, but be careful not to overuse them. Too many of them will make your writing sound artificial and awkward.

- To show a movement in time: *first, second, next, finally, then, soon, later, in the beginning, at first, meanwhile*
- To move to an example: *for example, to illustrate, for instance, as a case in point*
- To add another idea, example, or point: *in addition, furthermore, and, also, second, third, next, moreover, finally, similarly*

- To show a contrast: *on the other hand, however, but, yet, instead, on the contrary, nevertheless*
- To show a result: *so, therefore, as a result, consequently, hence, thus*
- To conclude: *finally, in conclusion, as a result, hence, therefore, clearly, obviously*
- Notice how the addition of these transitions helps improve the paragraph about Donald Duck cartoons:

> 1 Some television viewers claim that Donald Duck cartoons are immoral. 2 **For example**, for fifty years, Donald has kept company with Daisy, a relationship that to some seems suspicious and dishonorable. 3 **In addition**, Donald's nephews—Huey, Dewey, and Louie—are apparently the illegitimate children of a "Miss Duck," who was last seen in a comic book in 1937. 4 **Finally**, it seems improper and indecent to these critics that Donald is drawn without pants. 5 Donald's dressing habits clearly upset these particular television viewers. 6 **However**, the opinion of these persons have been largely ignored by the general public.

3. *Write your own transitional phrases, clauses, or full sentences.*   The most effective transitions are those written in your own words as phrases, clauses, or complete sentences. Transitions such as these often **repeat a word or idea** from the previous sentence. They also often **refer to the central idea** of a paper to introduce a new element of support.

Note the transitional phrases, clauses, and full sentences in the following paragraph:

> 1 Some television viewers claim that Donald Duck cartoons are immoral. 2 **According to these viewers, Donald's relationship with Daisy is an example of his immorality**. 3 For fifty years, Donald has kept company with Daisy, a relationship that to some seems suspicious and dishonorable. 4 In addition, **some people question the morality of a cartoon that features three children of unknown parentage**. 5 Donald's nephews—Huey, Dewey, and Louie—are apparently the illegitimate children of a "Miss Duck," who was last seen in a comic book in 1937. 6 Finally, it seems improper and indecent to these critics that Donald is drawn without pants. 7 **Although few people ever expect to see any animal in pants**, Donald's dressing habits clearly upset these particular television viewers. 8 **Luckily for the famous duck**, the opinions of these persons have been largely ignored by the general public.

In the above paragraph, sentence 2 is a full *transitional sentence*. It replaces the phrase *for example*, and it emphasizes the central idea of the paragraph by using the word *immorality*. Sentence 3 is another *transitional sentence*. Again, this sentence improves the coherence of the paragraph by emphasizing the central idea of *morality*. Sentence 7 now includes a *transitional clause*. Notice that the clause refers to the idea of animals "in pants," which was mentioned at the very end of sentence 6. Sentence 8 contains a *transitional phrase* that allows the reader to move easily into the concluding idea of the paragraph.

EXERCISE **4.2**

Work with several other students in a small group to identify the topic sentence and central idea in each of the following paragraphs. Write "CI" above all references to the central idea. Circle all words or ideas that are repeated from one sentence to the next. Finally, underline all common transitional words and phrases.

EXAMPLE

TOPIC
1 Folk remedies, which are passed on from one generation to another,
CENTRAL IDEA
are sometimes quite effective and sometimes absolutely worthless.
CI
2 One example of effective folk wisdom is the advice to eat chicken
soup when you have the flu. **3** Several scientific studies have shown
CI
that chicken soup improves the functioning of the fibers in the upper
respiratory tract that help people get rid of congestion caused by the
CI
flu. **4** Unfortunately, not all folk remedies are as effective as chicken
soup. **5** Scientists say, for example, that slices of raw potato placed on
CI
the forehead will do nothing for a fever, although many people believe
CI
otherwise. **6** Another bit of folk advice that scientists say is untrue is
that taping a child's ears back at night will change the position of ears
that sticks out too much. **7** Finally scientists say that boiling skim milk
CI
for children with diarrhea is dangerous as well as ineffective.

A.   1 If you think dainty butterflies are lily-livered weaklings, think again. 2 Most male butterflies are gutsy and aggressive within their own habitat and will pick a fight at the slightest provocation. 3 This trait is often seen when a male is on the prowl for a mate. 4 The European grayling butterfly, for example, will perch on a twig or leaf to wait for Ms. Right. 5 When he scents a female of his own species, he will begin an elaborate courtship dance and emit his own identifying scent. 6 But he will rough up almost anyone else who ventures into his territory, whether it's another butterfly twice his size, a dragonfly or a small bird. 7 He'll even lunge at his own shadow. 8 Black swallowtail butterflies, an especially aggressive species, have been known to chase after terrified birds for as long as half a minute. 9 When vying for the favors of the same female, two male butterflies will repeatedly ram each other in midair until one surrenders and flees.

—*Irving Wallace et al.,* Significa

B. 1 The idea that our minds should operate as high-speed data-processing machines is not only built into the workings of the Internet, it is the network's reigning business model as well. 2 The faster we surf across the Web—the more links we click and pages we view—the more opportunities Google and other companies gain to collect information about us and to feed us advertisements. 3 Most of the proprietors of the commercial Internet have a financial stake in the crumbs of data we leave behind as we flit from link to link—the more crumbs, the better. 4 The last thing these companies want is to encourage leisurely reading or slow, concentrated thought. 5 It's in their interest to drive us to distraction.

—*Nicholas Carr, "Is Google Making Us Stupid?"*

C. 1 When we think about sex, being male or being female, we may think that we have arrived at the bedrock of biology, at a category in which societal views or social constructions have no sway. 2 After all, we have no choice as to our sex (or so it may seem), and we think we simply are what we are, male or female—or so one might think. 3 However, when considering the question of identity and sex, one finds oneself fully immersed in the whirlpool of societal definitions: one may be male or female, but what does that mean beyond certain biological differentiations? 4 These biological differentiations themselves may be easily enough observed, though here, too, nothing is as easy as it seems. 5 But when we ask about identity, we ask what it means that women give birth and men do not, that men, on average, have greater upper body strength, and that men have a greater chance of growing bald than women. 6 In other words, as far as identity is concerned, the biological facts are less important than what we make of them.

EXERCISE **4.3**

Revise the following paragraphs to improve their coherence by referring more clearly to the central idea, by repeating words and ideas from one sentence to the next, and by adding appropriate transitional words and phrases. You may also need to add complete sentences to emphasize how the details are related to the central idea of the paragraph. Consider working with other students as you revise two of these paragraphs. Then revise one on your own.

A. 1 After spending two days observing people around me, I have come to the conclusion that there is no activity too important, no conversation too intimate, and no setting too sacred to counteract people's desire to text. 2 I saw at least two dozen people texting while driving. 3 I might have seen more, but I was occasionally texting myself. 4 I saw many more people text under their desk while attending class. 5 The less discreet ones were texting openly. 6 I see couples sitting at tables when I visit restaurants. They are talking to each other and texting at the same time. 7 Parents are talking to their children while texting. 8 I see children texting while talking to their parents. 9 People talking on the phone often text while they are talking, using their earphones to keep the conversation going. 10 I have seen people text both in churches and in temples. 11 I have not visited a mosque yet, but it would not surprise me to find the same phenomenon there. 12 If texting were an army, I'd say it has conquered the world.

B.   1 Most fathers that I know seem to be much more awkward and nervous than mothers when it comes to caring for their babies. 2 My brother's baby, Kaori, had a slight cold. 3 My brother insisted that she should be taken to the hospital. 4 His wife said that Kaori would be fine in a day or so. 5 The child recovered completely. 6 My brother became sick because he hadn't slept all night. 7 My father would always avoid holding my little brother when we were younger. 8 At Disneyland, my mother asked him to hold my brother while she used the restroom. 9 The entire time, my dad paced back and forth. 10 Whenever my mother held the child, she seemed completely at ease. 11 I suppose it is natural for mothers to feel comfortable with their young children. 12 I don't see any reason for fathers to be as awkward as they are.

C.   1 After reading G. Gordon Liddy's "Without Emotion," I was reminded of times in my own life when I felt that I had to act without emotion just to make it through an unpleasant experience. 2 I had to go through a divorce. 3 I had no financial support, and I had an eleven-month-old son to take care of. 4 I had to think about handling the pressing issues of finding food, clothing, shelter, and a job. 5 I was laid off from a typesetting position with a local newspaper. 6 I immediately busied myself with the task of finding another job. 7 Liddy was trying to get to the point where he could act without emotion if he ever really had to. 8 For me, it was either act without letting my emotions get to me or allow myself to be defeated by my circumstances.

IMPROVING UNITY AND COHERENCE WITH THESIS STATEMENTS AND TOPIC SENTENCES

So far we have discussed unity and coherence *within* paragraphs, but these elements of clear writing affect the entire essay, not just the single paragraph. Remember, *unity* refers to a writer's ability to stay focused on one central idea, and *coherence* involves clarifying relationships between ideas. When you move from one paragraph to another within an academic essay, you can stay focused on the central idea of the essay (unity) and clarify the relationships between paragraphs (coherence) by paying particular attention to the thesis statement of the essay and the topic sentence of each paragraph.

THESIS STATEMENTS AND TOPIC SENTENCES

1. *Write a thesis statement that clearly expresses the central idea of the essay.*   As we discussed in Chapters 1 and 2, academic essays need thesis statements that carefully and accurately state the central idea of the paper. Unless your instructor tells you otherwise, place the thesis statement at the end of your introductory paragraph.

2. *Write topic sentences that clearly express the central idea of each paragraph.*   This point has been discussed in Chapters 1 and 2. Unless your instructor tells you otherwise, place your topic sentences at the start of each body paragraph.

3. *Write topic sentences that clearly develop the central idea of the thesis statement.*   This point relates to both the *unity* and the *coherence* of your essay. One way to emphasize the relationship between each topic sentence and the thesis statement is to repeat words and ideas from the central idea of the thesis statement within each topic sentence. To avoid repetitive wording, don't repeat exact phrases.

4. *Write topic sentences that use transitions to move away from the topic in the previous paragraph.*   This point relates the *coherence* of your essay. A transition within a topic sentence might be a brief reference to the central idea of the previous paragraph, a common transitional phrase, or a transitional phrase or sentence of your own.

SAMPLE STUDENT ESSAY

Examine the following essay, and note how the unity and coherence are emphasized as the writer moves from one paragraph to another. The central idea in the thesis and in each topic sentence is in boldface. The transition that opens each paragraph is underlined once. The words in each topic sentence that repeat the central idea of the thesis statement are in parentheses.

The Benefits of Competition

In the article "School Sports—Latest New Age Target," John Leo tells us that   1
many gym teachers across America are opposed to competition in school sports because they think such competition harms the children who aren't outstanding players. He refers to an article from the *New York Times*, which he says "carries the implicit message that win-lose games are dangerous." Leo, however, disagrees with the *Times* article. He believes that one can "lose without humiliation and win without feeling superior." I agree with him. In fact, after the experiences

(continued)

I have had with school sports in my own life, **I believe that the competition in school sports benefits students in many ways.**

One of the (benefits of competition) in school sports is that it **motivates** stu- 2 dents to do their best. For example, when I was taking a swim class last semester, I could not swim one hundred yards without stopping. When the teacher said that he was going to time every one of us to see who could finish one hundred yards in the least amount of time, I was worried because I was sure I could not swim that far. During the competition, the only thought that came into my mind was that I did not want to be the last one to finish, and that thought motivated me to continue swimming even though I was very tired. When I reached the finish line, I was astounded to find that I was in fourth place. From this experience and from many others like it, I can say the competition did indeed bring out the best in me.

In addition to motivating students, competition in school sports **(prepares** 3 **young people)** for the competition they will face in real life. My younger brother has (benefited) from school sports this way. Since he is the youngest member of our family, we always used to let him win when we played games with him because that was the only way we could keep him happy. Then one day he came home from school depressed. When I asked him what had happened, he said that he had lost to a friend in a school race. After I heard his story, I realized that my brothers and I had spoiled him and that school sports were giving him a dose of reality. I decided that the next time he wanted to beat me at checkers, he would have to really compete with me because that is the only way to teach him what life is really like.

Not only does competition benefit people by motivating them and teaching 4 them about life, but it also (benefits them) by **revealing their own inner strengths and weaknesses.** My friends Minh and Hoa are good illustrations of this point. Minh is a quiet person who never seems very secure about his tennis talent. On the other hand, Hoa, a talkative person, always brags about how well he plays tennis. Hoa was sure that he was a better tennis player than Minh, but one day he had to face Minh in a school tennis tournament. When Hoa lost the game, he realized that he really could not play tennis as well as he thought. This competition pointed out Hoa's weakness, but it also revealed to Minh his own hidden strength. If they had not competed, neither would have discovered the truth about himself.

Clearly, competition in school sports can (benefit) people in many ways. It 5 motivates students to do their very best, it teaches them about real life, and it reveals to them their own strengths and weaknesses. Like John Leo, I believe that school sports are a valuable part of school life.

EXERCISE 4.4

Examine the following sets of thesis statements and topic sentences. In each set, consider the following questions:

1. Does each thesis statement present one clear central idea? What is it?

2. Does each topic sentence introduce a central idea? What is it?

3. Does each topic sentence clearly develop the central idea in the thesis statement? What words or ideas from the thesis statement does it repeat?

4. Does each topic sentence open with some kind of transition to move it away from a previous paragraph?

A. *thesis statement*   Knowing many people myself who have attended college as first-year students, I agree that survival skill courses are extremely helpful in dealing with all the stress that comes along with college life.

no

topic sentence   One of the main things that many first-year students stress about is the fact that they will no longer be living under the care of their parents.

topic sentence   In addition to the stress of being away from home, college also introduces new financial stress.

One

B. *thesis statement*   Will the A student or the C student get further in life and have what it takes to survive everyday troubles?   *opinion*

topic sentence   Surprisingly, most people would say that the A student would be better off because he or she puts academics first.

topic sentence   I feel that the so-called smart kids get far too much praise for excellence in academics.   *noe related*

topic sentence   Education is a great thing.   *not related*

topic sentence   I feel that education is incorrectly defined in other parts of the world, and that our international peers are becoming stupid by their schooling.   *not clear and related*

C. *thesis statement*   I did not find my first semester at college particularly stressful because I had read through much of the college catalog, I had friends who were going to college, and I asked questions of college faculty and staff when I needed help.   *too much*

topic sentence   Spending some time reading the college catalog makes for very useful preparation for the first semester.   *not related*

topic sentence   Having friends who already go to college takes the edge off the newness and nervousness that accompanies the first few weeks at college.

topic sentence   Most importantly, maybe, faculty and staff at college are there to help if students have questions both in the early days and as their studies continue.

D. *thesis statement*   Being academically smart and having straight A's might lead to career success, but success isn't everything in life.

topic sentence		Smart students sometimes lack the social graces and may not be popular.
topic sentence		Popularity is very important in this age of social networking.
topic sentence		Especially in job interviews, it is important to know how to get along with people.
E.	*thesis statement*	I agree that going through life "mindlessly" makes a person accept the norm and suppresses the creative side of human behavior.
	topic sentence	Being mindful involves forcing ourselves into looking at things from a different point of view.
	topic sentence	Being mindful also means using your imagination and creativity to learn what works best for you as an individual.
	topic sentence	One last definition of what being mindless means is best portrayed by elderly people at retirement homes.

READINGS

Most Freshmen Say Religion Guides Them   THOMAS BARTLETT

Thomas Bartlett is a reporter for The Chronicle of Higher Education, a weekly newspaper on higher education read by college and university faculty and administrators. "Most Freshmen Say Religion Guides Them" appeared as the Chronicle's cover on April 22, 2005. It reports on and summarizes a large national survey about college students' religious beliefs.

BEFORE YOU READ

1. Consider the title of this selection. Would you say it accurately describes you or the first-year students you know?
2. This reading selection uses the terms *religion* and *spirituality*. What is your understanding of these terms? In what ways are they similar and/ or different?

Most college freshmen believe in God, but fewer than half follow religious teachings in their daily lives. A majority of first-year students (69 percent) say their beliefs provide guidance, but many (48 percent) describe themselves as "doubting," "seeking," or "conflicted."   1

Those are some of the results of a national study released last   2
week that is believed to be the first broad, in-depth look at the
religious and spiritual views of college students. The study, "Spirituality in Higher Education: A National Study of College Students'
Search for Meaning and Purpose," was conducted by the Higher
Education Research Institute at the University of California at Los
Angeles (http://www.gseis.ucla.edu/heri). Last fall 112,232 freshmen
were asked how often they attended religious services, whether
they prayed, and if their religious beliefs affected their actions.

Among the findings was a strong correlation between students'   3
religious beliefs and their views on hot-button political issues. For
instance, students who considered themselves religious were more
likely to oppose same-sex marriage. Religious students were also
less likely to believe that abortion should be legal.

On other questions, however, there was little difference   4
between religious and nonreligious students. For instance, a majority of both groups believed that the federal government should do
more to control the sale of handguns and that colleges should ban
racist and sexist speech on campus.

The survey also found that while first-year students were not   5
always sure what they believed, most of them were interested in
grappling with big questions like the meaning of life.

What that suggests, according to Alexander W. Astin, direc-   6
tor of the research center at UCLA, is that colleges should be
searching for ways to incorporate spiritual and religious questions
into the curriculum—even if doing so makes some professors
uncomfortable.

"There's an unwritten assumption that we just don't talk about   7
these issues," says Mr. Astin. "I don't think we're taking advantage
of the opportunity to help students explore those questions with
each other and in their course work."

That is because higher education is "a little more repressed"   8
when the conversation turns to spiritual matters, according to
Claire L. Gaudiani, a former president of Connecticut College who
helped oversee the study. "For a lot of intellectuals, religion and spirituality are seen as a danger to intellectual inquiry," says Ms. Gaudiani.

She argues, however, that dealing with questions about mean-   9
ing and purpose "doesn't have to mean indoctrination." She
compares what she calls "educating the spirit" to teaching good
nutrition or physical fitness. "Right now students get the sense that
we don't do spirituality," she says.

Burning Questions. If most professors do not "do spiritual-   10
ity," then Mark Wallace is an exception. The associate professor of
religion at Swarthmore College teaches a first-year seminar called
"Religion and the Meaning of Life." He agrees that many professors
are reluctant to engage in what he calls "meaning teaching." Which
is a shame, he says, because meaning is exactly what students are
looking for. "They hunger and crave that sort of conversation in a
college environment," says Mr. Wallace.

He also agrees with Ms. Gaudiani that it is possible to deal with   11
religious questions without promoting a particular ideology. What
his students seem to want is an "open, safe place" for the discussion of universal issues where they won't be "censored or yelled
at or ignored." As proof, he cites the fact that he usually has three
times as many students sign up for his seminar as he can accept.
"They have burning questions about life issues," he says. "And they
feel those kinds of issues get ignored in the classroom."

Not in David K. Glidden's classroom: The professor of philoso-   12
phy at the University of California at Riverside teaches "The Care
of the Soul," a course that focuses on how to live a purposeful life.
While Mr. Glidden is not sure that students will complete his class
knowing how to care for their souls, he thinks such courses are
a good start and should be a part of a college's curriculum. "My
sense is that the students I've taught are a lot like what T.S. Eliot
called 'hollow men.' They are living in a world and they don't know
what they're here for—they don't know how to live their lives."

And they want to know how to live their lives, says Richard F   13
Galvin, a professor of philosophy at Texas Christian University. He
is part of a team-taught, freshman-level course called "The Meaning of Life." The course has two sections of 50 students and the
seats are always filled. "I can tell by talking to them in office hours,
looking at their faces in class, and reading their work that it affects
them," Mr. Galvin says. "They want to talk about these issues. What
I like to tell them is that there is plenty of time to be worried
about their careers but this might be the last time they get to talk
about big questions."

Readings for the course include Plato's dialogues and works by   14
Friedrich Nietzsche and John Stuart Mill.

Jeffrey Sebo took Mr. Galvin's class when he was a freshman.   15
The senior philosophy major was intrigued by the title of the
course and became fascinated by the discussions—so much so
that he has returned to the class twice as a teaching assistant. "It
was the big questions that got me hooked," he says.

The results of the UCLA study were heartening to Carol Geary 16
Schneider, president of the Association of American Colleges and
Universities, which has long advocated a more holistic and less
career-centered approach to higher education. "Students are more
idealistic than we thought," she says. "But what this data shows us is
that we have a long way to go. Students have idealism that can be
tapped but we're not doing all we can to help them connect that
idealism to important challenges in the world around us."

Figuring out how to do that is not simple, but colleges need 17
to start trying, according to Mr. Astin. "If you want to take seriously the claims we make about liberal learning, this is what you
have to do," he says. "There are large numbers of students who
are involved in spiritual and religious issues and who are trying
to figure out what life is all about and what matters to them. We
need to be much more creative in finding ways to encourage that
exploration."

Freshmen's Views on Religion and Spirituality. Last fall 18
the Higher Education Research Institute at the University of California at Los Angeles asked 112,232 college freshmen about their
views on religion and spirituality. Here are some of the findings:

Students' religious preferences	
Roman Catholic	28%
None	17%
Baptist	13%
Other Christian	11%
Methodist	6%
Lutheran	5%
Presbyterian	4%
Church of Christ	3%
Other religion	3%
Episcopalian	2%
Jewish	2%
Buddhist	1%
Eastern Orthodox	1%
Hindu	1%
Islamic	1%
United Church of Christ	1%
Latter-Day Saints (Mormon)	0.4%
Unitarian	0.4%
Quaker	0.4%

Current views about spiritual/religious matters

Secure	42%
Seeking	23%
Conflicted	15%
Not interested	15%
Doubting	10%

Note: Figures add up to more than 100% because students could choose more than one option.

Indicators of students' religiousness

Believe in God	79%
Pray	69%
Attend religious services*	81%
Discussed religion/spirituality with friends*	80%
Discussed religion/spirituality with family*	76%
Religious beliefs provide strength, support, and guidance**	69%
Follow religious teachings in everyday life***	40%

*Occasionally or frequently.
**Agree strongly or somewhat.
***Consider it essential or very important.

Indicators of students' spirituality

Believe in the sacredness of life*	83%
Have an interest in spirituality*	80%
Search for meaning/purpose in life*	76%
Have discussions about the meaning of life with friends*	74%
My spirituality is a source of joy**	64%
Seek out opportunities to help me grow spiritually***	47%

*Describes students to some or a great extent.
**Agree strongly or somewhat.
***Consider it essential or very important.

Source: Higher Education Research Institute.

AFTER YOU READ

Work with other students to develop responses to these questions or to compare responses that you have already prepared.

1. Use your own words to state the thesis of the article. Then identify any sentence or sentences in the article that seem to express the idea.
2. Divide the article into sections according to each major point that Bartlett makes.
3. In three or four sentences, briefly summarize the thesis of the article and its major supporting points.

4. Identify the types of support that Bartlett uses. Does he use brief or extended examples, statistics, or expert testimony?

5. Look at paragraphs 3, 4, and 11 (or other paragraphs assigned by your instructor), and explain how the coherence is maintained from sentence to sentence.

It's None of Your Business: The Challenges of Getting Public Information for the Public   KATHLEEN CARROLL

This essay is based on a speech given for the Associated Press Institute for Cultural Diplomacy at the International Freedom of Expression Forum in Berlin, Germany, on March 1, 2012. Kathleen Carroll is an executive editor and senior vice president of the Associated Press.

BEFORE YOU READ

1. The title of this essay suggests a contradiction. What is that contradiction? How does that contradiction hint at the central idea of the article?

2. In what countries do you think it might be difficult to access information from the government? Why do you think so?

Why do governments keep so many secrets? They do, of course, all of them. Kingdoms, dictatorships, democracies of every kind, single-party and multi-party governments—it doesn't matter what kind of system governs a nation, that system values and keeps a lot of secrets. To start, let's concede that some activities—diplomatic negotiations, military strategies—should remain secret, at least for a while. But that's a small part of what governments do. The vast majority of government activity should be out in the open and available to the citizens it serves.   1

More than 100 countries around the world agree. Those nations have laws that acknowledge their citizens have the right to know what is being done on their behalf. By the book, that means that more than 5 billion people around the world are free to ask questions of their government and expect clear and speedy answers. In reality, nearly half of those countries simply ignore their own laws. Citizens who seek information are ignored or, in the worst cases, punished just for asking.   2

Last year, Associated Press journalists conducted the first ever test of those transparency laws. We asked the same questions of the European Union and the 105 nations with open records laws.   3

And about half of the nations that mandate public disclosure had this answer: "It's none of your business."

What did we ask? Two simple questions: How many people have been arrested on terrorism charges since the Sept. 11, 2001, attacks in the United States? And how many have been convicted? Sixty-six countries gave us some kind of answer, most not complete. Even with the paltry responses, we could document a dramatic surge in terrorism arrests and convictions—nearly 120,000 arrests and more than 35,000 convictions. The actual amount is almost certainly higher. One third of the convictions—nearly 13,000—came from just two nations, Turkey and China, which are among the countries that human rights advocates complain use terrorism laws to crack down on dissenters. 4

And how do countries define terrorism? It depends. China, for example, arrested more than 7,000 people under a definition that counts terrorism as one of Three Evils, along with separatism and extremism. 5

How easy was it to gather those numbers? Only 14 countries answered in full within their own legal deadline, among them India, Armenia and the Cook Islands. Another 38 countries answered most questions, at least providing data, but days, weeks and even months late, including the UK, France, Germany, Canada and the United States. Belgium and Austria were among those that simply didn't respond at all. 6

In fact, more than half the countries did not release anything. A third didn't even acknowledge the request. Among those who didn't respond were Pakistan and China, which adopted open information laws in part because there were financial incentives: for China, it was a condition for joining the World Trade Organization; for Pakistan, it was in return for $1.4 billion in aid from the International Monetary Fund. These laws are not on the books to serve journalists, but to serve citizens. 7

Even if a national government is responsive to requests, regional and local officials may not yet be on board with transparency. In China, for example, one family in an industrial northeastern city tried to use the laws to flush out why local authorities were steamrolling a construction project that threatened the family matriarch's home. They got the records and proved the process was deeply flawed; the home was destroyed anyway. 8

There are places where the system works well. India is one. India's information law was passed in 2006 and since then, citizen requests have exploded—from 24,000 in the first year to more 9 than a million today. Politicians there describe right to information as a "fundamental human right" and dozens of blogs help people with right to information issues. A number of requests have uncovered local corruption and unethical behavior, just what information laws are intended to do. There are still issues. In some cases local officials suspected of corruption simply refuse to answer citizen questions or, in some cases, go after them instead.

Another model law is in Mexico's. Requests can be anonymous 10 and all responses are made public, usually within a month. The government processes more than 3,000 requests a week and fully answers 85 percent of them.

The U.S. gets about 600,000 requests a year, more than Mexico 11 but less than India. A large number of those requests are filed by people researching their family histories, seeking military records for ancestors, for example. There are a number of online resources— government and private—to help make the research easier.

More such laws are coming; they are under serious consid- 12 eration in at least two dozen countries. Indeed, the Internet has made transparency easier in many cases. Mexico's law went into effect in 2003, in the online era. The U.S. law went into effect in the paper-pushing year of 1966—and a Byzantine bureaucracy has grown up in the 46 years since. Each separate federal agency has an office to handle requests—meaning citizens have to know how the system works and where to ask before they ever file a request. Only half of the requests get a full answer, though rarely within the 20 days that the law requires. Requests can linger for years and there is no consequence for not answering. More than 10 years ago, we asked the State Department for information about a now-defunct Greek terror organization. At the latest check last year, a staffer said: "The information was sent to a senior reviewer."

The U.S. system clearly needs some updating and the Obama 13 administration has gotten a start, setting up an office to streamline things. One of Obama's first acts as president was to change the presumption about the federal law to one of disclosure. In other words, all questions about what was going on were expected to yield an answer. That same administration has stepped up investigation and prosecution of government whistleblowers—employees who have exposed waste or fraud within their agencies.

Obama is not the only politician to have mixed views of trans- 14 parency. Prime Minister Tony Blair pushed for a public information law in 2005 and now Britain has a thriving one. Today, Blair refers to his support of transparency as monumentally stupid, saying in

his autobiography "I quake at the imbecility of it." Like many officials, Blair's views on the need for open government changed after
he began, well, governing. His view these days is that officials can't
be effective if there is a chance the public might learn about their
deliberations. The public, it seems, must be protected from the
ugly business of government on their behalf. Philippine President
Benigno Aquino III was similarly worried about the downsides of
transparency; he has only recently decided to support a proposed
Freedom of Information law.

So what exactly are we being protected from? What is so bad   15
about secrets? Let's turn the questions on its head. What's so bad
about transparency? Why NOT tell your citizens what you are
doing for them? Let's take public safety, a fundamental function
of any government and a topic of keen interest to citizens, and
a topic of intense conversation in Japan, where in March 2011 a
tremendous tsunami damaged and ultimately melted the nuclear
reactors at the Fukushima Daiichi power plant.

The situation was terribly frightening—tens of millions of   16
Japanese citizens were worried about radiation in their food and in
their air and they were not getting straight answers from their government. Documents obtained through Japan's open information
laws show that both the government and the plant's operators
were aware of the tsunami risks well before the March 11 tsunami
but were in no hurry to deal with it. They planned a lengthy study
of the problem. A different set of documents from the U.S. nuclear
regulatory officials talking with their counterparts in Japan during
the crisis spell out the confusion in Tokyo and Washington's deep
mistrust of assurances about what was happening at the plant.

In New York City, the topic of public safety is utterly inter-   17
twined with the Sept. 11 terrorist attacks. City officials who no longer trusted the FBI, the CIA and other federal agencies to protect
the city, set up its own anti-terrorism unit and it has since become
one of the most aggressive intelligence gathering agencies in the
United States. The unit, set up with CIA help and at least $1 billion
from Washington, has been secretly spying on Muslim citizens by
infiltrating their mosques, coffee shops, businesses and clubs. And
not just in New York City, but in neighboring states and on university campuses throughout the northeastern U.S., almost always
without the consent or even knowledge of the local authorities.

And all of that activity was a secret until we revealed it begin-   18
ning last summer. The NYPD first denied the unit even existed

and the city council that governs the city wasn't told, either. Local Muslim groups have complained about citizens being targeted simply because of their faith. And officials at some of the universities and neighboring cities penetrated by the New York agents are none too happy, either. It's true that this kind of police activity is common in many countries around the world. But in the United States, one of the long enshrined values protects citizens from police investigation unless authorities have a legitimate reason to suspect illegal activity. New York's mayor and police chief say the unit is acting legally and they strongly defend its activities as vital to protecting the city against terrorists. They also imply that critics are not sufficiently worried about the next attack. Two of the city's newspapers not only agree, they howl that the AP's reporting may actually put the city at greater risk. Both views—strongly held and tartly worded—miss the point. Taxpayers are funding this unit. This unit was formed to protect those taxpayers. And yet the entire effort was not just secret, the NYPD even denied that it existed.

19   You can have a healthy discussion about whether or not this kind of intelligence gathering is ultimately helpful or harmful. You can debate the merits of targeting a group of people because heinous acts have been committed by others in the name of their shared religion. But you can only have those discussions if you know about the unit in the first place—if the government-funded activity is, in fact, no longer a secret.

AFTER YOU READ

Work with other students to develop responses to these questions or to compare responses that you have already prepared.

1. Use your own words to express the thesis of the article. Then identify any sentence or sentences in the article that seem to express that idea.

2. Divide the article into sections according to each major point that Carroll makes.

3. In three or four sentences, briefly summarize the thesis of the article and its major supporting points.

4. Paragraphs 6–8 serve a different purpose from paragraphs 9–10. Explain that difference.

5. Identify the types of support that Carroll uses.

6. Look at paragraph 14 (or other paragraphs assigned by your instructor) and explain how coherence is maintained from sentence to sentence.

We Treat Racism Like It's Going Extinct: It's Not

BRITTNEY COOPER

Brittney Cooper is assistant professor of women's and gender studies and Africana studies at Rutgers University. She is currently completing her first book, Race Women: Gender and the Making of a Black Public Intellectual Tradition. *Cofounder of the popular feminist blog,* Crunk Feminist Collective, *Cooper is also a sought-after social commentator on issues of race, gender, and popular culture.*

BEFORE YOU READ

1. Consider the title of this article. It makes two assertions. What are they? What is your reaction to them?
2. Would you say the younger generation of today is more or less racist than its counterparts of ten or twenty years ago?

When 28-year-old George Zimmerman killed 17-year-old Trayvon   1
Martin on a residential Sanford, Florida, street in February 2012,
after trailing the hoodie-clad, iced tea–carrying youth through the
neighborhood because he looked "suspicious," it became clear
that America's Millennial generation had not, in fact, disentangled
itself from the nation's sordid, bloody and lamentable history of
racial atrocity. For George Zimmerman, born in October 1983, fits
almost every standard definition of the Millennial generation.

Based upon most studies of Millennials, I loosely define them   2
(or us) as a generation of people born in the late 20th century
who have or will come of age in the first two decades of the
21st century. For instance, having turned 18 in 1998 (voting age)
and 21 in 2001 (drinking age), I usually reluctantly call myself a
cusp-Millennial.

Darren Wilson, the police officer who killed Michael Brown Jr.   3
on a residential street in Ferguson, Missouri, in Aug. 2014, defini-
tively fits the Millennial classification. Born in 1986, Wilson later
testified in reference to Brown that "it looked like a demon," and
that he (Wilson) felt like a child trying to wrestle "the Hulk." Both
Wilson and Brown stand at 6 feet 4 inches, and both weighed
between 200 and 300 pounds. Wilson also had a gun. Moreover,
Wilson's characterizations of Brown as less-than-human, as mon-
strous, and dangerous, fit within a long and enduring history of stereotypes of black men as criminals, animals and brutes.

Recent polling data also indicate that white Millennials   4
are nearly as likely as their parents (61 percent to 64 percent

respectively) to believe that white people are harder working and more intelligent than African-Americans. The paradox of progress, as historian Jelani Cobb calls it, is that these negative racial attitudes persist among young white Americans even though they are the same generation that played a pivotal role in the election of Barack Obama to the presidency. But it is important to recognize that mainstream acceptance of exceptionally accomplished black people is not an accurate indicator of the racial attitudes of the general populace.

Recently, young fraternity members at the University of Oklahoma were caught on video singing a chant that copiously used the N-word, proclaiming that there would never be one in their fraternity. Two students were expelled, and we were treated to the requisite white American morality tale of shock, disavowal and denouncement. The problem is that these incidents happen every year. In fall 2013, a white sorority at the University of Alabama rejected two pledges of color seemingly solely on the basis of race. Moreover each year, we hear stories of fraternities and sororities and other campus groups throwing race-themed parties that traffic in stereotypes about African-Americans and Latinos. 5

The shock and surprise from white Americans about these continued incidents baffle me. These clear racist and racially-tinged occurrences happen with a kind of quotidian regularity. The question is why we think the problem of racism is an evolutionary problem rather than an ideological one. We treat racism as though it is the contained characteristic of a specific species of human beings known as racists, that lived in a prior era of American history, but have now nearly become extinct. We keep missing that racism is ideological and institutional, rather than merely individual. 6

Or we treat racism like an outmoded technology, hoping that it will go the way of the rotary phone, the cassette tape and the VCR. 7

We keep missing that racism is the message, not the medium. The message more specifically is antiblackness and white supremacy. These messages have never been properly addressed or even remotely dismantled, and this is why they persist despite the medium. Such messages adapt to new media and new technologies—be they digital technologies or social phenomena like gentrification, segregation, over-policing and mass incarceration, which perpetuate the fundamental message of racism, namely black inferiority. 8

These messages—about racism and antiblackness and white   9
supremacy—persist because they resonate. Such messages mark
who belongs and who doesn't, who is worthy of America's promise and who is not, who is worthy of our national empathy, care,
and resources and who isn't.

Millennials have grown up in a world marked by these mes-   10
sages. And we have come of age and reached young adulthood in
a struggling economy, with a shrinking middle-class, rising college
costs, and limited job opportunities. When resources are scarce
in this way, the old messages about who is worthy resonate and
often come to predominate.

Despite this dismal picture, I still think Millennials have a   11
chance to shift the generational narrative on racism. Young black
Millennials and Millennials of color have taken to the streets proclaiming a new message—Black Lives Matter. Unbowed by the
recalcitrant racial attitudes of their white Millennial counterparts,
these young people of color are demanding that America change,
demanding a dismantling of the social technologies of racism,
demanding that black lives be treated with value. And I believe
that we will win.

AFTER YOU READ

1. Use your own words to state the thesis of the article. Then identify any sentence or sentences in the article that seem to express the idea.
2. Divide the article into sections according to each major point that Cooper makes.
3. In three or four sentences, briefly summarize the thesis of the article and its major supporting points.
4. Identify the types of support that Cooper uses. Does she use brief or extended examples, statistics, or expert testimony?
5. Look at paragraphs 3, 6, and 8 (or other paragraphs assigned by your instructor) and explain how the coherence is maintained from sentence to sentence.

Video Games Can Be Helpful to College Students
SCOTT CARLSON

Scott Carlson is a staff reporter for The Chronicle of Higher Education. *In the following selection, he discusses a report that suggests video games have little effect on a college student's performance.*

BEFORE YOU READ

1. Consider your own experience with video games. Do you play them? If so, what kind do you play and how often?
2. In your experience, do video games interfere with your education? If you play video games, would you be a better student without them?

A report released last month suggests that video games are a vital and positive part of college students' social lives, even though games may be keeping them from their studies.   1

The study on which the report was based was conducted by the Pew Internet and American Life Project, which sponsors research to gauge the effect of the Internet on various aspects of everyday life. The researchers made distinctions among video games played online, those played through a personal computer, and those using a dedicated video-game console, such as a Sony PlayStation.   2

The study shows that for this generation of college students, gaming does not edge out other activities, says Steve Jones, a professor of communication at the University of Illinois at Chicago, who supervised the research.   3

"It's been with them forever, and they have never had to choose between gaming and other things," he says. "It's already been in the mix for them since the kindergarten days…. It's not that disruptive as a result."   4

The researchers distributed paper surveys to more than 1,100 students at colleges across the country. The findings are accurate to within 3.5 percentage points, the report says.   5

The study's least surprising finding is that most respondents—65 percent—said they were regular video-game players. One in five college students said games had helped them develop, and even improve, friendships. Sixty percent said games provided a pastime when friends are not around.   6

The genders showed differences in the ways that they approached games: Women play computer and Internet games more than men, while the two sexes play console games at about the same rate. The researchers speculate that because console games are generally more violent and feature stereotyped gender roles, they are less attractive to women.   7

"The men were telling us that gaming was a standard part of the entertainment and media mix for them, and it was something they looked forward to doing," Mr. Jones says. "Women were telling   8 us that they were doing it to kill time, so it wasn't as prominent an activity in their everyday lives."

The time spent on gaming and socializing does seem to cut into classwork. About half of the students said gaming distracts them from studying.   9

For one in 10, gaming is a procrastination tool. A third of the respondents said they played games during class.   10

However, in a somewhat contradictory finding, two-thirds of the students said video games had no effect on their college performance. The researchers noted that the amount of time the students spent studying closely matched the results of other surveys. Sixty-two percent of the students said they studied about 7 hours a week, and 15 percent said they studied 12 hours a week.   11

James Gee, a professor of education at the University of Wisconsin at Madison, is not heartened by the figures on students' reported study habits—merely an hour a day for a full load of college courses.   12

But the professor, whose book *What Video Games Have to Teach Us about Learning and Literacy* was published in May, says that in his research on high-school and middle-school students, he has had a hard time finding any whose schoolwork is, in fact, damaged by video games. "From the earliest ages, the game is one among multiple tasks that people do and switch between," he says.   13

Gaming is a much more integral part of students' social lives than the Pew study suggests, Mr. Gee believes. "The report is a good first swipe, but with any new technology, you want to know what the niches are," he says.   14

Mr. Jones says the study is only a beginning for research on video games—something that could be used to push the creation of educational games for students.   15

"Those of us working in higher education could do more to show some of the positive sides of gaming," he says. "In some ways, it's unfortunate that we call them games, because that makes it hard for us to take them seriously."   16

AFTER YOU READ

1. State the thesis of the article in your own words. Then identify any sentences in the article that express that idea.

2. Divide the article into sections according to each major point that Carlson makes.

3. In three or four sentences, briefly summarize the thesis of the article and its major supporting points.

4. Identify the types of support that Carlson uses.

5. Choose one or more paragraphs from the article, and explain how its coherence is maintained from sentence to sentence.

WRITING ASSIGNMENTS

1. In "Most Freshmen Say Religion Guides Them," Thomas Bartlett writes, "A majority of first-year students (69 percent) say their beliefs provide guidance, but many (48 percent) describe themselves as 'doubting,' 'seeking,' or 'conflicted.'" What do you think of these statements? Can a person find guidance from spiritual or religious beliefs while also feeling doubt and conflict? Write a paper in which you illustrate your response with examples drawn from your own experiences and/or the experiences of people you know.

2. Bartlett refers to Professor Richard Galvin, who says that students want to know how to live their lives. He goes on to say, "They want to talk about these issues. What I like to tell them is that there is plenty of time to be worried about their careers but this might be the last time they get to talk about big questions." What might be one of the "big questions" Professor Galvin refers to? Write a paper in which you explain how that question or issue affects you and/or people with whom you are familiar. Illustrate your explanations with examples drawn from your own experiences and/or the experiences of people you know.

3. In "It's None of Your Business: The Challenges of Getting Public Information for the Public," Kathleen Carroll argues that citizens have a right to know what governments do in the name of citizens. Do you agree that this is so? Why or why not? Are there situations in which you have thought you would like to know more about what the government is doing? Write a paper in which you support your responses with specific examples.

4. Carroll admits that there might be times when governments need to use secrecy. She alludes to times of war and to potential threats to citizens. How important is transparency for democracy? At what point does a government's refusal to be transparent interfere with the ideals of democracy? In other words, are secrecy and democracy compatible? Write a paper in which you use specific examples to support your responses.

5. In "We Treat Racism Like It's Going Extinct: It's Not," Brittney Cooper writes, "America's Millennial generation [has] not, in fact, disentangled itself from the nation's sordid, bloody and lamentable history of racial atrocity." Consider your own experiences with and knowledge of racism as it exists today. Where do you see racist attitudes in action? Write a paper in which you use specific examples drawn from observations from your own life or the lives of people you know.

6. Cooper writes, "These messages—about racism and antiblackness and white supremacy—persist because they resonate.... Millennials have grown up in a world marked by these messages." Do your own experiences confirm or contradict this view? Write a paper in which you illustrate either in what ways attitudes of younger Americans are racist, intolerant, and bigoted or in what ways they are open, tolerant, and accepting of other races, religions, lifestyles, or cultures. Or, if you perceive people as a blend of contradictory characteristics, write a paper illustrating how that might be so. Support your ideas with examples drawn from your own experiences and observations.

7. In "Video Games Can Be Helpful to College Students," Scott Carlson discusses a study that examined the effect of video games on college students. The report, he says, "suggests that video games are a vital and positive part of college students' social lives, even though games may be keeping them from their studies." What do you think of this statement? Is it true for you or for people you know? Write a paper in which you offer your own analysis of the effects of video games on the people who play them. Use specific examples drawn from your personal experiences or observations.

8. According to Carlson, the study of video games "made distinctions among video games played online, those played through a personal computer, and those using a dedicated video-game console, such as a Sony PlayStation." In your experience, what distinctions might one make among these three types? Do they offer different types of games? Do they attract different types of people? Does one type attract or repel one gender over another? Write a paper in which you use specific examples drawn from your personal experiences or observations.

EVALUATING SAMPLE PAPERS

As you read and evaluate the quality of the essays on the following pages, consider these areas:

1. Thesis Statement
   Underline the thesis statement of the essay. Does it express a clear and specific central idea?

   1   2   3   4   5   6

2. Topic Sentences
   Underline the topic sentence of each paragraph. Does it clearly state the central idea of the paragraph?

   1   2   3   4   5   6

3. Support

Examine the supporting details in each paragraph. Are they specific and clear? Should they be more detailed, or should more support be included?

1   2   3   4   5   6

4. Unity

Does each paragraph clearly relate to and develop the central idea expressed in the thesis statement? Do the supporting details *within* each paragraph clearly relate to and develop the *central idea* expressed in the topic sentence of that paragraph?

1   2   3   4   5   6

5. Coherence

Does each paragraph open with a transition, a reference to the central idea of the thesis statement, and an identification of its own central idea? Are the sentences within each paragraph clearly related to each other by the use of transitions or by references to the central idea of the paragraph?

1   2   3   4   5   6

6. Sentence Structure

Do the sentences combine ideas that are related, using coordination and subordination when appropriate? Are there too many brief, choppy main clauses?

1   2   3   4   5   6

7. Mechanics, Grammar, and Spelling

Does the paper contain a distracting number of errors of these kinds?

1   2   3   4   5   6

8. Overall Ranking of the Essay

1   2   3   4   5   6

Student Essay 1

Do I have to go to church to have spirituality? Does God not hear me when I pray if I don't pick and follow a traditional religion? These have been my personal "big questions" about Religion. But I have not known a time or a place where I felt comfortable asking them. I remember the day that I became disillusioned with organized religion. The preacher at the church I attended as a young girl would rant and rave about how Baptist were the chosen religion and all other people were going to hell, but I didn't agree with him. I had always thought that there was a heaven for each religion. I just couldn't believe that God would be like that. So I decided that I didn't want to go to church anymore. Yet I still searched for my own spirituality. In Thomas Bartlett's article, "Most Freshmen Say Religion Guides Them," he states that most college freshmen believe in God but fewer than half follow religious teachings in their daily lives. He talks about how students are not always sure what they believe, but most of them wanted to explore the meaning of life. Bartlett is correct in his thinking. Students should be offered courses that help them explore their spirituality and allow them to have open dialogue about their big questions on "the meaning of life" and feel comfortable about doing so.

Providing a forum for open dialogue would create an environment without judgment where students can feel comfortable expressing their views honestly. In religion today, the extremist seem to be the loudest voice. And critical thinkers might fear that speaking out about their feelings and questions regarding religion can give people a wrong impression of them. I have experienced this myself. I have been with friends and wanted to say, "I have prayed about that, and I feel that whatever Gods will is that I accept it." But I stopped myself from saying what I wanted to say because I did not want to be judged a fanatic. I also fear that my friends will lump me into the group of religious people who do not believe in same sex marriage and abortion. These are very controversial things that seem to be attached to religion. If religion or spirituality was a subject that people felt free to discuss; as a result, these very few extremist would not be able to speak for so many.

Students hunger for answers to big questions like who am I-and where am I going in my life, and college should allow curriculum to assist them to answer or at least ponder these questions in a spiritual way. According to Claire L. Gaudiani, who helped over-see this study, "Right now students get a sense that colleges do not do spiritually" (127). That is not entirely true though, in our class we have had readings on religion and had to write papers on the subject, and I have noticed that these assignments have created a dialogue among my classmates and I. We are feeling more comfortable about having conversations that might be considered taboo. I might even be able to discuss my spirituality with them now with no judgment. This is because we are speaking more freely in your class. I do believe that in not understanding each other's beliefs then misconceptions can happen. With a proper arena students can help each other answer their big questions about life too.

Some students have deep problems that they keep to themselves. And in the most extreme causes have used guns to hurt people and themselves. I wonder what could make a student feel so all alone and suicidal. And in the less extreme, students can have the same feelings but not act on them. If these students were able to find hope within themselves and develop their spirituality I think it would really help them. They could even find friendship in the professors and see them as mentors assisting them in finding their meaning of life. Either way it sure could not hurt. If there are professors out there willing to create this curriculum, others willing to teach it and students wanting to learn it then that is all the answer I need.

College professors who are willing and have the desire must have the power to mentor, teach respect and create open dialogue in classrooms. They need to have the freedom to bring students closer together, instead of allowing students to continue feeling isolated. Their classrooms should feel personal and comfortable to harbor growth and critical thinking, so extremist views can be examined in the open and hopefully purged. If a student feels the need to attend classes regarding religion and spiritually that help him explore the "Meaning of life," they should be available to him without going to Seminary School.

In reflection, my experience as a new college student has felt personal. My professors have encouraged creating friendships and helped us students to have dialogue about tough issues. I graduated high school in 1983 and grew up in the 1960s and 70s, a time when in my opinion, these kinds of things were not encouraged in classrooms, or allowed to be spoken in home. I feel lucky to be in college now, during a time where freethinking is encouraged. If a course on religions and spiritually were offered here at Palomar College, I would definitely sign up.

Student Essay 2

This essay was written in response to a reading selection not included in this text.

In Richard Cohen's article "A Generation of Bigots Comes of Age," he suggests we should all be concerned that our children are growing up intolerant of other races. This reminds me of the billboard with a picture of an African-American child and a white child with their arms around each other's backs and a caption that read, "They are not born hating each other." The billboard reflects what I have experienced with children today. I believe children have a more open and accepting attitude toward other races. I think this can be credited to the education of children.

One example of how we are educating our children is through the television set. Television is often the sole exposure to images of minorities. The persuasiveness of the media can profoundly influence children's ideas of the world they live in. For example, Barney the dinosaur uses a variety of different races in his "backyard gang." There are Hispanic, African-American, and Asian, as well as Caucasian. Another example would be *Sesame Street*, where they promote friendship between children of many different races. Furthermore, they also use animals and friendly monsters to demonstrate that it is not important what you look like but how you treat others.

Through school, children are also being educated about racial tolerance. My oldest son started school in Valley Center, where he was enrolled in bilingual education. He was taught in both English and Spanish. One day all his lessons would be in English whether it be math or colors and shapes then the next day he would be taught in Spanish. Not only that but they encouraged friendship with all the children in class by making sure that they mixed the Spanish speaking students into study groups with the English speaking students, so that they could help each other understand the lessons. They have a large number of migrant workers and also Indians from a nearby reservation. They educated the children on the different cultures on national and religious holidays. For instance, St. Patrick's Day comes with a social studies lesson on Ireland. The students also celebrate the Chinese New Year, Cinco de Mayo, and they have a study of African-American history during which they celebrate Martin Luther King, Jr. Day.

Similarly, children are being taught tolerance through neighborhood friendships. When you come into our neighborhood, you will see all of the children playing together. We have children from all different races. None of them are concerned with what color skin the other has. Some examples are Vanessa and David, who are American Indian; Aaron, Javier, and Claudia, who are Hispanic; Jovonne, Huesson, and Anjenneta, who are African-American; and Jennifer, Mark, and Kevin, who are Caucasian. This is a vastly different situation from when I was growing up, because we had no other races, the only differences were our hair or eye color. Of course, I had heard it said that friendship has a color all its own. I believe children today have proven that statement.

Consequently, as our children grow we will see many changes in this nation. One change is already taking effect at this time. This nation is moving toward a global economy, and with this move we need to understand that people, regardless of skin color, are a very important part of the picture. Furthermore, the friendships children are building now will last as they grow. As a result, the ignorance and bigotry of the past will continue to shrink. In fact, through education and knowledge bigotry cannot survive.

Student Essay 3

Video Games are entertaining but for students they are only a distraction. I do not agree with Scott Carlson's essay "Video Games Can Be Helpful to College Students," when he claims, "video games are a vital and positive part of College students social lives," because video games take students away from their school work. I know from personal experiences that video games are big part of the life of college students, but they need to realize that video games are bringing their grades down. The negative effects of Video Games cripple students' ability to focus and be successful in school.

From my own experience, I can give a valid stand on my argument saying video games are detrimental to a college student's grades. My old habit back in high school and first year at Palomar College was to go to school, eat, sleep, and of course play lots of video games. In this routine there was no time for homework or studying, my grades reflected my work ethic. In high school, I could be lazy and play video games all night and my grades were not that bad. But once I got to college I could not keep my grades up and play tons of video games at once. I would have two days of school a week and I did not work at the time so the rest of the week I did nothing but play video games for ten to twelve hours a day. In this span of time, I went from having a 3.0 grade point average in high school to a 2.0 grade point average in college. At this point in time I had to tell myself, "Dylan you need to get your life in check and start going somewhere with your life."

Once I realized my video game playing was negatively affecting my school work, I then changed my ways by getting a job and focusing on getting all my school work done and actually studying. This semester is when I started getting serious and my grades have vastly improved once I cut out video games. To this day it is still hard not to throw down my textbook and just pick up a controller but then I have to tell myself, "Video Games will not help keep your grades up. Get your school work done." With this mindset and non-video game playing I hope to transfer to a University where I will socialize with people in real life instead of through a headset in a video game.

Video games are not healthy for college students lives. Most college students I know drive to school and then spend all day in a desk at school; how can a student get any exercise if they sit all day and then go home to sit more while they play video games. The Freshmen 15, when a college freshman gains 15 pounds in their first year of college, can be countered by not playing video games and instead by working out. This is what I started doing when I got to college, I was forced to attend 36 hours or more at the school gym in my Health class. Health class showed me the positive aspects of living a healthy life and now I go to my own gym to 4-5 days a week.

The life of a college student is busy and they cannot be distracted by things such as video games. Video Games aid in the procrastination of school studies and reflect poorly on the grades of college students. Through my own experiences in college and video games makes Carlson's argument about video games being good for college students seems ridiculous to me.

SENTENCE COMBINING: VERBAL PHRASES

The verbal phrase is an easy and effective way to add more information to your sentences without using a full clause to do so. In fact, you already use verbal phrases every day, both in your speech and in your writing. When you write "The man crossing the street waved at the irate motorists," you use a verbal phrase ("crossing the street"). The sentence "The plan to rob the bank was nearly flawless" also contains a verbal phrase ("to rob the bank").

Although people use verbal phrases unconsciously in their speech and writing, learning how to use them in a planned, conscious manner can improve your writing in two ways. First, using verbal phrases will allow you to add more action and description to your writing without using additional sentences. As a result, your writing will have a sense of depth and detail that will distinguish it from the prose of the average writer. Second, using these phrases will allow you to vary the structure of the sentences that you write, and a varied sentence structure makes for more interesting reading than sentence after sentence written exactly the same way.

A **verbal** is simply a verb form that is not used as a verb. For example, in the following sentences, the underlined verb forms are used as adjectives, not as verbs.

> The <u>singing</u> cowboy made everybody angry.
>
> The police officer assisted the <u>confused</u> motorist.

Each type of verbal has its own specific name. In the above examples, *singing* is a **present participle** and *confused* is a **past participle**.

PRESENT AND PAST PARTICIPLES

The *present participle* is the "-ing" form of a verb used as an adjective.

> A <u>traveling</u> sales representative decided that he needed a new pair of shoes.
>
> Mr. Ingham did not know what to do about the <u>barking</u> dogs.

The *past participle* is also used as an adjective. Some past participles end in "-d" or "-ed" *(picked, fired, tossed)*; others end in "-n" or "-en" *(eaten, thrown, spoken)*; still others have their own unique forms *(sung, brought, gone)*. To determine the past participle form of any verb, ask yourself how you would spell the word if "have" preceded it.

> The <u>exhausted</u> jogger decided to rest for an hour.
>
> The patient with the <u>broken</u> leg was ready to leave the hospital.

PRESENT AND PAST PARTICIPIAL PHRASES

Present and past participial phrases consist of present and past participles with other words added to them to give more details. The following examples are drawn from reading selections in this text.

> <u>Revealing their own tensions over gender,</u> the mothers claim that the children's fathers are more likely to buy the kids brand-name shirts or sneakers.

> The evidence for that awful prognostication can be found in a recent public opinion survey <u>conducted for the Anti-Defamation League by the Boston polling firm of Marttila & Kiley</u>....

> A report <u>released last month</u> suggests that video games are a vital and positive part of college students' social lives....

> We circle the wagons, <u>watching out for our own.</u>

INFINITIVE PHRASES

The **infinitive** is another type of verbal. It consists of the base form of a verb preceded by "to" *(to throw, to breathe, to eat)*. The **infinitive phrase** consists of the infinitive with other words added to it to give more details. Here are some examples:

> Legions of women band together <u>to revive the self-esteem they lost in supposedly loving relationships</u> and <u>to learn to love a little less.</u>

> Even healthy families need outside sources of moral guidance <u>to keep the internal tensions from imploding....</u>

USING VERBAL PHRASES

Participial and infinitive phrases can be used to improve your writing in several ways:

1. *Use verbal phrases to develop sentences by adding details and ideas.* Participial phrases are particularly effective for adding details to your sentences. Since participles are verbals, they work especially well when you are describing actions. Notice how the writers of the articles in this text used verbal phrases to expand their sentences:

> Through sports, children learn how to handle defeat as well as victory.

> Through sports, children learn how to handle defeat as well as victory— <u>no sulking, gloating or rubbing it in.</u>

> Giving directly to the street person—well, that's another matter.

> Giving directly to the street person <u>shambling across my pathway</u>— well, that's another matter.

2. Use verbal phrases to combine related sentences.   Verbal phrases often can be used to create one sentence from two or more related sentences. Note how the following sentences can be combined using verbal phrases:

> **Two sentences:** Seymour stared at his lottery ticket in amazement. He could not believe that he had just won ten million dollars.

> **One sentence using a present participial phrase:** <u>Staring at his lottery ticket in amazement,</u> Seymour could not believe that he had just won ten million dollars.

> **Two sentences:** A body was found in the Alps last year. It had been frozen for over three thousand years.

> **One sentence using a past participial phrase:** A body <u>frozen for over three thousand years</u> was found in the Alps last year.

> **Two sentences:** Michelle wanted to pass the midterm on Monday. She knew that she should study all weekend.

> **One sentence using an infinitive phrase:** Michelle knew that she should study all weekend <u>to pass the midterm on Monday.</u>

3. Use verbal phrases to be concise.   Many subordinate clauses can easily and more concisely be written as verbal phrases.

> The sycamore tree <u>that is growing next to our driveway</u> has started to drop its leaves.

> The sycamore tree <u>growing next to our driveway</u> has started to drop its leaves.

> <u>Because he thought that he had seen a ghost,</u> Herman began to scream.

> <u>Thinking that he had seen a ghost,</u> Herman began to scream.

> The person <u>who was accused of shoplifting</u> insisted that she had paid for all her items.

> The person <u>accused of shoplifting</u> insisted that she had paid for all her items.

EXERCISE 4.5

Develop the following sentences by adding verbal phrases to them where indicated. Use verbals derived from the verbs in parentheses.

EXAMPLE

> ^ Lyle stared at the paper in front of him. (confuse, determine)
> Confused by the unclear directions but determined to pass the test, Lyle stared at the paper in front of him.

1. ^ Natalie started to draw a cartoon. (hope)
2. ^ Li Na resigned from playing competitively. (feel)

3. Robinson went in search of food ^. (look, climb)

4. Gabriel ^ began to write his novel. (determine, inspire)

5. Leilani and Kalolo had time ^ before getting back to the hotel. (eat, drink, sightsee)

6. ^ Susan B. Anthony refused to apologize for voting. (arrest, fine)

7. The newcomer to Korean food ^ (sweat, drink) very much enjoyed the extra-spicy kimchi.

8. The hamburger ^ on the shelf showed no signs of decay two years later. (forget, leave)

9. ^ The student was completely unaware that the instructor had asked him a question. (text, update)

10. Julius Caesar's plan ^ was almost sidetracked when he bathed too long in the Rubicon River. (come, see, conquer)

EXERCISE **4.6**

Combine each of the following groups of sentences into one sentence. Change each underlined sentence into the type of verbal phrase suggested in parentheses.

EXAMPLE

The macaw emitted an earsplitting shriek.

It flew from the tree.

(present participial phrase)
  Emitting an earsplitting shriek, the macaw flew from the tree.

1. A rogue elephant separates itself from the herd and roams alone.
   It is often quite dangerous.
   (present participial phrase)

2. A solitary rogue elephant can be savage.
   It attacks and kills everyone it can.
   (present participial phrase)

3. A. A. Kinlock, a British authority, wrote that a rogue will often haunt a particular road.
   It will stop traffic for as long as it remains.
   (present participial phrase)

4. One particular rogue in India seemed determined.
   It killed many people and even destroyed their homes.
   (infinitive phrase)

5. <u>Carl Ackley was seized and mutilated by a rogue elephant.</u>
   Carl Ackley, the father of modern taxidermy, became convinced that the elephant was the most dangerous of all animals.
   (past participial phrase)

6. <u>The Asian elephant is considered less temperamental than the African elephant.</u>
   It nevertheless more commonly turns rogue.
   <u>It accounts for the deaths of more than fifty persons per year.</u>
   (past participial phrase and present participial phrase)

7. <u>A rogue elephant wants to destroy its victim.</u>
   It will catch him and dismember him.
   <u>It will smash him against the ground or a tree.</u>
   <u>It will toss him into the air.</u>
   (infinitive phrase and two present participial phrases)

8. An elephant may turn rogue because it is suffering from a wound.
   <u>The wound may have been inflicted by another elephant or by hunters.</u>
   (past participial phrase)

9. In many instances, elephants were found to have been suffering from painful sores and old wounds.
   <u>These elephants had been identified as rogues and killed.</u>
   (past participial phrase)

10. <u>One Indian rogue suffered from a huge sore at the end of its tail.</u>
    It caused great damage.
    <u>It chased travelers.</u>
    <u>It killed several natives.</u>
    (present participial phrases)

   Adapted from Lawrence D. Gadd, The Second Book of the Strange (Amherst, NY: Prometheus Books). © 1981 by Newspaper Enterprise Association. Reprinted by permission of the publisher.

AVOIDING DANGLING MODIFIERS

Because verbal phrases are not verbs, they do not have subjects. However, they do express an action, and the "doer" of that action is usually the subject of the sentence. Whenever you open a sentence with a verbal phrase, be sure that the subject of the sentence is also the "doer." If the subject cannot logically perform the action in the verbal phrase, you have a dangling modifier that needs to be rewritten. (See Chapter 16 for a more thorough discussion of dangling modifiers.)

DANGLING MODIFIER

<u>Sighing with relief,</u> the golf ball rolled into the cup.
A golf ball cannot sigh with relief.

POSSIBLE CORRECTION

<u>Sighing with relief,</u> the golfer watched as his golf ball rolled into the cup.
A logical subject has now been supplied. A golfer can sigh with relief.

POSSIBLE CORRECTION

<u>As the golfer sighed with relief,</u> the golf ball rolled into the cup.
The verbal phrase has been rewritten into a subordinate clause with its own subject and verb.

EXERCISE 4.7

Revise any dangling modifiers in the following sentences, either by supplying a logical subject or by rewriting the verbal phrase as a subordinate clause. Some sentences may be correct.

EXAMPLE

INCORRECT
<u>Surprised by the unexpected rainstorm,</u> our clothing was soon soaked.

CORRECT
<u>Surprised by the unexpected rainstorm,</u> we were all soon soaked.

CORRECT
<u>Because we were all surprised by the unexpected rainstorm,</u> our clothing was soon soaked.

1. Recognizing the implications of her joke, the comedian's eyebrows went up.
2. Ignored by all but the most discerning music critics, the audience couldn't believe how good the band was.
3. Revealing the secret ingredient to his infamous cupcake, an apology was offered to the studio guests.

4. Disgusted by their Instagram posts, Stefan ended his association with Carl and Carlos.

5. Hidden for over two centuries, the mayor and an assembled group of journalists opened the time capsule.

EXERCISE **4.8**

Combine the following sentences using verbal phrases. In each case, the first sentence is the main sentence. Each following sentence should be revised as a verbal phrase and added to the beginning or to the end of the main sentence or, occasionally, within the main sentence. Be careful not to write a dangling modifier when you start a sentence with a verbal phrase.

1. According to many legends, a creature lives in the Himalayas of Nepal.

   The creature is named the "abominable snowman" or "Yeti."

2. This creature is said to look half-human, half-ape.It stands eight feet tall.

   It is covered in long, white fur.

3. It has icy blue eyes and a second transparent eyelid.

   The second eyelid allows it to see in blowing snow.

   It also prevents its eyes from freezing in cold temperatures.

4. Some people refer to large, unidentifiable footprints.

   These people want to prove that the Yeti exists.

   The footprints have been discovered in the snows of Nepal.

5. The Sherpa, native people, keep the legend of the Yeti alive with stories.

   They live high in the Himalayas.

   Their stories describe their encounters with the creature.

6. Another huge, apelike creature has been reported.

   It is called Bigfoot in the United States.

   It is called Sasquatch by Canadian Indian tribes.

   It has been reported to exist in the northern United States and Canada.

7. Such a creature has reportedly been sighted in the Pacific Northwest, California, New Jersey, Pennsylvania, Ohio, Illinois, and British Columbia.

   It stands six to eight feet tall.

   It weighs eight hundred or more pounds.

8. Some researchers point to an ancient apelike creature.

   It is named Gigantopithecus.

   They point to Gigantopithecus to support their theory that Bigfoot might be descended from it.

9. Brazilians tell stories about the Mapinguary.

   The Brazilians are frightened by attacks on their cattle and farms.

   They describe the Mapinguary as an immense, apelike animal.

10. The Mapinguary fearlessly attacks wild cattle.

    It is also called the Bigfoot of Brazil.

    It leaves behind human-like footprints as long as eighteen inches.

Part Two

Writing about Reading

In the first four chapters of this text, you have written papers on topics similar to those in the reading selections. In a sense, you have used the topics in the reading selections as springboards for your own ideas, and then you have supported those ideas with examples drawn from real-life experiences.

In the next four chapters, you will move from writing on topics that are similar to those in the reading selections to writing about the reading selections themselves. Often called *academic papers* because they are required in many college-level courses, the writing assignments in the next four chapters will introduce you to summarizing accurately what you have read, to evaluating and responding to the ideas in a reading selection, to synthesizing ideas from several articles, and to arguing a point based on information drawn from a number of sources. In other words, you will be asked to write *about* what you have read.

Of course, academic writing does not mean that you will no longer use personal experiences to support your points. As a means of supporting your ideas, the real experiences of real people are just as important as ever. You will find, however, that much of your support will also be drawn from the articles you read. For that reason, the clear and accurate reading you have been practicing in Chapters 1 through 4 will be of critical importance. Obviously, you cannot write thoughtfully about an article if you have not first read it in a thoughtful manner.

Summarizing and Responding to Reading

5

Clear and accurate summarizing is one of the most important skills you can learn in college. Your ability to summarize effectively will help you study for and take tests; write reports and papers (particularly papers involving research); and give thorough, convincing oral presentations. Summarizing is also a skill in demand in the business world, especially when you must report information to other people. The person who can read and *accurately* report what he or she has read will always have an advantage over the person who cannot.

It seems as if summarizing should be such a simple task. After all, when you summarize, you merely explain what you have read to somebody else. And in many ways summarizing *is* simple. Yet it also can be quite a challenging assignment. A good summary demands that you read carefully, that you accurately identify the main points of what you have read, and that you then successfully communicate those ideas to another person. The following explanations should help you write successful summaries.

Characteristics of a Successful Summary

- A summary accurately communicates the author's ideas.
- It includes all of the author's main points.
- It usually does *not* include supporting details.
- It does *not* include your opinions or reactions.
- It does *not* alter the author's meaning in any way.
- It uses your own words and writing style.

WRITING A BRIEF SUMMARY

Because most summaries present only the central idea and main points of a reading selection, they are usually quite brief, often no more than one or two paragraphs long. To write a summary, follow these steps:

1. As you read the material that you intend to summarize, underline or highlight whatever seems significant to you. Mark statements that seem to express the central idea and the main points of the reading selection. Even particularly vivid facts or other supporting details may be marked.
2. Reread the material, annotating it and dividing it into major sections so that each section reflects one main point.
3. Write the opening sentence of your summary. It should identify the name of the reading selection, the author, and the central idea, purpose, thesis, or topic of the reading.
4. After the opening sentence, briefly summarize each of the author's main ideas. Often you will need no more than one sentence to summarize each main idea.
5. Revise what you have written so that your summary is expressed in your own words and in your own style of writing. Where needed, add transitions that refer to the author between main points.

READING

Read the following article. As you do, identify its central idea and main points. Then reread the article, annotating it and dividing it into major sections. A sample brief summary follows the article. Note how the central idea and main points of the article are incorporated into the summary.

What America Has Gained, What America Has Lost

GEORGE PACKER

George Packer is an award-winning American journalist, novelist, and playwright. Currently, he writes about foreign policy for The New Yorker. *His recent book,*

The Unwinding: An Inner History of the New America, *covers the history of America from 1978 to 2012. In the following selection, Packer discusses the "common temptation" to think that things in American life have gotten worse and cautions the reader to balance all that has gone right with what has gone wrong.*

It's a common temptation of middle age to think that the present   1
is significantly worse than the past—to mistake a herniated disc in
the L4-L5 region with America's declining global power, or annoy-
ance at public iPhone conversations with the erosion of all social
norms. Certain pieces I've written in this space and elsewhere, not
to mention a new book being published today (*The Unwinding: An
Inner History of the New America*), might lead readers to believe
that I spend my days wallowing in nostalgia for Jimmy Carter and
Boz Scaggs, if not J.F.K. and Perry Como. Not true! There are many,
many things about the year 2013 that I would not want undone,
and many other things about the year 1978 that I would not
want back. It's worth remembering them, as a kind of fact-check
exercise, before considering whether—as so many Americans I've
interviewed over the past few years believe—something has gone
wrong.

Recent additions to American life that I would fight to hang   2
onto: marriage equality, Lipitor, a black President, Google searches,
airbags, novelistic TV shows, the opportunity for women to be as
singlemindedly driven as their male colleagues, good coffee, safer
cities, cleaner air, photographs of the kids on my phone, anti-bullying,
Daniel Day Lewis, cheap communications, smoke-free airplanes,
wheelchair parking, and I could go on.

In general, the things in my list fall into two categories: tech-   3
nological advances that make life easier, tastier, more entertaining,
healthier, longer; and socio-political changes that have made the
country a more tolerant, inclusive place. Over the past generation,
America has opened previously inaccessible avenues to previously
excluded groups, although in some cases the obstacles remain
formidable, and in others (immigrant farm laborers, for example)
there has hardly been any change at all. More Americans than ever
before are free to win elective office or gain admission to a good
college or be hired by a good company or simply be themselves in
public. And they have more freedom to choose among telephones,
TV shows, toothpastes, reading matter, news outlets, and nearly
every other consumer item you can think of.

The bottom line in all these improvements is freedom. In   4
America, that's half the game.

The other half is equality. Not equality of result—no success-   5
ful political tendency or President in this country, not even F.D.R.'s
New Deal, has promised that. As Richard Hofstadter shows in his
great 1948 book, *The American Political Tradition*, the deal in this
country has always been equal opportunity. That was Jefferson's
meaning when he inscribed in the annals of our civic religion
the conviction that "all men are created equal." Even a populist
like Andrew Jackson demanded only "the classic bourgeois ideal,
equality before the law, the restriction of government to equal
protection of its citizens." But when the results are distributed
as unequally as they are at this moment, when the gap between
promise and reality grows so wide, when elites can fail repeatedly
and never lose their perches of privilege while ordinary people
can never work their way out of debt, equal opportunity becomes
a dream. We measure inequality in numbers—quintiles, average
and median incomes, percentages of national wealth, unemployment statistics, economic growth rates—but the damage it is doing
to our national life today defies quantification. It is killing many
Americans' belief in the democratic promise—their faith that the
game is fair, that everyone has a chance. That's where things have
unquestionably deteriorated over the past generation. The game
seems rigged—and if it is, following the rules is for suckers.

We usually think of greater inclusiveness as a blow struck for   6
equality. But in our time, the stories of greater social equality and
economic inequality are unrelated. The fortunes of middle-class
Americans have declined while prospects for many women and
minorities have risen. There's no reason why they couldn't have
improved together—this is what appeared to be happening in the
late nineteen-sixties and early seventies. Since then, many women
and minorities have done better than in any previous generations,
but many others in both groups have seen their lives and communities squeezed by the economic contractions of the past generation. Like almost everything else, the new inclusiveness divides the
country into winners and losers. It's been good for those with the
education, talent, and luck to benefit from it; for others—in urban
cores like Youngstown, Ohio; rural backwaters like Rockingham
County, North Carolina; and the exurban slums outside Tampa—
inclusiveness remains mostly theoretical. It gives an idea of equality,
which makes the reality of inequality even more painful.

No iPhone app or biotech breakthrough can do anything   7
about this disparity. It's not a problem that the most brilliant start-
up entrepreneurs are equipped to solve. It seems immune to

engineering solutions, since it has coincided with a period of rapid technological change. It's one of those big, structural problems that requires action on many fronts, from many institutions—from government at all levels, from business, from the media and universities. It needs a shift in laws, priorities, social relations, modes of production, and in the ways people think of their rights and obligations as citizens.

In *The Unwinding*, which looks at the past generation of American life, there are many stories of institutional corrosion. Politics turns bitterly divisive, government agencies founder, corporations abandon any sign of loyalty or vision beyond their quarterly earnings, great media organizations lose their financial foundation and their compass, the dream of home ownership turns into a Ponzi scheme. But there are also life stories of ordinary Americans— Dean Price, Tammy Thomas, Jeff Connaughton, Michael Van Sickler, Nelini Stamp, and others—who continue to chase their version of the American dream. They remain invested in it, whether or not it remains invested in them. They hold off any temptation to resign myself to the narrative of decline. It's impossible to have spent the past several years traveling the country and talking to people like these without feeling hope.

8

A SAMPLE BRIEF SUMMARY

In "What America Has Gained, What America Has Lost," George Packer argues that it is important to consider how America has improved over the years as well as how it has declined before drawing any conclusion that "something has gone wrong." He points out many advances that he would not want to lose, both technological advances and sociopolitical changes. He especially appreciates that America is "a more tolerant, inclusive place" than in the past. He sees more freedom in America. On the other hand, he is concerned that economic equal opportunity has decreased in our country. Although he believes we have greater social equality, he goes so far as to say that economically, "The game seems rigged." And yet, Packer says, the interviews he has conducted around the country, the "life stories of ordinary Americans," are filled with stories of people invested in the American dream, and those stories give him a feeling of hope.

EXERCISE 5.1

Identify the paragraph or paragraphs from "What America Has Gained, What America Has Lost" that are covered in each sentence of the above summary. Are all of the main points clearly and accurately summarized?

WRITING PARAPHRASES AND QUOTATIONS

Paraphrasing

As you can see from the above sample summary, most of what you write in a summary consists of the author's ideas put into your own words. Each time you reword what an author has written so that the *author's idea* is now expressed in *your writing style*, you have **paraphrased** the author. Here are some points to consider when you paraphrase:

1. Paraphrases must reflect your own writing style, not the author's.
2. Paraphrases must not change or distort the author's ideas in any way.
3. Paraphrases must be clearly identified as presenting the author's ideas, not your own.
4. Paraphrases use the present tense when referring to the author.

Here are some paraphrases that appeared in the sample summary of "What America Has Gained, What America Has Lost," along with the original passages:

ORIGINAL | In general, the things in my list fall into two categories: technological advances that make life easier, tastier, more entertaining, healthier, longer; and socio-political changes that have made the country a more tolerant, inclusive place. Over the past generation, America has opened previously inaccessible avenues to previously excluded groups, although in some cases the obstacles remain formidable, and in others (immigrant farm laborers, for example) there has hardly been any change at all.

PARAPHRASE | He points out many advances that he would not want to lose, both technological advances and sociopolitical changes. He especially appreciates that America is "a more tolerant, inclusive place" than in the past. He sees more freedom in America.

ORIGINAL | That's where things have unquestionably deteriorated over the past generation. The game seems rigged—and if it is, following the rules is for suckers.

PARAPHRASE | Although he believes we have greater social equality, he goes so far as to say that economically, "The game seems rigged."

Note that both of the above paraphrases accurately state the ideas in the original, yet they do so in a writing style quite different from that of the original. Both paraphrases clearly refer to the author of the article, and the words that refer to the author are written in the present tense.

Quoting

A quotation is an exact reproduction of an author's words. To let the reader know that the words are not your own, you must use quotation marks.

However, you should be careful to use quotations sparingly in your writing. For the most part, *your* writing should be in *your* style, not in someone else's, so most references to what you have read should appear as paraphrases, not as quotations. In general, quote only those words, phrases, or sentences that you really want to emphasize or that would not be as emphatic if they were paraphrased. In fact, notice how *few* quotations appear in the brief summary of "What America Has Gained, What America Has Lost," above. With that said, let's discuss the points you should keep in mind when you use quotations in your writing:

1. Quotations must be accurate.

ORIGINAL   It's one of those big, structural problems that requires action on many fronts, from many institutions—from government at all levels, from business, from the media and universities.

INACCURATE   As Packer claims, "It's one of those big, structural problems that requires <u>actions</u> on <u>lots of</u> fronts, from many institutions—from government at all levels, from <u>businesses, and even</u> from the media and universities."

2. *Every* quotation should be integrated into your text with a transition that refers to its source.

And yet, <u>Packer says,</u> the interviews he has conducted around the country, the "life stories of ordinary Americans," are filled with stories of people invested in the American dream, and those stories give him a feeling of hope.
<u>He especially appreciates</u> that America is "a more tolerant, inclusive place" than in the past.

3. Use correct punctuation to separate transitions from quotations.

a. Use commas to set off transitional phrases that introduce a complete-sentence quotation.

<u>According to Packer,</u> "It's one of those big, structural problems that requires action on many fronts, from many institutions—from government at all levels, from business, from the media and universities."
"It's one of those big, structural problems that requires action on many fronts, from many institutions," <u>according to Packer,</u> "from many institutions—from government at all levels, from business, from the media and universities."
"It's one of those big, structural problems that requires action on many fronts, from many institutions—from government at all levels, from business, from the media and universities," <u>according to Packer.</u>

b. Use a colon to separate a complete-sentence quotation from a complete-sentence transition.

Packer stresses his assertion that Americans perceptions about America are distorted: "More Americans than ever before are free to win elective office or gain admission to a good college or be hired by a good company or simply be themselves in public."

c. Do not use any punctuation to set off partial quotations unless you would have used punctuation even if the quotation marks were not there.

Packer points out that more Americans today can run for public office or enroll in colleges or get a good job or even "simply be themselves public."

4. Use brackets if you need to add one or more of your own words for clarity and an ellipsis (three spaced dots) if you leave out material.

ORIGINAL	Like almost everything else, the new inclusiveness divides the country into winners and losers.
QUOTATION	Packer claims, "Like almost everything else, the new inclusiveness [in the United States] divides the country into winners and losers."
ORIGINAL	It's been good for those with the education, talent, and luck to benefit from it; for others—in urban cores like Youngstown, Ohio; rural backwaters like Rockingham County, North Carolina; and the exurban slums outside Tampa—inclusiveness remains mostly theoretical.
QUOTATION	According to Packer, "It's been good for those with the education, talent, and luck to benefit from it; for others . . . inclusiveness remains mostly theoretical."
ORIGINAL	That's where things have unquestionably deteriorated over the past generation. The game seems rigged—and if it is, following the rules is for suckers.
QUOTATION	Parkers says, "[Economic inequality is] where things have unquestionably deteriorated over the past generation. The game seems rigged. . . ."

Note   Words added in brackets must *not* alter the author's idea, and words omitted need *not* be replaced with an ellipsis if it is obvious that they have been omitted. Notice that none of the partial quotations in any of the above examples need ellipses. Also notice that the last example has *four* spaced dots. The fourth dot is a period.

5. Use single quotation marks to indicate a quotation that appears within another quotation.

According to Packer, "That was Jefferson's meaning when he inscribed in the annals of our civic religion the conviction that 'all men are created equal.'"

6. Punctuate the end of a quotation correctly.

a. Place periods and commas within quotation marks.

Packer also states, "That was Jefferson's meaning when he inscribed in the annals of our civic religion the conviction that 'all men are created equal.'"

b. Place semicolons and colons outside quotation marks.

Packer concludes, "It's impossible to have spent the past several years traveling the country and talking to people like these without feeling hope"; however, the general American public may not agree with him.

c. Place question marks and exclamation points within quotation marks if the quotation is a question or exclamation. In all other situations, place them outside.

Do you agree when Packer writes, "It is killing many Americans' belief in the democratic promise—their faith that the game is fair, that everyone has a chance"?

In "Live Each Moment for What It's Worth," Erma Bombeck asks, "Does the word *refrigerator* have no meaning for you?"

Note

For a further discussion of using and integrating paraphrases, summaries, and quotations within your paper, see "Documenting Your Sources" in the Appendix.

EXERCISE 5.2

Write a brief summary of Michael Ryan's "Are You Living Mindlessly?" on pages 430–433 or an article assigned by your instructor. Your summary should identify the central point and main ideas of the article. Follow the above suggestions for writing paraphrases and quotations in your summary.

WRITING AN EXTENDED SUMMARY

Although brief summaries are handy for expressing the main ideas of something you have read, many papers, reports, or presentations will require a more detailed summary of your source, one that explains the main ideas more thoroughly, pointing out which ideas the author has emphasized and how the author has supported those ideas. Writing an extended summary is excellent practice for such assignments. To write a successful extended summary, you need to read carefully and accurately and communicate what you have read clearly and completely to someone else.

The steps in the writing of an extended summary are essentially the same as those in the writing of a brief summary. However, the extended summary is written as a brief essay, with individual paragraphs explaining the author's points in more detail than in a brief summary. Below is an extended summary of "What America Has Gained, What America Has Lost." Notice how each paragraph focuses on one of the article's main points.

A SAMPLE EXTENDED SUMMARY

In "What America Has Gained, What America Has Lost," George Packer examines the tendency to believe that America has generally declined over the years, that somehow things have gotten worse. He says, however, that it's important to consider how America has improved over the years as well as how it has declined before drawing any conclusion that "something has gone wrong."

One of the first points he makes is that in two general areas he sees much improvement: technological advances and sociopolitical changes. More specifically, he says that technological advances "make life easier, tastier, more entertaining, healthier, longer." Sociopolitical advances, he says, "made the country a more tolerant, inclusive place." He claims that there is more freedom in America today, that avenues that in the past were closed to many groups are now open. He says that Americans have more freedom in choosing to run for office, attend college, get a job, and just be themselves.

He does not, however, see as much improvement in the area of economic equal opportunity. Of economic inequality, he says "It is killing many Americans' belief in the democratic promise—their faith that the game is fair, that everyone has a chance." He goes on to say that generally an increase in inclusiveness would be seen as also increasing equality, but that does not seem to be the case as far as economic equality is concerned. He acknowledges that the economic prospects for women and minorities have improved, but he also says that, in general, "The fortunes of middle-class Americans have declined. . . ."

Finally, Packer concludes that the problem of such inequality will not be easily resolved, that "It's one of those big, structural problems" requiring many different approaches. Nevertheless, he does not resign himself "to the narrative of decline" because he has found in his interviews of ordinary Americans that they remain invested in the American dream, "whether or not it remains invested in them," and that gives him hope.

EXERCISE 5.3

Work with other students to develop responses to these questions or to compare responses that you have already prepared.

1. Examine the introductory paragraph of the sample extended summary above. Where does it state the central idea of "What America Has Gained, What America Has Lost"? What other information does it include?

2. Identify the topic sentence of each body paragraph. Which paragraph or paragraphs from "What America Has Gained, What America Has Lost" does that topic sentence introduce?

3. Identify the transitions between paragraphs.

4. Examine the support within each paragraph. Have any points been left out of it that you think should have been included?

WRITING A SUMMARY-RESPONSE ESSAY

Many college writing assignments will ask that you both summarize what you have read and respond to it. After all, your ability to express your own reaction to a topic is certainly as important as your ability to summarize that topic. Although the structure of such an essay will vary, depending on the topic and the expectations of your instructor, one common format consists of a brief summary in your introductory paragraph, followed by a clear thesis statement of your own in the same introductory paragraph, followed by several body paragraphs that support and develop your thesis statement. When you write a summary-response essay, keep the following points in mind:

1. The introduction should include a brief summary of the article and its main points.

2. The introduction should include a thesis statement that expresses your response to the topic.

3. Each body paragraph should open with a topic sentence that clearly refers to and develops the thesis statement.

4. Each body paragraph should support its topic sentence with explanations, facts, examples, statistics, or references to authority.

5. Each sentence should reflect a sense of coherence by exhibiting a clear relationship to the sentence before it or to the topic sentence of the paragraph.

A SAMPLE SUMMARY-RESPONSE ESSAY

In "What America Has Gained, What America Has Lost," George Packer says that it's important to consider how America has improved over the years as well as how it has declined before drawing any conclusion that "something has gone wrong." He points out many technological and sociopolitical advances that he would not want to lose. He especially appreciates that America is "a more tolerant, inclusive place" than in the past. On the other hand, he is concerned that economic equal opportunity has decreased in our country, that economically, "The game seems rigged. . . ." And yet, he says, the interviews he has conducted around the country give him a feeling of hope. I have a very similar reaction to his. Although I see many areas of improvement that give me hope, there are also areas of American life that worry me.

I am particularly pleased by the improvement in "inclusiveness." Specifically, I see improvement in the acceptance of people with non-traditional sexual roles and identities. I'm delighted that more and more states are legalizing gay marriages, and I'm thrilled that those in LGBTQIA communities are more and more accepted in our society. I have seen these improved attitudes in action in my own brother, who for years held homophobic and judgmental opinions about gay men and women. When my daughter, who is a gay woman, and her partner visited him for two weeks several years ago, he began to loosen and eventually abandoned his negative attitudes. Today, he is still a man devoted to his church and politics, but he is also a vocal supporter of gay rights.

Another area of improvement that pleases me is a growing awareness that our prison system is not working. It seems to me that more and more people are realizing that something is very wrong when the United States incarcerates more people per capita than any other country in the world. The prison overcrowding has forced many states, especially California, where I live, to reconsider their prison policies, replacing some of them with valuable drug and alcohol diversion programs. As a person who works regularly in prisons, I have been very pleased to see a strong movement toward the creation of programs to assist the inmates and parolees in achieving and maintaining a clean and sober lifestyle.

And yet, regardless of these hopeful signs, I am concerned by a number of changes in our society, particularly in the area of politics. I am especially worried by a growing unwillingness on the part of our politicians to compromise. It's almost as if the extremist elements of both sides—left and right—have hijacked their parties and placed roadblocks to prevent any bipartisan agreement. In fact, in 2011, the gridlock in Washington came within one hour of a literal government shutdown. I do not understand the political finger-pointing and absolute refusal to budge from a position that our current politicians demonstrate. If there is one lesson from our Founding Fathers that they seem to have forgotten, it is the need to compromise in a country of multiple and various voices.

In the end, I must admit that I feel more hopeful than discouraged about our country. Like Packer, I worry about the growing economic inequality and about other issues in our society; however, I believe that Americans will ultimately make the right choices and move in a positive direction. Perhaps I am an optimist. Perhaps I am naïve. But I do trust that we will ultimately make the right choices as we move forward.

EXERCISE 5.4

Work with other students to develop responses to these questions or to compare responses that you have already prepared.

1. The introduction to the summary-response essay is much more developed than the introduction to the extended summary essay. Why? What is it doing that is different?

2. Identify the thesis statement of the essay.

3. Identify the topic sentence of each body paragraph. Does it clearly introduce the topic of the paragraph?

4. Identify the transitions between paragraphs. Also, explain how each topic sentence is clearly connected to the thesis statement.

5. Examine the support in each paragraph. Point out which sentences are generalized explanations and which are specific examples.

6. Examine the concluding paragraph, and explain what it does to bring the essay to a satisfactory close.

READINGS

The Bachelor: Silly, Sexist, and, to Many, Irresistible

MIMI AVINS

In the following selection, Mimi Avins, a staff writer for the Los Angeles Times, *considers the popularity of ABC's* The Bachelor, *and, by extension, the popularity of other similar "reality" shows. She finds the show "stupid, contrived, and ... boring." And yet, she writes, "I was addicted too."*

BEFORE YOU READ

1. Have you watched *The Bachelor* or similar "reality" shows? If you have, what was your reaction to them?

2. Why do you think such shows have become so popular in the past few years?

Well, excuse me for coming late to the party, but it took "The Bachelor" to seduce me. Until Alex Michel, the highly eligible, soul mate–shopper of ABC's hit "reality" show came along, I was a confirmed hater of the unscripted programs that surfaced on television a few seasons ago. 1

Without ever having seen "Survivor," I decided it was stupid, contrived and boring. When "Who Wants to Be a Millionaire" was on at the gym, I'd leave the room. I feared that those relentlessly hyped phenomena and their sorry offspring would elbow out the unreal series I enjoy: well-crafted fare like "The West Wing" and "Six Feet Under." 2

I wish I could say I would have spent this spring's Monday evenings rereading the complete works of Virginia Woolf if I hadn't been flattened by a nasty bout of pneumonia. But, if truth be told, I didn't tune into "The Bachelor" just because I was weak and 3 feverish. About halfway through its six-week run, in which 31-year-old Michel fishes for Mrs. Right in a pool of 25 carefully selected women, I began hearing murmurs from smart, sophisticated, highly evolved female friends. "I know it's sexist and ridiculous, but I'm addicted to 'The Bachelor,'" they confessed.

So I watched Episode 4. Ensconced in a Malibu mansion that is   4
to the new millennium what the "Dynasty" homestead was to the '80s, Michel had winnowed the group down to a quartet of beauties. In a hometown-hopping hour, he met each of their families. Then, in the show's final minutes, one of the hopefuls was eliminated. Oh, my God, I thought. This is stupid, contrived and often slow enough to be boring. I was addicted too.

The scholarly component of my fascination stemmed from   5
analyzing how cleverly a drama was constructed from the basic one-man, 25-women premise. "The Bachelor" (and for all I know, its unscripted predecessors) is a triumph of clever editing. The most romantic, amusing or titillating moments from hours of undoubtedly tedious encounters are shown. I write nonfiction for a living. Why wouldn't I be transfixed by the show's skill at spinning a compelling narrative from the dross of life? Part of the fun is busting the essential manipulativeness of the format.

For example, Michel has a wonderful time with Trista's family   6
in St. Louis. They're warm and welcoming. Talk flows, laughs come easily. When he meets Shannon's parents in Dallas, the atmosphere is so chilly it's a wonder he didn't put on a parka. Were the good times in Texas edited out? Were the conversational dead ends in Missouri trashed? Call me cynical, but I think so.

In a "reality" show, reality is plastic. The players' appeal, their vul-   7
nerability and even wit can be adjusted as deliberately as a TV set's volume control. Michel would have been insufferable if he'd been too perfect. Thus the decision to show him losing his lunch, as he and Trista hover above Hawaii in a helicopter, only made him more endearing.

Enough intellectual rationalization. There's much more to a   8
"Bachelor" fixation than a desire to bust the show for being faux. Millions of women, and some men, have become obsessed with the program, whose audience and media presence steadily grew. As Diane Sawyer said on "Good Morning America" after admitting she'd fallen under "The Bachelor's" spell, "It's a strange thing we're all doing when we watch, but we are watching." Inquiring minds wonder why.

Everyone's a Voyeur. With the exception of Monica Lewinsky   9
and her married boyfriend, we don't usually become privy to

what goes on between men and women behind closed doors. But we are curious. "The Bachelor" is part of a genre that finds sport in the brutality of modern courtship. It's less cheesy than "Blind Date," "Shipmates," "Temptation Island" or "Change of Heart." Michel is a poised, personable management consultant with an MBA from Stanford. The show's bevy of bachelorettes is uncommonly telegenic, outgoing and seems to have triple-digit IQs. "The Bachelor" lets us see the sort of genetically blessed population you'd think would be immune to the more barbaric aspects of singlehood being humiliated. There's a certain wicked comfort in knowing no one is safe from the dating jungle's hazards.

Shallow Is Good. We come to know the characters we care   10
about in dramatic series over time. We know their back stories and idiosyncrasies. If "The Bachelor" moved at a more leisurely pace, it would have more depth. Yet its effectiveness is in direct proportion to its shallowness. Its cast is reduced to archetypes. Michel is the catch, choosing among the good girl, the ditz, the hottie, the mystery woman and the neurotic handful. By skimming the surface, the show lets the audience fill in its many blanks, sparking the sort of debate that fueled its popularity.

Pass the Popcorn. Let us not underestimate the howl factor.   11
It's so easy to mock Michel and the girls for their verbal tics, hairstyle goofs or awkward giggles. Nothing like sitting in front of the TV feeling superior to cap off a hard day.

Take this cringe-inducing exchange: As they ride home from a   12
date in one of the show's ubiquitous stretch limos, Michel asks Kim, a nanny from Arizona, what she likes to do in her free time. She tells him she finds turning the pages of magazines relaxing, but she doesn't really "read fiction/nonfiction." The very thought that a guy who majored in history and literature at Harvard might stroll into the sunset with a gal who confines her reading to Us magazine and self-help tomes makes you screech at the screen.

Women have organized "The Bachelor" watching parties,   13
because the urge to nudge a friend while cackling is often irresistible. Most of the time, everyone involved seems in on the joke. On a pre-show broadcast just before Thursday's finale, it was evident that the producers and most of the participants have a sense of humor about themselves.

Champagne Wishes and Caviar Dreams. Perhaps "The   14
Bachelor" hooked me when "Survivor" and "The Mole" didn't because romance is more entertaining than power struggles. The show has put Michel and his inamoratas into soft-focus fantasies

sure to warm the heart of every woman who believed the glass slippers didn't give Cinderella blisters.

At every turn, Michel and the woman he's with are pampered. The dazzling settings they find themselves in obscure the fact that nothing that might pass for interesting conversation ever occurs. In the snippets we see, the dates have all the charm of job interviews, as Michel grills the women about everything from the authenticity of their body parts to whether they expect relationships to follow a preordained sexual timetable. Michel may sound platitudinous when he tells each woman she's "awesome," but style trumps content. It can be hard to quibble with such a pretty fairy tale. 15

Repeat Steps 1 through 4. There's a notion currently rampant in the culture that the right way to find a mate can be diagramed the way Popular Mechanics teaches you how to install a carburetor. Some women are looking for tips, as if whatever wiles "The Bachelor" winner used could be practiced at home. For them, "The Bachelor" is the "Name That Tune" of relationship shows—"I can get that man to propose in six dates!" 16

If the mysteries of attraction could be reduced to a strategy, everyone would follow it. If there were a love potion, everyone would drink it. Just because Michel ultimately chose the bustiest, most blandly agreeable and sexually adventurous woman who, he said, "made him feel good," doesn't mean there aren't terrific single men looking for flat-chested, high-maintenance brunets who'll make them miserable. Just don't tell that to the faithful who think the show is a dating manual. 17

The big complaint about "The Bachelor" has been that it's demeaning to women. ABC, already casting for a sequel, may try to eviscerate that charge by letting one bachelorette choose from 25 men in a future edition. The really bold move would be to have a geriatric version, or even a middle-aged one. That would never fly, because the show is about people who look good in a mud bath looking for a partner. And it is very much about almost regular folks who want, more than anything, to be on TV. Women can't imagine why Michel would have to wife-hunt so publicly. Men don't understand why the women would risk getting their hearts broken in prime time. 18

In fact, the show is as much about the quest for fame as the search for love. As they've been doing the rounds on talk shows, the women who were dumped admitted that falling in love would have been nice. But being on TV was cool enough. "The Bachelor" isn't the story of the perfect union of Alex and Amanda Marsh. 19

Between commercials for diamond rings and herpes medications, it celebrates the wedding of a voyeuristic audience and a group of exuberantly exhibitionist players—a match made in TV heaven.

AFTER YOU READ

Work with other students to develop responses to these questions or to compare responses that you have already prepared.

1. State the thesis of the article in your own words. What sentences in the article, if any, best express the idea?

2. Divide the article into sections according to each major point that Avins makes.

3. Briefly summarize the thesis of the article and its major supporting points.

4. Avins offers several reasons for the popularity of *The Bachelor*, most of which seem to describe common human tendencies. Choose one and explain where you see it at work in other areas of life.

5. Avins says that the biggest complaint about *The Bachelor* is that it's demeaning to women. Do you agree? What other shows on television might be said to demean women?

For Better, For Worse: Marriage Means Something Different Now
STEPHANIE COONTZ

Stephanie Coontz teaches family history at Evergreen State College in Olympia, Washington. She is author of six books about American families, including Marriage, a History: From Obedience to Intimacy, or How Love Conquered Marriage. *"For Better, For Worse" was first published in* the Washington Post *in 2005. In this reading selection, she takes issue with "traditional" ideas and images of marriage and family.*

BEFORE YOU READ

1. What is the source of the phrase "For Better, For Worse"? What is its meaning in that source? In what way is its meaning different in this title?

2. In what ways has the meaning of "marriage" changed? What changes would you expect this reading selection to discuss?

Thirteen years ago, Vice President Dan Quayle attacked the producers of TV sitcom's *Murphy Brown* for letting her character bear a child out of wedlock, claiming that the show's failure to defend traditional family values was encouraging America's youth to abandon marriage. His speech kicked off more than a decade

1

of outcries against the "collapse of the family." Today, such attacks have given way to a kinder, gentler campaign to promote marriage, with billboards declaring that "Marriage Works" and books making "the case for marriage." What these campaigns have in common is the idea that people are willfully refusing to recognize the value of traditional families and that their behavior will change if we can just enlighten them.

But recent changes in marriage are part of a worldwide   2 upheaval in family life that has transformed the way people conduct their personal lives as thoroughly and permanently as the Industrial Revolution transformed their working lives 200 years ago. Marriage is no longer the main way in which societies regulate sexuality and parenting or organize the division of labor between men and women. And although some people hope to turn back the tide by promoting traditional values, making divorce harder or outlawing gay marriage, they are having to confront a startling irony: The very factors that have made marriage more satisfying in modern times have also made it more optional.

The origins of modern marital instability lie largely in the tri-   3 umph of what many people believe to be marriage's traditional role—providing love, intimacy, fidelity, and mutual fulfillment. The truth is that for centuries, marriage was stable precisely because it was *not* expected to provide such benefits. As soon as love became the driving force behind marriage, people began to demand the right to remain single if they had not found love or to divorce if they fell out of love.

Such demands were raised as early as the 1790s, which   4 prompted conservatives to predict that love would be the death of marriage. For the next 150 years, the inherently destabilizing effects of the love revolution were held in check by women's economic dependence on men, the unreliability of birth control and the harsh legal treatment of children born out of wedlock, as well as the social ostracism of their mothers. As late as the 1960s, two-thirds of college women in the United States said they would marry a man they didn't love if he met all their other, often economic, criteria. Men also felt compelled to marry if they hoped for promotions at work or for political credibility.

All these restraints on individual choice collapsed between   5 1960 and 1980. Divorce rates had long been rising in Western Europe and the United States, and although they had leveled off following World War II, they climbed at an unprecedented rate in the 1970s, leading some to believe that the introduction of no-fault divorce laws, which meant married couples could divorce if they simply fell out of love, had caused the erosion of marriage.

The so-called divorce revolution, however, is just one aspect of the worldwide transformation of marriage. In places where divorce and unwed motherhood are severely stigmatized, the retreat from marriage simply takes another form. In Japan and Italy, for example, women are far more likely to remain single than in the United States. In Thailand, unmarried women now compete for the title of "Miss Spinster Thailand." Singapore's strait-laced government has resorted to sponsoring singles nights in an attempt to raise marriage rates and reverse the birth strike by women.   6

In the United States and Britain, divorce rates fell slightly during the 1990s, but the incidence of cohabitation and unmarried child-raising continues to rise, as does the percentage of singles in the population.   7

Both trends reduce the social significance of marriage in the economy and culture. The norms and laws that traditionally penalized unwed mothers and their children have weakened or been overturned, ending centuries of injustice but further reducing marriage's role in determining the course of people's lives. Today, 40 percent of cohabiting couples in the United States have children in the household, almost as high a proportion as the 45 percent of married couples who have kids, according to the 2000 Census. We don't have a TV show about that yet, but it's just a matter of time.   8

The entry of women into the workforce in the last third of the 20th century was not only a U.S. phenomenon. By the 1970s, women in America and most of Europe could support themselves if they needed to. The 1980s saw an international increase in unmarried women having babies (paving the way for Murphy Brown), as more people gained the ability to say no to shotgun marriages, and humanitarian reforms lowered the penalties for out-of-wedlock births. That decade also saw a big increase in couples living together before marriage.   9

Almost everywhere, women's greater participation in education has raised the marriage age and the incidence of non-marriage. Even in places where women's lives are still largely organized through marriage, fertility rates have been cut in half and more wives and mothers work outside the home.   10

From Turkey to South Africa to Brazil, countries are having to codify the legal rights and obligations of single individuals and unmarried couples raising children, including same-sex couples. Canada and the Netherlands have joined Scandinavia in legalizing   11

same-sex marriage, and such bastions of tradition as Taiwan and
Spain are considering following suit.

None of this means that marriage is dead. Indeed, most people   12
have a higher regard for the marital relationship today than when
marriage was practically mandatory. Marriage as a private relationship between two individuals is taken more seriously and comes
with higher emotional expectations than ever before in history.

But marriage as a public institution exerts less power over peo-   13
ple's lives now that the majority of Americans spend half their adult
lives outside marriage and almost half of all kids spend part of their
childhood in a household that does not include their two married
biological parents. And unlike in the past, marriage or lack of marriage does not determine people's political and economic rights.

Under these conditions, it is hard to believe that we could   14
revive the primacy of marriage by promoting traditional values.
People may revere the value of universal marriage in the abstract,
but most have adjusted to a different reality. The late Pope John
Paul II was enormously respected for his teaching about sex and
marriage. Yet during his tenure, premarital sex, contraception use
and divorce continued to rise in almost all countries. In the United
States, the Bible Belt has the highest divorce rate in the nation.
And although many American teens pledged abstinence during
the 1990s, 88 percent ended up breaking that pledge, according
to the National Longitudinal Study of Adolescent Youth that was
released in March.

Although many Americans bemoan the easy accessibility of   15
divorce, few are willing to waive their personal rights. In American
states where "covenant" marriage laws allow people to sign away
their right to a no-fault divorce, fewer than 3 percent of couples
choose that option. Divorce rates climbed by the same percentage
in states that did not allow no-fault divorce as in states that did. By
2000, Belgium, which had not yet adopted no-fault divorce, had the
highest divorce rates in Europe outside of Finland and Sweden.

Nor does a solution lie in preaching the benefits of marriage   16
to impoverished couples or outlawing unconventional partner-
ships. A poor single mother often has good reason not to marry
her child's father, and poor couples who do wed have more than
twice the divorce risk of more affluent partners in the United
States. Banning same-sex marriage would not undo the existence
of alternatives to traditional marriage. Five million children are
being raised by gay and lesbian couples in this country. Judges
everywhere are being forced to apply many principles of marriage

law to those families, if only to regulate child custody should the couple part ways.

We may personally like or dislike these changes. We may wish to keep some and get rid of others. But there is a certain inevitability to almost all of them.   17

Marriage is no longer the institution where people are initiated into sex. It no longer determines the work men and women do on the job or at home, regulates who has children and who doesn't, or coordinates care-giving for the ill or the aged. For better or worse, marriage has been displaced from its pivotal position in personal and social life, and will not regain it short of a Taliban-like counterrevolution.   18

Forget the fantasy of solving the challenges of modern personal life by re-institutionalizing marriage. In today's climate of choice, many people's choices do not involve marriage. We must recognize that there are healthy as well as unhealthy ways to be single or to be divorced, just as there are healthy and unhealthy ways to be married. We cannot afford to construct our social policies, our advice to our own children and even our own emotional expectations around the illusion that all commitments, sexual activities and care-giving will take place in a traditional marriage. That series has been canceled.   19

AFTER YOU READ

Work with other students to develop responses to these questions or to compare responses that you have already prepared.

1. State the thesis of the article in your own words. What sentences in the article, if any, best express the idea?
2. Divide the article into sections according to each major point that Coontz makes.
3. Briefly summarize the thesis of the article and its major supporting points.
4. What are the basic changes that Coontz discusses in this article? What are the causes of these changes?
5. Explain Coontz's claim that basing marriage on "love, intimacy, fidelity and mutual fulfillment" has destabilized marriage. How does she explain and support this claim?

Let Them Eat Dog: A Modest Proposal for Tossing Fido in the Oven   Jonathan Safran Foer

Jonathan Safran Foer is the author of Everything Is Illuminated *(Houghton Mifflin, 2002) and* Eating Animals *(Little, Brown and Company, 2010). He teaches creative writing at New York University.*

BEFORE YOU READ

1. Consider the title. What sort of attitude does it suggest on the part of Jonathan Foer? Are you familiar with an essay titled "A Modest Proposal"?
2. Some Americans eat beef—others eat pork. Would you eat dog? Why or why not?

Despite the fact that it's perfectly legal in 44 states, eating "man's best friend" is as taboo as a man eating his best friend. Even the most enthusiastic carnivores won't eat dogs. TV guy and sometimes cooker Gordon Ramsay can get pretty macho with lambs and piglets when doing publicity for something he's selling, but you'll never see a puppy peeking out of one of his pots. And though he once said he'd electrocute his children if they became vegetarian, one can't help but wonder what his response would be if they poached the family pooch.   1

Dogs are wonderful, and in many ways unique. But they are remarkably unremarkable in their intellectual and experiential capacities. Pigs are every bit as intelligent and feeling, by any sensible definition of the words. They can't hop into the back of a Volvo, but they can fetch, run and play, be mischievous and reciprocate affection. So why don't they get to curl up by the fire? Why can't they at least be spared being tossed on the fire? Our taboo against dog eating says something about dogs and a great deal about us.   2

The French, who love their dogs, sometimes eat their horses.   3

The Spanish, who love their horses, sometimes eat their cows.   4

The Indians, who love their cows, sometimes eat their dogs.   5

While written in a much different context, George Orwell's words (from *Animal Farm*) apply here: "All animals are equal, but some animals are more equal than others."   6

So who's right? What might be the reasons to exclude canine from the menu? The selective carnivore suggests: 7

Don't eat companion animals. But dogs aren't kept as companions in all of the places they are eaten. And what about our petless neighbors? Would we have any right to object if they had dog for dinner?   8

OK, then: Don't eat animals with significant mental capacities. If by "significant mental capacities" we mean what a dog has, then good for the dog. But such a definition would also include the pig, cow and chicken. And it would exclude severely impaired humans.   9

Then: It's for good reason that the eternal taboos—don't fiddle with your crap, kiss your sister, or eat your companions—are taboo. Evolutionarily speaking, those things are bad for us. But dog   10 eating isn't a taboo in many places, and it isn't in any way bad for us. Properly cooked, dog meat poses no greater health risks than any other meat.

Dog meat has been described as "gamey," "complex," "buttery" 11 and "floral." And there is a proud pedigree of eating it. Fourth-century tombs contain depictions of dogs being slaughtered along with other food animals. It was a fundamental enough habit to have informed language itself: the Sino-Korean character for "fair and proper" (yeon) literally translates into "as cooked dog meat is delicious." Hippocrates praised dog meat as a source of strength. Dakota Indians enjoyed dog liver, and not so long ago Hawaiians ate dog brains and blood. Captain Cook ate dog. Roald Amundsen famously ate his sled dogs. (Granted, he was really hungry.) And dogs are still eaten to overcome bad luck in the Philippines; as medicine in China and Korea; to enhance libido in Nigeria and in numerous places, on every continent, because they taste good. For centuries, the Chinese have raised special breeds of dogs, like the black-tongued chow, for chow, and many European countries still have laws on the books regarding postmortem examination of dogs intended for human consumption.

Of course, something having been done just about every-   12 where is no kind of justification for doing it now. But unlike all farmed meat, which requires the creation and maintenance of animals, dogs are practically begging to be eaten. Three to four million dogs and cats are euthanized annually. The simple disposal of these euthanized dogs is an enormous ecological and economic problem. But eating those strays, those runaways, those not-quite-cute-enough-to-take and not-quite-well-behaved-enough-to-keep dogs would be killing a flock of birds with one stone and eating it, too.

In a sense it's what we're doing already. Rendering—the con-   13 version of animal protein unfit for human consumption into food for livestock and pets—allows processing plants to transform useless dead dogs into productive members of the food chain. In America, millions of dogs and cats euthanized in animal shelters every year become the food for our food. So let's just eliminate this inefficient and bizarre middle step.

This need not challenge our civility. We won't make them suffer 14 any more than necessary. While it's widely believed that adrenaline makes dog meat taste better—hence the traditional methods of slaughter: hanging, boiling alive, beating to death—we can all agree that if we're going to eat them, we should kill them quickly and painlessly, right? For example, the traditional Hawaiian means of holding the dog's nose shut—in order to conserve blood—must be regarded (socially if not legally) as a no-no. Perhaps we could include dogs under the Humane Methods of Slaughter Act. That doesn't say anything about how they're treated during their lives, and isn't subject to any meaningful oversight or enforcement, but surely we can rely on the industry to "self-regulate," as we do with other eaten animals.

Few people sufficiently appreciate the colossal task of feeding a   15
world of billions of omnivores who demand meat with their pota-toes. The inefficient use of dogs—conveniently already in areas of high human population (take note, local-food advocates)—should make any good ecologist blush. One could argue that various "humane" groups are the worst hypocrites, spending enormous amounts of money and energy in a futile attempt to reduce the number of unwanted dogs while at the very same time propagat-ing the irresponsible no-dog-for-dinner taboo. If we let dogs be dogs, and breed without interference, we would create a sustain-able, local meat supply with low energy inputs that would put even the most efficient grass-based farming to shame. For the ecologically-minded it's time to admit that dog is realistic food for realistic environmentalists.

For those already convinced, here's a classic Filipino recipe   16
I recently came across. I haven't tried it myself, but sometimes you can read a recipe and just know.

Stewed Dog, Wedding Style   17
First, kill a medium-sized dog, then burn off the fur over a hot fire.   18
Carefully remove the skin while still warm and set aside for later (may be used in other recipes). Cut meat into 1" cubes. Marinate meat in mixture of vinegar, peppercorn, salt, and garlic for 2 hours. Fry meat in oil using a large wok over an open fire, then add onions and chopped pineapple and sauté until tender. Pour in tomato sauce and boiling water, add green pepper, bay leaf, and Tabasco. Cover and simmer over warm coals until meat is tender. Blend in purée of dog's liver and cook for additional 5–7 minutes.

There is an overabundance of rational reasons to say no to   19
factory-farmed meat: It is the No. 1 cause of global warming, it systematically forces tens of billions of animals to suffer in ways that would be illegal if they were dogs, it is a decisive factor in the development of swine and avian flus, and so on. And yet even most people who know these things still aren't inspired to order something else on the menu. Why?

Food is not rational. Food is culture, habit, craving and iden-   20
tity. Responding to factory farming calls for a capacity to care that
dwells beyond information. We know what we see on undercover
videos of factory farms and slaughterhouses is wrong. (There are
those who will defend a system that allows for occasional animal
cruelty, but no one defends the cruelty, itself.) And despite it being
entirely reasonable, the case for eating dogs is likely repulsive to
just about every reader of this paper. The instinct comes before
our reason, and is more important.

AFTER YOU READ

Work with other students to develop responses to these questions or to compare responses that you have already prepared.

1. State the thesis of the article in your own words. What sentences in
   the essay, if any, best express the idea?
2. Divide the article into sections according to each major point that Foer
   makes.
3. Briefly summarize the thesis of Foer's essay and its major supporting
   points.
4. Why do you believe Foer wrote "Let Them Eat Dog"? What do you
   think he wanted the reader to consider?
5. Analyze Foer's writing style, specifically sentence variety. What type of
   sentences does his essay present?

Why You Should Think Twice before Shaming Anyone on Social Media   LAURA HUDSON

Laura Hudson is a freelance writer and editor. She is a regular contributor to
WIRED *and senior editor at* Offworld. *Hudson writes about video games, feminism, comics, and digital media for the* Los Angeles Times, Publishers Weekly,
and The New York Times. *"Why You Should Think Twice before Shaming Anyone on Social Media" first appeared on* WIRED.

BEFORE YOU READ

1. Have you ever witnessed a person shaming someone on an influential
   social media site? How did you react to such digital exposure?
2. What is your immediate reaction when you witness someone being
   publicly shamed on the Internet?

Earlier this year, at a tech conference called PyCon, the consultant   1
Adria Richards overheard some indelicate puns—involving the
terms "dongles" and "forking"—from a couple of male attendees

sitting behind her. The jokes made Richards uncomfortable, so in the heat of the moment she decided to register her displeasure by tweeting a picture of the two guys, calling their behavior "not cool."

In the context of a tech culture that often fails to make women feel welcome, it's easy to see why Richards, sitting there in the (roughly 80 percent male) PyCon audience, felt like she wasn't the one with the power in that room.   2

But online it was a different story. The two men were social-media nobodies, whereas Richards had more than 9,000 Twitter followers, some highly connected in the tech world. Her grievance quickly received more than 100 retweets and press coverage that stretched from The Washington Post to MSNBC.   3

PyCon soon responded—sympathetically—to her complaint, but the damage was done. One of the men was recognized by his employer and lost his job. The backlash against his firing then triggered a massive onslaught of online abuse against Richards, who also got fired. No one emerged happy. "I have three kids, and I really liked that job," wrote the newly unemployed jokester. "Let this serve as a message to everyone, our actions and words, big or small, can have a serious impact." Later, Richards made a similar assessment: "I don't think anyone who was part of what happened at PyCon that day could possibly have imagined how this issue would have exploded into the public consciousness . . . I certainly did not, and now . . . the severest of consequences have manifested."   4

Shaming, it seems, has become a core competency of the Internet, and it's one that can destroy both lives and livelihoods. But the question of who's responsible for the destruction—the person engaging in the behavior or the person revealing it—depends on whom you ask. At its best, social media has given a voice to the disenfranchised, allowing them to bypass the gate-keepers of power and publicize injustices that might otherwise remain invisible. At its worst, it's a weapon of mass reputation destruction, capable of amplifying slander, bullying, and casual idiocy on a scale never before possible.   5

The fundamental problem is that many shamers, like Richards, don't fully grasp the power of the medium. It's a problem that lots of us need to reckon with: There are millions of Twitter accounts with more than 1,000 followers, and millions on Facebook with more than 500 friends. The owners of those accounts might think they're just regular people, whispering to a small social circle. But in fact they're talking through megaphones that can easily be turned up to a volume the entire world can hear.   6

Increasingly, our failure to grasp our online power has become a liability—personally, professionally, and morally. We need to think twice before we unleash it.   7

Consider a form of shaming that a lot of us might want to get behind: calling out people who say indefensibly terrible things online. Numerous Tumblr and Twitter accounts have cropped up to document racist and sexist remarks on social media. Following a feed like @EverydaySexism or @YesYoureRacist can be a powerful experience; after a while, the shocking ugliness fades to a dull, steady ache, an emotional corrosion that simulates how the dehumanization of prejudice can become almost mundane. These feeds shame the jerks they highlight by broadcasting their ignorance far beyond their typically small, like-minded audiences to tens of thousands of people.   8

When the website Jezebel cataloged a series of racist tweets by high school students about President Obama, it not only published their names but also called their high schools and notified the principals about their tweets. In some cases, Jezebel listed the hobbies and activities of the students, essentially "SEO-shaming" them to potential colleges. Most of the kids have since deleted their Twitter accounts, but search any of their names on Google and you'll likely find references to their racist tweets within the first few results.   9

Yes, what these kids wrote was reprehensible. But does a 16-year-old making crude comments to his friends deserve to be pilloried with a doggedness we typically reserve for politicians and public figures—or, at the very least, for adults?   10

We despise racism and sexism because they bully the less powerful, but at what point do the shamers become the bullies? After all, the hallmark of bullying isn't just being mean. It also involves a power differential: The bully is the one who's punching down.   11

And this is precisely the differential that so many of us fail to grasp when our friends and followers are just abstract numbers on a social-media profile. Indeed, the online elite don't always wield the same sort of social power and influence in their offline lives and jobs; many have been victims of bullying themselves.   12

When Mike "Gabe" Krahulik, the artist behind the popular webcomic Penny Arcade, heard that an unprofessional PR rep for a game controller had been insulting and taunting one of his readers, he gleefully posted the damning emails to his website, along with the man's Twitter name, for the express purpose of unleashing the Internet kraken.   13

"I have a real problem with bullies," Krahulik wrote, after the   14
marketer was deluged with hate mail. "I spent my childhood
moving from school to school and I got made fun of every place
I landed. I feel like he is a bully and maybe that's why I have no
sympathy here. Someday every bully meets an even bigger bully,
and maybe that's me in this case."

But even if you think your bullying is serving a greater good,   15
the fact remains that you're still just a bully.

Internet speech can be cruder and crueler than our real-life   16
interactions, in large part due to our literal distance from the
people we're talking to and their reactions. That detachment can
sometimes be liberating, and it's often a good thing that people
speak bluntly online, especially against injustice that they see
around them. But a sense of proportion is crucial. These days, too
many Internet shame campaigns dole out punishment that is too
brutal for the crime. Using an influential social media account to
call out individuals, as Richards did, isn't simply saying something is
"not cool"; it's a request to have someone put in the digital stocks,
where a potentially unlimited number of people can throw digital
stones at them. And it turns out to have real-life consequences for
everyone involved.

That's why starting a shaming campaign is not a decision   17
to be taken lightly—especially because the Internet doesn't do
take-backs if you change your mind later. The bigger the so-called
Donglegate story became, the more disproportionate and unfair
Richards' original tweet seemed, even if that level of exposure was
never her intent. As Krahulik wrote after the PR bully pleaded with
him to make the abuse stop, "Once I had posted the emails I didn't
have the power anymore. The Internet had it now, and nothing
I said or did was going to change that."

Online shaming is a door that swings only one way: You may   18
have the power to open it, but you don't have the power to close
it. And sometimes what rushes through that door can engulf
you too.

AFTER YOU READ

Work with other students to develop responses to these questions or to compare responses that you have already prepared.

1. State the thesis of the article in your own words. What sentence or
   sentence in the article, if any, best express the idea?
2. Divide the article into sections according to each major point that
   Hudson makes.

3. Briefly summarize the thesis of the article and its major supporting points.

4. Besides shaming wrongdoers publicly, how else can people deal with cyber bullies? Compare your answers with those from other members of the class.

WRITING ASSIGNMENTS

1. Write a brief summary of one of the reading assignments in this chapter or of a reading assignment from Part Four of this text.

2. Write an extended summary of one of the reading assignments in this chapter or of a reading assignment from Part Four of this text.

3. Write a summary-response essay in reaction to Mimi Avins's "*The Bachelor: Silly, Sexist, and, to Many, Irresistible*." After briefly summarizing her article, your introduction should include a thesis of your own that responds to one of the following topics or to a topic assigned by your instructor:

   a. Mimi Avins offers several reasons for the popularity of *The Bachelor*. Consider another popular television program, and write a paper in which you explain why that program is so popular. As you present each reason for the show's popularity, support that reason with specific examples drawn from actual episodes that you have seen.

   b. Toward the end of her article, Avins writes, "The big complaint about 'The Bachelor' is that it's demeaning to women." Consider in what way this show or other shows with which you are familiar may demean women or any other group of people. Support your points with specific examples drawn from shows that you have watched.

   c. Choose one of the reasons that Avins proposes for the popularity of *The Bachelor*, and consider in what way it makes a true statement about human nature. You might, for example, explain what she means by "Everyone's a Voyeur" and then write a paper supporting that idea with examples of your own drawn from various areas of life. Or consider "Champagne Wishes and Caviar Dreams." What does she mean by that? Consider writing a paper illustrating what her point reveals about human nature, illustrating your understanding with examples of your own.

4. Write a summary-response essay in reaction to Stephanie Coontz's "For Better, For Worse: Marriage Means Something Different Now." After briefly summarizing his article, your introduction should include a thesis of your own that responds to one of the following topics or to a topic assigned by your instructor:

   a. Stephenie Coontz discusses a variety of trends that suggest that the meaning of marriage has changed radically since the 1960s: changes in divorce laws, the tendency to remain single, the willingness to live together without marriage, the acceptance of single motherhood, the prevalence of same-sex couples. Examine the attitudes toward marriage that you have encountered in your family and/or in the people you know. Write a paper in which you examine the attitudes revealed by the relationships of those around you, supporting your points with examples and clear explanations.

b. Coontz writes: "We may personally like or dislike these changes. We may wish to keep some and get rid of others. But there is a certain inevitability to almost all of them." Which of these changes do you "personally like or dislike"? Write a paper in which you explain the reasons for your reactions, supporting your points with examples and clear explanations.

c. According to Coontz, "None of this means that marriage is dead. Indeed, most people have a higher regard for the marital relationship today than when marriage was practically mandatory." Consider your own attitudes toward marriage. What do you consider to be the elements of a successful marriage? Write a paper in which you define such a marriage, supporting your points with examples and clear explanations.

5. Write a summary-response essay in reaction to Jonathan Safran Foer's "Let Them Eat Dog." After briefly summarizing the article, your introduction should include a thesis of your own that responds to one of the following topics or to a topic assigned by your instructor:

a. In "Let Them Eat Dog," Foer proposes, "If we let dogs be dogs, and breed without interference, we would create a sustainable, local meat supply with low energy inputs that would put even the most efficient grass-based farming to shame." When it comes to meat consumption in the United States, are Americans hypocritical? Why is it acceptable to slaughter chickens, cows, and pigs for food consumption—and not dogs? Write a paper in which you analyze why Americans turn a blind eye when it comes to poultry, beef, and pork meat. Support your points with specific examples and clear explanations.

b. Foer writes. "There is an overabundance of rational reasons to say no to factory-farmed meat: It is the No. 1 cause of global warming, it systematically forces tens of billions of animals to suffer in ways that would be illegal if they were dogs, it is a decisive factor in the development of swine and avian flus, and so on." Should Americans know how their meat is processed? Should the conditions of animals in factories concern consumers? Write a paper in which you analyze in what ways Americans would benefit from and/or suffer the consequences of knowing or not knowing where their meat comes from. Support your points with specific examples and clear explanations.

c. In "Let Them Eat Dog," Foer presents a Filipino recipe called "Stewed Dog, Wedding Style." He even writes, "I haven't tried it myself, but sometimes you can read a recipe and just know." Foer later adds, "Food is not rational. Food is culture, habit, craving and identity." Write a paper in which you focus on a particular food you crave and connects you to your culture and identity. Is that food a healthy choice or not? Support your points with specific examples and clear explanations.

6. Write a summary-response essay in reaction to Laura Hudson's "Why You Should Think Twice before Shaming Anyone on Social Media." After briefly summarizing the article, your introduction should include a thesis of your own that responds to one of the following topics or to a topic assigned by your instructor:

    a. What is your position on online shaming and its power? Write a paper in which you support or oppose public shaming using public media—using your own examples and explanations.

    b. Hudson provides several reasons to dissuade readers from shaming people online. She provides several examples where shaming has backfired, arguing that there is "no room for sexism, racism, and other bad behavior on the internet." Write a paper in which you focus each of your body paragraphs on a separate point discussed by Hudson. Then, use your own examples and explanations to support or refute what Hudson claims.

7. Write a summary-response essay in reaction to one of the reading assignments in Part Four of this text. After briefly summarizing the article, your introduction should include a thesis of your own that responds to a topic assigned by your instructor.

EVALUATING SAMPLE PAPERS

EXTENDED SUMMARIES

As you read and evaluate the following extended summaries, consider these areas:

1. Introduction

    Underline the sentences that state the central idea of the article. Is it accurate and clear? Does the introduction prepare the reader for an extended summary and not for a summary response?

    1   2   3   4   5   6

2. Unity

    Does each paragraph have a clear and specific topic sentence that accurately introduces one of the major sections of the article? Does the material in each paragraph clearly relate to its topic sentence?

    1   2   3   4   5   6

3. Support

Are all of the major points in the article summarized? Is each point accurately and fully explained?

1   2   3   4   5   6

4. Coherence

Are transitions used between paragraphs? Where needed, are transitions used between sentences within each paragraph?

1   2   3   4   5   6

5. References to the Text

Are direct quotations and paraphrases correctly introduced and smoothly incorporated into the text? Do they reflect the author's points accurately?

1   2   3   4   5   6

6. Sentence Structure

Do the sentences combine ideas that are related, using coordination, subordination, or verbal phrases when appropriate? Are there too many brief, choppy main clauses?

1   2   3   4   5   6

7. Mechanics, Grammar, and Spelling

Does the paper contain a distracting number of errors of these kinds?

1   2   3   4   5   6

8. Overall Ranking of the Essay

1   2   3   4   5   6

Student Summary 1

The reading selection "TV Can't Educate" can be found in Part 4.

In "TV Can't Educate," Paul Robinson argues that TV and movies are not suited for educational purposes. He introduces the critics of the NBC program about the narcissism in Marin County and his German scholar friend who criticized the biographical movie of Hitler as people who misunderstand the concept of TV and movies. He writes that, although both of them consider TV and movies as "a source of knowledge," TV and movies can't teach people. According to Robinson, "By knowledge and learning I obviously don't mean an assortment of facts. Rather I have in mind the analytic process that locates pieces of information within a large context of argument and meaning. Movies and TV are structurally unsuited to that process."

The first reason why TV is not suited for education is "a simple matter of time." As Robinson says, although TV moves forward automatically, people need enough time to absorb, to test, and to compare the information with their known facts, and he points out that reading is the only way to satisfy the process. Robinson also indicates that TV can't explain complicated phenomena such as "Hitler's relations with the German industrialists" and "life in Marin County" in one hour-long TV show because there are too many questions, more than can be covered in an hour-long TV program. He points out again, "If these questions have answers, they are to be found in the books and articles of sociologists, not on TV."

In addition to the problems of time, Robinson writes about the incompleteness of educational TV. He even says, "the worst thing on TV is educational TV." According to Robinson, viewers are taught authoritatively by the hosts who act as if they know everything. However, viewers can only learn the segment of knowledge which is shown on "60 Minutes" programs. Robinson insists, "Complete ignorance really would be preferable, because ignorance at least preserves a mental space that might someday be filled with real knowledge, or some approximation of it."

Although TV is totally unsuited for education, Robinson says TV is perfect entertainment. He says that the reason that TV is suited for entertainment but not for education is that actors can manipulate timing. He introduces several examples to show how important the manipulation of time is for entertainment, such as Jack Benny, Art Carney, and Audrey Meadows. According to Robinson, television can provide enjoyable time and make people escape from the real world. He says, "Television can provide all this. But it can't educate."

Robinson writes not only about TV but also about movies, and points out, "Movies are faced with the same dilemma." He compares two movies, *Julia* and *Jazebel*, to show the movies' dilemma. According to Robinson, *Jazebel* moves swiftly and entertains viewers. On the other hand, *Julia* tries to deal with too difficult and uncinematic issues to be covered in the movie, even though those issues are perfectly written in Lilian Hellman's memoir. Robinson writes, "The issues of the memoir—despite all those meaningful silences—inevitably eluded the movie."

In conclusion, Robinson insists that people should not consider TV and movies as educational devices and must recognize TV can't educate.

Student Summary 2

The reading selection "TV Can't Educate" can be found in Part 4.

Using the examples of a documentary aired by NBC on July 20, 1978, entitled "I Want It All Now" and a German movie about Adolf Hitler called *Hitler: Eine Karriere*, Paul Robinson in his article "TV Can't Educate," suggests that the critics of these programs suffered from the same wrong assumption "that television and movies can be a source of knowledge, that one can learn from them." He further explains, "By knowledge and learning I obviously do not mean an assortment of facts. Rather, I have in mind the analytic process that locates pieces of information within a larger context of argument and meaning. Movies and T.V. are structurally unsuited to the process." In his article, Robinson provides several opinions and examples to support his theory.

For example, Robinson states that learning takes time not found in the time allotted for television and movies. He describes in the learning process the ability to stop the absorption of fact or proposition at any time, which allows time for conscious comparison as necessary. He says that television can never teach because it does not allow the time for mental debate. He suggests that the only true way to learn is through reading and shows how that is the way in which information can be found that is often not able to be portrayed in television and movies. This is because the information in its entirety is difficult to be reduced to a scene in a movie.

Robinson then attacks educational television, stating "The worst thing in T.V. is educational T. V.." He goes on to say how many of us take information we receive from television and regurgitate it back as if we've become authorities on the subject, yet we truly have no basis for our proclamations, only the statements by a media personality who also has just been introduced to the idea. He concludes that thought with "complete ignorance would be preferable, because ignorance at least preserves a mental space that someday might be filled with real knowledge. . . ."

Mr. Robinson does not totally discount T.V., though. He says that T.V. is a good form of entertainment, fit to amuse but not to educate. By illustrating the timing used in comedy sketches of Jack Benny or *The Honeymooners*, he shows that the timing is crucial in conveying the comedic points or punchlines, whereas they would not be as humorous in writing. He points out the irony in the fact that television is tied to the clock, which is the reason it is unsuitable for learning.

Movies also are faced with the problem of trying to educate. According to Robinson, directors do this by setting the pace of a picture. He writes, "It's as if the director were trying to provide room within his time-bound narrative for the kind of reflection associates with analysis." He uses the examples of movies he had recently seen—*Julia* and *Jezebel*—and the speed at which the movies moved along. One movie, *Jezebel*, was very entertaining and moved quite rapidly. The other movie was slow and tried to address issues beyond the scope of a media presentation. Although the issues were eloquently captured in Lillian Hellman's memoir, even two gifted actors (Jane Fonda and Jason Robards) were unable to sufficiently convey the meaning once it was transferred from memoir to movie scene.

In his conclusion, Robinson asks that we do not ask of movies and television more than they can deliver, which is entertainment. He says, "In fact, let us discourage them from trying to 'educate' us."

SUMMARY-RESPONSE ESSAYS

As you read and evaluate the following summary-response essays, consider these areas:

1. Introduction
   Does the introduction contain a clear and accurate brief summary of the central idea and major supporting points of the article? Does it prepare the reader for a summary-response essay by moving to a thesis of the writer's own?

   1   2   3   4   5   6

2. Thesis Statement
   Underline the thesis statement of the essay. Does it express a clear and specific central idea?

   1   2   3   4   5   6

3. Topic Sentences
   Underline the topic sentence of each paragraph. Does it clearly state the central idea of the paragraph?

   1   2   3   4   5   6

4. Support

Examine the supporting details in each paragraph. Are they specific and clear? Should they be more detailed, or should more support be included?

1   2   3   4   5   6

5. Unity

Does each paragraph clearly relate to and develop the *central idea* expressed in the thesis statement? Do the supporting details *within* each paragraph clearly relate to and develop the *central idea* expressed in the topic sentence of that paragraph?

1   2   3   4   5   6

6. Coherence

Does each paragraph open with a transition, a reference to the central idea of the thesis statement, and an identification of its own central idea? Are the sentences within each paragraph clearly related to each other by the use of transitions or by reference to the central idea of the paragraph?

1   2   3   4   5   6

7. Sentence Structure

Do the sentences combine ideas that are related, using coordination, subordination, and verbal phrases when appropriate? Are there too many brief, choppy main clauses?

1   2   3   4   5   6

8. Mechanics, Grammar, and Spelling

Does the paper contain a distracting number of errors of these kinds?

1   2   3   4   5   6

9. Overall Ranking of the Essay

1   2   3   4   5   6

Student Essay 1

Does the "happily ever after" exist? For years, love books, love movies and love stories made us believe that someday we will find a true love—that one special person who we will spend the rest of our lives with. In Stephanie Coontz's "For Better, For Worse, Marriage Means Something Different Now," she claims now on the twenty first century marriage is not considered to be as serious as it once was. Some people tend to get married as an impulse; as a result, most marriages do not seem to last. However, there are still those select few people who still follow traditional customs of marriage. To have a successful marriage, couples might consider keeping up with some elements that may make their marital relation strong and stable such as happiness, trust between them, and always respect each other.

First, as we all know love is the most important factor for couples to grow together. "Love is a condition in which the happiness of another person is essential to your own," claimed Robert Heinlein, who was an American science fiction writer. For instance, my grandparents, José and Carmen, had a long lasting marriage; they last 52 years together. I remember every time my grandfather used to listen to their favorite song, he would automatically put it all the way up and go find my grandmother wherever she was just to ask her if she would like to dance with him one more time. While they were dancing, my family and I could see how much they loved each other. It was just as beautiful as a fairytale story where you could literally breathe love. My grandfather was a remarkable man known as gentleman. He grew up having his parents as an example of love, which probably affected him in a good way his behavior towards his wife. Some people say that love is like a flower that to make it grow we need to water it every day with the same happiness as we did the first day.

Second, the base to have a stable and happy marriage is to trust each other. Trust is earned used to tell Carmencita to all her grandchildren. This happened ten years ago, I still remember some lady came to my house asking desperately for my grandma. My mom and my aunt welcomed the lady to the house and asked her to have a seat. When my grandma got to the living room, the lady automatically told her that she was having a baby with my grandpa. Carmen could not believe it, and my mom and her sister were furious. My grandma just asked her to leave, but all my family could see that she was not even mortified with that shocking news. Looking us desperate and anxious, she just replied, I trust José. After a few days, we all figured out that the lady was just planning to separate them so that she could marry my grandpa. Because of my grandmother's plenty trust toward him and their good communication, my grandma did not believe the woman's or anybody else's comments. Bad people who are trying to break marriages exist everywhere, but if we believe on our partners nothing of these will affect us.

In addition, one more element is the respect as partners and as individuals. To be respected, we first need to respect. Before my grandparents got married, my grandma was married. Her first husband died. A couple years ago, my family and I went to the cemetery to leave some flowers to some of our family members. Suddenly I saw that my grandma left some flowers to a man who was not my family. I asked Jose, why is she leaving flowers in that man's grave if he is not part of our family? Even though I was still a kid, José thought it was a good moment to let me know. He replied to me, "That man was her husband"; I did not know that little detail. I was shocked! Then I asked him, "Do you still love her knowing that she was married with a man who was not you?" He answered, "Of course, I respect her past and I decided to marry her." My grandpa taught me that day a good lesson that I will never forget. Respect the past of the person you love, it should not affect your present. The fact that he was the man that my grandmother had once loved made my grandpa have a respect for that person. José accepted Carmen as his wife and at the same time he was accepting her past, her present and her future.

In conclusion, even though marriages are not that successful anymore, some people are still trying to rescue their marital lives. Marriage is about love, communication, trust, respect and some other elements that must be applied. Thanks to my grandparents, I happened to experience what a real marriage is, what love is and what family means. Sadly, my grandfather died two years ago but before he left he taught us the value of a family and how to support it. He also showed us that he was not lying in their wedding when he said to my grandmother, "Till death do us part."

Student Essay 2

Mimi Avins writes in "*The Bachelor*: Silly, Sexist, and, to Many, Irresistible," about her own and many others' addiction to the TV show *The Bachelor*. She says that although many other shows never got her interest, this show did. Many of her smart and sophisticated female friends enjoyed the show, and soon enough she was addicted too. One of the reasons she enjoyed the show was because she enjoyed "analyzing how cleverly a drama was constructed." In addition, she says that the world liked the show because of its shallow aspect. By just skimming the personality of each person we are able to fill in the blanks on the rest of their lives and personalities. Another factor in why we enjoy seeing the show is because people make mistakes and we like to know that they're not that far from our own reality. Her sub-heading "Champagne wishes and caviar dreams" suggests that it's more entertaining to watch the rich and stylish and imagine ourselves in those situations than anything else. America also watched because it was a guide to "find a mate." One major complaint was that the show was sexist. She says that "in fact the show is as much about the quest for fame as the search for love." One of her major points about why America liked to watch the show was because everyone is a voyeur. I believe this is so true in many aspects of human nature.

Everyone secretly enjoys watching other people. This is evident in everyday life. How many people slow down when an accident happens and become "looky-loos," even though I'm sure the drivers know that looking will probably cause another accident. The accident can be so minor or a major serious fender bender and everyone slows down to watch. When anyone in public raises their voices don't we all turn and watch what is happening. We watch just because something might happen and it might be juicy. We don't want to be ridiculed for being nosey so we watch secretly from the corner of our eyes.

America enjoyed watching the show *The Bachelor* because they liked watching people make idiots of themselves. These moments of mistakes made it easier for us to watch because we knew that the people on TV weren't robots. It made us feel normal and not so idiotic ourselves. We laugh at those men who approach women who are obviously way out of their league trying to impress them. We laugh under our breath when someone trips over a rock or the sidewalk when they are walking. We enjoy sophisticated men and women on TV embarrassing themselves because they are supposed to be above such things. Men and women who jump through loops and run through mud to impress someone is a hilarious factor.

I think that human nature also prompts us to watch when other people hit emotional roads. We take pleasure in watching human nature at its most raw form. When we see someone crying and sobbing we want to know why, even if we don't know the whole story or who the person is. *The Bachelor* had many emotional ups and downs during it's duration on TV. The different women leaving each week and the cat fights that made for such excellent TV are just some rare moments of emotional roads that we loved to watch. We also liked to see the emotional highs that the show had. When the "bachelor" chose his "soul mate" on the season finale, we all watched as the couple cried and it made our own heart feel with joy. These moments are so enjoyable because its in our nature to be emotional.

Mimi Avins writes that she was addicted and the rest of America was addicted too. She gave many good examples of why she was addicted and many reasons of why America was addicted. I believe that she was right and I think a major reason was that everyone is a voyeur and we secretly and openly enjoy it. Human nature makes us more apt to watching others whether it's on TV or in real life.

Student Essay 3

The reading selection "Killing Women: A Pop-Music Tradition" can be found in Chapter 2.

In "Killing Women: A Pop-Music Tradition," John Hamerlinck writes that accepting violence toward women in pop music has somehow made society less sensitive to domestic abuse. Hamerlinck believes many artist have incorporated these kinds of lyrics into their songs. Even the MTV generation is not concerned with these disturbing images that can be produced by these kinds of woman—killing lyrics. He also points out that these songs do not cause violence but "reflect a disturbingly casual level of acceptance in society when it comes to so-called crimes of passion." We as a society have let ourselves understand and rationalize with why people commit these types of crimes. I believe Hamerlinck's view of woman in pop music is accurate. I feel music is extremely powerful and certain lyrics in songs can glamorize drug-induced lifestyles, while other lyrics in songs embrace drinking as a part of everyday life. Even a person's style of dressing and attitude can change.

Music lyrics have been known through the ages to glamorize drug-induced life-styles. In Eric Clapton's "Cocaine" Clapton sings "If you wanna hang out, you've gotta take her out—cocaine," or "If you got that lose, you wanna kick them blues—cocaine." These lyrics could suggest that, if you want to have a good time or if you want to hang out and be cool you should take cocaine. I feel these lyrics send a false representation of drug use to people. These lyrics just mention the glamorous side of drugs use and not the deadly addiction it can have on a person. Another example are the musicians who lived drug-induced lifestyles. Janis Joplin and Jimi Hendrix are always being portrayed as wild drug-loving hippies that lived fast glamorous lives. On the cover of *Pearl*, Janis Joplin has a bottle of whiskey in one hand and a smoke in the other. This might send a negative message to people who want to be like their favorite musician. They could decide that they want to drink and use drugs like Janis Joplin did. I enjoy listening to these artists, but I do not feel we should glamorize their lifestyles.

In addition to lyrics that glamorize drug-induced lifestyles, there are also the lyrics in songs that seem to say, It's alright to have a drink or to get drunk whenever you feel like it. Country music is always portraying booze and bars as just a natural part of life. David Allan Coe writes "Mamma, train, truck, prison, and getting drunk, is the perfect country western song." I personally listen to country music and I realize that most of my country CD's I own have at least one song about getting drunk. People might get carried away with the lyrics and drink whenever they feel like it because the CD they are listening to promotes drinking. Country music can be good music, but I think some of these artists need to stop using alcohol as a way to fix problems. Next is another example of lyrics in pop music promoting drinking. In the famous song "Margaritaville" Jimmy Buffett tells the story of a man who is constantly drunk in order to forget about his lost love. I do not feel these lyrics will turn a person into an alcoholic, but these lyrics could urge someone to drink if they have had a fight with their boyfriend or girlfriend. The lyrics seem to say it's alright to drink when you are depressed and have problems in life.

Finally, some types of lyrics can influence people to dress a certain way and can change a person's attitude. Some people like to dress in clothes that reflect what kind of music they like. People who listen to country like to wear cowboy hats, Wrangler jeans, and ropers while rap music lovers like to dress in baggy, loose, hip-hop clothes. I think dressing this way is fine, but sometimes people attitudes reflect negatively on the music they listen to. When I worked in a music shop in high school young kids that listen to rap would come in and act rude. On some occasions they used vulgar language when they talked. Some of theses boys had no respect for women because many of the rap artists use insulting language about women in their music. This is not a message that we want to be sending our youth. Artist should be more careful when they write music because they have the power to mold young people in our society.

Clearly, music is powerful and wonderful today, but I feel artist need to be more observant when writing lyrics that could have negative effects on people that are looking for role models and are trying to deal with problems in their life.

SENTENCE COMBINING: APPOSITIVES

As you know from the earlier sentence-combining sections of this text, in English there are many ways to add information to the basic sentence. So far, you have practiced using adjectives, prepositional phrases, main clauses, subordinate clauses, and verbal phrases in your sentences. The **appositive** is yet another way to add interest and depth to your writing. Like most of the other sentence-combining methods you have studied, the appositive allows you to consolidate ideas into one sentence that otherwise might be expressed in two or more separate sentences.

At its simplest level, an appositive is simply a noun or a pronoun renaming or identifying another noun or pronoun. Usually the appositive is set off by commas, and it normally follows the noun or pronoun it is renaming. Here are some examples from the articles from Part Four of this book:

> Lam Ton, from Viet Nam, is already a U.S. citizen, and he did well with a restaurant, **the Mekong**, at the intersection of Broadway and Argyle Street in Chicago.

> Cash recently released a single called "Delia's Gone" from his latest album, **American Recordings**.

Notice that in each of the above examples a noun renames a noun. The noun *the Mekong* renames *restaurant* in the first sentence, and *American Recordings* renames *album* in the second. As is usually the case, each appositive follows and is set off by a comma from the noun it renames.

Another characteristic of the appositive is that it usually includes modifiers of its own—adjectives, adverbs, or other modifiers that add information to the appositive word. Notice the modifiers of the appositive word in the following examples from "Serve or Fail" and "Killing Women: A Pop-Music Tradition":

> Alternatively, colleges could limit the service requirement to a student's junior year—**a time when the students are settled and have more hours and stability in their schedules**.

> The Beatles provide harsh and frightening imagery in "Run for Your Life," **a song that features premeditation along with traditional blues lines**.

PUNCTUATING APPOSITIVES

Most appositives are set off with commas. However, occasionally they are set off with dashes or with a colon. In general, follow these guidelines:

1. Use commas to set off most appositives.

   Two dogs, **an Irish setter and a German shepherd**, ran into the lobby of the hotel.

2. Use dashes to set off an appositive that consists of a series, that already uses internal commas, or that seems to require a strong break.

   Only three people—**a real estate agent, the manager of the local grocery store, and the town's only banker**—attended the Chamber of Commerce mixer.

3. Use a colon to set off an appositive at the end of a sentence if you want to establish a formal tone.

   Last Christmas, Jason visited only one person: **his father**.

   (Note that the above appositive could also have been set off with a comma or with a dash.)

RECOGNIZING WHEN TO USE APPOSITIVES

You have the opportunity to use an appositive almost anytime you have a sentence consisting of a form of the verb *be* followed by a noun or pronoun. If you omit the verb, set off the resulting phrase with commas, and then continue with your sentence, you have created an appositive.

ORIGINAL SENTENCE WITH FORM OF *BE*
Alex Haley was the author of *Roots*.

OMIT THE VERB AND SET OFF THE RESULTING PHRASE WITH COMMAS
Alex Haley, the author of *Roots*,

COMPLETE THE SENTENCE
Alex Haley, the author of *Roots*, died in 1992.

If you watch for them, you will find many opportunities to create appositives when you have written sentences using a form of the verb *be* followed by a noun or pronoun. Notice, for example, how two of the following three sentences use *was* and *is* to introduce a noun.

   Mr. Erickson **was** the winner of the Florida lottery. He gave all of his money to Helping Hands. Helping Hands **is** a small orphanage in New York.

Now notice how those same three sentences can be written as one sentence with two appositives.

   Mr. Erickson, **the winner of the Florida lottery**, gave all of his money to Helping Hands, **a small orphanage in New York**.

EXERCISE 5.5

Use appositives and appropriate punctuation to combine the following sentences. In each case, the words to be made into an appositive are underlined.

EXAMPLES

Robert Louis Stevenson was <u>a British novelist.</u> He wrote *Treasure Island*.
  Robert Louis Stevenson, a British novelist, wrote *Treasure Island*.

Johann von Goethe lived from 1749 to 1832. He was a <u>poet, dramatist, and novelist.</u>
  Johann von Goethe—a poet, dramatist, and novelist—lived from 1749 to 1832.

1. Anyone who looked at Medusa was immediately turned into stone. Medusa was <u>the mythological Gorgon with a head full of snakes.</u>
2. Perseus was <u>the son of the god Zeus and the human princess Danae.</u> He used a reflecting shield to avoid looking at Medusa while he cut off her head.
3. From blood of the severed head of Medusa came Pegasus. Pegasus was <u>a beautiful winged horse</u>.
4. Pegasus was ridden by the Greek muses as well as by Apollo. He was <u>a symbol of the poetic imagination.</u>
5. Athena was <u>the Greek goddess of wisdom.</u> Perseus gave the severed head of Medusa to Athena, who placed it on her own shield.

CHANGING ADJECTIVE CLAUSES TO APPOSITIVES

Another opportunity to use an appositive arises whenever you write an adjective clause containing a form of the verb *be* followed by a noun or pronoun. In such cases, you can omit the relative pronoun that starts the adjective clause and the verb. The result will be an appositive.

EXAMPLE

USING AN ADJECTIVE CLAUSE
Amoxil, **which was** the most frequently prescribed drug in 1991, is an antibiotic.

USING AN APPOSITIVE
Amoxil, the most frequently prescribed drug in 1991, is an antibiotic.

EXERCISE 5.6

Use appositives and appropriate punctuation to combine the following sentences or to change adjective clauses to appositives. In each case, the words to be made into an appositive are underlined.

1. Frederick Hart, who is <u>a contemporary American sculptor,</u> creates sensual, innovative cast figurative sculptures with clear acrylic resin.
2. Sonya Romero, who is <u>a first-grade teacher,</u> was awarded $20,000 by Target for her altruistic work at Lew Wallace Elementary.
3. The kalimba is <u>an African musical instrument.</u> It produces a melodious sound.
4. My grandfather's Impala will be displayed at this year's Chicano Park Day's Lowrider Show. The Impala is <u>a green 1964 Chevrolet.</u>
5. Erma Bombeck wrote over four thousand columns in her lifetime. She was <u>a humorist and newspaper columnist.</u>

EXERCISE 5.7

Use appositives and appropriate punctuation to combine the following sentences or to change adjective clauses to appositives.

1. In Greek mythology, Hades was the name of the underworld as well as of the god Hades. The god Hades was king of the Underworld.
2. Hades is described by Homer as a shadowy place inhabited by the dead. Homer is the famous writer of the *Iliad* and the *Odyssey*.
3. Cerberus was a fierce dog with three heads and the tail of dragon. It guarded the gates of Hades, allowing the dead in but no one out.
4. Hades was the ruler of Hades, and Persephone was his queen. Persephone was the daughter of Demeter.
5. Hades kidnapped Persephone, who was the maiden of spring, when she strayed too far from her companions.
6. When Demeter heard the news, she withheld her gifts from the world. Demeter was the goddess of grain.
7. The earth, which was once a green and flowering land, now turned into a frozen desert.
8. Zeus was the king of all gods and brother of Hades. To save the earth, Zeus told Hades to allow Persephone to return to the upper world.
9. Before she left, Hades tricked her into eating some food; unfortunately, the Fates required anyone who ate food in Hades to remain there forever. The food she ate was several pomegranate seeds. The Fates were Clotho, Lachesis, and Atropos.
10. When Persephone returned, the earth, which was a barren world without any vegetation, came alive once again, but each year she must return to Hades, which is her underworld realm, for four months.

EXERCISE 5.8

Combine the following sentences, using coordination, subordination, verbal phrases, or appositives.

1. The "Trail of Tears" refers to one of the many forced "removals" of Native Americans from their native lands.
   These "removals" resulted in the deaths of thousands of men, women, and children.

2. In the 1830s, these so-called removals focused on what are generally referred to as the Five Civilized Tribes of the Southeast.
   These were the Choctaw, Chickasaw, Creek, Cherokee, and Seminole nations.

3. Each of these Native American societies had developed a culture.
   The culture was compatible with white society.
   It even emulated European styles in many respects.

4. There was a problem, however.
   It was that these tribes resided in valuable territory.
   The territory was cotton-growing land.

5. The Indian Removal Act was passed in 1830.
   Thousands of Choctaws, Chickasaws, and Creeks were forced to move.
   They moved from the Southeast to territory west of Arkansas.

6. The forced move caused many hardships.
   Hundreds and eventually thousands of Native Americans died.
   They suffered from pneumonia, cholera, and other diseases.

7. Gold was discovered in Cherokee country in Georgia.
   The state of Georgia tried to force the Cherokee to leave.
   The Cherokee took their case to the United States Supreme Court.

8. At this time, the Cherokee were not nomads.
   They were a nation of Native Americans.
   They had built roads, schools, and churches.
   They even had a system of representative government.

9. The Supreme Court ruled against them.
   Seventeen thousand Cherokee were forced to travel the "Trail of Tears" to Oklahoma.

10. Along the way, 4,000 of the 17,000 died.
    Another 1,000 escaped.
    They hid in the Great Smoky Mountains.

11. In the following years, the Cherokee eventually won back 56,000 acres.
    Seven million acres of land had been taken from them.

Evaluating Reading Selections 6

The students in the Trudeau cartoon seem to be doing an excellent job of recording what their instructor has to say. Since they are listening carefully, their notes will probably be accurate summaries of the lecture. However, wouldn't you agree that something is missing from the students' activities in this cartoon? Shouldn't they have some reaction to the statements "Jefferson was the Antichrist! Democracy is Fascism! Black is white! Night is day!"? The problem, of course, is that taking careful notes is just not enough. These students need to **evaluate** as well as record.

Evaluating what you read (or hear) is a valuable skill. We have all heard the old saying "Don't believe everything that you read," and certainly most people follow that advice. Unfortunately, what we do or do not believe is often not based on careful evaluation. Instead, many people merely accept material that confirms what they *already* believe and reject material that does not confirm their previously held beliefs.

Evaluation demands that you approach an idea with an open mind—that you be willing to consider its validity on the basis of the evidence presented, not on the basis of any preconceptions you may have. It demands that you be willing to change your ideas if the evidence suggests that you should. And it demands that you make an effort to understand the purpose of what you are reading so that you don't criticize something for failing to do what it was not intended to do.

AUDIENCE AND PURPOSE

Perhaps the first step in evaluating anything that you read is to determine the audience and the purpose of the article. The **audience** of an article is its intended readers. Obviously, an article in *Ms.* magazine on the sexual exploitation of women will have a different audience from an article on the same subject published in *Playboy*, and those different audiences may influence the authors' choices of ideas to be covered. Of course, no matter who the audience is, a writer must still provide reasonable support for his or her points.

An evaluation should also consider the **purpose** of any article that you read. Clearly it would be unfair to criticize a writer for failing to discuss the responsibilities of parenthood if that writer's purpose was to entertain you with humorous stories about the frustrations of living with a teenager. Here are four common purposes that you should consider whenever you read.

To Inform

This type of writing is often called *expository*. It generally consists of facts rather than opinions or arguments. Most newspaper reporting has *informing* as its purpose, as does most of the material that you read in textbooks.

To Entertain

Generally, nonfiction *entertainment* writing tends to be humorous and often focuses on situations that are common to the average person. Dave Barry, for example, is a nationally syndicated entertainment columnist.

To Persuade

Persuasive writing tends to focus on controversial issues, presenting opinions and arguments that are supported (effectively or ineffectively) with facts, examples, explanations, statistics, and/or references to authority. Editorials in newspapers and magazines are common examples of persuasive writing.

To Raise an Issue or Provoke Thought

This type of writing is similar to persuasive writing in that it examines controversial issues, but its purpose is not necessarily to persuade the reader that the writer's particular argument is the correct one. Instead, its intent is often to unsettle the reader, to raise questions that need to be answered but that are not fully answered in the article itself. Such articles are often found in newspaper and magazine editorials.

In this chapter, you will write evaluations of articles designed to persuade, to raise an issue, or to provoke thought. As you read each article in this chapter, you must ask yourself if the article's purpose is to convince you of a particular argument or if it is merely to get you to think about the issue at hand. Of course, at times the purpose may be a little of both, so you should consider that possibility too.

EVALUATING SUPPORT

In addition to considering the audience and the purpose of what you read, you need to examine the evidence or support that is presented to you. For example, if a writer claims that we should do away with the minimum wage, you should look to see not only what reasons he gives but also what facts, statistics, examples, or references to authority he offers to explain his reasons.

When you do look closely at a written argument—especially an editorial in a newspaper or magazine—you will often find that the support is quite sketchy. Much of the argument may consist of opinions or explanations rather than facts or other specific types of support. In such cases, you must decide whether more support is needed or whether the argument is reasonably convincing as it stands. However, an argument without sufficient support should be looked at skeptically, no matter how well it is written.

FACTS

Facts are tricky things. Most people consider a fact to be something "true" or "correct" or "accurate." But not everyone agrees about what is or is not true. For example, is it a fact that drinking coffee is bad for your health? Some people might *claim* that such a statement is accurate, but just as many others would say it is not. And science itself has provided few answers about the long-term effects of coffee drinking. So is it or is it not true that coffee is bad for your health? Surely such a statement cannot be treated as a fact if there is so much disagreement about it.

The best way to define a fact is to move away from the idea of "truth" or "correctness" and toward the idea of objective, physical verification. Treat as a fact any statement that has been objectively verified through direct experience, measurement, or observation. Statistics, then, are facts, as are historical or current events, scientific observations, and even personal experience. If it has been verified that caffeine increases a person's blood pressure, then such a statement is a fact. If you visited a Toyota dealership yesterday and felt uncomfortable talking to the salesperson, your statement that such an event occurred and that you reacted the way you did are facts. If the distance between the sun and the earth has been measured as 92,900,000 miles, such a statement is a fact.

Of course, even using objective verification, you cannot assume all facts are always accurate. For many years, people believed it was a fact that the sun circled the earth, not vice versa. After all, anyone could see that each day the sun rose in the east and set in the west. In this case, objective verification was not accurate enough to lead us to the fact that the earth circled the sun. So how do you know which facts have been accurately verified and which have not? Often you must consider the source. If the writer of an article says that 24,700 murders were committed in the United States in 1991, you will probably accept that statement as a fact if the writer is a professional reporter or columnist whose career is riding on his or her accuracy. Of course, that does not mean that you should accept the writer's *conclusions*, especially if the writer is trying to persuade you to accept his or her particular point of view.

EXERCISE 6.1

Discuss which of the following statements can and which cannot be objectively verified as facts.

1. Noodles and gunpowder were invented in China.
2. If more than five people go on this trip, we'll have trouble having any meaningful conversations.
3. No loyal American would ever burn the American flag.
4. Julia Butterfly Hill sat in a redwood tree that she named Luna for 738 days.
5. Ethiopia is the point of origin for most Semitic languages.
6. Betsy Ross sewed the first American flag.
7. When the Lakers won the 2010 NBA championship, Ron Artest thanked his psychiatrist in a postgame interview.
8. Kanye West has a habit of interrupting award ceremonies.
9. Private businesses do everything more efficiently than the government.
10. Dark chocolate tastes better than milk chocolate.

As you can see from the above sentences, some statements are more clearly facts than others. That Ron Artest of the Los Angeles Lakers thanked his psychiatrist in a postgame interview in 2010 could easily be verified if you had to do so, but how would you verify the statement that private businesses always do everything more efficiently? You would need to find a study of all private businesses in America; they would all have to operate more efficiently than all government entities, and one would have to find private businesses that do the same work as government entities in order to set up a valid comparison. How likely is it that you will find such a study?

For that matter, how would you verify that dark chocolate tastes better than milk chocolate? Such a statement would be a fact only if it were worded this way: "I like dark chocolate better than milk chocolate." Do you see the difference? The second statement refers only to the speaker's personal preference, which the speaker verifies merely by making the statement. By the way, one of the ten sentences above has long been accepted as a fact by most people even though scholars know that it has never been verified and is probably not a fact at all. Which sentence is that?

OPINIONS

When people say something like "That's just my opinion," they usually mean that they don't want to argue about the point. In fact, "That's just my opinion" is often a way of saying that you don't have any facts to support your idea. Of course, at one time or another we all hold opinions without having examined the facts behind them. Perhaps we hold them because people we respect—our parents, friends, or teachers—hold them or because they reinforce what we already believe to be true about the world or the society in which we live.

Clear, responsible thinking, however, demands that we examine our opinions and discard those that are not well-supported. Although it is true that we are all entitled to our own opinions, certainly the unexamined, unsupported opinion is not as valuable as the opinion formed after one has carefully considered the facts. When you think about opinions, consider these three distinctions.

Personal Opinion

The term *personal opinion* is often used when the speaker really means *unsupported* or *unexamined opinion*. If you hear someone say (or if you yourself say) "Well, that's just my personal opinion," be aware that such a statement probably means the opinion has not been very thoroughly examined. In addition to referring to an unexamined opinion, a personal opinion may also refer to matters of personal taste, such as "Suspense novels are more fun to read than science fiction novels."

Considered Opinion

A *considered opinion* is one reached after you have considered the relevant facts and other types of support. If, for example, you have read various articles on the pros and cons of handgun control, you can be said to have developed a considered opinion of your own. Remember, however, that any considered opinion should be open to change if new evidence or support demands it.

Expert Opinion

As you learned in Chapter 3, one type of support is *reference to authority*. For the most part, you should be able to accept an opinion held by experts in a particular field as long as their opinion is related to their field of expertise. For example, you would probably accept an orthopedic surgeon's opinion about the usefulness of a particular knee brace, but there would be no reason to accept that surgeon's opinion about a particular political issue. In addition, even an expert's opinion about an issue in his or her own field must be questioned if other experts in the same field disagree.

EXERCISE **6.2**

Indicate which of the following opinions you would take more seriously than others. Which of these opinions are more likely to be personal opinions, considered opinions, or expert opinions?

1. Your uncle says that German bread tastes better than Swedish bread.
2. A person at a party says that capital punishment discriminates against those who cannot afford expensive attorneys.
3. Your dentist tells you who will win the Super Bowl in 2020.
4. One homeless person tells another that a particular police officer will not care if he sleeps on the park bench.

5. Your English instructor says that college is a prerequisite for a successful life.

6. The owner of a local convenience store says that the state lottery takes money from the people who can least afford to spend it.

7. A scientist from the Scripps Institute of Oceanography warns that rising ocean acidity levels endanger worldwide fish populations.

8. A member of the city council says that crime will not be reduced until we start locking up criminals and throwing away the key.

9. Your mother tells you that you are far more cynical than you used to be.

10. A real estate salesperson says that now is the time to buy because housing prices are sure to rise.

GENERALIZATIONS VERSUS SPECIFIC STATEMENTS

Much of your ability to evaluate what you read will depend on how well you can distinguish between a generalization and a specific statement. A *specific statement* will refer to specific people, places, events, or ideas, usually giving names and dates as it does, while a *generalization* will refer to groups of people, places, events, or ideas.

SPECIFIC STATEMENT
Yesterday, John McIntyre, a homeless man in San Diego, California, went the entire day without eating anything.

GENERALIZATION
Many homeless people often go an entire day without eating anything.

Both specific statements and generalizations can be facts or opinions, depending on what they say. For example, one of the following specific statements is clearly a fact, and one is clearly an opinion.

FACT
This morning Samantha spilled a cup of coffee on Angelo.

OPINION
This morning Samantha's carelessness caused her to spill a cup of coffee on Angelo.

As you can see, both of the above statements are specific, but only one can be called a fact.

Like specific statements, generalizations may be either facts or opinions. Generalizations that are based on obviously verified facts rarely require support and are usually treated as facts, while generalizations requiring further support are treated as opinions. Of the following generalizations, which should be treated as a fact and which should not?

People who smoke face a higher risk of developing lung cancer than people who don't smoke.

Students' sloppy style of dress today reflects a general "I don't care" attitude toward all of society.

As you can see, both specific statements and generalizations can express facts, so both can be used to support a writer's ideas. However, most writing instructors will ask you to provide specific statements as often as possible, primarily because specific statements are more interesting to read and are more persuasive than generalizations. It is simply more compelling to hear that someone's best friend, who smoked two packs of cigarettes a day, died two days ago after a painful battle with lung cancer than it is to hear the generalization that people who smoke die of lung cancer more often than people who don't.

EXERCISE **6.3**

First, explain whether each of the following statements is a generalization or a specific statement. Then explain whether each statement should be considered a fact or an opinion. If it is an opinion, discuss whether or not it could be reasonably supported with facts.

1. Throughout most of civilized history, people have relied on animals or on their own feet for transportation.
2. From 2000 to 2010, the National Highway Traffic Safety Administration received over 6,200 complaints of unintended acceleration in some Toyotas.
3. Listening to the speed metal band Dragonforce made him take a sledgehammer to my brother's 2015 Mustang.
4. Today's social problems are indicators of our immoral society.
5. Colleges and universities have not done a very good job in preventing rape or punishing rapists.
6. The latest earthquake in California was caused by people not living according to God's will.
7. Some of the earthquakes in Oklahoma are caused by hydraulic fracking.
8. SpongeBob SquarePants is a cartoon character who lives in a pineapple under the Pacific Ocean with his pet snail, Gary.
9. Whether raising the minimum wage will help more people enter the middle class is an issue on which economists disagree.
10. Lee Harvey Oswald was not the only person who fired shots when John F. Kennedy was assassinated.

CONSIDERING YOUR OWN KNOWLEDGE AND EXPERIENCE

Evaluating the support in a text demands that you also think about what *you* know to be true and compare it to what you are reading. For example, if you are a single mother who is successfully raising a happy, well-adjusted child, your experience will certainly contradict an article that asserts that single mothers cannot provide a healthy home environment for their children. You must then consider whether the argument in the article is flawed or overgeneralized or whether your own experience is an unusual exception. Whatever you decide, remember that your own knowledge and experience are important sources of information that you should consult before accepting the support offered by any writer.

CONSIDERING UNSTATED OBJECTIONS

A final step to take as you evaluate an argument is to determine whether the writer has ignored ideas that might contradict or otherwise weaken his or her position. For instance, if you are reading a newspaper editorial arguing that competition in school sports damages our children, consider what objections may not have been addressed by the writer. Do school sports benefit children in any ways that the writer has ignored? Is competition a valuable quality in any way?

Of course, a writer does not have to cover every—or any—objection to write an interesting, thought-provoking paper. If the purpose of the article is to raise issues that the reader should think about, you may not find any objections considered at all. However, the more a paper is intended to convince or persuade the reader, the more thoroughly the writer must consider and respond to major objections.

STEPS IN EVALUATING A TEXT

1. Read the text actively.
   - Determine its purpose and intended audience.
   - Identify its thesis.
   - Identify its main points.
2. Determine how well the main points are supported.
   - Distinguish between facts and opinions.
   - Distinguish between specific support and generalizations.
   - Identify statistics, examples, and references to authority.
3. Test the article's points against your own knowledge and experience.
4. Consider any obvious objections that have been ignored.

READINGS

Uncle Sam Doesn't Always Want You   Mark Arax

Mark Arax is a former Los Angeles Times *staff writer and the author of several books, including, most recently,* West of the West. *In the following review of a book titled* Not Fit for Our Society, *Arax discusses "the spasms of anti-immigration that have defined our nation from the very beginning."*

BEFORE YOU READ

1. On what grounds can the inhabitants of one country say that the inhabitants of another can or cannot enter? Is a country like a private home? Or is it something altogether different?

2. What issues or problems might cause someone to leave his or her country?

One long ago morning in California, as debate raged over the anti-immigration initiative known as Proposition 187, I walked into a coffee shop in the town of Selma, the "raisin capital of the world," to feel the pulse of the farmer.   1

From counter to booth, it was all gloom. If Prop. 187 passed, requiring legal residency for public schooling and other services, disaster was next, the farmers said: There would be no Mexican illegals to pick the crops.   2

I was about to leave when a grape grower with a Middle Eastern last name stopped me. Yes, 80% of his pickers came from Mexico without legal documents. Yes, these migrants were among the hardest working people on earth. But he was going to vote for Prop. 187 anyway.   3

"We need to send a message to these Mexicans that the state of California isn't for sale," he said. Then he added, with a touch of rural realpolitik, "Even if 187 passes, they're going to find a way to get to my fields."   4

What is it about immigration that drives America crazy mad, makes us forget who we are?   5

Peter Schrag takes up that question in *Not Fit for Our Society*, a thoughtful, especially timely look at the spasms of anti-immigration that have defined our nation from the very beginning. He writes: "The history of American attitudes about immigration and immigration policy has long been a spiral of ambivalence and inconsistency, a sort of double helix, with strands of welcome and rejection wound tightly around one another."   6

How else to explain the paradox implicit in the anti-immigration rants of former Rep. Tom Tancredo (R-Colo.)? He's the grandson of a Sicilian immigrant whose "race" was once officially listed as among the most inferior in morals and intelligence of any group entering the U.S.   7

"If this book tells anything about that three-hundred-year narrative," Schrag writes, "it's that almost everything that's being said in the arguments for closing the border and shutting down immigration has been said before, often in literally the same terms and tones."   8

A longtime newspaper columnist, Schrag is an old-school dig-   9
ger and thinker who approaches immigration from the political left
but never with a partisan's shrillness. Deftly, often powerfully, he
traces the contradictions to our nation's DNA.

The Declaration of Independence stated that "All men are cre-   10
ated equal." Puritan John Winthrop envisioned the new land as the
"City upon a Hill," a beacon to the rest of the world. Who would
fell the trees, clear the fields and plant the crops, if not the immigrant drawn by that light?

Yet we were also a place that saw itself as God's manifestation,   11
a land of innocence and exceptionalism in a world of decadence.
We could hardly allow such a place to be defiled by the dreg, the
criminal, the anarchist, the too fertile. So it became that the noble
Saxon forbid the German, and the German forbid the Irish, and
the Irish forbid the Italian, and the Italian forbid the Jew, and the
Jew forbid the Chinese, and the Chinese forbid the Mexican, and
the Mexican forbid the Muslim.

We were a great melting pot. From forbidden to forbidder, it   12
took but a generation or two.

In the late 1700s, as the U.S. vacillated from one of the world's   13
most liberal naturalization laws to one that required 15 years of
residency, Thomas Jefferson could be heard moaning about immigrants from foreign monarchies. The Rev. Lyman Beecher, the Lou
Dobbs of the mid-1800s, railed against the Catholic hordes from
Europe—the "contents of the poor house and the sweepings of
the streets."

Soon, Boston would elect its first Irish-Catholic mayor.   14

Nativism is our most stubborn trait. Dormant for long   15
stretches—boom times when the factories and fields needed
more workers—it inevitably showed itself with hard times. Fear
gave rise to laws that rigged the numbers in such a way that quo-
tas favored Nordic immigrants over those from Southern and
Eastern Europe. In a 1910 survey of schools, the U.S. Immigration
Commission concluded that 63% of children of southern Italian
descent were "retarded." They were exceeded only by the children
of Polish Jews, at nearly 67%.

Schrag uncovers a long list of statesmen—conservationists,   16
founders of the New York Zoological Society, the esteemed Sen.
Henry Cabot Lodge and progressive California newspaperman V.S.
McClatchy—who became rabid nativists. The more shameful of
the lot pushed an American brand of eugenics that made its way
to Hitler.

Now and then, a kind of consensus was achieved when the   17
various immigrants found one immigrant to beat up on. For a good
part of a century, the Chinese and Japanese—"mongrels" who
would never blend in—played the role of whipping boy.

Is the Mexican the new "Oriental"? Is the recent Arizona law   18
allowing police to demand the papers of Mexican-looking people
engaged in suspicious activity a knee jerk of the same old nativism?
Or is 21st century America finally stretched too thin to absorb the
great press of Mexico's undocumented?

Addressing this last question, Schrag fails to fully explore   19
the pathologies of migrant families. In the San Joaquin Valley, for
instance, more than half of the high school students of Mexican
descent are dropping out; large numbers are joining gangs and having children out of wedlock. Might this be a different story than the
narrative of the Chinese, Armenian and Jew? Schrag doesn't say.

Quibble aside, "Not Fit for Our Society" is an important   20
reminder that the music of anti-immigration is a tired old piece of
vinyl, the same warps and scratches, over and over, sung by a babel
of voices.

AFTER YOU READ

Work with other students to develop responses to these questions or to compare responses that you have already prepared.

1. State the thesis of the article in your own words. What sentences in
   the article, if any, best express the idea?
2. This article was originally published in the *Los Angeles Times*. Who
   would you say is Arax's audience? What is the purpose of his essay?
3. Divide the article into sections according to each major point that is
   made.
4. Consider the support that is provided for each point. Are generalizations or specific statements used? Facts or opinions? Are the opinions
   reasonably supported?
5. Consider your own experience or the discussions people you know
   have about immigration. Do they confirm or contradict the ideas in
   this article?
6. Are there any objections to these points that you should consider?
7. Neither Native Americans nor African Americans are mentioned in
   this article. Is there a reason for that?
8. The second-to-last paragraph of Arax's essay makes a number of statements that need further scrutiny or might be considered generalizations. They are not backed up by facts. Should or shouldn't he, as a
   reporter, make such generalizing statements?

Education Is Not a Luxury   STEPHEN JOEL TRACHTENBERG

Stephen Joel Trachtenberg was the 15th president of the George Washington University and currently holds the title of president emeritus and university professor of public service. He is the author of numerous books including The Art of Hiring in America's Colleges & Universities, Thinking Out Loud, Reflections on Higher Education, Speaking His Mind, *and* Big Man on Campus. *In the following article, he argues that our current school calendar does a disservice to both students and teachers.*

BEFORE YOU READ

1. Consider the title. It suggests that some people consider education a luxury. Do you? In what way might someone consider education a luxury?
2. What do you think might be the benefits and/or drawbacks of extending the primary and secondary school years so that students attend all year long?
3. What might be the benefits and/or drawbacks of extending the primary and secondary school day so that students meet a full day, such as from 9:00 A.M. to 5:00 P.M.?

Even less than a hundred years ago, America was an agricultural society. Most people worked in farming or in finishing agricultural crops—such as the famous butcher, brewer, and baker cited at the beginning of Adam Smith's *Wealth of Nations*, published in 1776. This last century has seen an incredible transformation of our society into one that produces information and services. But one thing has not changed. Though we are no longer agrarian, the agrarian calendar continues to dominate one facet of American life—education. The school year still begins late in the summer and ends late in the spring. It accommodates farming. Eighty years ago it made as much sense as it did ten thousand years ago, when some of our ancestors gave up hunting and gathering because they had learned to cultivate crops and domesticate animals.

For them, as for Americans eighty years ago, tending the crops was the most important thing. Schooling was a luxury, which could be carried on when the demands of the fields and the pastures were not pressing. But schooling—the long process of educating the young—is not in our world and time a luxury. We claim to believe this, to take it for granted. Yet we still maintain a school calendar that reflects life eighty years ago and maybe ten thousand years ago.

This creates many problems in American education, but the   3
worst of them are these:

- America will never take schools seriously as long as they operate
  on the ancient agrarian calendar—even if few people use the
  phrase.
- And it will never take them seriously as long as they are open
  from only nine to three o'clock or some equivalent.

A short school year and school day cause people to reach the   4
conclusion that this schooling business is a part-time occupation,
that it is not serious. That is a melancholy opinion. Although it is
not thoroughly justified, either, it is nevertheless prevalent, and, of
course, in part accurate. It seems to me that we could make much
better use of our whole year.

Recently I mentioned this issue to a friend. One of the prob-   5
lems, he said, was that the schools were doing things that they
should not be doing—teaching sex and drugs and driver's ed, as he
put it. These things, he pointed out, should be the business of the
family. He claimed that they are wasting classroom time.

He made a good point, but I don't agree with it. Topics like   6
these may be putting a squeeze on the time spent on literacy and
numeracy, but they are important. Moreover, I asked him, where's
the family these days? In our poorest neighborhoods, the family has
often ceased to be. In our richest neighborhoods, we often have
two busy parents in the household, but not so often in the house.

Making the Case

I'm not for letting parents off the hook, no matter how busy they   7
are. But facts are facts. So, I said to my friend what I have just written here and added that his argument and my counter to it could
together make a case for a longer school day and a longer school
year. Consider:

If we accept the facts (or at least opinions) that

- Schools must take on some of the instruction traditionally
  associated with families;
- These obligations are diminishing the time spent on learning
  those things that children need to learn;
- Schools are not in many cases adequately preparing young
  people for university work;
- Children have only one shot, or maybe two, at primary and
  secondary education, since by the time the nontraditional

student reaches his twenties, he is not quite suited to most third-grade classes; and

- Education is not a luxury.

Then we must conclude that the schools can teach both aca-   8
demic subjects and other things provided we make it possible for
the schools to do so.

How do we do that? As I've been suggesting, by lengthening   9
the school year, say, to eleven months, and the school day from 9
to 5, or a full shift, whatever the starting and quitting times may be.
This, I think, would have a number of benefits.

First, it would convince the rest of the world that the schools   10
are, at last, serious. Second, with teachers working conventional
hours and a typical work year, it would be possible to begin to pay
teachers what they are really worth. That, in turn, would be certain to
attract more capable young people who would see school teaching
as a career worth pursuing in the first place and, more to the point,
staying with. And finally, it would accommodate all the things that
teachers need to teach and young people need to learn.

Now, a few footnotes to what I have just proposed: 11

A 9-to-5 day would not be spent entirely in the classroom. It   12
couldn't be. Eight hours is an exhausting teaching schedule and a
fidgety learning schedule. But the time could be well spent otherwise—by providing teachers more preparation time, by giving
more office hours, by permitting time for research, and by engaging students in other activities, many of which are now reserved
for after school, such as organized sports, clubs, and even work for
the older ones. Please understand that I am merely offering some
possibilities.

The University Model

What I am proposing may look very much like the university   13
model. That's exactly what it is. Universities, like schools, are driven
by their double missions of learning and service. But universities
are also driven by the compelling need to be efficient, to get the
most out of their staffs and their plants. While universities typically
have more of both than schools, the size is not the issue.

An idle school building is costly because it produces nothing   14
while still needing to be maintained. Even worse, it represents, in
its idleness, missed opportunities for teaching and learning. I know
there are movements for using schools after hours for other
purposes—for community activities, adult education, and so forth.

All those are praiseworthy. But, if there can be a hierarchy of praise, I would save mine for using more of the day—and of the plant and staff—for teaching the young.

Another footnote: applying the university model to schools would help to create what university administrators like me spend a lot of time and effort doing—promoting an atmosphere of learning. I think one of the problems of education in America is that, to a lot of boys and girls, school is not their real occupation. It is something they have to do, in many cases want to do, but it is not what they are really about. Their lives begin when they are furloughed for the day.   15

I confess that universities are not populated exclusively with young men and women whose thirst for learning and knowledge is so great that they will sit in classrooms, libraries, and laboratories until they keel over from sheer exhaustion or hunger. I will even confess that some have no idea why they are there. I will confess even worse in some cases.   16

But after twenty-five years as a university president, I will not confess but assert that by far most of the students I have observed quickly realize that they are here to learn and the opportunities are everywhere. All they have to do is look around and seize them. In other words, they are responding to the atmosphere.   17

They are also responding to what is available. An atmosphere of learning without the first-rate instruction or the various tangibles and intangibles that make learning possible is nothing but a disappointment. But if you have the teachers and the school facilities, then you already have the means for teaching. Lengthening the school day and convincing the young that they are present for long hours because this is what their occupation really is will, I believe, go a long way to create an atmosphere of learning.   18

Expanding Offerings

What I am proposing implies more than just additional time to teach what is already being taught; it implies expanding academic offerings. It is dismaying to me that many students come to us without any training in foreign languages, or that only a couple of languages, typically Spanish and French, were offered to them; they were offered no classics, no Russian, no Arabic, no Asian languages. I could say the same about other subjects, including art history, advanced math, and so on. The result, in any case, is a deficit.   19

Speaking of languages, let me add this: many school districts must deal with immigrant children who, among them, may speak   20 twenty-five or even fifty languages other than English. One thing is clear: the children are learning another language—which is good—but at the expense of learning other essential things such as history, math, and science. Certainly something is being sacrificed, because there are not enough hours in the teaching day and not enough days in the teaching year, as those are currently constituted, to do all that should be done. Again, this is a deficit.

But with more time in the day, more days in the year, and an atmosphere of learning, all these deficits can be made up. Perhaps not everything is possible—budgets are not infinite. But give talented teachers more time and a great deal more becomes possible. 21

One more note, on collateral amelioration. The benefits to schools and education that I believe would follow from a twenty-first-century school calendar would provide something for teachers—two things, in fact. First, a greater sense of pride, both for emulating the university model and for being able to accomplish more. In turn, such benefits would aid in recruiting gifted young potential teachers and help to retain those, of any age and experience, who are already teaching. 22

At least three objections can be raised against this proposal. First, that there's not enough money available to pay teachers for working conventional hours and a typical work year. Second, that time off from school allows real learning to take place while the preconscious mind processes the past. Third, that any additional resources that are made available would deprive the community the opportunity to spend money on helping single mothers cope with the educational needs of their children or to help families understand that mastery, not mere familiarity, is the aim of education. 23

The first and third objections are, at heart, issues of resource allocation. I'll attempt a brief answer with questions of my own. Are our teachers better at their professions because they work at other jobs during the summer—often menial jobs with trivial pay and benefits? Would our youngsters be better off learning from teachers who devote their full effort to teaching rather than scrabbling for a living? Will we persuade families that their children need to excel when their role models, their teachers, are overworked and underpaid? 24

The second objection is more interesting. No doubt time for reflection and debate is critical to learning. But simply because we ask teachers to work longer doesn't mean we must ask them 25 to do the same thing hour after hour. Additional time can be devoted to individual instruction, tutoring, and creating challenging assignments and projects for different talents. We can find ways to encourage reflection and debate and still allow our children sufficient time for frolic and for the preconscious mind to do its cogitation.

It is very important to note that I have not meant anything I   26
have said to be an indictment of schools or parents. The problem here, like many institutional problems, can be explained in the same way—inertia. This is the way things have always been, we say; this is what has always worked and will continue to work. Maybe, but I do not really think so, if only because the world has changed, and not just in the last century, but in the last twenty years.

The computer revolution put a lot of jobs out of business, and   27
it will be the undoing of more as time goes by. Other changes—social as well as technological—have reset the clock we live by. Thus, we must reset our calendar. We cannot be sure what boys and girls entering school today will need to know in twenty years. But it is certain that they are going to need as much basic preparation in literacy and numeracy as possible—and as early as possible—if they are going to be able to adapt to more change. What they miss in second grade or eleventh can disable them, or at least harm them, forever.

Having made my case, I offer it to you, if you want to make it   28
your own. I hope you share my outlook that an education is not a luxury for subsistence farmers but a box full of tools for a lifetime, an endless series of points of departure, and a full-time joy.

AFTER YOU READ

Work with other students to develop responses to these questions or to compare responses that you have already prepared.

1. State the thesis of the article in your own words. What sentences in the article, if any, best express the idea?

2. This article was originally published in *The World and I*. The magazine describes itself as "a multifaceted monthly publication that presents a broad range of thought-provoking reading in politics, science, culture, humanity, and more in these seven sections—Current Issues, The Arts, Life, Natural Science, Culture, Book World, and Modern Thought." Who would you say is Trachtenberg's audience? What is the purpose of his essay?

3. Divide the article into sections according to each major point that Trachtenberg makes.

4. Consider the support that Trachtenberg provides for each of his points. Does he use generalizations or specific statements? Facts or opinions? Are his opinions reasonably supported?

5. Consider your own experience or the experiences of people you know. Do they confirm or contradict Trachtenberg's points?

6. Are there any objections to Trachtenberg's points that you should consider?

History 101: Pass the Popcorn, Please   ELAINE MINAMIDE

Elaine Minamide, a freelance writer who lives in southern California, is an adjunct instructor at Palomar Community College. In the following article, first published in the San Diego Union-Tribune, *she raises questions about the use and misuse of films in the classroom.*

BEFORE YOU READ

1. What do you think about the use of movies in the classroom? Do movies help students learn the subject matter?

2. Make a list of both the advantages and disadvantages of using movies in a classroom setting.

3. Which seems stronger, the advantages or the disadvantages?

On the face of it, the arguments make sense: 1

"Films provoke students to not only think about history, but to experience it to its fullest."   2

"Movies give educators a priceless opportunity to connect to young students bored by textbooks."   3

"Anything that gets the kids thinking and talking can only be positive."   4

It's difficult to argue with success. Opening to chapter eight in a history book rarely evokes the kind of hand-flailing, call-on-me-teacher response most educators only dream about. Switching on the VCR is a different story. From the opening credits, kids are hooked, involved, and—dare we say it?—learning.   5

That's the bottom line, isn't it? So what if *Amistad* has, as some critics have charged, "rewritten history"? Who cares if *Titanic* is merely a backdrop for a hyped-up, modern love story? Does it matter, as long as kids are thinking about the grander issues, like slavery or the tragic arrogance of man?   6

The debate over the use of contemporary films in the classroom may be stimulating, but something else is at stake that has nothing to do with blurring the line between fact and fiction. Any   7 competent teacher can address head-on disputes over historical accuracy or propaganda. That's what education is all about, after all: guiding students into becoming discriminating, critical thinkers.

The greater issue has to do with declining literacy and can be traced back to the days when the letter "b" first danced across the television screen. While older siblings sweated through math problems and penmanship at school, the preschool set of the '70s sat cross-legged on their carpets, mesmerized by Bert and Ernie singing catchy jingles about the alphabet. Parents, of course, were delighted: What better way for your precocious 3-year-old to learn her ABCs than to plop her in front of the TV while you made a few phone calls? *Sesame Street* was a godsend.   8

Wouldn't you know it—most educators didn't agree. By the time those preschoolers entered kindergarten, not only did they already know their ABCs, but they sat in their little chairs, waiting for the song and dance to begin. The Entertain Me pupils were in their seats, and they're seated still. Today's high schoolers are yesterday's *Sesame Street* watchers, clamoring to be entertained.   9

Evidently, teachers are accommodating them. A recent feature article in the *San Diego Union-Tribune* focused on local teachers who frequently supplement classroom instruction with contemporary films. One eighth-grade history teacher, for example, has a must-see list of flicks that she either encourages her students to see or brings to the classroom herself.   10

A high school social-studies teacher uses movies to introduce new subjects to his students. And they're not alone. Some film companies (notably, the producers of *Amistad*) now supply schools across the nation with study guides to accompany their current releases.   11

It's been argued that since students spend so much more time watching TV and movies than reading books, it's best to meet them on common ground if you want them to learn. Furthermore (the argument goes), since movies motivate students to further inquiry (researching the sinking of the *Titanic* is currently in vogue), their use in the classroom is not only justifiable but highly innovative.   12

Their arguments contradict sound educational philosophy. The purpose of education is to challenge students, not cater to them. Children may prefer cookies and candy, but wise parents still serve fruits and vegetables. The issue should be explored from a broader perspective. To what degree do the apparent short-term gains become long-term liabilities?   13

As time goes by, will students' dependency upon audio-visual learning make it difficult, if not impossible, for them to extract   14 meaning from books alone? In our quest to capture the wayward attention of kids raised on song and dance, do we handicap them instead? It doesn't take much mental acumen to be inspired and even informed by a well-made Hollywood movie. The question is not do movies enhance learning, but rather, are they becoming a substitute for actual learning?

That's not to say movies shouldn't be utilized in the classroom. 15 By all means, use them, but as dessert, not the main course. Incorporate film into the curriculum after the historical subject matter is fully grasped, not before, and only then as part of a broader process of research and analysis. Use films to teach critical thinking, to train students to look for bias, propaganda, commercial exploitation, historical accuracy. Allow students' knowledge of a subject to influence their appreciation of a movie, rather than the reverse.

More to the point, however, require that they read. If one 16 of the goals of education is to foster literacy, it seems counterproductive to assign movies as a supplement to learning when historical fiction may be just as effective. Assigning books like *Les Miserables* or *Gone with the Wind* has the added benefit of broadening students' literary background. Teachers should be providing students with a must-read book list rather than a must-see movie list.

Why should kids read *Les Miserables* when they can see the 17 movie instead? Answer: They probably won't. That's why acquiescing to the "entertain me" style of learning serves little purpose other than to reinforce students' reluctance to read. Movie-watching is one more marshmallow in the sugar-laden diet of popular curricula. We have no one to blame but ourselves if all kids know about history or culture is what they learned from their VCRs. After all, they came to us expecting a song and dance. And we haven't disappointed.

AFTER YOU READ

Work with other students to develop responses to these questions or to compare responses that you have already prepared.

1. State the thesis of the article in your own words. What sentences in the article, if any, best express the idea?
2. This article was originally published in a San Diego newspaper. Who would you say is Minamide's audience? What is the purpose of her essay?
3. Divide the article into sections according to each major point that Minamide makes.

4. Consider the support that Minamide provides. Does she use general-izations or specific statements? Facts or opinions? Explain why you do or do not find her support convincing.

5. Consider your own experience or the experiences of people you know. Do they confirm or contradict Minamide's points?

6. Are there any objections to Minamide's points that you should consider?

Public Universities Should Be Free   AARON BADY

Aaron Bady is a postdoctoral fellow at the University of Texas and formerly a doctoral candidate at the University of California at Berkeley. He is an editor and blogger at The New Inquiry.

BEFORE YOU READ

1. Consider the title. What does it suggest will be the point of this reading selection?

2. Has the money paid for education by you, your family, or people you know affected your education in some way?

Public education should be free. If it isn't free, it isn't public education.   1

This should not be a controversial assertion. This should be   2
common sense. But Americans have forgotten what the "public" in
"public education" actually means (or used to mean). The problem
is that the word no longer has anything to refer to: This country's
public universities have been radically transformed. The change has
happened so slowly and so gradually—bit by bit, cut by cut over
half a century—that it can be seen really only in retrospect. But
with just a small amount of historical perspective, the change is
dramatic: public universities that once charged themselves to open
their doors to all who could benefit by attending—that were, by
definition, the public property of the entire state—have become
something entirely different.

What we still call public universities would be more accurately   3
described as state-controlled private universities—corporate entities that think and behave like businesses. Whereas there once was
a public mission to educate the republic's citizens, there is now the
goal of satisfying the educational needs of the market, aided by PR
departments that brand degrees as commodities and build consumer interest, always with an eye to the bottom line. And while
public universities once sought to advance the industry of the state
as a whole, with an eye to the common good, shortfalls in public

funding have led to universities' treating their research capacity as a source of primary fundraising, developing new technologies and products for the private sector, explicitly to raise the money they need to operate. Conflicts of interest are now commonplace.

Should public universities be free? Only because our public universities have been so fundamentally privatized over the last 40 years does the sentence "Public universities should be free" even make sense. Of course they should be free! If an education is available only to those who can afford it—if an education is a commodity to be purchased in the marketplace—in what sense can it really be called public?   4

Let There Be Light

In the early 1960s, California formulated a master plan for higher education—a single name for a set of interlocking policies developed by University of California president Clark Kerr. The idea was that any Californian who wanted a postsecondary education would have a place to go in the state's three-tiered system. Students could go to a community college for free, and from there they could transfer to a California State University or a University of California—where no tuition was charged, only course fees that were intended to be nominal. New universities were swiftly planned and built to meet the dramatic increase in demand expected from baby boomers and the state's growing population; as more and more citizens aspired to higher education, California opened more and more classrooms and universities to give them that opportunity. The master plan was not a blank check, but it was a commitment: any Californian who wanted a postsecondary education could get one.   5

Today that is simply not true. For one thing, institutions like the University of California have not grown to meet the rising demand; year by year, bit by bit, as the state's population has continued to grow, a larger percentage of California students have been turned away or replaced by out-of-state students (who pay much higher tuition). In fact, university officials are quite explicit about the fact that they are admitting more out-of-state and international students (and fewer Californians) in order to raise money. Historically, about 10 percent of the U.C.'s student population was from out of state, but that number has more than doubled since the 2008 financial crisis. (In Michigan, which has been hit even harder than California, out-of-state enrollment in the University of Michigan system is closer to 40 percent.)   6

Most important, as tuition steadily rises to the level of com-   7
parable private universities, the word "public" comes to mean less
and less. Indeed, when Mark Yudof was appointed president of
the University of California in 2008, he was known as an advocate
of what he had called in 2002 the hybrid university: an institution
that retained some of the characteristics of a public university but
would draw the bulk of its revenue from student tuition.

Yudof's vision of the "public" university would have been unrec-   8
ognizable to the architects of the master plan: instead of providing
the tools for the state's citizens to better themselves, state universities are to survive by thinking like a business, selling their product
for as much as the market will bear. From the point of view of
higher-education consumers—which are what its students have
effectively become—the claim that the U.C. system is public rings
increasingly false with every passing year.

For my parents, by contrast, distinction between public and pri-   9
vate was very clear. Both baby boomers and the first in their families to get college degrees, they went to public universities because
they were affordable and private universities were not. By that
definition, are there any public universities left? Schools that are at
least partially funded and controlled by elected officials, usually at
the state level, are nominally public, and the broad range of universities that are not owned by the government—from nonprofit
corporations like Harvard to explicitly for-profit corporations like
the University of Phoenix or Udacity—truly inhabit the private
sector. But if the price tag is the same, if the product is the same
and if the experience is the same, what difference does a university's tax status make? A university that thinks and behaves like a
private-sector corporation—charging its consumers what the market will bear, cutting costs wherever it can and using competition
with its peers as its measure of success—is a public university in
name only.

Open Roads and Toll Roads

A better way to compare public and private would be to consider   10
the difference between public roads and toll roads. Some toll
roads are owned and operated by state governments and some by
the private sector. But does the driver care who owns the road? I
doubt it; the important thing is whether the road is free and open
to all or whether it can be used only by those who can afford to
drive on it. The same is true of public and private universities: A
university is public only if those who need to use it can do so.

In this sense, it seems to me that the malaise that afflicts our   11
public universities is not really about dollars and cents. If this country can build the world's largest military and fight open-ended
wars in multiple theaters across the globe, it can find a way to pay
for public education, as it once did in living memory. But doing so
has ceased to be a real priority. Affordable public education is no
longer something we expect, demand or take for granted; to argue
that public education should be free makes you sound like an
absurd and unrealistic utopian. Meanwhile, we take it for granted
that roads should be free to drive on, a toll road here or there not
withstanding. You provide the car and the gas; the state provides
the road.

This used to be how we thought about our public universi-   12
ties, before they became exorbitant toll roads. If you had the
grades and the ambition, there was a classroom open to you. But
if every road were a toll road, no one would expect to drive for
free. If every road were a toll road, the very idea that the government would build and maintain a massive system of roads and
highways—and then let anyone use it (for free!)—would seem
fantastical, ridiculous, even perverse. People expecting the right to
drive anywhere they pleased, for free, would be branded utopian,
socialist and deluded, soft-hearted liberals demanding a free lunch.
That's the world we live in when it comes to highways. When the
roads that drive our economy and make modern life possible get
too crowded or too congested, we expect the state to build new
roads. When the old roads wear out, they are repaved. When a
tree or a landslide obstructs a thoroughfare, the state clears the
way. When there are not enough classrooms, on the other hand,
the state no longer builds new universities; it simply charges more.

For most of the 20th century, when the overwhelming major-   13
ity of this country's public universities were built, it was simply
common sense that a growing college-age population had to
be matched by a growing system of accessible higher education,
something that—as everyone agreed—only the government could
provide and that only the government did provide. They were
explicitly chartered to bring a college degree within the reach of
as many citizens as possible and to advance the greater good by
disseminating knowledge as widely as possible. Without that common sense, that bipartisan consensus, our public universities would
never have been built in the first place. And judged by that original
standard, there are few, if any, public universities left.

AFTER YOU READ

Work with other students to develop responses to these questions or to compare responses that you have already prepared.

1. State the thesis of the article in your own words. What sentences in the article, if any, best express the idea?

2. This article was originally published on the Al Jazeera website. (Al Jazeera is an international news organization similar to CNN but based in Qatar.) Who would you say is Bady's audience? What is the purpose of his essay?

3. Divide the article into sections according to each major point that Bady makes.

4. Consider the support that Bady provides. Does he use generalizations or specific statements? Facts or opinions? Explain why you do or do not find his support convincing.

5. Consider your own experience or the experiences of people you know. Do they confirm or contradict the view that public universities are no longer truly public?

6. Are there any objections to Bady's points that you should consider?

WRITING ASSIGNMENT

Choose one of the reading selections from this chapter or a selection assigned by your instructor. After a discussion with other members of your class, determine whether or not you find the reading selection convincing by identifying which points seem particularly weak or particularly strong. Then write a paper in which you evaluate the reading selection. Focus each body paragraph of your paper on a separate point from the article, explaining why it is or is not convincing to you.

EVALUATING SAMPLE PAPERS

As you read and evaluate the following essays, consider these areas.

Evaluation Essay

1. Introduction

Does the introduction accurately and clearly state the central idea and purpose of the article? Does it smoothly and easily move the reader into the paper?

1   2   3   4   5   6

2. Thesis

Does the introduction end in a clear statement of evaluation of the effectiveness of the article?

1   2   3   4   5   6

3. Unity

Does each paragraph have a clear and specific topic sentence that accurately introduces and states an evaluation of one of the main points of the article? Is the material in each paragraph clearly related to its topic sentence?

1   2   3   4   5   6

4. Development

Is each topic sentence supported with clear references to the article as well as to details and examples from the writer's own knowledge and experience? Are references to ideas from the article accurately explained?

1   2   3   4   5   6

5. Coherence

Are transitions used between paragraphs? Where needed, are transitions used between sentences within each paragraph?

1   2   3   4   5   6

6. References to the Text

Are direct quotations and paraphrases correctly introduced and smoothly incorporated into the text? Do they reflect the writer's point accurately?

1   2   3   4   5   6

7. Subordination and Sentence Variety

Do the sentences combine ideas that are related, using coordination, subordination, or verbal or appositive phrases when appropriate? Are there too many brief, choppy main clauses?

1   2   3   4   5   6

8. Grammar and Mechanics

Does the paper contain fragments, comma splices, fused sentences, errors in subject-verb agreement, pronoun use, modifiers, punctuation, or spelling?

1   2   3   4   5   6

9. Overall Ranking of the Essay

1   2   3   4   5   6

Student Essay 1

The reading selection "Why Competition" can be found in Part Four.

In his essay "Why Competition?" Alfie Kohn attacks a trait embedded in the very fabric of American society, competition. By concluding that relationships between both teammates and rivals are undesirable and illustrating the pitfalls competition holds for both individuals and American society, Kohn tries to prove that "competition by its very nature is always unhealthy." Although Kohn uses several strong personal examples to support his claims, the essay contains little substantiated support. However, since Kohn's purpose was "to at least have opened up some provocative, and largely neglected, lines of inquiry," he was successful.

I disagree in part with Kohn's first point which concerns relationships between both teammates and rivals. Kohn believes that the relationships between teammates lack depth and fullness and also observes that rivalry causes the teammates to not only exclude their rivals from "any possible community," but often to regard them with "suspicion and contempt." Kohn supports this two pronged attack with his personal experiences as a camp counselor and also compares teammates to soldiers. After attending scores of high school football games, I cannot disagree with Kohn's observations about rivals, but, as an athlete, I always played on teams with people who were my true friends and not just "comrades."

Kohn's second point is that "the desire to win . . . tends to edge out other goals and values in the context of any given competitive activity." He claims that when people are competing, winning becomes all important, and values fly out the window. His support is another personal experience which consists of his participation on a debate team. Perhaps these "debaters" are just overzealous, or they just take themselves too seriously. When I compete recreationally, whether I'm arguing a point or dribbling a basketball, I'm concerned with having fun first and winning second.

After making it clear that none among us is above behaving competitively, Kohn states his third and most convincing argument, that the cost of competition in human terms is immeasurable. With individual success, says Kohn, comes anxiety. A person's self worth starts becoming conditional. Kohn says, "my . . . values become contingent on how much better I am than so many others in so many activities." With this kind of pressure on us, Kohn continues, we can never be satisfied. Kohn doesn't rely solely on personal experiences to support this argument, but also includes a quote from a psychologist. I agree with this final argument because during my eight years of ballet school, I often felt the envy competition breeds and also found myself measuring my own accomplishments in terms of other, more experienced, dancers.

Although Kohn does bring up some interesting points, his support is mainly from personal experience. The basis of the argument is strong and, with further development, could be pretty convincing. Despite its weaknesses, this essay definitely made me rethink the term "healthy competition."

Student Essay 2

Everyone agrees that children cannot afford to be uneducated. It is simply the means of educating children that provokes a controversy. In the article "History 101: Pass the Popcorn, Please," Elaine Minamide quotes those with opposing views in saying, "Movies give educators the priceless opportunity to connect to young students bored by textbooks." However, Minamide believes that watching contemporary films in class makes students dependent on audio-visual learning instead of books. She points out that students get used to the "song-and-dance" routine from *Sesame Street*. Unlike Minamide, I feel that kids need a more intriguing, interactive approach in order to learn and retain the material. I did not find Minamide's arguments very effective. Watching movies in the classroom is beneficial to the student because it is a more interesting way of presenting the material.

Minamide asks, "As time goes by, will students' dependency upon audio-visual learning make it difficult, if not impossible, for them to extract meaning from books alone?" To answer her question, I would say that's unlikely, but even if it that were the case, the students would still be learning, only in a more interesting fashion. In fact, one of the educational advantages of audio-visual learning is the interest it sparks in students. Most kids can't get an education from dry textbooks and boring lectures. Kids learn in many different ways, so the material must be presented in an interesting fashion. While I was doing an internship in a seventh-grade classroom at Diegueno Junior High School, the students were learning about Chinese dynasties. The teacher divided them into groups that would rotate through five stations. They would watch a movie about the dynasties, research it on the Internet, read from the text, listen to a lecture, and discuss it in groups. The kids ended up enjoying the movie most because it gave them a true sense about the different Chinese dynasties, and it provided a mental picture as well. Another example of audio-visual learning being successful is when my eleventh-grade history class watched *Schindler's List*. We had read about the Holocaust in the textbook, but none of us had a clear picture, and the fragments of the history we had learned were not put together. As we watched the movie, most everyone was in tears, and I must say that I've never seen quite such a reaction from reading a textbook.

Besides the benefit of providing more interesting ways to educate by using movies, the so-called song-and-dance routine, which Minamide thinks will handicap students, is really an effective way to learn. In order to learn the material, the students must enjoy themselves. Did you every wonder why kids in kindergarten have smiles on their faces while many high school students wear frowns? It's because the younger students are intrigued by the teacher's presentation, causing them to learn more. My history teacher sings songs to our class with his guitar. We listen to the lyrics and get lost in true history. As we all look pleasantly at our teacher, we find ourselves experiencing history instead of reading it. We must be involved; it is essential. As Benjamin Franklin put it, "Tell me and I forget. Teach me and I remember. Involve me and I learn."

Minamide writes, "More to the point, require that they read." Unlike the "song-and-dance" routine, reading is only beneficial if you enjoy it. Unless a student has an astounding imagination, he/she probably cannot absorb as much knowledge from textbooks as they would from historical films. When I was in fifth grade, my class was learning about the American presidents. Our class was split into two groups, the "readers" and the "watchers." Half of us reading the textbook, the other half watching a film. The next day, both groups were tested on the material, and the "watchers'" average test scores were double that of the "readers." Need I say more?

I most definitely believe that using audio-visual technology is beneficial to the students. It allows the student to learn from whatever means of education helps them the most. As Minamide quoted her critics, "Films provoke students to not only think about history, but to experience it to the fullest." Maybe students do need to be entertained, but is that such a bad thing? It's human nature to be interested in interesting things. As time goes on, we must move and advance along with it. Why keep students in the past with only reading books when they can learn from so many different methods? Children cannot afford to be uneducated. It is our job to spark their interests, which will soon grow into bright, luminous flames.

Student Essay 3

The following essay evaluates an article titled "Teenagers in Dreamland" by Robert J. Samuelson.

In "Teenagers in Dreamland," Robert J. Samuelson states that children live in a dreamland, curious and disorienting "mixture of adult freedoms and childlike expectations." Children are becoming more and more independent at an earlier age and adult authority is becoming less. He also explains the difference of children's attitudes if they attend private and public schools. Children are also working while they are attending school which causes problems with their schoolwork. Working while going to school makes kids think they are more independent and have more freedom. Society thinks the kids are growing up fine, but statistics show differently. I feel that Samuelson's argument about private schools educating students better than public school is weak; however, I agree with his arguments that students want more responsibility and freedom, and that students have jobs that demand more time than they have to do schoolwork.

I disagree with Samuelson's idea that private schools educate students better than public schools. He states that private schools give 50% more homework and have "rigorous courses in math, English, and history." When I was in high school, I felt that I had the same amount of homework as my friends in private schools. I also feel that they were more rebelling than I was because they had more authority watching over them. Private schools may provide better education for a small group, but Samuelson overlooks the fact that private schools have fewer students so they can focus more on their students. On the other hand, public schools can't limit their attendance so they have to focus on students with more needs. I feel that if I went to a private school, I would have turned out totally different. I think I would be more rebelling and not willing to go to college.

Samuelson states that children are growing up too soon. For example, they want to own their own cars and want to have more freedom to do what they please and do it when they want. Students move out of their parent's houses earlier than when their parents were their age. I see youths getting married really young and depending on others for support. When I was a high school student, I saw pregnancy within the high school population. Most of the girls were just about to finish high school and now they have a long road ahead of them. For example, one of my friends is 17 and pregnant. Her boyfriend is 25 and they thought they had all this freedom to do what they wanted. Now he is going off to Okinawa, and she will have to depend on others to help take care of the child. This is a case of a young woman growing up too fast.

Students are running into the dilemma of going to school and having a job. They feel that the only way to get freedom is to have a job. I had a job when I was going to high school, and it took away time from my schoolwork. It was hard to budget my time so I had time for schoolwork and still be able to spend time with my friends. My job was demanding more of my time from my friends and schoolwork. I liked the money because I was able to buy what I wanted, but my grades were bad.

I feel that Samuelson has a strong point that when children work while they are going to school, it takes away from their education. I also agree that children are growing up too soon. They want to be adults while in some ways they want to be kids. However, I disagree that private schools are better than public schools because he has not concerned the size of the populations in the school.

SENTENCE COMBINING: PARALLELISM

You were introduced to the concept of parallelism in Chapter 2 when you used coordination to combine sentences. At that time, you learned that ideas joined with coordinating conjunctions should be worded similarly. For example, two words joined with a coordinating conjunction, such as *and*, should both be nouns, or both adjectives, or both adverbs—the point is that they should both be the same type of word.

The same is true of two phrases or clauses joined with a coordinating conjunction. You can join two prepositional phrases or two participial phrases with a coordinating conjunction, but you should not join a prepositional phrase to a participial phrase with one.

ITEMS IN A SERIES

When you write three or more ideas in a series, you should word them similarly, just as you do when you join two ideas with a coordinating conjunction. The key is to use similar types of words, phrases, or clauses as you write the series. *The principle of parallelism requires that you use similar grammatical constructions when you join two ideas with coordinating conjunctions or when you join several ideas in a series.*

The following sentences are drawn from the reading selections in this text. Note that each sentence uses parallel sentence structure.

Parallel Words

NOUNS

Our culture stresses <u>freedom</u>, <u>individuality</u>, and <u>choice</u>.

ADJECTIVES, NOUNS

But it will be <u>easier</u> and <u>happier</u> for us knowing that our grandson will be spared the continued <u>explanation</u> and <u>harassment</u>, the <u>doubts</u> and <u>anxieties</u>, of being a child of unmarried parents.

Parallel Phrases

INFINITIVES

To be a hero you have <u>to stand out</u>, <u>to excel</u>, <u>to take risks</u>....

VERB PHRASES

Like millions of Americans, the cabdriver was probably a decent human being who had never <u>stolen anything</u>, <u>broken any law</u>, or <u>willfully injured another</u>....

PARTICIPIAL PHRASES

The only reason debaters sacrifice their free time <u>collecting thousands of pieces of evidence</u>, <u>analyzing arguments</u>, and <u>practicing speeches</u>, is to win.

Parallel Clauses

SUBORDINATE CLAUSES	A fellow commits a crime <u>because he's basically insecure,</u> <u>because he hated his stepmother at nine,</u> or <u>because his sister needs an operation.</u>
MAIN CLAUSES	<u>Strategy is planned for the next battle;</u> <u>troops are taught the next cheer.</u>

As you can see from the above examples, you can use parallelism to join all kinds of sentence parts, as long as they are the same type of sentence part. You can join nouns to nouns, infinitives to infinitives, and subordinate clauses to subordinate clauses.

ITEMS JOINED BY CORRELATIVE CONJUNCTIONS

Correlative conjunctions are pairs of words that combine related ideas. The most common correlative conjunctions are *either . . . or, neither . . . nor, not only . . . but also,* and *both . . . and.* Follow the principles of parallel sentence structure when you use these correlatives. Each word, phrase, or clause joined to another by a correlative conjunction should be worded similarly to the other. The following examples illustrate both correct and incorrect usage.

INCORRECT

The timber wolf will **either** <u>adapt to its new environment</u> **or** <u>it will die a slow death.</u> (verb phrase combined with main clause)

CORRECT

The timber wolf will **either** <u>adapt to its new environment</u> **or** <u>die a slow death.</u> (verb phrase combined with verb phrase)

CORRECT

Either the timber wolf will adapt to its new environment **or** it will die a slow death. (main clause combined with main clause)

EXERCISE **6.4**

Use parallel sentence structure to combine each group of sentences into one sentence.

EXAMPLE

Chelsea was startled by the sudden applause. She was also confused by the bright lights. She stuttered a few words. Then she ran from the stage.

> Startled by the sudden applause and confused by the bright lights, Chelsea stuttered a few words and then ran from the stage.

1. Edmonia Lewis was an American sculptor. She worked for most of her career in Rome. She gained fame and recognition in the international arts world as a sculptor utilizing the neoclassical style.

2. Lewis was praised as the first professional African American and Native American sculptor. Edmonia Lewis had little training. She overcame numerous obstacles to become a revered and respected artist.

3. She was born on July 4, 1844, in Greenbush, New York. However, she was often evasive when it came to personal details. Lewis mentioned varying years of birth throughout out her life.

4. Lewis was the daughter of an African American father and a part-Ojibwa (Chippewa) mother. She was orphaned at an early age. She was raised by some of her mother's relatives.

5. Lewis grew up with a band of Chippewa Indians. They lived near Niagara Falls. They made baskets, moccasins, and blouses. They sold them as souvenirs to tourists.

6. She was supported by her older brother. He also encouraged her. She enrolled in Oberlin College in Ohio. It was one of the first colleges in the United States to admit African Americans. It also admitted Native Americans. It admitted women of all colors.

7. Oberlin is where Lewis began her art studies. It is also where she struggled with her dual African American and Native American heritage. She encountered much prejudice and violence. She eventually settled for a mostly African American identity.

8. Lewis left for Boston. She befriended abolitionist William Lloyd Garrison. She met sculptor Edward A. Brackett. Brackett taught Lewis sculpture. Brackett also helped her set up her own studio.

9. By the early 1860s, her small measure of commercial success gave her the opportunity to further refine her artistic skills. It allowed her to move to Rome, Italy. She was able to develop her skill sculpting in marble. She focused on themes and images relating to African American and Native American subjects.

10. One highlight of her career was her participation in the 1876 Centennial Exposition in Philadelphia, for which she created a 3,015-pound marble sculpture, *The Death of Cleopatra*. Another highlight of her career was the commission of a portrait by former U.S. President Ulysses S. Grant in 1877, who sat for her as a model. He was very pleased with her finished piece.

11. In the late 1880s, the neoclassical genre became less popular. Lewis's popularity declined. She was lost to history, so much so that only recently, scholars established that by 1901 she had moved to the Hammersmith area of London. They also established that she died on September 17, 1907, in the Hammersmith Borough Infirmary from chronic Bright's disease.

EXERCISE 6.5

Revise the following sentences to correct any errors in parallelism.

EXAMPLE

The farmer knew that for the rest of his life he would be planting seeds, his crops needed tending, and prayers for a good harvest.

The farmer knew that for the rest of his life he would be planting seeds, tending his crops, and praying for a good harvest.

1. History has recorded many changes initiated by Columbus's travels to the Americas, such as the devastating impact of European diseases on indigenous populations, the gold and silver imported to Europe, and that many settlers were part of the immigration from Europe.

2. An often overlooked impact of the so-called Columbian exchange has been the number of foods introduced to Europe from the Americas, such as potatoes, maize (or corn), peanuts, tomatoes, and people in Europe started to grow beans.

3. It is impossible today to imagine Italy without tomatoes, many countries in Africa without peanuts, or that Germans and Russians wouldn't eat potatoes, but such was the case before the Columbian exchange.

4. A report by the United Nations has shown that rice, maize, potatoes, and the farming of wheat are the most important staple foods globally.

5. However, because these staples were often grown by poor people first, it is difficult to establish when people in Africa, Asia, or Europe started either to cultivate maize or potatoes were first grown.

6. Why did farmers start growing crops that were unfamiliar to them, tasted different from what they knew, and cooking them needed different techniques as well?

7. One reason is that potatoes not only produce about four times the calories per acre compared to wheat but also planting them on fallow fields is possible.

8. Maize, too, produces more calories than either rye or than wheat produces.

9. In short, the introduction of crops from the Americas, especially potatoes, led to rapid population growth in northern Europe, the number of famines was reduced, and easier storage was allowed for.

EXERCISE 6.6

Use parallel sentence structure to combine each group of sentences into one sentence.

1. Mark Twain, one of America's greatest writers, grew up in Hannibal, Missouri. Then he spent several years as a riverboat pilot on the Mississippi. Later he worked on newspapers in Nevada and California.

2. His literary career took him from the shores of the Mississippi. He traveled to the silver-mining boomtowns of Nevada. He lectured in the literary salons of Boston.

3. He was born Samuel Clemens, but he used many pseudonyms. One that he used was Thomas Jefferson Snodgrass. He also wrote as W. Epaminandos Adrastus Blab. Another was Sergeant Fathom. He finally settled on Mark Twain.

4. In Hannibal, Missouri, Twain was surrounded by the soft drawls of Virginia transplants. He also listened to the hard twangs of immigrants from Arkansas. There were many other accents that he heard.

5. As a boy, Mark Twain would love to load his pockets with small knives and his favorite marbles. His pockets would hold extra fishhooks and string. He would even carry toads in them. Later in life he was always interested in what people had in their pockets.

6. In Hannibal, Samuel Clemens would listen intently to ghost stories. He also would listen to Bible narratives. Adults would tell tall tales that he enjoyed hearing. Then he would retell them to his friends.

7. Both Mark Twain and Tom Sawyer, his famous literary double, cut school to play with friends. They sneaked out of the house at night to roam the streets of his town. They both played practical jokes on parents and siblings.

8. Mark Twain's clear, economical style is one of his strengths. So is his ability to reproduce the informal sounds of ordinary American speech. His unique sense of humor is also a strength. These are the chief characteristics of works like *The Adventures of Huckleberry Finn*.

9. Twain would edit his work ruthlessly. He would rework passages. He would change wording He would cut out entire sections if they didn't add to the story or the humor.

10. In the later years of his life, Twain experienced bankruptcy. He also suffered through the death of his favorite daughter. He also faced illness and death of his wife.

EXERCISE 6.7

Combine the following sentences, using coordination, subordination, verbal phrases, appositives, and parallel sentence structure where appropriate.

1. Urban legends are humorous, embarrassing, strange, or horrific stories.
   The stories are about ordinary people and places.
   They are told as if they are true events.
   They are told as if they recently happened.

2. They often contain names of familiar places.
   These names further confirm the validity of the story.
   With the aid of email and the Internet, these stories spread quickly.

3. One such urban legend involves the discovery of skeletons.
   This legend started in 2002.
   The skeletons were of a race of giants.
   These giants existed in Saudi Arabia during biblical times.

4. Emails showed photos of skeletons.

They were being unearthed by the Aramco gas exploration team.
The emails reported that the military had immediately sealed off the area.

5. The photographs of the giant skeletons actually came from a Photoshop contest.

The contest was run by the site Worth1000.com in 2002.
Those photographs were added to a completely different photograph.
It was of a Cornell University excavation of a mastodon skeleton.

6. Other common urban legends are located closer to home.

There is the one about the boy being bitten by a poisonous snake.
He was playing in the plastic ball pit in a local Carl's Jr.

7. A current urban legend comes as an email.

It warns that women are being killed by terrorists.
The terrorists are sending poisonous perfume samples through the mail.

8. The "poisoned perfume" urban legend appeared in 2002.

That was shortly after Dillard's department store issued a press release.
The press release said its December mailings would include a sample.
The sample would be of perfume-scented powder.

9. Not every strange story is an urban legend.

The one about Mike demonstrates that.
Mike was a chicken.
It lived for eighteen months without a head.

10. You can learn more about Mike, the headless chicken.

Conduct a Google search.
Then decide for yourself whether the story is true or an urban legend.

The Small Society. © *King features syndicate.*

Synthesizing Ideas from Reading Selections

7

One of the goals of a college education is to learn to search out new ideas and to consider those that are different from our own. After all, we really can't claim to be educated about an issue if we know only one side of it. Many college assignments will ask you to discuss or explain the various issues involved in a particular topic. A philosophy instructor, for example, might ask you to explain the concept of love as it is developed by a number of philosophers; a health instructor might ask you to discuss different theories about the best way to prevent high cholesterol; and a political science instructor might ask you to write about the arguments involved in the debate over the powers delegated to the Department of Homeland Security.

People who are able to consider ideas from a number of sources, to see the relationships among those ideas, and to pull those ideas together into one coherent whole possess a valuable skill. They are the people who will be able to consider all sides of an issue and then reach reasonable, considered judgments about how they should vote, where they should work, or why they should accept one idea rather than another. They are also the people who will not oversimplify a complex issue, who will recognize that sometimes there is no one "correct" answer but merely one alternative that is only slightly better than other possible alternatives.

A **synthesis** is a paper or report that pulls together related ideas. In one sense, a synthesis is similar to a summary in that both papers require careful reading and accurate reporting. However, writing a synthesis is often more difficult than writing a summary because a synthesis requires that you read a number of sources, identify the related ideas, and then explain how those ideas are related. Sometimes several sources on the same topic will discuss very different points yet reach the same conclusion, and your synthesis will need to reflect that. Sometimes related sources will discuss the same points but reach quite different conclusions. And sometimes sources will simply repeat ideas you have already read in other sources.

PREPARING YOUR SOURCES AND NOTES

CLARIFY YOUR PURPOSE

The first step in writing a synthesis is to make sure you understand what you are and are not being asked to do. As you prepare this paper, think of yourself as a teacher. Your job is to educate those who read your paper about the issue at hand—*not to convince them to hold a particular opinion about it.* In other words, in this paper you will explain all sides of the issue, but you will *not* take a stand on the issue. (You will do that in Chapter 8.)

READ AND HIGHLIGHT YOUR SOURCES

Active, careful reading is very important when you write a synthesis. Read your source material with a pen, pencil, or highlighter in hand. Mark whatever seems like it might be important even on your first reading of the article. You can decide later whether you want to use everything you have marked.

TAKE NOTES

- Use a separate sheet of paper for each source.
- Write the title or author's name at the top of the page to keep each set of notes clearly separate from the others.
- Now start rereading the places you marked in the article, briefly summarizing or paraphrasing those ideas on your sheet of paper.
- Write the page number next to each note.
- If you write a direct quotation, be sure to place it within quotation marks.
- In addition to important ideas, make a note of any striking examples, statistics, or facts.

ORGANIZING YOUR MATERIAL

GROUP RELATED IDEAS

Once you have listed the ideas that each writer discusses, look for the relationships among those ideas. Take time with this step. Deciding which ideas are related requires careful reading.

Sometimes the relationships are easy to see. For instance, let's say you have read articles discussing the potential effects of television on its viewers. (Two reading selections on the effects of television appear in Part Four.) While reading the articles, you will have noticed that several of them are concerned with television's ability to educate. You might group those ideas under the heading "Is Television Educational?"

As you continue to read your notes, you might observe that some writers discuss the idea that television affects our character, influencing who we are or how we act. You might group those ideas under the heading "Does Television Make Us Better People?"

As you continue to group ideas, you might find it difficult to decide which ideas should be grouped. Perhaps some ideas seem only somewhat related to others. In such cases you will have to decide whether or not to group them. You might also discover that one article discusses an important idea that is not discussed anywhere else. In such a case, create a separate category for that idea. You may or may not decide to use it in your synthesis.

Finally, you will probably discover that you need to go back and reread parts of some of the articles. Perhaps you remember that one of them discussed the educational value of television even though you had not made a note of it. Now is the time to quickly reread the article to find that idea.

Below is a sample grouping of ideas from four reading selections, one of which is in Part Four. Notice that the entries have been divided into columns to keep opposing ideas clearly separated. Also notice that each entry includes the author's last name in parentheses.

Is Television Educational?

Yes	No
• TV can provide learning. (Henry)	• TV cannot provide the time needed to learn. (Robinson)
• Children learn alphabet from *Sesame Street*. (Henry)	• Learning requires time to absorb facts. It requires reading. (Robinson)
• High school students learn about toxic waste on beaches. (Henry)	• A documentary about Marin County cannot really be accurate because it does not have the time to cover the complexities of life there. (Robinson)
• A study by psychologist Daniel Anderson says children learn to think and draw inferences as they watch TV. (Drexler)	• Educational TV is the worst kind—it makes people think they know something when they really don't. (Robinson)
• Same study—TV does not replace reading; it replaces other recreational activities. (Drexler)	
• Same study—TV watching does not lower IQ, although people with lower IQ do tend to watch more TV. (Drexler)	

Does Television Make Us Better People?

Yes

- TV's characters embody human truths.

  (Henry)

- They epitomize what we feel about ourselves.

  (Henry)

- They teach behavior and values. The character of Mary Richards summed up the lives of a whole generation of women.

  (Henry)

- Without TV we might be less violent, have more respect for institutions, be healthier, but we also might be less alert, less informed, less concerned about world matters, lonelier.

  (Henry)

No

- Opinion of psychologist Daniel Anderson—The violence, sexism, and materialism on TV are having a major social impact on our children.

  (Drexler)

- TV is often used as a form of escapism.

  (Drexler)

- TV causes confusion between reality and illusion.

  (Woolfolk Cross)

Is Television Valuable as Entertainment?

Yes

- TV is very good at entertaining. Jack Benny and Art Carney would not be nearly as funny in print. You need to see them and watch their timing.

  (Robinson)

- A study by psychologist Daniel Anderson says when parents and kids watch together, kids tend to think about what they see.

  (Drexler)

No

- Many times watching TV is a default activity because there is nothing else to do.

  (Woolfolk Cross)

- TV entertainment mesmerizes viewers. Kids prefer videos to real life.

  (Woolfolk Cross)

- Boys on raft were disappointed because it was more fun on TV.

  (Woolfolk Cross)

- Children preferred to watch a video of a fight rather than the real thing.

  (Woolfolk Cross)

- UPI reported children watching TV next to the corpse of their dead father.

  (Woolfolk Cross)

- Former DA Mario Merola says a jury wants the drama of TV and is less likely to convict if it doesn't get it.

  (Woolfolk Cross)

- In a Univ. of Nebraska study, over half of children chose TV over their fathers.

  (Woolfolk Cross)

DEVELOP A ROUGH OUTLINE OF THE ISSUES

Now that you have divided your notes into separate groups, arrange them in an order that will help your readers understand the issue. You will probably devote one paragraph to each group, but which group should you present first? Does the reader need to understand one particular idea first? Does one idea lead to another, suggesting it should be placed before the other one? Does one idea seem more significant than the others? These are all questions you should consider as you experiment with different possible paragraph arrangements.

Try writing out a few rough outlines—nothing formal, just some possible paragraph arrangements. Choose the one that seems to present your ideas in the most understandable order.

WRITING THE DRAFT

WRITE A PRELIMINARY THESIS STATEMENT

You have been developing thesis statements the entire semester, so this step will seem obvious to you by now. Your thesis states the central idea of your paper and should appear as the last sentence of your introductory paragraph. But what is the central idea of a synthesis? Your papers up to this point have asserted your own ideas about your life, experiences, or reading. The synthesis paper, however, asks you *not* to assert your opinions but to report on the ideas and opinions of others.

Let's consider the discussion about the effects of television. A reading of several articles on the topic might result in the following rough outline:

- the educational value of television
- the entertainment value of television
- the social or behavioral value of television

Although there are many ways to write a successful thesis for such a paper, two common techniques are the **open thesis** and the **closed thesis**. The open thesis makes it clear to the reader that the paper will explain the issues, but it does not list them. The closed thesis, on the other hand, lists the material to be covered in the order that it will be covered.

OPEN THESIS

Although most would agree that television has had a profound effect on many of its viewers, there is little agreement about whether that effect has been for the better or the worse.

CLOSED THESIS

In the debate over the effects of television on its viewers, three particularly interesting questions involve television's ability to educate its audience, its value as a source of entertainment, and its effects upon our behavior.

Which type of thesis should you use? They both have advantages. The open thesis is more concise and does not lock you into a specific organization. The closed thesis clearly forecasts the direction of the paper, a clarity that you might prefer. (If you write a closed thesis, be sure to present the points in the body of your paper in the same order that they appear in the thesis.)

WRITE THE FIRST DRAFT

As with most first drafts, you want to get your ideas onto paper without worrying too much about how well you have written them. So try to *write* as much as possible at this point, not *correct*. (You can correct and improve later.)

Perhaps the most difficult task of writing a synthesis is to present the ideas in your own words, not as a list of quotations. Use the skills of paraphrasing and summarizing (discussed in Chapter 5 as well as in the Appendix) as you write each paragraph. Remember that your purpose is to explain the issues, not to argue one way or the other.

DOCUMENTING YOUR SOURCES

Whenever you use someone else's words or ideas in your writing, you must let the reader know the source of those words or ideas. It doesn't matter whether you have paraphrased, summarized, or quoted—in each case, you must let the reader know whose material you are using.

Up to this point, your writing assignments have focused on one reading selection at a time. In them you have used simple transitions to tell the reader when you were using material from the reading selection. (See Chapter 5 as well as the Appendix for a discussion of transitions with paraphrases, summaries, and quotations.) There are, however, more formal methods of documentation that you will need to learn to use as you write in college classes.

The two most common methods of documentation are the MLA (Modern Language Association) method, used primarily in the humanities, and the APA (American Psychological Association) method, used mostly in the social sciences. Both methods use parentheses within the paper to identify the author and page number of a particular passage that is paraphrased, summarized, or quoted. They also use a separate page at the end of the paper to give more detailed and complete identification of the sources used. In most classes, your instructor will tell you which method to use and will suggest a documentation guide that you should purchase.

Because this text includes its own reading selections, you do not need to write a separate page (called a Works Cited page) that gives detailed identification about the sources you use. However, the papers you write for Chapters 7 and 8 will be clearer if you learn to use parentheses to identify the particular article you are referring to at any given time. Use these guidelines to help you:

- Each paraphrase, summary, and quotation should be identified by author and page number in parentheses. Do not use the author's first name within the parentheses.

According to one writer, "Educational TV corrupts the very notion of education and renders its victims uneducable" (Robinson 432).

In defense of television, another writer claims that many schoolchildren learn the alphabet from *Sesame Street* and that high school students learn about the problems that our planet faces (Henry 428).

- If the author's name is already included in the transition, it does not need to be repeated in the parentheses.

According to Paul Robinson, "Educational TV corrupts the very notion of education and renders its victims uneducable" (432).

In defense of television, William Henry III claims that many schoolchildren learn the alphabet from *Sesame Street* and that high school students learn about the problems that our planet faces (428).

- When your source quotes or paraphrases someone else and you want to use that material, indicate it by using "qtd. in" as is done in the following example. (Here the quotation of Daniel Anderson comes from an article by Madeline Drexler.)

According to Daniel Anderson, a psychologist at the University of Massachusetts at Amherst, children watching TV "muse upon the meaning of what they see, its plausibility and its implications for the future—whether they've tuned in to a news report of a natural disaster or an action show" (qtd. in Drexler 437).

- No punctuation is placed between the author's last name and the page number (see above examples).
- The parenthetical citation is placed at the end of the borrowed material but before the period at the end of the sentence (see above examples).

Note

Further instruction in the use of MLA parenthetical documentation as well as in the writing of a Works Cited page (if your instructor requires one) can be found in the Appendix.

REVISING AND REFINING THE SYNTHESIS

As with all papers, the difference between the average and the superior essay is often determined by the time and effort put into the revising and refining of it. Consider these suggestions as you revise.

REFINE THE THESIS STATEMENT

Once the first draft is finished, reread your thesis. Does it still accurately introduce what you have written? Would a rewriting of the thesis improve it?

ADD OR REFINE TOPIC SENTENCES

As you know, each paragraph in an academic essay should open with a clear topic sentence. Do your topic sentences clearly introduce the topic of each paragraph? Do they contain transitions that move them smoothly away from the topic of the preceding paragraph?

RETHINK WEAK PARAGRAPHS

Do any of your paragraphs seem weak to you? Perhaps one is much shorter than the others. The ideas in that paragraph might need more explanation. Consider rereading the sections of the articles that discuss the ideas in that paragraph and adding more explanation to it. Or perhaps the ideas in that paragraph should be grouped within another paragraph.

Does any paragraph read as if it jerks along from one confusing idea to the next? Consider taking out a new sheet of paper and completely rethinking it. Sometimes you need to rewrite a rough paragraph from start to finish.

PROOFREAD FOR ERRORS IN GRAMMAR, SPELLING, AND PUNCTUATION

Use but do not rely only on grammar and spelling checkers. Consider having someone whose judgment you trust read your final draft. Many colleges have free tutors available to students. Make use of them.

READINGS: PHYSICIAN-ASSISTED SUICIDE

BEFORE YOU READ

1. Should physician-assisted suicide be permitted? Why or why not?
2. Make a list of reasons you would expect to hear both for permitting physician-assisted suicide and for prohibiting it.

In Defense of Voluntary Euthanasia   SIDNEY HOOK

Sidney Hook (1902–1989) was considered by many to be one of America's most controversial public philosophers. Beginning his career as the first American scholar of Marxism, a leading disciple of John Dewey, and an early supporter of Soviet Communism, Hook eventually renounced Marxism and came to be one of the most vehement supporters of the Cold War. An outspoken participant in many of the principal political debates of this century, he was best known for his vigorous defense of political and academic freedom and his stand against totalitarianism in all forms. The following essay was published in The New York Times *in 1987.*

A few short years ago, I lay at the point of death. A congestive heart failure was treated for diagnostic purposes by an angiogram that triggered a stroke. Violent and painful hiccups, uninterrupted for several days and nights, prevented the ingestion of food. My left   1 side and one of my vocal cords became paralyzed. Some form of pleurisy set in, and I felt I was drowning in a sea of slime. At one point, my heart stopped beating; just as I lost consciousness, it was thumped back into action again. In one of my lucid intervals during those days of agony, I asked my physician to discontinue all life-supporting services or show me how to do it. He refused and told me that someday I would appreciate the unwisdom of my request.

A month later, I was discharged from the hospital. In six   2
months, I regained the use of my limbs, and although my voice still lacks its old resonance and carrying power I no longer croak like a frog. There remain some minor disabilities and I am restricted to a rigorous, low sodium diet. I have resumed my writing and research.

My experience can be and has been cited as an argument   3
against honoring requests of stricken patients to be gently eased out of their pain and life. I cannot agree. There are two main reasons. As an octogenarian, there is a reasonable likelihood that I may suffer another "cardiovascular accident" or worse. I may not even be in a position to ask for the surcease of pain. It seems to me that I have already paid my dues to death—indeed, although time has softened my memories, they are vivid enough to justify my saying that I suffered enough to warrant dying several times over. Why run the risk of more?

Secondly, I dread imposing on my family and friends another   4
grim round of misery similar to the one my first attack occasioned.

My wife and children endured enough for one lifetime. I know   5
that for them the long days and nights of waiting, the disruption of their professional duties and their own familial responsibilities counted for nothing in their anxiety for me. In their joy at my recovery they have been forgotten. Nonetheless, to visit another prolonged spell of helpless suffering on them as my life ebbs away, or even worse, if I linger on into a comatose senility, seems altogether gratuitous.

But what, it may be asked, of the joy and satisfaction of living,   6
of basking in the sunlight, listening to music, watching one's grandchildren growing into adolescence, following the news about the fate of freedom in a troubled world, playing with ideas, writing one's testament of wisdom and folly for posterity? Is not all that one endured, together with the risk of its recurrence, an acceptable price for the multiple satisfactions that are still open even to a person of advanced years?

Apparently those who cling to life, no matter what, think so. I   7
do not.

The zest and intensity of these experiences are no longer   8
what they used to be. I am not vain enough to delude myself
that I can in the few remaining years make an important discovery useful for mankind or can lead a social movement or do
anything that will be historically eventful, no less event-making.
My autobiography, which describes a record of intellectual and
political experiences of some historical value, already much too
long, could be posthumously published. I have had my fill of joys
and sorrows and am not greedy for more life. I have always
thought that a test of whether one had found happiness in
one's life is whether one would be willing to relive it—whether,
if it were possible, one would accept the opportunity to be
born again.

Having lived a full and relatively happy life, I would cheerfully   9
accept the chance to be reborn, but certainly not to be reborn
again as an infirm octogenarian. To some extent, my views reflect
what I have seen happen to the aged and stricken who have been
so unfortunate as to survive crippling paralysis. They suffer, and
impose suffering on others, unable even to make a request that
their torment be ended.

I am mindful too of the burdens placed upon the community,   10
with its rapidly diminishing resources, to provide the adequate and
costly services necessary to sustain the lives of those whose days
and nights are spent on mattress graves of pain. A better use could
be made of these resources to increase the opportunities and
qualities of life for the young. I am not denying the moral obligation
the community has to look after its disabled and aged. There are
times, however, when an individual may find it pointless to insist on
the fulfillment of a legal and moral right.

What is required is no great revolution in morals but an   11
enlargement of imagination and an intelligent evaluation of alternative uses of community resources.

Long ago, Seneca observed that "the wise man will live as long   12
as he ought, not as long as he can." One can envisage hypotheti-
cal circumstances in which one has a duty to prolong one's life
despite its costs for the sake of others, but such circumstances are
far removed from the ordinary prospects we are considering. If
wisdom is rooted in the knowledge of the alternatives of choice,
it must be reliably informed of the state one is in and its likely
outcome. Scientific medicine is not infallible, but it is the best we
have. Should a rational person be willing to endure acute suffering
merely on the chance that a miraculous cure might presently be

at hand? Each one should be permitted to make his own choice—especially when no one else is harmed by it.

The responsibility for the decision, whether deemed wise or   13
foolish, must be with the chooser.

Promoting a Culture of Abandonment   TERESA R. WAGNER

Teresa Wagner is an attorney who is employed in the library at the University of Iowa College of Law. She specializes in human rights and right-to-life issues and has been affiliated with the Family Research Council, a Washington-based organization with the following mission statement: "The Family Research Council champions marriage and family as the foundation of civilization, the seedbed of virtue, and the wellspring of society. We shape public debate and formulate public policy that values human life and upholds the institutions of marriage and the family. Believing that God is the author of life, liberty, and the family, we promote the Judeo-Christian worldview as the basis for a just, free, and stable society."

The death toll in Oregon will really begin to rise now. Attorney   1
General Janet Reno has decided that a federal law regulating drug
usage (the Controlled Substances Act) somehow does not apply
to the use of lethal drugs in Oregon, the only state in the country
to legalize assisted suicide. The evidence will begin pouring in on
how deadly assisted suicide can be, not just for the individuals subject to it, of course, but for the culture that countenances it.

There are frightening and compelling policy reasons to oppose   2
assisted suicide. Foremost is the risk of abuse. Proponents of
assisted suicide always insist that the practice will be carefully limited: It will be available, they claim, only for those who request it
and only for those who are dying anyway (the terminally ill).

Such limitations are virtually impossible. People will inevitably   3
be killed without knowing or consenting to it. Several state courts
have already ruled as a matter of state constitutional law that any
rights given to competent patients (those who can request death)
must also be given to incompetent ones (those who cannot). Third
parties make treatment decisions for this latter group. Now legal,
assisted suicide will be just another treatment option for surrogate
decision makers to select, even if the patient has made no indication of wanting to die.

What's more, the cost crunch in medicine virtually guarantees   4
that hospitals and doctors will eventually pressure, and then coerce,
patients to avail themselves of this easy and cheap alternative.

Similarly, the confinement of this right to the terminally ill is   5
impossible. As many groups opposing assisted suicide have noted,
the term itself is hardly clear. The Oregon law defines terminal
disease as that which will produce death within six months. Is that
with or without medical treatment? Many individuals will die in
much less than six months without very simple medical treatment
(insulin injections, for example). They could be deemed terminal
under this law and qualify for this new right to death.

More importantly, the rationale for providing this new right   6
almost demands its extension beyond limits. After all, if we are
trying to relieve pain and suffering, the non-terminal patient, who
faces years of discomfort, has a more compelling claim to relief
than the terminal patient, whose hardship is supposed to be short-
lived. Courts will quickly recognize this and dispense with any terminal requirement.

So much for limits.   7

The tragedy, of course, is that we have the ability right now to   8
relieve the suffering of those in even the most excruciating pain.
Anesthesiologists and others in pain centers around the country
claim that we can provide adequate palliation 99 percent of the time.

Unfortunately, certain obstacles prevent patients from getting   9
the pain relief they need: Many in medicine fear, mistakenly, that
patients will become addicted to analgesic medications; overzealous regulatory agencies penalize doctors who prescribe the large
doses needed (or they penalize the pharmacies that stock them);
and medical professionals generally are not trained adequately in
pain and symptom management.

The more important reasons to oppose assisted suicide, how-   10
ever, are moral: We must decide what type of people we are and
how we will care for the weak and sick among us, for it is only to
these dependents, not to all individuals, that we are offering this
new right. Is this because we respect their autonomy (allegedly the
basis of the right to die) more than our own? Or do we unconsciously (or consciously) believe their lives are of less worth and
therefore less entitled to make demands of care (not to mention
money) on us?

Make no mistake: Despite incessant clamor about rights, ours is   11
actually a culture of abandonment. The acceptance of assisted suicide and euthanasia in this culture is almost inevitable. Abortion, of
course, was the foundation. It taught (and still teaches) society to
abandon mothers, and mothers to abandon their children. Divorce
(husbands and wives leaving or abandoning each other) sends the

same message. The commitment to care for others, both those who have been given to us and those we have selected, no longer exists. We simply do not tolerate those we do not want.

What to do about the advance of this culture? Replace it with a culture of care, a culture of commitment.   12

This is obviously no easy task, for it is neither easy to administer care nor easy to receive it. (Indeed, the elderly cite the fear of dependence most often when indicating why they might support assisted suicide.) But it is precisely within this context of care, of giving and receiving, that we enjoy the dignity particular to human beings. Otherwise we would simply shoot the terminal patient as we do the dying horse.   13

The assisted suicide question is really the battle between these two cultures. We can follow the way of Jack Kevorkian or of Mother Teresa. The life of Mother Teresa was a witness to nothing if not to commitment and care. She was simply there to care for the sick and the old, to assure them of their worth. Jack Kevorkian and our culture of abandonment, epitomized by assisted suicide and all the abuses to follow, surely will not.   14

The Right to Choose Death   KENNETH SWIFT

In the following selection from the June 25, 2005, issue of the Los Angeles Times, *Kenneth Swift argues in support of California's proposed Assembly Bill 654, which "is intended to expand the range of care for dying patients to 'include choices for those relatively few whose suffering is extreme and cannot be palliated despite the best efforts.'" The bill failed to get through the Assembly.*

We were finally able to bring our little girl home, a joyful event that seemed unlikely just a short time before. She had developed an infection that turned out to be quite virulent, threatening her internal organs and, potentially, her life. After weeks of hospitalization, including a few days when her prognosis was particularly grim, she showed the same resolve and fortitude that had often been on display throughout her 14 years of life. With the help of a wonderful staff of doctors and a state-of-the-art facility, she beat the odds, overcame her affliction, and our family is whole once again.   1

I can't say that I am afraid of death, but I do find the prospect of dying quite frightening, especially for loved ones like my Megan. Actually, when living turns into dying, when the quality of life becomes instead a daily struggle with pain and hopelessness, death can be a relief.   2

There were a few days when we wondered if Megan had 3
crossed that invisible line between living and dying and whether
we would be strong enough to help her find that relief. During her
hospital stay, we saw others who had confronted the same issue,
their decision easily discerned by the puffy eyes, glistening cheeks
and empty collar in their hands, leash still attached.

Yes, Megan is a dog, though for my wife and me, that is a fact 4
relevant only for health insurance purposes (she is not covered).
Although she does not qualify as our legal dependent, she more
than qualifies as a full-fledged, loved and loving member of our
family. Yet, being "just a dog" and therefore no more than property
under the law, she is afforded a right denied to most of her fellow
mammalians of the bipedal variety: the right to die with dignity,
spared of pain and suffering if that should be her fate.

Only residents of Oregon are able to exercise a similar right. 5
However, a bill in the Assembly, AB 654, would provide the same
right to Californians that Oregonians have had since 1998.

This is not the first time that assisted suicide has been consid- 6
ered by the California Legislature. Bills were introduced in 1995
and 1999 but never presented for a floor vote. In addition, Proposition 161 was on the ballot in 1992 but rejected by 54% of the
voters. According to information on the Assembly's website, AB
654 is intended to expand the range of care for dying patients
to "include choices for those relatively few whose suffering is
extreme and cannot be palliated despite the best efforts." Makes
sense to me.

Life is a precious gift. Yet when a life turns tragic through dis- 7
ease or injury and the joy of living yields to the pain of interminable suffering, surely an enlightened society such as ours can accept
that from death there can be peace.

Critics make the usual "slippery slope" argument that the right 8
to die is just the first step toward an eventual policy of euthanasia.
In fact, the Assembly website notes the fear of the critics that "the
right to die may become a responsibility to die" for those considered "socially disadvantaged," such as the elderly and the disabled.

In response to those fears, AB 654 is narrowly written to 9
apply only to the terminally ill and only after ascertaining the competence of the patient. Also, it requires two doctors to attest to
the condition of the patient and the fact that the patient is acting
voluntarily.

The bill is modeled on the law in Oregon, where, in the seven 10
years since the measure was passed, just over 200 residents have

exercised their right to end their suffering and none of the concerns of the critics have been realized.

The more religious of the critics would argue that assisted   11
suicide attempts to usurp an authority that can only be the province of God. Yet even the religious support the taking of life for capital crimes and even the use of war when the cause is considered "just." So what could be more just than allowing a person to choose to end a life that is bereft of hope and consumed with pain? It is time for compassion to replace unfounded fears.

If life is for the living, then surely death should be an option for   12
the dying. Megan shouldn't be the only one with that right.

Death and the Law: Why the Government Has an Interest in Preserving Life
Lawrence Rudden and
Gerard V. Bradley

Lawrence Rudden is the former director of research for the Graham Williams Group in Washington, D.C. He writes on politics and culture. Gerard V. Bradley is a professor of law at the University of Notre Dame. In this selection from the May 2003 issue of World and I, *they argue that government must take "an unyielding stand in favor of life."*

Attorney General Ashcroft wants to stop doctors who kill. He   1
has good reason: doctors have a special responsibility to show by word and deed, in season and out, that intentionally killing another person is simply wrong. Yes, even if that person is, like Evelyn, terminally ill.

A doctor's calling is always to heal, never to harm. A doc-   2
tor's calling is special, though not unique. None of us possesses a license, privilege, or permission to kill, but the healer who purposely kills puts into question, in a unique way, our culture's commitment to the sanctity of life. The scandal created by doctors who kill is great, much like that caused by lawyers who flout the law, or bishops—shepherds—who do not care about their flocks. Whenever someone whose profession centers upon a single good—healing or respect for law or caring for souls—tramples that good, the rest of us cannot help but wonder: is it a good after all? Maybe it is for some, but not for others? Who decides? Is all the talk of that good as supremely worthwhile idle chatter or, worse, cynical propaganda?

Do not intentionally kill. This is what it means—principally and   3
essentially—to revere life. Making intentional killing of humans a

serious crime is the earmark of society's respect for life. All our criminal laws against homicide (save for Oregon) make no exception—none whatsoever—for victims who say they want to die. Our law contains no case or category of "public service homicides," of people who should be dead. People hunting season is never open. Our laws against killing (except Oregon's) make no exception for those who suffer, even for those near death. None.

When someone commits the crime of murder, all we can say   4
is that the victim's life was shortened. We know not by how much; the law does not ask, or care. After all, no one knows how much longer any of us shall live. Many persons who are the picture of health, in the bloom of youth, will die today in accidents, by another's hand, or of natural causes. Yes, we can say with confidence that someone's death, maybe Evelyn's, is near at hand. But so long as she draws breath, she has the same legal and moral right that you and I have not to be intentionally killed.

It is not that life is the only good thing which we, and our laws,   5
strive to protect. Life is not always an overriding good; we accept certain risks to life. What is the alternative? Do nothing at all that creates some (even a small) chance of death? Would we get up in the morning? Drive our cars? Take medicine? Go swimming? Fly in airplanes? Some risk to life is acceptable where the risk is modest and the activities that engender it are worthwhile.

Sometimes the risk can be great and still worth accepting. We   6
might instinctively step in front of a car, or jump into a freezing lake to save a loved one, or a stranger's wandering toddler. We might do the same upon reflection, but we do not want to die. We do not commit suicide.

Religious martyrs may face certain death, but they do not   7
want to die. They submit to death as the side effect of their acts, whether these be described as witnessing to the truth, or, in the case of Saint Thomas More, avoiding false witness. The axman, the lion tamer, the firing squad—they kill. They intend death.

This distinction between intending and accepting death is not   8
scholarly hairsplitting. This distinction is real, as real as space shuttles. The Columbia crew knew all along that they risked death by flying into space. That which they risked came to be, but they were not suicides.

Of course doctors may—even must—prescribe analge-   9
sics. Doctors should try to relieve the suffering of their terminal patients, up to and even including toxic doses. Not because they want to kill, any more than they want to kill patients in exploratory

surgery. Doctors who prescribe strong painkillers want to help, even to heal. Given how ill some patients are, the risk of death is worth running, just as some very risky surgeries are a risk worth taking.

Evelyn wants to let go, and she needs help to do so. Yet, none 10 of us walks into a doctor's office and demands a certain treatment. Doctors do not fetch medicines upon demand. They are not workmen at our service. Yes, doctors work toward our health in cooperation with us. They have no right to impose treatment we do not want. But we have no right to drugs, surgery, or anesthesia.

Or to lights out—even for Evelyn.   11

Why? Because autonomy, or self-rule, is not an all-consuming 12 value. It is not a trump card. Evelyn honestly wishes to bring down the curtain. We may find her condition hideous, as she evidently does, but our feelings (of repulsion, sympathy, or whatever) are unreliable guides to sound choosing. Feelings certainly do not always, or even usually, mislead us. Often, though, they do.

Pause a moment and you will, if you try, think of something 13 attractive and pleasing you did not choose today, because it would have been wrong, and something unappealing, even repulsive, you chose to do because it was right. For me, some days, it has to do with my mother, who suffers from advanced Alzheimer's. Enough said.

On what basis does a society and its governing authorities decide 14 that life is a great common good? Because it is true: life is good. The law is a powerful teacher of right and wrong. Like it or not, what our laws permit is thought by many to be good, or at least unobjectionable. What the law forbids is believed to be, well, forbidden.

Why should our government take such an unyielding stand 15 in favor of life? Because we are all safer where everyone's life is prized, not despised.

AFTER YOU READ

Work with other students to develop responses to the following suggestions or to compare responses that you have already prepared.

1. Identify the thesis of each article. Then divide each article into major sections.

2. To clarify the arguments presented by each article, ask yourself, "What are this writer's reasons for his position?" Examine each major division, and make a list of the different reasons offered.

3. Once you have developed such a list, consider ways the various writers' points can be grouped. Which points from different articles would you put together? Why?

READINGS: ONLINE DATING

BEFORE YOU READ

1. Do you or does anybody you know participate in online dating? What experiences have you or people you know had?
2. What do you believe are the benefits of online dating? What do you believe are the drawbacks of dating online?

Overwhelmed and Creeped Out   ANN FRIEDMAN

Ann Friedman has a regular column about politics, culture, and gender for NYmag.com. *She also contributes to* New Republic, Columbia Journalism Review, ELLE, The Guardian, Los Angeles *magazine,* Bookforum, The Gentlewoman, *and other publications. She cohosts a podcast, "Call Your Girlfriend," with her friend Aminatou Sow. The following selection was published in* The New Yorker *in February 2013.*

The eligible men are laid out like items on a menu that I can scroll   1
through by flicking my thumb. I haven't even tapped on a single
photo yet when—*brrring*—a new message appears: "Wassup?" I
ignore it and return my attention to the sea of forty-five-year-old
men with usernames like "Drunky." Anyone worth messaging in
here? I don't have much time to think about it—*brrring brrrring*—
because two new messages arrive in the chat window. "Whaat
are you up to?" and "hey there." Ignore; ignore. I'm seeing so many
men with questionable facial hair that I double-check my profile
to make sure that I haven't accidentally indicated a preference
for goatees. *Brrring brrrring brrrrrring*. I scream and toss the phone
to the other end of the couch, as if this action will repel the men
within it. Even though I know these men can't see my exact location, I feel cornered, overwhelmed.

Blendr is the most high-profile of a series of new location-   2
based dating apps for straight people. It was created by the same
folks who made *Grindr*, the hookup app that's become ubiquitous
in the gay community. In June, *Grindr* announced it now has four
and a half million users (six hundred thousand of them in the U.S.),
and that they spend an average of ninety minutes browsing every
single day. Contrast *Grindr*'s success with that of *Blendr*: the founders weren't willing to disclose the number of users, opting instead
to send me an anodyne statement that they "are thrilled with the
pace of *Blendr*'s growth," which, they say, "was faster in the first six

months of launch than *Grindr's* adoption rate during its first six months." The company declined to say how many of those users are actually, well, using the app. If my own reaction is any indication, it's no wonder. After my initial session, I only opened the app to show it to friends, scrolling through pages and pages of unappealing men in what resembled a masochistic digital-age performance-art piece titled "Why I'm Single."

In truth, though, I tried *Blendr* not to find love, but at the   3
behest of a bevy of Web developers. Around the time that *Blendr* launched in September 2011, I wrote a short article declaring that the app was destined to fail. I argued that it didn't take seriously the concerns of women—safety, proximity, control—even though the founder Joel Simkhai told *GQ*, "As a gay man, I probably understand straight women more than straight guys do." Yeah, but probably not enough. Since airing my skepticism, I've received an e-mail or *Facebook* message every couple of months from a male entrepreneur who wants to pick my brain about how to make a location-based dating app appeal to women. "*Blendr* is generally useless, and there is a huge, untapped market for a hookup app for straights (or everyone other than gay men, really)," one of them wrote to me. "Attitudes towards sex have shifted massively in the past decade or so, not just amongst young people."

And not just among men. But you wouldn't know it by looking   4
at the founders of every major dating start-up. From the Web-based heavy hitters like *OkCupid*, *eHarmony*, and *Plenty of Fish* on down to newer apps like *Skout*, *How About We*, and *MeetMoi*, they're all developed by men. This might not seem like a big deal, until you consider one read on why *Grindr* has been so successful: the app has a "for us by us" appeal to gay men. But when it comes to heterosexual-dating technology, all-male co-founders represent the wants and needs of only half of their target audience. Sure, they can try to focus-group their way out of the problem, but if an app for "straight" people is to get anywhere close to *Grindr's* level of success, women have to not just join out of curiosity. They have to actually use it.

Men are slightly overrepresented among dating-service   5
users, according to a 2010 Duke University study, and when it comes to apps, men tend to be more willing to use location-based dating features. On either platform, they're far more likely to use the services aggressively. A Northwestern University study found that men viewed more than three times as many profiles as women and were about forty per cent more likely

than women to send a message or chat after viewing a profile. "The most desirable partners, especially the most desirable women, are likely to find the process of sifting through so many first-contact e-mails aversive, perhaps causing them to disengage from the process altogether," the researchers write. They call this "the deluge problem."

Both Web entrepreneurs and armchair sociologists will tell you   6
that women are different. Despite our commitment to baseline feminist ideals, most of us don't like to be relationship aggressors. We prefer to meet someone in person, not just browse pics of his pecs. We respond to emotional cues and pheromones and all sorts of subtle factors. But what if that isn't entirely true? What if women are just as open to spontaneously meeting a man for a drink—and maybe more? After all, in a survey of a hundred thousand *OkCupid* users, over half the women said they've had casual sex. Women may initiate contact less frequently, but they are comfortable reaching out first if they see a profile that appeals to them. Maybe the real failure is that no one has built an app that women want to use.

Some men are trying. When the French online-dating mar-   7
keter Yannick Rolland helped to make a U.S.-based dating site that "empowers women," he held round after round of focus groups with the opposite sex. "The main problem was women, especially attractive women, busy women, would stop using a dating Web site after their first experience, because it was a disaster. They got creeped out by thousands of e-mails with sometimes harsh messages," Rolland told me. "The goal behind it was to make a Web site where women have the power. Where only women can make the first move."

The result is a ham-fisted site called *Checkhimout.com*, on which   8
women are "shoppers" and men are "products." Only women can initiate contact, though men can "favorite" profiles. Rolland says that fifty-nine per cent of their users are women, and I decided to join their ranks to "shop" for myself. The site suggested I check out "products" as far away as Vancouver. (I live in Los Angeles.) Not a sign of a very robust user base. I didn't see a single man I'd be interested in messaging. Plus the whole shopper-product dynamic made me feel gross. Rolland says that he hears this complaint occasionally—from women, but not from men. He acknowledges that "it can be frustrating for men to be a product. It's like in the store: If you're a tin can, you're on the shelf, and women pass in front of you, and you don't have a hand to wave at them."

However, he has no plans to change the shopping conceit. However, male users can pay to be highlighted as "featured products" on the home page.

So what do women want? If you look at the precious few   9
dating sites and apps with female founders, a pattern emerges: women want authenticity, privacy, a more controlled environment, and a quick path to a safe, easy offline meeting. *Coffee Meets Bagel*, which is both an app and a Web site founded by three sisters, sends you a match and then sets a deadline by which you have to either "like" or "pass." If you get a mutual "like," you're instantly connected to your match via text message (without the other person seeing your real phone number). You can choose to be shown only friends-of-friends through *Coffee Meets Bagel* by connecting the service to your Facebook account, or you can choose to keep it private and anonymous.

"Women are more selective with their own personal agency,   10
with regards to contact," says Jessica Carbino, a Ph.D. candidate in sociology at U.C.L.A. who studies online dating. "Even women who are looking for something more casual, I don't think they're wanting to waste their time." Carbino works with Talia Goldstein and Valerie Brennan, the co-founders of *Three Day Rule*, an L.A.-based matchmaking service, dating site, and singles event series. It started as a blog on which they advised women where to grab a drink based on the type of guy they were interested in—the corporateer, weekend warrior, laid-back surfer. And they've carried over this philosophy to their dating site, keeping it L.A.-only, and focused on matching people based on which of nineteen personality categories they fall into. The lessons they've learned may not apply to hookup apps, however. *Three Day Rule* caters to women who are searching for Mr. Right as opposed to Mr. Right Now. Women may be averse to mobile apps because they "might feel that men might only be looking for a hot piece of ass. They're not going to be looking for women who have a lot to offer in other areas, their intellect or their sense of humor," Carbino says. But even for women "the visual becomes more important when it's a Mr. Right Now issue."

The *Three Day Rule* view of "empowering women" in a dating   11
context is, perhaps unsurprisingly, more complicated than that of *Checkhimout.com*. "Women are in a unique position these days," says Brennan. "On one hand, women are extremely powerful and we're leading the workforce and climbing to jobs that are simply amazing. But, on the same note, we want to be feminine, we may

not necessarily want to be the ones approaching the guys. How does that work? You still want to be the girl at the bar where the guy is the one who comes up to you."

Their answer was to create a dating site that functions as an intermediary. It shows just a few carefully selected matches at a time—bypassing the deluge problem, and saving busy professionals (who are a target demographic for online dating precisely because they're too busy to meet people) from scrolling through pages and pages of profiles. After hearing Brennan's pitch, I filled out the questionnaire for *Three Day Rule*. The site is still in beta mode and not open to the general public, and will eventually be for paying users only. After the onslaught of creepy messages on *Blendr* and other mobile apps, I was relieved at the promise of getting just a few curated matches a day. 12

Three Day Rule is working on its own mobile app. "We're blending the concept of types and also the privacy concerns that we've addressed with our members in coming up with a non-Grindresque mobile app that definitely connects people in offline venues," Brennan says. This seems to be a dominant theme of other woman-led online-dating efforts. Match.com, which now has a female president, is one of the few big dating sites to stay out of the location-based app game. Instead, the company has been hosting in-person meet-ups for its members. 13

"A lot of people want to meet organically," Carbino says. Even though the stigma is largely gone, "people tell me that online-dating seems forced. They say, 'I don't really want to meet my partner online.' If you had a mobile app to let people know where men who meet their criteria are and lets women initiate, it could work. As long as women feel comfortable." 14

And right now, heterosexual women aren't the only ones who are uncomfortable with the existing mobile-dating-app options. I asked a male friend of mine—someone who has used the Web-based version of *OkCupid* for awhile—whether he also used the *OkCupid* Locals app. "I've been tempted to use it," he told me, "but it's hard to figure out the hidden codification of the app. Am I meant to just look for rando hookups or bar dates, or am I actually supposed to court a woman through this? It all seems weird." And it's likely to stay that way until a start-up comes along that manages to make mobile dating *not weird* by offering women—and the men they want to meet—control, incredible filters, and clarity of mission. Until then, we're left to scroll through page after page of unappealing options. 15

How Racist Is Online Dating?   SHAUNACY FERRO

Shaunacy Ferro is a writer based in Brooklyn. She is a regular contributor to Popular Science. *Ferro's work has appeared in* The Huffington Post, Ventura County Reporter, *and* PopSci.com.

How racist are Americans when it comes to selecting a mate? 1
Though the rate of interracial marriages in the U.S. has doubled
in the past 30 years, according to online dating habits, we're still
pretty racist. Surprise!

But. A new study of racism in *OkCupid* messaging finds a *little* 2
bit of hope in a sea of largely same-race interactions. To examine
how racial prejudice affects our romantic decisions, Kevin Lewis,
a sociologist at the University of California at San Diego, analyzed
messages sent by more than 126,000 *OkCupid* users over a two-
and-a-half-month period. He only included heterosexual interactions between users who self-identified with the site's five largest
racial categories: Black, White, Asian (East Asian), Hispanic/Latino
and Indian. He found that people from all racial backgrounds
disproportionately contacted users from their same racial background. However people were more willing to reply to a user of
a different race than they were to initiate contact. And right after
they did so, for about a week, they were more likely to start a conversation with someone of another race.

OkCupid'sOkTrends blog detailed the prevalence of racial preju- 3
dice on its own service back in 2009. According to the site's internal stats, white males get the most responses to their messages
than any other group, and that white, Asian and Hispanic women
reply to non-white men less than a quarter of the time. Lewis
found similar patterns: "Most men (except black men) are unlikely
to initiate contact with black women, all men (including Asian men)
are unlikely to reply to Asian women, and although women from
all racial backgrounds tend to initiate contact with men from the
same background, women from all racial backgrounds also disproportionately reply to white men." *OkCupid*, like so many places, is
good place to be a white dude.

Lewis suggests that one factor in online dating's racial seg- 4
regation could be what he calls preemptive discrimination. "In
other words, part of the reason site users, and especially minority
site users, do not express interest in individuals from a different
racial background is because they anticipate—based on a lifetime
of experiences with racism—that individuals from a different

background will not be interested in them." This, according to the paper, could be a mediating factor in why people are more likely to reply to users of another race than message them first—they're sure the person is interested in them if they receive a message.

Some limitations of this study: It only looked at a subset of heterosexual interactions on one dating site, whose users, co-founder Christian Rudder wrote on *OkTrends*, "are better-educated, younger, and far more progressive than the norm." (A 2010 Pew report found Millennials were far more likely than other age groups to accept interracial marriage.) So the findings may not apply to all dating demographics. And the actual content of the messages wasn't included in the data, so there's no guarantee the reply wasn't "LOOLOL IN UR DREAMS."

5

But online dating provides a new vantage point from which to examine interracial dating preferences, since the dating pool is virtually unlimited. With traditional dating networks, scholars have found it hard to qualify how much of self-segregation in the dating pool has to do with internal prejudice, versus structural issues in an already-segregated society. Offline, you might have fewer opportunities to meet someone of another race to begin with, based on where you live or how homogeneous your networks of family and friends are, but online, there's less of a barrier. Which apparently we still don't try to surmount.

6

Online Dating Odds Getting Better KATHERINE P. HARVEY

Katherine P. Harvey has won awards for news photography and community service reporting. Currently, Harvey covers small-business trends in San Diego's competitive market. She is a regular contributor to the San Diego Union-Tribune.

It's hard to imagine needing more online dating options in a world that already offers *eHarmony, Tinder, Meet-an-Inmate.com* and everything in between.

1

But online dating has a reputation for failing. The failures are so comically pervasive that Instagram accounts like *Bye Felipe* and *Tinder Nightmares* exist just to chronicle people's Internet dating misadventures.

2

Still, the odds are actually improving for people looking for love online—and the companies selling virtual dating services are making more money than ever as they come up with more creative ways to help people find their match.

3

One in four online daters now say they have met a spouse or   4
long-term mate through websites or mobile apps, according to
Pew Research.

The $2.2 billion dating industry is growing fast and is expected   5
to reach $2.7 billion by 2019. Three-quarters of the industry's rev-
enue already comes from online and mobile dating services. Market research firm IBISWorld says its future growth will be driven
largely by startups launching new mobile apps and carving out
their own niches.

Three companies doing just that are based here in San Diego   6
County.

SingldOut, a service that uses LinkedIn profiles and DNA cheek   7
swabs to help you identify who you'll have chemistry with, raised
$600,000 in a seed round last year.

Neqtr, a "socially conscious" dating app that connects people   8
based on their philanthropic interests and sends them to group
volunteer events for their first date, launched in January.

Then there's *Wyldfire*, an app that lets the women vet and   9
pick which men are allowed into their dating community. *Wyldfire*,
based in Carlsbad, just raised $450,000.

Room for Improvement

"It's very inspirational to see all these newcomers, because we   10
haven't had enough innovation in this industry," said Mark Brooks,
an online dating analyst and consultant.

The matchmaking industry has been behind the technology   11
curve for years, Brooks said, because of the stigma toward online
dating. But a declining marriage rate, increasing number of singles
and rising comfort level with the Internet and smartphones are
all driving new products and ideas in the centuries-old business of
matchmaking.

People like Internet dating, Brooks said, because it gives them   12
more options and lets them get the tough questions out of
the way up front. It's fraught with challenges, though, as people
become too picky about arbitrary criteria like height and eye color,
and men emboldened by the anonymity of online identities harass
and chase off the women—sometimes intentionally.

It's also tough to tell online whether someone is telling the   13
truth about things like age, height and weight. If not, it makes for an
awkward first date.

Industry leaders like *InterActiveCorp*, which owns *Match.com*,   14
Chemistry.com, *Delightful.com*, *Tinder*, *OkCupid*, *Meetic* and *Twoo*, have

still not effectively addressed many of those challenges, said *Singld-Out* owner Elle France.

"The market is so full, there are so many apps and sites out   15
there, but nobody's really offering a solution that's fulfilling and last-ing," she said.

Brooks said that's bound to change now that it's easier to get   16
into the online dating business.

"Development costs are down, it's growing in popularity, every-   17
body knows somebody who's met someone through a site," he said. "It's a very sexy business. I'm hooked."

That's where new apps like *Wyldfire, Neqtr* and *SingldOut* come   18
in. Each offers a piece of the solution to the online dating puzzle.

"Everyone's offering a piece, and they're interesting pieces,"   19
Brooks said.

The big question, he said, is whether they will be able to attract   20
a critical mass of people and then find a way to make money with-out turning those people off.

"We're selling people to people, so if we don't have people, we   21
don't have a service," he said.

Here's where the newcomers fit into the online dating puzzle.   22

Online Dating and Relationships   Aaron Smith and Maeve Duggan

Aaron Smith is a Pew Center researcher. He is an expert in the growing impact of mobile technologies, the role of the Internet in connecting Americans to political and civic issues, and ongoing demographic trends in technology adoption. Maeve Dug-gan is a research analyst at the Pew Research Center's Internet Project.

One in ten Americans have used an online dating site or mobile   1
dating app themselves, and many people now know someone else who uses online dating or who has found a spouse or long-term partner via online dating. General public attitudes towards online dating have become much more positive in recent years, and social networking sites are now playing a prominent role when it comes to navigating and documenting romantic relationships. These are among the key findings of a national survey of dating and relation-ships in the digital era, the first dedicated study of this subject by the Pew Research Center's Internet Project since 2005.

**11% of American adults—and 38% of those who are   2
currently "single and looking" for a partner—have
used online dating sites or mobile dating apps**

One in every ten American adults has used an online dating   3
site or a mobile dating app. We refer to these individuals throughout this report as "online daters," and we define them in the following way:

11% of internet users (representing 9% of all adults) say that   4
they have personally *used an online dating site* such as Match.
com, eHarmony, or OK Cupid.

7% of cell phone apps users (representing 3% of all adults) say   5
that they have *used a dating app on their cell phone*.

Taken together, 11% of all American adults have done one   6
or both of these activities and are classified as "online daters." In
terms of demographics, online dating is most common among
Americans in their mid-20's through mid-40's. Some 22% of 25–34
year olds and 17% of 35–44 year olds are online daters. Online
dating is also relatively popular among the college-educated, as
well as among urban and suburban residents. And 38% of Americans who are single and actively looking for a partner have used
online dating at one point or another.

66% of online daters have gone on a date with someone they met   7
through a dating site or app, and 23% of online daters say they
have met a spouse or long-term relationship through these sites.

Compared with eight years ago, online daters in 2013 are   8
more likely to actually go out on dates with the people they meet
on these sites. Some 66% of online daters have gone on a date
with someone they met through an online dating site or app, up
from 43% of online daters who had done so when we first asked
this question in 2005. Moving beyond dates, one quarter of online
daters (23%) say that they themselves have entered into a marriage or long-term relationship with someone they met through a
dating site or app. That is statistically similar to the 17% of online
daters who said that this had happened to them when we first
asked this question in 2005.

Attitudes towards online dating are becoming more positive over   9
time.

Even today, online dating is not universally seen as a positive   10
activity—a significant minority of the public views online dating
skeptically. At the same time, public attitudes towards online dating
have grown more positive in the last eight years: 59% of all internet
users agree with the statement that "*online dating is a good way to*

meet people," a 15-point increase from the 44% who said so in 2005.

53% of internet users agree with the statement that "*online dat-* 11
ing allows people to find a better match for themselves because they can get to know a lot more people," a 6-point increase from the 47% who said so in 2005.

21% of internet users agree with the statement that "*people who* 12
use online dating sites are desperate," an 8-point decline from the 29% who said so in 2005.

Additionally, 32% of internet users agree with the statement 13
that "*online dating keeps people from settling down because they always have options for people to date.*" This is the first time we have asked this question.

Opinions of online dating, 2005–2013

% of Internet users who agree with each of the following statements

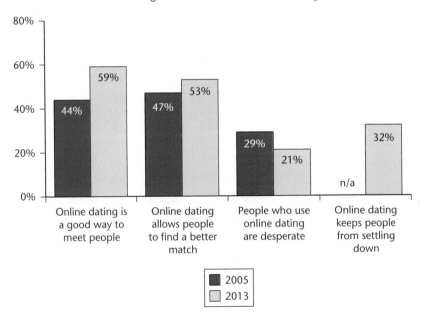

Pew Research Center's Internet & American Life Project Spring Tracking Survey, April 17–May 19, 2013. N = 2,252 adult ages 18+. Interviews were conducted in English and Spanish and on landline and cell phones. 2005 survey was conducted September 14–December 8, 2005, n = 3,215 adults ages 18+.

In general, online daters themselves give the experience high 14
marks. Some 79% of online daters agree that online dating is a good way to meet people, and 70% of them agree that it helps people find a better romantic match because they have access to a wide

range of potential partners. Yet even some online daters view the process itself and the individuals they encounter on these sites somewhat negatively. Around one in ten online daters (13%) agree with the statement that "people who use online dating sites are desperate," and 29% agree that online dating "keeps people from settling down because they always have options for people to date."

*42% of all Americans know an online dater, and 29% know some-   15
one who has used online dating to find a spouse or other long-
term relationship.*

Familiarity with online dating through usage by friends or family   16
members has increased dramatically since our last survey of online dating in 2005. Some 42% of Americans know someone who has used online dating, up from 31% in 2005. And 29% of Americans now know someone who met a spouse or other long-term partner through online dating, up from just 15% in 2005.

Familiarity with online dating through others, 2005–2013

% of American adults who . . .

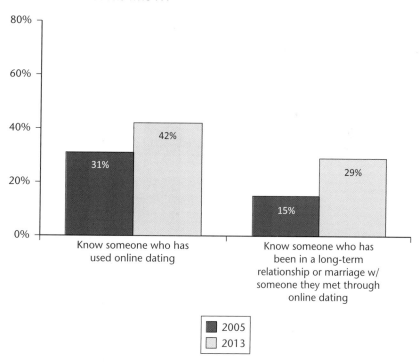

Pew Research Center's Internet & American Life Project Spring Tracking Survey, April 17–May 19, 2013. N = 2,252 adult ages 18+. Interviews were conducted in English and Spanish and on landline and cell phones. 2005 survey was conducted September 14–December 8, 2005, n = 3,215 adults ages 18+.

People in nearly every major demographic group—old and   17
young, men and women, urbanites and rural dwellers—are more
likely to know someone who uses online dating (or met a long-
term partner through online dating) than was the case eight years
ago. And this is especially true for those at the upper end of the
socio-economic spectrum:

57% of all college graduates know someone who uses online   18
dating, and 41% know someone who has met a spouse or other
long-term partner through online dating.

57% of Americans with an annual household income of $75,000   19
or more know someone who uses online dating, and 40% know
someone who met a spouse or partner this way.

Negative experiences on online dating sites are relatively common.   20

Even as online daters have largely positive opinions of the   21
process, many have had negative experiences using online dating.
Half (54%) of online daters have felt that *someone else seriously
misrepresented themselves in their profile.* And more seriously,
28% of online daters have been *contacted by someone through an
online dating site or app in a way that made them feel harassed or
uncomfortable.* Women are much more likely than men to have
experienced uncomfortable contact via online dating sites or
apps: some 42% of female online daters have experienced this
type of contact at one point or another, compared with 17% of
men.

40% of online daters have used dating sites designed for people   22
*with shared interests or backgrounds, and one in three have paid
to use a dating site or app. One in five online daters have asked
someone to help them review their profile.*

Paid dating sites, and sites for people who are seeking partners 23
with specific characteristics are popular with relatively large numbers of online daters:

40% of online daters have *used a site or app for people with shared* 24
interests or backgrounds.

33% of online daters have *paid to use an online dating site or app.* 25

Organized outings are much less common, as just 4% of online 26
daters have attended a group outing or other physical event organized by an online dating site.

Additionally, 22% of online daters have *asked someone to*   27
help them create or review their profile. Women are around twice

as likely as men to ask for assistance creating or perfecting their profile—30% of female online daters have done this, compared with 16% of men.

5% of Americans who are currently married or in a long-term partnership met their partner somewhere online. Among those who have been together for ten years or less, 11% met online.   28

Even today, the vast majority of Americans who are in a mar-   29
riage, partnership, or other serious relationship say that they met their partner through offline—rather than online—means. At the same time, the proportion of Americans who say that they met their current partner online has doubled in the last eight years. Some 6% of internet users who are in a marriage, partnership, or other committed relationship met their partner online—that is up from 3% of internet users who said this in 2005. On an "all-adults" basis, that means that 5% of all committed relationships in America today began online.

This question was asked of everyone in a marriage or other   30
long-term partnership, including many whose relationships were initiated well before meeting online was an option. Looking only at those committed relationships that started within the last ten years, 11% say that their spouse or partner is someone they met online.

Younger adults are also more likely than older ones to say that   31
their relationship began online. Some 8% of 18–29 year olds in a marriage or committed relationship met their partner online, com-pared with 7% of 30–49 year olds, 3% of 50–64 year olds, and just 1% of those 65 and older.

In addition, people who have used online dating are signifi-   32
cantly more likely to say that their relationship began online than are those who have never used online dating. Fully 34% of Ameri-cans who are in a committed relationship and have used online dating sites or dating apps in the past say that they met their spouse or partner online, compared with 3% for those who have not used online dating sites.

Using the internet to flirt, research potential partners, and check   33
up on old flames have all become much more common in recent years.

Compared with when we conducted our first study of dating   34
and relationships in 2005, many more Americans are using online

tools to check up on people they used to date, and to flirt with potential (or current) love interests:

24% of internet users have *searched for information online about* 35 *someone they dated in the past,* up from 11% in 2005.

24% of internet users have *flirted with someone online,* up from 36 15% in 2005.

Young adults are especially likely to flirt online—47% of inter- 37 net users ages 18–24 have done this before, as have 40% of those ages 25–34. And while younger adults are also more likely than their elders to look up past flames online, this behavior is still relatively common among older cohorts. Some 21% of internet users ages 45–54, and 15% of those ages 55–64, have gone online to look up someone they used to date.

Additionally, 29% of internet users with recent dating experi- 38 ence have gone online to *search for information about someone they were currently dating or about to meet for a first date.* That is more than double the 13% of such internet users who did so when we last asked about this behavior in 2005.

Social networking sites offer a new online venue for 39 navigating the world of dating and relationships.

Today six out of every ten Americans use social networking 40 sites (SNSs) such as Facebook or Twitter, and these sites are often intertwined with the way they experience their past and present romantic relationships:

One third (31%) of all SNS users have gone on these sites to 41 *check up on someone they used to date* or be in a relationship with.

17% have *posted pictures or other details from a date* on a social 42 networking site.

Younger adults are especially likely to live out their relation- 43 ships through social networking sites. Some 48% of SNS users ages 18–29 have used these sites to check up on someone they dated in the past, and 31% have posted details or pictures from a date on a social networking site.

These sites are also being used as a source of background 44 research on potential romantic partners. Nearly one third (30%) of SNS users with recent dating experience1 have used a social networking site to *get more information about someone they were interested in dating.* And 12% of SNS users with recent dating

Checking on past relationships and posting details from dates on social networking sites

% of SNS/Twitter users who have used a social networking site to . . .

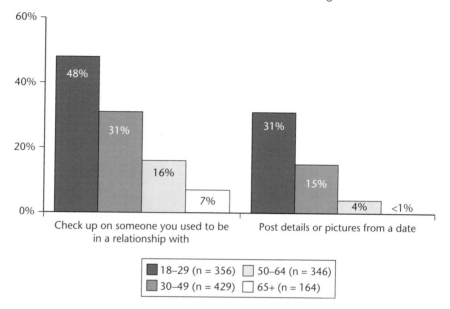

Pew Research Center's Internet & American Life Project Spring Tracking Survey, April 17–May 19, 2013. N = 2,252 adult ages 18+. Interviews were conducted in English and Spanish and on land-line and cell phones.

experience have friended or followed someone on a social net-working site specifically because one of their friends suggested they might want to date that person.

Beyond using these sites as a tool for researching potential partners, some 15% of SNS users with recent dating experience have *asked someone out on a date* using a social networking site.

For young adults especially, social networking sites can be the site of "relationship drama."

As more and more Americans use social networking sites, these spaces can become the site of potential tension or awk-wardness around relationships and dating. Some 27% of all social networking site users have unfriended or blocked someone who was flirting in a way that made them feel uncomfortable, and 22% have unfriended or blocked someone that they were once in a relationship with. These sites can also serve as a lingering reminder of relationships that have ended—17% of social networking site users have untagged or deleted photos on these sites of them-selves and someone they used to be in a relationship with.

Negative relationship experiences on social networking sites

% of SNS/Twitter users who have . . .

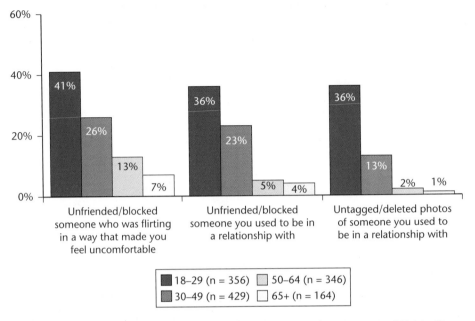

Pew Research Center's Internet & American Life Project Spring Tracking Survey, April 17–May 19, 2013. N = 2,252 adult ages 18+. Interviews were conducted in English and Spanish and on landline and cell phones.

Not surprisingly, young adults—who have near-universal rates   48
of social networking site use and have spent the bulk of their dating lives in the social media era—are significantly more likely than
older social media users to have experienced all three of these
situations in the past. And women are more likely than men to
have blocked or unfriended someone who was flirting in a way
that made them uncomfortable.

AFTER YOU READ

Work with other students to develop responses to the following suggestions
or to compare responses that you have already prepared.

1. Identify the thesis of each article. Then divide each article into major
   sections.
2. To clarify the arguments presented by each article, ask yourself, "What
   are this writer's reasons for his or her position?" Examine each major
   division, and make a list of the different reasons offered.
3. Once you have developed such a list, consider ways the various writers' points can be grouped. Which points from different articles would
   you put together? Why?

WRITING ASSIGNMENTS

Note Working with several sources can be substantially more difficult than working with only one source. As you respond to one of these assignments, consider working with other students to clarify and organize your ideas.

1. Write a synthesis of the ideas presented in the articles grouped under the headings "Physician-Assisted Suicide" or "Online Dating." After taking careful notes of each article, divide related ideas into separate groupings and then decide on a logical organization of those groups. Remember that your purpose is to explain the issues, not to take a stand.

2. Write a synthesis of the ideas presented in the articles grouped under the headings "Online Worlds: Friend or Foe" or "School, Teenagers, and Part-Time Jobs" in Chapter 8. Or write a synthesis of the articles grouped under the headings "Should Drugs Be Legalized" or "Should the Minimum Legal Drinking Age Be Lowered" in Part Four.

EVALUATING SAMPLE PAPERS

Synthesis Essay

Use the following criteria to evaluate the student essays below.

1. Introduction

Does the first paragraph introduce the topic and establish its complexity? Does the thesis make it clear that the point of the paper is to explain the issues discussed by a number of writers?

1   2   3   4   5   6

2. Unity

Does each paragraph have a clear and specific topic sentence that accurately introduces an idea discussed by one or more of the articles? Is the material in each paragraph clearly related to its topic sentence?

1   2   3   4   5   6

3. Support

Are all of the major points discussed? Is each point accurately and fully explained?

1   2   3   4   5   6

4. Coherence

Are transitions used between paragraphs? Are they used within paragraphs, especially when the writer is moving from what one article says to what is said in another?

1   2   3   4   5   6

5. References to the Text

Are direct quotations and paraphrases correctly introduced and smoothly incorporated into the text? Do they reflect the articles' points accurately?

1   2   3   4   5   6

6. Sentence Structure

Do the sentences combine ideas that are related, using coordination, subordination, verbal phrases, or parallelism when appropriate? Are there too many brief, choppy main clauses?

1   2   3   4   5   6

7. Mechanics, Grammar, and Spelling

Does the paper contain a distracting number of errors of these kinds?

1   2   3   4   5   6

8. Overall Ranking of the Essay

1   2   3   4   5   6

Evaluate the following student essays. Use the criteria above to determine which essay is most effective.

Student Essay 1

If you or a loved one were in excruciating pain, should mercy killing be an option available to either of you? After sustaining severe damages or illness, for some people ending a life can be thought of as a cure for suffering, a benefit to society, and a matter of autonomy. In contrast, others believe giving up on life is regarded as a deplorable mistake and a threat to the practice of medicine. The legality of euthanasia is rare throughout the world, yet a dangerous black market supplies people the means to end their own life. Death is an unpleasant, personal subject; however, assisted suicide has been a contentious procedure in today's politics.

Concerns for the intense pain that terminally ill patients endure are significant in debates over voluntary euthanasia. Sidney Hook, a philosopher and political pundit, described his agonizing survival after suffering a heart attack:

> A congestive heart failure was treated for diagnostic purposes by an angiogram that triggered a stroke. Violent and painful hiccups, uninterrupted for several days and nights, prevented the ingestion of food. My left side and one of my vocal cords became paralyzed. Some form of pleurisy set in, and I felt I was drowning in a sea of slime. At one point, my heart stopped beating; just as I lost consciousness, it was thumped back into action again (243).

When he requested his doctor to cease life support, the doctor "refused and told me that someday I would appreciate the unwisdom of my request" (243). Following his recovery, Hook noticed his condition worried his family and predicted his health would falter again, which would cause another episode of grieving for his family. Even though a critically ill patient's burden on society can impact their desire to die, Teresa Wagner blames those feelings on "a culture of abandonment," intolerant of dependence (247). When culture is devoted to health instead of mercy killing, Wagner adds, "But it is precisely within this context of care, of giving and receiving, that we enjoy the dignity particular to human beings" (247).

Another disputed issue is the value society has for forcing people to remain alive until their natural death. Sidney Hook detests the use of resources to "sustain the lives of those whose days and nights are spent on mattress graves of pain" when they could be used to benefit the young (244). Furthermore, Hook declares, "I am not vain enough to delude myself that I can in the few remaining years make an important discovery useful for mankind or can lead a social movement or do anything that will be historically eventful, no less event making" (244). Similarly, Kenneth Swift asserts, "the joy of living yields to the pain of interminable suffering" (248). Lawrence Rudden and Gerard Bradley insist on criminalizing assisted suicide because laws against killing distinguish value for life. In addition, they both regard survival as a traditionally noble pursuit; for example, they write, "Doctors who prescribe strong painkillers want to help, even to heal. Given how ill some patients are, the risk of death is worth running, just as some very risky surgeries are a risk worth taking" (250). When Teresa Wagner argues society must evaluate life in two ways: "We can follow the way of Jack Kevorkian or of Mother Teresa" (247). She considers the role of Mother Teresa is "to care for the sick and the old, to assure them of their worth," whereas Jack Kevorkian resembles "our culture of abandonment, epitomized by assisted suicide and all the abuses to follow" (247).

Additionally, arguing the right to voluntary euthanasia is pivotal in forming opinions on the legality of the procedure. When speaking about his pet dog's freedom to be euthanized, Kenneth Swift concludes human rights are diminished by having less autonomy than man's best friend, the canine. Lawrence Rudden and Gerard Bradley disagree, and proclaim, "A doctor's calling is always to heal, never to harm" (249). They juxtapose a doctor with the authority to kill with job positions that shouldn't neglect their moral purpose, such as "lawyers who flout the law" (249). Teresa Wagner warns, "Make no mistake: Despite incessant clamor about rights, ours is actually a culture of abandonment" (247).

The debate also centers on the legal parameters of assisted suicide and violations consequent to legalizing the practice. "Several state courts have already ruled as a matter of state constitutional law that any rights given to competent patients (those who can request death) must also be given to incompetent ones (those who cannot)," laments Teresa Wagner (245). She predicts, "Hospitals will eventually pressure, and then coerce, patients to avail themselves of this easy and cheap alternative" (246). Lastly, Teresa Wagner suggests courts will strike away Oregon's requirement for patients to be expected to die within six months because the limit is arbitrary for being nonspecific when medical treatment is available and excluding patients who could suffer years of illness. Kenneth Swift mentions a bill, AB 654, in California that would only allow consenting, terminally ill patients who receive approval by two doctors to be voluntarily euthanized. Moreover, he notes, "The bill is modeled on the law in Oregon, where, in the seven years since the measure was passed, just over 200 residents have exercised their right to end their suffering and none of the critics have been realized" (249).

There are diverse opinions on the practice of voluntary euthanasia. Each writer provides substantial reasoning and evidence to make his or her case. Although there were no agreements between the authors from both sides on assisted suicide, the arguments presented by either side of the issue were oftentimes similar. This is a complex issue, nonetheless, with far reaching consequences should the wrong conclusion about mercy killing prevail in society. Proper evaluation of the evidence shall give everyone the opportunity to make the right decision.

Student Essay 2

Two of the reading selections in this synthesis can be found in Part Four.

United States citizens debate the right age deemed *appropriate* for adults to start drinking alcohol. Should adults in the United States be able to drink when they are legally considered adults or are adults not allowed to make adult decisions? The country allows everyone of age eighteen or older to make many different choices regarding responsibilities, but drinking falls short. Should adult citizens be able to drink unconsidered an adult and give power back to states regardless of a possible increase in *driving under the influence*-related accidents?

Legally United States citizens are considered adults at the age of eighteen. As considered adults, citizens are given responsibilities such as obeying laws, voting and expected independency. In Elizabeth Whelon's "The Perils of Prohibition," she states "At 18 they're considered adults. Yet when they want to enjoy a drink like other adults, they are, as they put it, "disenfranchised." The United States considers citizens adults at eighteen years of age with everything except their ability to drink. Also, in Andrew Stuttaford's "De-Demonizing Rum" What's Wrong with "Underage Drinking," Stuttaford states "A typical Texan of 19—let's call her Jenna—is judged to be responsible enough to vote, drive, marry, serve in the military and (this is Texas) be executed, but she is not, apparently, sufficiently mature to decide for herself whether to buy a margarita." The country may hold double standards when it comes to drinking in comparison to other *adult* responsibilities. No other examples of laws may be found that can provide the same standard. So why is it that drinking can be held to such standards?

Some authors argue that once states within the United States were all individually allowed to decide what the legal drinking age for citizens should be. This allowed the states more power than the central government. "The legal drinking age has been raised to 21 in every state" (Stuttaford). Whelon also writes, "But laws in all 50 states say that no alcoholic beverages may be sold to anyone until that magic 21st birthday." The Federal government took over the legality of the drinking age and made a country-wide law for drinking. According to the United States Government smaller sections of the country should not decide the best interest for their particular state.

Automobile crashes are one of the leading causes of deaths in the United States each year. Some argue lowering the drinking age means more people driving under the influence. Toomey Rosenfeld wrote in his essay, "The Minimum Legal Drinking Age," "Several studies in the 1970's found that motor vehicle crashes increased significantly among teens when the MLDA was lowered." Rosenfeld argues that with more teenagers being able to drink, more teens will drink and drive. Stuttaford admits, "While it is possible to debate the numbers, there can be little doubt that the higher drinking age has coincided with a reduction in the number of highway deaths." Authors argue against adults being able to drink based on the possibility that an individual may choose to drive while drinking.

If the United States government considers citizens adults at age eighteen, then should citizens be treated as adults? Huge life decisions are allowed to be made at age eighteen except for drinking. Is drinking the only exception to the rules? If we as citizens are treated and punished as adults for everything else at age eighteen then is it only fair we can drink like adults at age eighteen or is it a decision to be made at a later age?

SENTENCE COMBINING: SENTENCE VARIETY

Have you ever listened to someone talk who never varies the pitch or tone of his or her voice? Have you ever had to listen to a speaker (perhaps an instructor?) who drones on and on with no changes in the sound of her voice to help emphasize the important points or just to make what she is saying more interesting? If you have heard such a person, you know—as we do—how *boring* such a voice can be. Even if you aren't sleepy to begin with, you are ready to nod off within five minutes, right?

Writers have the same problems as speakers. They need to express their ideas in ways that will prevent their readers from taking a big yawn, closing their eyes, and starting to snore. **Sentence variety** is one technique that writers use to add interest to what they write. As the term implies, *sentence variety* means that the sentences in your paragraph or essay are somehow different from each other—they are *varied*—just as a good speaker's voice is frequently varied to keep the attention of the audience.

Actually, you have been practicing sentence variety throughout the sentence-combining sections of this text. When you embedded adjectives, adverbs, and prepositional phrases in Chapter 1; when you practiced using main and subordinate clauses in Chapters 2 and 3; when you used verbal phrases in Chapter 4 and appositives in Chapter 5; and when you practiced parallelism in Chapter 6—in each case, you were learning ways to vary the kinds of sentences that you write. In this section, you will work on writing sentences that are varied both in length and in structure.

SENTENCE LENGTH

One of the chief causes of monotonous writing is a series of relatively brief sentences, one after the other. Take a look at the following paragraph:

> It was a warm, miserable morning last week. We went up to the Bronx Zoo. We wanted to see the moose calf. We also needed to break in a new pair of black shoes. We encountered better luck than we had bargained for. The cow moose and her young one were standing near the wall of the deer park. The wall was below the monkey house. We wanted a better view. We strolled down to the lower end of the park. We were by the brook. The path there is not much traveled. We approached the corner where the brook trickles under the wire fence. We noticed a red deer getting to her feet. Beside her was a spotted fawn. Its legs were just learning their business. The fawn was small and perfect. It was like a trinket seen through a reducing glass.

Wouldn't you agree that this writing is rather lackluster? The constant repetition of separate, short sentences makes the writing seem childlike and overly simple. However, with just a little work, many of the ideas in the excessively short sentences can be combined into longer sentences. Here is how the passage was actually written by the well-known essayist E. B. White:

> On a warm, miserable morning last week we went up to the Bronx Zoo to see the moose calf and to break in a new pair of black shoes. We encountered better luck than we had bargained for. The cow moose and her young one were standing near the wall of the deer park below the monkey house, and in order to get a better view we strolled down to the lower end of the park, by the brook. The path there is not much traveled. As we approached the corner where the brook trickles under the wire fence, we noticed a red deer getting to her feet. Beside her, on legs that were just

learning their business, was a spotted fawn as small and perfect as a trinket seen through a reducing glass.

—*E. B. White, "Twins"*

What do you think? Isn't the difference dramatic? E. B. White's paragraph is effective not just because he is a master of descriptive detail (both paragraphs contain the same details), but because his sentences have a rhythm and flow that result from his ability to vary the lengths of his sentences.

EXERCISE 7.1

1. Count the number of sentences in E. B. White's paragraph, and compare that to the number of sentences in the choppy paragraph.
2. Now look at the lengths of the sentences in E. B. White's paragraph, and point out where the lengths vary. Try to explain the effect of the shorter and longer sentences.
3. Point out where details from the choppy paragraph are embedded in E. B. White's paragraph as prepositional phrases.
4. Point out where E. B. White's paragraph uses coordination and subordination to combine ideas that were separate sentences in the choppy paragraph.

SENTENCE STRUCTURE

Although a series of short, choppy sentences can be quite distracting, a more common cause of lifeless writing is a repetitive sentence structure. Perhaps the most commonly repeated sentence structure—and the easiest to vary—is the sentence that opens with the subject and verb of its main clause. Here are some examples of this common sentence pattern:

>   S   V
> Television has been blamed for a number of problems in our society.

>   S   V
> The house slid into the ravine after the rain weakened the cliffs below it.

>   S   V
> The committee voted to reduce the homeowners' fees.

As you can see, each of the above sentences opens with a main clause, and the subject and verb of each main clause are quite close to the start of the sentence. To add some variety to your writing, try opening many of your sentences with something other than the main clause. Here are some possibilities:

1. Open your sentence with a subordinate clause.
   <u>After the rain weakened the cliffs below it</u>, the house slid into the ravine.

2. Open your sentence with a prepositional phrase.
   <u>Over the past forty years</u>, television has been blamed for a number of problems in our society.

3. Open your sentence with a verbal phrase.

<u>Responding to the complaints from a majority of the owners</u>, the committee voted to reduce the homeowners' fees. (present participial phrase)

<u>Concerned about the rising cost of living</u>, the committee voted to reduce the homeowners' fees. (past participial phrase)

<u>To prevent people from having to sell their homes</u>, the committee voted to reduce the homeowners' fees. (infinitive phrase)

Of course, another way to vary your sentence structures is to use subordinate clauses, prepositional phrases, verbal phrases, and appositives within as well as at the ends of sentences. The trick is to avoid using the same sentence pattern from one sentence to another to another.

EXERCISE 7.2

Rewrite the following paragraphs to improve their sentence variety. In both the original and revised versions, compute the average number of words in each sentence by counting all the words and dividing by the number of sentences. In each revised copy, underline any words, phrases, or subordinate clauses that open sentences before the appearance of the main clause.

1. Huge numbers of migrating birds die every year. They crash into brightly lit skyscrapers. Birds in the city have learned to avoid the bright lights and reflective glass. Migrating birds are attracted to the light. They get lost in the maze of tall buildings. Some collide with the glass. Others die from exhaustion. In coastal cities, sea gulls feed off the corpses. In Toronto, seagulls have learned to use tall buildings as tools. They herd migrating birds into them like sheep. It is estimated that 10,000 birds a year die in the 180 acres of Toronto's financial district. Visitors complained about bird carcasses littering the grounds. In response, the CN Tower in Toronto now reduces its exterior lighting during the spring and fall migration seasons.

Average number of words per sentence: ___
Average number of words per sentence in your revision: ___

2. Not too many people know about the Chinese Exclusion Act. The Chinese Exclusion Act was enacted in 1882. After the Gold Rush of 1849, Chinese were drawn to the West Coast. They were drawn to the West Coast for economic opportunity. Americans feared and blamed unemployment on Chinese immigrants. Americans viewed Chinese as racially inferior. President Chester A. Arthur halted Chinese immigration. He signed the Act in 1882. For ten years Chinese could not immigrate to the United States. The restriction was extended in 1892. It was made permanent in 1902. In addition, Chinese immigrants living in the United States could not become U.S. citizens. The federal court had the power to deport Chinese, as well. The law was repealed by the Magnuson Act in 1943. The Magnuson Act is also known as the Chinese Exclusion Repeal Act. President Franklin D. Roosevelt signed the act. The exclusion was repealed because China was an ally with the United States against Japan during World War II.

Average number of words per sentence: ___
Average number of words per sentence in your revision: ___

Arguing from Several Reading Selections

8

WHAT IS AN ARGUMENT?

Well, an argument is probably *not* what Calvin proposes in the cartoon on the facing page ("I say, either agree with me or take a hike!"). Attitudes like Calvin's usually lead to quarrels and angry confrontations, which are, unfortunately, what many people think of when they hear the word *argument*.

The "argument" that you will write in this chapter will not be a quarrel in which you beat your reader into submission. Instead, it will be exactly the kind of writing you have been practicing all semester—a reasonable presentation of facts, statistics, examples, and other support in an attempt to convince your reader that your thesis makes sense. To a degree, you have been arguing every time you have written a paper this semester, for in each assignment you have attempted to support a thesis statement with reasonable and convincing evidence.

The difference between the earlier assignments and what is normally called an "argumentative" paper is that an argumentative thesis takes a stand on a *debatable* subject. As a result, your readers may already have opinions about your subject. Your job is to convince them that the opinion you express in your thesis is reasonable and worthy of their serious consideration. That's easier said than done.

To write a convincing argument, you will need to draw upon the writing skills you have been practicing so far:

- You will need to choose an appropriate topic, one that you can support with facts, examples, statistics, and statements from authority.
- You will need to organize your support into unified paragraphs that are introduced by clear and accurate topic sentences.

- You will need to summarize, paraphrase, and quote accurately when you draw material from reading selections.
- You will need to distinguish between facts and opinions as well as between specific and general statements.

THE ATTITUDE OF THE EFFECTIVE ARGUER

When you argue a position, no matter what the situation, your *attitude* can make all the difference in the world. Obviously, if your attitude, like Calvin's, is "I'm right, period! End of discussion!" you will not have much success. But even if you present evidence to support your ideas, you probably will not have much success if you are close-minded and show no understanding of your opposition's point of view. In fact, on many debatable issues, you should not expect to write a completely convincing argument; after all, an issue is debatable precisely *because* there are convincing arguments on both sides of it. As you approach any complicated, debatable issue, keep in mind the following points.

Keep an open mind until you have looked closely at the issue. Perhaps the biggest mistake that many people make is *first* to decide what they think and *then* set out to prove that they are right. This is probably a natural thing to do—after all, nobody likes to be wrong—but will not lead to clear thinking and well-written arguments.

Whatever your beliefs are, set them aside until you have completed your study of the issue. As you read articles, talk to people, and consider your own experience, *be willing to change your mind* if the evidence suggests that you should—that willingness is one of the characteristics of a clear thinker.

Don't write as if your evidence completely resolves the issue. Debatable topics exist because the "one, true" answer is not at all clear, so don't take the attitude that your evidence proves your opinion is right and all others are wrong. It probably doesn't. What it *may* prove—if your support is effective enough—is that your opinion is *reasonable* and should be considered by reasonable people. Too often people approach arguments as battles in which the other side must be thoroughly destroyed and discredited. But the "other side" is usually a figment of our imagination. There may be two or three or four or more ways of approaching a debatable issue—not one right way (yours) and one wrong way (theirs).

Don't misunderstand us. You *should* support your argument as well as you can, and you *should* be willing to take a stand. But you should also be willing to recognize points that might weaken your argument and to qualify your position if you need to.

PREPARING THE ARGUMENT

COLLECTING INFORMATION

As you have already read, the first step is *not* to take a stand or write a thesis statement. Even though you may already have an opinion on your topic, remember that the sign of a good thinker is the willingness to modify, qualify, or change an opinion if the information that has been collected and examined requires such a change. For example, suppose you think that watching too much television can cause serious problems, especially for children, so you decide to make television viewing the subject of your essay. Your *first* step is to try your best to set aside your personal opinion, keep an open mind, and start collecting information related to *both sides* of your topic. Your goal should be to come to an understanding of the opposing arguments related to television viewing and *only then* to draw a conclusion of your own. For the most part, the information you collect will come from material you read, from people you talk to, and from your own experiences.

LISTING AND EVALUATING INFORMATION

As you collect information, organize it into lists that reflect opposing attitudes toward the subject. For instance, a writer investigating the benefits and drawbacks of television viewing might develop the lists presented below after examining the article by Paul Robinson in Part Four of this book as well as other articles (not in this text) by William Henry III, Madeline Drexler, and Donna Woolfolk Cross and after considering her personal experiences and the experiences of people she knows. If you have worked through the synthesis assignment in Chapter 7, you will recognize this list. Although an argument paper takes a stand while the synthesis does not, both assignments require that you understand all sides of the issue before you write the paper. (When you list an item, remember to identify its source so you can return to the article for more information when you evaluate the arguments.)

Is Television Educational?

Yes	No
• TV can provide learning. (Henry)	• TV cannot provide the time needed to learn. (Robinson)
• Children learn alphabet from *Sesame Street*. (Henry)	• Learning requires time to absorb facts. It requires reading. (Robinson)
• High school students learn about toxic waste on beaches. (Henry)	• A documentary about Marin County cannot really be accurate because it does not have the time to cover the complexities of life there. (Robinson)

- A study by psychologist Daniel Anderson says children learn to think and draw inferences as they watch TV.
  (Drexler)
- Same study—TV does not replace reading; it replaces other recreational activities.
  (Drexler)
- Same study—TV watching does not lower IQ, although people with lower IQ do tend to watch more TV.
  (Drexler)
- Personal experience—I have used movies like *Gone with the Wind* to discuss history with my kids. A special about Bill Cosby led to questions about typical lifestyle of African Americans.

- Educational TV is the worst kind— it makes people think they know something when they really don't.
  (Robinson)

Does Television Make Us Better People?

Yes

- TV's characters embody human truths.
  (Henry)
- They epitomize what we feel about ourselves.
  (Henry)
- They teach behavior and values. The character of Mary Richards summed up the lives of a whole generation of women.
  (Henry)
- Without TV we might be less violent, have more respect for institutions, be healthier, but we also might be less alert, less informed, less concerned about world matters, lonelier.
  (Henry)

No

- Opinion of psychologist Daniel Anderson—the violence, sexism, and materialism on TV are having a major social impact on our children.
  (Drexler)
- TV is often used as a form of escapism.
  (Drexler)
- TV causes confusion between reality and illusion.
  (Woolfolk Cross)
- Personal knowledge—I have seen news reports about children imitating violent acts on television.

Is Television Valuable as Entertainment?

Yes

- TV is very good at entertaining. Jack Benny and Art Carney would not be nearly as funny in print. You need to see them and watch their timing.
  (Robinson)

No

- Many times watching TV is a default activity because there is nothing else to do.
  (Woolfolk Cross)

- Personal experience—I use TV to relax and entertain myself.
- A study by psychologist Daniel Anderson says when parents and kids watch together, kids tend to think about what they see.

(Drexler)

- Personal experience—My children have never confused TV with reality as far as I know, but we watch TV together and talk about what we see.

- TV entertainment mesmerizes viewers. Kids prefer videos to real life.

(Woolfolk Cross)

- Boys on raft were disappointed because it was more fun on TV.

(Woolfolk Cross)

- Children preferred to watch a video of a fight rather than the real thing.

(Woolfolk Cross)

- UPI reported children watching TV next to the corpse of their dead father.

(Woolfolk Cross)

- In a Univ. of Nebraska study, over half of children chose TV over their fathers.

(Woolfolk Cross)

- Former DA Mario Merola says a jury wants the drama of TV and is less likely to convict if it doesn't get it.

(Woolfolk Cross)

As you can see, there is quite a bit of material to consider before you decide exactly where you stand, and not all of the material can be neatly divided into pro/con arguments. This writer, however, has attempted to divide the points she has found into three general groupings. The first focuses primarily on the educational value of television; the second seems to concern itself with television's impact on our behavior and values; and the third discusses both television's entertainment ability and the fear that television blurs the distinction between what is real and what is not.

At this point, you are in a position to evaluate the evidence. You have before you several major arguments about the benefits and drawbacks of television, some of which seem to directly contradict each other. Which seem more convincing? Consider which arguments use facts, examples, and expert testimony and which seem to rely more on unsupported opinions. Compare your own personal experiences to the arguments presented to see if they support or refute them.

As you evaluate the arguments, do not fall into the trap of thinking that one side must be right and the other must be wrong. Often that is just not the case. Do you see, for example, that it is possible that television has some benefits *and* some drawbacks, that the question is not necessarily a black-or-white or a right-or-wrong issue? Such complexity is exactly why debatable, controversial issues *are* debatable and controversial. Both sides usually have points that need to be taken seriously. If you recognize the valid points on both sides of an issue and are willing to admit it when your opposition makes a good argument, then you have a better chance of convincing your reader that your own stand is a reasonable one that you have carefully thought out.

TAKING A STAND

Perhaps the most important point to note here is that taking a stand is the *final* step in preparing an argument, not the first step. Once you have collected, listed, and evaluated the various arguments related to your topic, you need to decide what your opinion is. Remember that you do not have to prove that everything your opposition says is wrong for you to hold a differing opinion. Nor do you have to pretend that the reasons you give for your opinion should convince a reasonable person that you are right. What you *will* have to do is take a stand that you can reasonably support with the evidence available and that does not require you to simply ignore evidence that refutes your opinion.

OUTLINING AND ORGANIZING THE ARGUMENT

Several methods can be used to organize the material in an effective argument, but they all involve presenting points in support of your position and responding to points that seem to refute your position. *Before* you write the first draft of your paper, you should outline the points you intend to cover and the organizational pattern that will best serve your argument.

Below are some possible organizational patterns you can use. For shorter essays, each Roman numeral indicates a separate paragraph, but for longer essays, each numeral might indicate two or more paragraphs. In either case, you must remember to support each point with facts, examples, statistics, and references to authority, drawn either from your reading or from your own experiences or the experiences of people you know.

    I. Introduction and thesis
   II. First point in support of your thesis
  III. Second point in support of your thesis
  IV. Third point in support of your thesis (more points as needed)
   V. Major objection to your thesis and your response to it
  VI. Concluding paragraph

As you can see, this organization focuses primarily on presenting points that support your thesis, saving your discussion of any major objection until the end of the essay. Some topics, however, work better if the major objection is covered first, as in an organization like this:

    I. Introduction and thesis
   II. Major objection to your thesis and your response to it
  III. First point in support of your thesis
  IV. Second point in support of your thesis
   V. Third point in support of your thesis (more points as needed)
  VI. Concluding paragraph

Sometimes you may be taking a particularly unpopular stand, to which there are many obvious objections. In such a situation, consider this kind of organization:

  I. Introduction and thesis
 II. First objection and your response to it
III. Second objection and your response to it
 IV. Third objection and your response to it (more objections and responses as needed)
  V. First point in support of your thesis
 VI. Second point in support of your thesis (more points as needed)
VII. Concluding paragraph

Obviously, the organization and length of your argument can vary greatly, depending on how many objections you need to respond to and how many points you intend to cover. Here is an outline for a possible paper on the benefits of television:

  I. Introduction and thesis
- Open with example of when I came home and kids were watching *The Simpsons*.
- Tentative thesis: TV has more benefits than drawbacks.

 II. One benefit: It's entertaining and relaxing.
- Support with personal experience of how it helps me after a long day as a student, employee, and mom.
- Use Robinson's point about importance of entertainment.

III. Another benefit: It can educate us and make us better thinkers.
- Use examples from Henry article.
- Use personal examples of *Gone with the Wind* and the special about Bill Cosby.

 IV. Another benefit: It makes people more aware of the world they live in.
- Use personal examples of my kids asking questions about reruns of *I Love Lucy* and *Roseanne*.
- Use Drexler's article about psychologist who says children think when helped by parents.

  V. Major objection: Woolfolk Cross says TV blurs reality and fantasy.
- If TV is used incorrectly, she is right.
- Refer to Drexler article again about parents guiding their children.

 VI. Another objection: TV hinders education because it replaces reading.
- Use personal experience of my kids to show this isn't so.

VII. Conclusion

WRITING THE ARGUMENT

If you have outlined and organized your points, writing the first draft of your paper should be no more difficult than writing the first drafts of every other paper you have written so far. Consider these points as you write:

1. Open your paper with an interesting lead-in. See Chapter 3 for a discussion of the many possibilities available to you.

2. Write a thesis statement that takes a clear position, but do not hesitate to qualify it if you need to. Notice, for example, how the qualification before this thesis helps the writer sound like a reasonable person: "*I know that the television can be abused and misused, but so can any good thing. On the whole, it seems to me that television watching has far more benefits than drawbacks.*"

3. Write clear topic sentences that refer to the central idea expressed in your thesis.

4. Support your topic sentences with facts, examples, statistics, and references to authority drawn either from your reading or from your own experiences or the experiences of people you know.

5. Respond to major objections in a reasonable manner. If the objection is simply inaccurate, explain why, giving support of your own. If the objection is reasonable yet does not change your point of view, explain why the reader should find your overall argument more persuasive.

6. See Chapter 3 for effective ways to conclude your essay.

PARAPHRASING, QUOTING, AND DOCUMENTING YOUR SOURCES

When you use material from the reading selections, identify the sources of all paraphrases, summaries, and quotations. Use clear transitions to introduce borrowed material as well as parentheses to identify the author and page number of each source. Refer to "Writing Paraphrases and Quotations" (pages 162–165), "Documenting Your Sources" (pages 242–243), and the Appendix (pages 447–465).

READINGS: ONLINE WORLDS: FRIEND OR FOE?

BEFORE YOU READ

1. What is your initial reaction to the idea that experiences on the Internet can be as negative as they are positive? Would you call your reaction a personal opinion or a considered opinion?

2. What arguments do you expect to find regarding the benefits of the Internet versus its drawbacks?

3. As you read the following articles, set aside any personal opinions you may hold. Try to keep an open mind as you collect information about the issue.

Is Internet Addiction a Real Thing?   Maria Konnikova

Maria Konnikova writes for The New Yorker *online, focusing on psychology and culture. Her first book,* Mastermind: How to Think Like Sherlock Holmes *(Viking/Penguin, 2013), was a* New York Times *bestseller and has been translated into seventeen languages. She graduated magna cum laude from Harvard University, where she studied psychology, creative writing, and government, and received her Ph.D. in psychology from Columbia University. In the following selection, published in 2014 in* The New Yorker, *she examines the reasons compulsive Internet activity may or may not be classified as an addiction.*

Marc Potenza, a psychiatrist at Yale and the director of the school's 1
Program for Research on Impulsivity and Impulse Control Disorders, has been treating addiction for more than two decades. Early in his career, he, like most others studying addiction at the time, focused on substance-abuse problems—cocaine and heroin addicts, alcoholics, and the like. Soon, however, he noticed patients with other problems that were more difficult to classify. There were, for example, the sufferers of trichotillomania, the inescapable urge to pull your hair until it falls out. Others had been committed for problem gambling: they couldn't stop no matter how much debt they had accumulated. It was to this second class of behaviors— at the time, they were not called addictions—that he turned his attention. Were they, he wondered, fundamentally the same?

In some sense, they aren't. A substance affects a person physi- 2
cally in a way that a behavior simply cannot: no matter how severe your trichotillomania, you're not introducing something new to your bloodstream. But, in what may be a more fundamental way, they share much in common. As Potenza and his colleague Robert Leeman point out in a recent review of the last two decades of research, there are many commonalities between those two categories of addiction. Both behavioral and substance addictions are characterized by an inability to control how often or how intensely you engage in an activity, even when you feel the negative consequences. Both come with urges and cravings: you feel a sudden and debilitating need to place a bet or to take a hit in the middle of a meal. Both are marked by an inability to stop.

Substance and behavioral addictions also both seem to have   3
some genetic basis, and, Potenza has found, the genetics seem
to share many common characteristics. Some of the same gene
mutations found in alcoholics and drug addicts, for instance, are
often found in problem gamblers. Furthermore, the neurochem-
istry that these addictions evoke in the brain is similar. Drugs, for
example, are known to affect the mesolimbic dopamine pathway—the pleasure center of the brain. Behaviors like gambling
similarly activate the same parts of the brain's reward circuitry.
Earlier this year, Trevor Robbins, a cognitive neuroscientist at the
University of Cambridge, and the psychologist Luke Clark, then
at Cambridge and now the director of the Centre for Gambling
Research at the University of British Columbia, came to a similar
conclusion after conducting an overview of the existing clinical
research into behavior addictions. The basic neuroscience of the
two types of addiction showed a substantial overlap.

In recent years, however, Potenza has been increasingly treat-   4
ing a new kind of problem: people who come to him because
they can't get off the Internet. In some ways, it seems exactly like
the behavioral addictions that he has been treating for years, with
much of the same consequences. "There are core features that cut
across those conditions," Potenza says. "Things like the motivation
to engage in the behaviors and put aside other important elements of life functioning, just to engage in them." Or, in the words
of Robbins and Clark, "behavior for behavior's sake."

There's something different, and more complicated, about   5
Internet addiction, though. Unlike gambling or even trichotillomania, it's more difficult to pin down a quantifiable, negative effect of
Internet use. With problematic gambling, you're losing money and
causing harm to yourself and your loved ones. But what about
symptoms like those of a woman I'll call Sue, who is a patient of
Potenza? A young college student, Sue first came to Potenza at the
behest of her parents, who were becoming increasingly concerned
about the changes in their daughter. A good—and social—student
in high school, she found herself depressed, skipping or dropping
classes, foregoing all college extracurricular activities, and, increasingly, using the Internet to set up extreme sexual encounters with
people she had never met in real life. Sue spends the majority of
her time online social networking, but does that mean that she has
a problem with the Internet or with managing her social life and
her sex life? What if she were obsessively online, for the rest of her
life, but learning languages or editing Wikipedia?

The Internet, after all, is a medium, not an activity in and of   6
itself. If you spend your time gambling online, maybe you have a
gambling addiction, not an Internet addiction. If you spend your
time shopping online, maybe it's a shopping addiction. "Some
people have posited that the Internet is a vehicle and not a target
of disorder," Potenza said. Can you be addicted to a longing for
virtual connectivity in the same way that you can be addicted to a
longing for a drink? As far back as 1997, before the days of ubiquitous smartphones and laptops, when dial-up and AOL dominated
the landscape, psychologists were already testing the "addictive
potential" of the World Wide Web. Even then, certain people were
exhibiting the same kinds of symptoms that appeared with other
addictions: trouble at work, social isolation, and the inability to cut
back. And, to the extent that there was something that people
referred to as an addiction, it appeared to be to the medium
itself—the feeling of connectedness to something—rather than to
an activity that could be accomplished via that medium.

By 2008, the worry about Internet addiction progressed to   7
such a point that *The American Journal of Psychiatry* published an
editorial strongly suggesting that Internet Addiction be included
in the next, and fifth, version of the so-called bible of psychiatry,
the *Diagnostic and Statistical Manual* (DSM). A decade of research,
wrote the psychiatrist Jerald Block, had only proven what the 1997
study had suspected, that the Internet could inspire the same patterns of excessive usage, withdrawal, tolerance, and negative reper-
cussions as more traditional substance use. What's more, Block
concluded, "Internet addiction is resistant to treatment, entails
significant risks, and has high relapse rates." It was a disease that
needed treatment as much as any other disease did.

The realization that the Internet may be inducing some   8
addictive-seeming behaviors in its own right has only grown more
widespread. One study, published in 2012, of nearly twelve thousand
adolescents in eleven European countries, found a 4.4 percent
prevalence of what the authors termed "pathological Internet use"
or using the Internet in a way that affected subjects' health and life.
That is, through a combination of excessive time spent online
and that time interfering with necessary social and professional
activities, Internet use would result in either mental distress or clinical impairment, akin to the type of inability to function associated
with pathological gambling. For maladaptive Internet use—a milder
condition characterized by problematic but not yet fully disruptive
behavior—the number was 13.5 per cent. People who exhibited

problematic use were also more likely to suffer from other psychological problems, such as depression, anxiety, A.D.H.D., and O.C.D.

Internet addiction ultimately did not make the list of offi-   9
cially recognized behavioral addictions in DSM-V, but compulsive
gambling did. It had taken gambling several decades of extensive
research to make the cut, and there simply wasn't enough sys-
tematic, longitudinal data about Internet addiction. But, to Potenza,
Block's conclusions rang true. Sue wasn't the first patient that he'd
seen for whom the Internet was causing substantial, escalating
problems; that number had been rising slowly over the last few
years, and his colleagues were reporting the same uptick. He had
been working with addicts for decades, and her problems, as well
as those of her fellow sufferers, were every bit as real as those of
the gambling addicts. And it wasn't just an iteration of college angst
in a new form. It was something endemic to the medium itself. "I
think there are people who find it very difficult to tolerate time
without using digital technologies like smartphones or other ways
of connecting via the Internet," Potenza said. It's the very knowledge of connectivity, or its lack, that's the problem.

He agrees that the subject remains far more disputed than   10
other behavioral areas: psychiatrists are no longer debating that
behavioral addictions exist, but they are ambivalent about whether
Internet use can be classified as one of them. The difference,
Potenza feels, is one of degree. Internet use remains so disputed
because it's changing too rapidly for researchers to keep up, and,
though the immediate effects are fairly visible, there's no telling
what the condition will look like over the long term.

Internet addiction remains a relatively minor part of Poten-   11
za's work—he estimates that fewer than ten out of every forty
patients he sees come in for an Internet problem. These patients
tend to be younger, and there seems to be a gender divide: male
patients are more likely to be addicted to activities like online gaming; women, to things like social networking. But it's hard to make
generalizations, because the nature of the problem keeps changing.
"The truth is, we don't know what's normal," Potenza says. "It's not
like alcohol where we have healthy amounts that we can recommend to people." In other words, just because you're online all day
doesn't mean you're an addict: there are no norms or hard numbers that could tell us either way.

Behavioral addictions are quite real, and, in a number of respects, 12
Internet addiction shares their core features. But the differences
that set it apart mean that the avenues of treatment may differ

somewhat from those typically associated with behavioral—and substance—addictions. One of the most effective ways of treating those addictions is by identifying and removing the catalysts. Cancel the credit card. Get rid of the bottles. Avoid the places you go to drink or to gamble, and, at times, avoid the people you do these activities with. Be aware of your triggers. With the Internet, though, that solution is far more problematic. Computers and virtual connections have become an integral part of daily life. You can't just pull the plug and expect to function. A student may be suffering from what she's doing online, but she also might need to use the Internet for her classes. The thing she needs to avoid in order to do well is also the thing she needs to use to reach the same end.

But Potenza hopes that that very ubiquity can, ultimately, be   13
enlisted as part of the solution. You may not be able to remove the triggers, but you can reprogram the thing itself, a kind of virtual bottle that automatically clamps shut when you've had too much to drink or a casino that turns off its lights as you move into dangerous territory. "The hope is to harness these same technologies within the mental-health field to promote health," Potenza said. Already, there are apps that block certain Web pages or that disable a computer's Internet connectivity. There are also ones that tell you when to put your smartphone away. Why not customize them, in conjunction with a therapist, to avoid the pitfalls that are most likely to lead to problem use for you personally? As is so often the case, technology may end up being both the problem and the answer.

Lost in an Online Fantasy World:
As Virtual Universes Grow, So Do Ranks
of the Game-Obsessed   OLGA KHAZAN

Olga Khazan is a freelance journalist based in Los Angeles and a graduate student in online journalism at the University of Southern California, where she also works in the New Media department. She graduated magna cum laude from American University in 2008 with a dual degree in political science and communications, law, economics and government. While in D.C., she worked as a freelance writer for the Northwest Current, *a local newspaper, and for a number of Web-based publications. The following reading selection was published in* The Washington Post *on August 18, 2006.*

They are war heroes, leading legions into battle through intricately   1
designed realms. They can be sorcerers or space pilots, their

identities woven into a world so captivating, it is too incredible to ever leave. Unfortunately, some of them don't.

Video games have often been portrayed as violence-ridden   2
vehicles for teen angst. But after 10 people in South Korea—mostly teenagers and young adults—died last year from game-addiction causes, including one man who collapsed in an Internet cafe after playing an online game for 50 hours with few breaks, some began to see a new technological threat.

Participation in massively multiplayer online role-playing games,   3
also called MMORPGs or MMOs, has skyrocketed from less than a million subscribers in the late 1990s to more than 13 million worldwide in 2006. With each new game boasting even more spectacular and immersive adventures, new ranks of gamers are drawn to their riveting story lines. Like gambling, pornography or any other psychological stimulant, these games have the potential to thrill, engross and completely overwhelm.

The most widely played MMO, Blizzard Entertainment's *World*   4
of Warcraft, has 6.5 million players worldwide, most of whom play 20 to 22 hours per week. Thousands can be logged in simultaneously to four different WoW servers (each its own self-contained "realm"), interacting with players across the globe in a vast virtual fantasy setting full of pitched battles and other violent adventures.

Brady Mapes, a 24-year-old computer programmer from   5
Gaithersburg, Md., and an avid *WoW* fan, calls it a "highly addictive game—it sucks the life out of you."

An MMO differs from an offline game in that the game world   6
evolves constantly as each player's actions directly or indirectly influence the lives of other players' characters. In *WoW*, players can simply attack one another, interact with the environment, or role-play in more complex relationships. More time playing means greater virtual wealth and status, as well as access to higher game levels and more-exciting content.

In addition, online gamers can join teams or groups (called "guilds"   7
in *WoW*) that tackle game challenges cooperatively. Fellow team members see membership as a commitment and expect participation in virtual raids and other joint activities. The constant interaction with other players can lead to friendships and personal connections.

"All I Could Think about Was Playing"
"The main reason people are playing is because there are other   8
people out there," said Dmitri Williams, an assistant professor at the University of Illinois at Urbana–Champaign, who has

researched the social impacts of MMOs. "People know your name, they share your interests, they miss you when you leave."

As MMO fan sites filled with raving gamers proliferate, so have online-addiction help blogs, where desperate recluses and gamers' neglected spouses search for a way out.   9

"I don't want to do everything with [my husband], but it would be nice to have a meaningful conversation once in a while," writes one pregnant wife on Everquest Daily Grind, a blog for those affected by excessive use of another popular fantasy MMO. "He does not have much interest in the baby so far, and I am worried that after it is born, he will remain the same while I am struggling to work and take care of the baby."   10

Another gamer writes that she was angry at her boyfriend for introducing her to online gaming, which began consuming her life at the expense of her personal and academic well-being.   11

"But I think deleting [your] character doesn't work, because the game haunts you," she said. "All I could think about was playing."   12

Kimberly Young, who has treated porn and chat-room addicts since 1994 at her Center for Internet Addiction Recovery, said that in the past year video game fixation has grown more than anything else.   13

"In MMOs, people lead wars and receive a lot of recognition," Young said. "It's hard to stop and go clean your room. Real life is much less interesting."   14

The trend echoes across the continents, with game-addiction treatment centers cropping up in China in 2005 and this summer in Amsterdam. In South Korea, where 70 percent of the population has broadband Internet access, the Korea Agency for Digital Opportunity offers government-funded counseling for the game-hooked.   15

"The Real World Gets Worse"

The games are set up to be lengthy, with a quest taking six hours or more to complete. The organization of players into cooperative teams creates a middle-school-esque atmosphere of constant peer pressure.   16

"You're letting other people down if you quit," Young said. "If you are good, the respect becomes directly reinforcing."   17

According to research performed by Nick Yee, a Stanford graduate student and creator of the Daedalus Project, an online survey of more than 40,000 MMO players, the average player is 26 years old; most hold full-time jobs. Seventy percent have played for 10 hours straight at some point, and about 45 percent would describe themselves as "addicted."   18

Yee believes escapism to be the best predictor of excessive   19
gaming. A person who plays MMOs in order to avoid real-life
problems, rather than simply for entertainment or socialization, is
more likely to experience what he calls "problematic usage."

"People feel like they lack control in real life, and the game   20
gives them a social status and value that they are less and less able
to achieve in the real world," Yee said. "As a result, the real world
gets worse and the virtual world gets better in comparison."

Liz Woolley, a Wisconsin software analyst and veteran of Alco-   21
holics Anonymous, founded Online Gamers Anonymous in May
2002 by adapting AA's 12-step addiction recovery model to help
gamers quit cold-turkey. Woolley recommends getting professional
help for underlying issues and finding other hobbies and real-world
activities to replace gaming.

"Addicts want to live in a fantasy life because you can't do a   22
'do-over' in real life," she said. "It can be hard to accept. You have to
let them know, 'Hey, this is real life. Learn to deal with it.'"

"Every Player Has a Choice"

"People are reluctant to point a finger at themselves," said Jason   23
Della Rocca, executive director of the International Game Developers Association. Excessive use "is a reflection of friction in that
person's life. They shouldn't use the game as a scapegoat."

Casual gamers may find it difficult to advance to the game's   24
highest levels in the face of more dedicated rivals, such as Mapes,
the Gaithersburg *WoW* fan, whose highest-level warrior character
is a force to be reckoned with. "If I go up against someone who
only plays for one to two hours, I'll decimate them," he said. "There
are other games out there if you only want to play a couple hours
at a time."

That dedication sometimes pushes Mapes to see the game as   25
more of a chore than a pastime. "Sometimes I realize that I'm not
having any fun, but I just can't stop," he said.

Several of the MMO researchers interviewed for this story   26
pointed out that many game companies employ psychologists who
analyze the games and suggest ways to make them easier to play
over long stretches of time.

Della Rocca argues that because online games' monthly sub-   27
scription rates remain constant regardless of how many hours a
subscriber spends on the network, developers profit less when
gamers play more intensively.

The psychologists "monitor subjects playing the games in order   28
to eliminate flaws and points of frustration," Della Rocca said. "The
notion that we are trying to seduce gamers is a fabrication of people who don't understand how games are developed."

Since Blizzard Entertainment released *WoW* in 2004, calls to   29
Online Gamers Anonymous have more than tripled, according to
Woolley, who said the industry is directly at fault for the suffering
of the people she tries to help.

"I think the game companies are nothing more than drug push-   30
ers," she said. "If I was a parent, I wouldn't let them in my house. It's
like dropping your kids off at a bar and leaving them there."

The signs of excessive MMO use are similar to those of alco-   31
holism or any other dependency—tolerance, withdrawal, lying or
covering up, to name a few. However, many in the industry are
hesitant to call it an addiction because, in the case of MMOs, the
nature of the problem is based on how it affects the user's life, not
the amount of time spent playing.

According to tvturnoff.org, Americans spend an average of   32
28 hours a week watching television, a fact that has yet to spawn a
bevy of dependence clinics.

"If a person was reading novels excessively, we'd be less likely   33
to call that 'addiction' because we value reading as culture," said the
University of Illinois's Williams. "We see game play as frivolous due
to our Protestant work ethic. There's plenty of anecdotal evidence
out there to suggest this is a problem, but it's not the role of science to guess or bet."

Mapes, who has played other engrossing titles such as Medal of   34
Honor and Diablo and eventually set them aside, said the decision
to control excessive gaming is one any player can make.

"Ultimately, every player has a choice to stop," he said. "I've   35
stopped before, and I've seen other people stop if they get
burned out."

"No One Was Talking about It"

Woolley disagrees, especially after witnessing the bitter outcome of   36
her son's Everquest obsession.

Shawn had played online games before, so she didn't suspect   37
anything different when he picked up the newest MMO from Sony.
Within months, Woolley said, Shawn withdrew from society, losing
his job and apartment and moving back home to live a virtual life
he found more fulfilling.

After a number of game-induced grand mal seizures sent   38
Shawn, who was epileptic, to the emergency room repeatedly, he
chose to pay ambulance bills rather than stop playing. The medical
professionals he saw treated his external symptoms but dismissed
his gaming condition.

"They told me, 'Be glad he's not addicted to something worse,   39
like drugs,' and sent him home," Woolley said.

On Thanksgiving Day 2001, Woolley found 21-year-old Shawn   40
dead in front of his computer after having committed suicide. Everquest was on the screen.

Readers' responses to an article written about the incident   41
in a local Wisconsin paper poured in, and the national attention
Shawn's story subsequently received prompted Woolley to start
up a self-help Web site. In the four years since its launch, Online
Gamers Anonymous (http://www.olganon.org/) has had 125 million
hits and registered more than 2,000 members, Woolley said.

"I realized that gaming addiction was an underground epidemic   42
affecting thousands of people, but no one was talking about it," she
said. "I wasn't worried about pressure from the gaming industry. I
thought, 'You already took my kid, you can't take anything else.'"

Dream Machines   WILL WRIGHT

*Will Wright is cofounder of Maxis, a game development company, and creator of The
Sims and many other games. He has been called one of the most important people
in gaming, technology, and entertainment by publications such as* Entertainment
Weekly, Time, PC Gamer, Discover, *and* GameSpy. *Wright was also awarded
the PC Magazine Lifetime Achievement Award in January 2005. The following
article appeared in* Wired *magazine in April 2006.*

The human imagination is an amazing thing. As children, we spend   1
much of our time in imaginary worlds, substituting toys and make-
believe for the real surroundings that we are just beginning to
explore and understand. As we play, we learn. And as we grow, our
play gets more complicated. We add rules and goals. The result is
something we call games.

Now an entire generation has grown up with a different set of   2
games than any before it—and it plays these games in different ways.
Just watch a kid with a new videogame. The last thing they do is read
the manual. Instead, they pick up the controller and start mashing
buttons to see what happens. This isn't a random process; it's the
essence of the scientific method. Through trial and error, players

build a model of the underlying game based on empirical evidence collected through play. As the players refine this model, they begin to master the game world. It's a rapid cycle of hypothesis, experiment, and analysis. And it's a fundamentally different take on problem-solving than the linear, read-the-manual-first approach of their parents.

In an era of structured education and standardized testing, this generational difference might not yet be evident. But the gamers' mindset—the fact that they are learning in a totally new way— means they'll treat the world as a place for creation, not consumption. This is the true impact videogames will have on our culture.   3

Society, however, notices only the negative. Most people on the far side of the generational divide—elders—look at games and see a list of ills (they're violent, addictive, childish, worthless). Some of these labels may be deserved. But the positive aspects of gaming— creativity, community, self-esteem, problem-solving—are somehow less visible to nongamers.   4

I think part of this stems from the fact that watching someone play a game is a different experience than actually holding the controller and playing it yourself. Vastly different. Imagine that all you knew about movies was gleaned through observing the audience in a theater—but that you had never watched a film. You would conclude that movies induce lethargy and junk-food binges. That may be true, but you're missing the big picture.   5

So it's time to reconsider games, to recognize what's different about them and how they benefit—not denigrate—culture. Consider, for instance, their "possibility space": Games usually start at a well-defined state (the setup in chess, for instance) and end when a specific state is reached (the king is checkmated). Players navigate this possibility space by their choices and actions; every player's path is unique.   6

Games cultivate—and exploit—possibility space better than any other medium. In linear storytelling, we can only imagine the possibility space that surrounds the narrative: What if Luke had joined the Dark Side? What if Neo isn't the One? In interactive media, we can explore it.   7

Like the toys of our youth, modern videogames rely on the player's active involvement. We're invited to create and interact with elaborately simulated worlds, characters, and story lines. Games aren't just fantasy worlds to explore; they actually amplify our powers of imagination.   8

Think of it this way: Most technologies can be seen as an enhancement of some part of our bodies (car/legs, house/skin, TV/   9 senses). From the start, computers have been understood as an extension of the human brain; the first computers were referred to as mechanical brains and analytical engines. We saw their primary value as automated number crunchers that far exceeded our own meager abilities.

But the Internet has morphed what we used to think of as a fancy calculator into a fancy telephone with email, chat groups, IM, and blogs. It turns out that we don't use computers to enhance our math skills—we use them to expand our people skills. 10

The same transformation is happening in games. Early computer games were little toy worlds with primitive graphics and simple problems. It was up to the player's imagination to turn the tiny blobs on the screen into, say, people or tanks. As computer graphics advanced, game designers showed some Hollywood envy: They added elaborate cut scenes, epic plots, and, of course, increasingly detailed graphics. They bought into the idea that world building and storytelling are best left to professionals, and they pushed out the player. But in their rapture over computer processing, games designers forgot that there's a second processor at work: the player's imagination. 11

Now, rather than go Hollywood, some game designers are deploying that second processor to break down the wall between producers and consumers. By moving away from the idea that media is something developed by the few (movie and TV studios, book publishers, game companies) and consumed in a one-size-fits-all form, we open up a world of possibilities. Instead of leaving player creativity at the door, we are inviting it back to help build, design, and populate our digital worlds. 12

More games now include features that let players invent some aspect of their virtual world, from characters to cars. And more games entice players to become creative partners in world building, letting them mod its overall look and feel. The online communities that form around these imaginative activities are some of the most vibrant on the Web. For these players, games are not just entertainment but a vehicle for self-expression. 13

Games have the potential to subsume almost all other forms of entertainment media. They can tell us stories, offer us music, give us challenges, allow us to communicate and interact with others, encourage us to make things, connect us to new communities, and let us play. Unlike most other forms of media, games are inherently malleable. Player mods are just the first step down this path. 14

Soon games will start to build simple models of us, the players. 15 They will learn what we like to do, what we're good at, what interests and challenges us. They will observe us. They will record the decisions we make, consider how we solve problems, and evaluate how skilled we are in various circumstances. Over time, these games will become able to modify themselves to better "fit" each individual. They will adjust their difficulty on the fly, bring in new content, and create story lines. Much of this original material will be created by other players, and the system will move it to those it determines will enjoy it most.

Games are evolving to entertain, educate, and engage us individually. These personalized games will reflect who we are and what we enjoy, much as our choice of books and music does now. They will allow us to express ourselves, meet others, and create things that we can only dimly imagine. They will enable us to share and combine these creations, to build vast playgrounds. And more than ever, games will be a visible, external amplification of the human imagination. 16

Searching Online May Make You Think You're Smarter Than You Are
PONCIE RUTSCH

Poncie Rutsch is a writer at the National Public Radio Science Desk and also blogs for Shots, *the* Salt, *and* Goats and Soda. *This essay appeared on NPR in 2015.*

Using the Internet is an easy way to feel omniscient. Enter a search 1 term and the answers appear before your eyes.

But at any moment you're also just a few taps away from 2 becoming an insufferable know-it-all. Searching for answers online gives people an inflated sense of their own knowledge, according to a study. It makes people think they know more than they actually do.

"We think the information is leaking into our head, but really 3 the information is stored somewhere else entirely," Matthew Fisher, a doctoral student in cognitive psychology at Yale University, tells Shots. Fisher surveyed hundreds of people to get a sense of how searching the Internet affected how they rate their knowledge. His study was published Tuesday in the *Journal of Experimental Psychology: General.*

Fisher began with a simple survey: he asked questions such as 4 "How does a zipper work?" or "Why are there leap years?" He allowed just half of his subjects to use the Internet to answer the questions.

Then he asked the subjects to rate how well they thought 5
they could answer a question unrelated to the first question, such
as "Why does Swiss cheese have holes?" or "How do tornadoes
form?" People who had been allowed to search online tended to
rate their knowledge higher than people who answered without
any outside sources.

To reveal factors that might explain why the Internet group 6
rated their knowledge higher, he designed follow-up experiments
using different groups of people. First, he asked people to rate
their knowledge before the test; there was no difference between
subjects' ratings. But afterwards, the Internet-enabled subjects again
rated their knowledge better than the others.

Next, Fisher tried to make sure that people saw the exact 7
same information. He told the Internet-enabled group, "Please
search for the scientificamerican.com page with this information." The non-search group was sent directly to the page. Fisher
checked that the two groups used the same URL. Still, the people
who could actively search rated their knowledge higher than those
who simply saw the information.

And this is just a taste of the experiments Fisher ran. He also: 8

- Compared different search engines.
- Reworded his questions to make it clear that he was asking for
  only the subjects' knowledge, not the Internet's.
- Made the online searchers use filters that would keep any
  relevant results from showing up.
- Asked questions for which there were no answers online, such
  as "How do wheat fields affect the weather?"
- Asked people to choose one of seven brain scans that most
  resembled their brain. The people who had been searching
  online picked the image with the most activity.

The results kept coming back the same: searching online led to 9
knowledge inflation.

There are practical consequences to this little exercise. If we 10
can't accurately judge what we know, then who's to say whether
any of the decisions we make are well-informed?

"People are unlikely to be able to explain their own shortcom- 11
ings," says Fisher. "People aren't aware of the quality of explanation
or the quality of arguments they can produce, and they don't realize it until they encounter the gaps."

The more we rely on the Internet, Fisher says, the harder it will 12
be to draw a line between where our knowledge ends and the

web begins. And unlike poring through books or debating peers, asking the Internet is unique because it's so effortless.

"We are not forced to face our own ignorance and ask for   13
help; we can just look up the answer immediately," Fisher writes in
an email. "We think these features make it more likely for people
to consider knowledge stored online as their own."

AFTER YOU READ

Work with other students to develop responses to these questions or to compare responses that you have already prepared.

1. As in most debates, you should be able to find reasonable arguments about the dangers of the Internet as well as its benefits. Make a list of the arguments outlining the positive and negative impacts of Internet/computer usage.
2. As you evaluate the arguments and take a stand, consider also your own experiences or the experiences of people you know. In what way has the Internet affected you and the society in which you live? Have the arguments you have read in these articles affected your opinion?

READINGS: SCHOOL, TEENAGERS, AND PART-TIME JOBS

BEFORE YOU READ

1. Consider whether or not you think it is a good idea for teenagers to work part-time while they are going to school. What are the advantages and/or disadvantages involved?
2. Did you work as a teenager? If you did, explain in what ways your experience benefited you. Did your experience have any negative results?

The Fast-Food Factories: McJobs Are Bad for Kids
AMITAI ETZIONI

Amitai Etzioni received his Ph.D. from the University of California, Berkeley, in 1958. He served as professor of sociology at Columbia University for twenty years, as a professor at The George Washington University, and as senior advisor to the White House from 1979 to 1980. In 2001, he was named as being among the top one hundred American intellectuals as measured by academic citations. Dr. Etzioni is married and has five sons.

McDonald's is bad for your kids. I do not mean the flat patties   1
and the white-flour buns; I refer to the jobs teen-agers undertake,
mass-producing these choice items.

As many as two-thirds of America's high-school juniors and   2
seniors now hold down part-time paying jobs, according to studies.
Many of these are in fast-food chains, of which McDonald's is the
pioneer, trend-setter and symbol.

At first, such jobs may seem right out of the Founding Fathers'   3
educational manual for how to bring up self-reliant, work-ethic-
driven, productive youngsters. But in fact, these jobs undermine
school attendance and involvement, impart few skills that will
be useful in later life, and simultaneously skew the values of
teen-agers—especially their ideas about the worth of a dollar.

It has been a long-standing American tradition that youngsters   4
ought to get paying jobs. In folklore, few pursuits are more deeply
revered than the newspaper route and the sidewalk lemonade
stand. Here the youngsters are to learn how sweet are the fruits
of labor and self-discipline (papers are delivered early in the morning, rain or shine) and the ways of trade (if you price your lemonade too high or too low …).

Roy Rogers, Baskin-Robbins, Kentucky Fried Chicken, et al., may   5
at first seem nothing but a vast extension of the lemonade stand.
They provide very large numbers of teen jobs, provide regular
employment, pay quite well compared to many other teen jobs
and, in the modern equivalent of toiling over a hot stove, test one's
stamina.

Closer examination, however, finds the McDonald's kind of job   6
highly uneducational in several ways. Far from providing opportunities for entrepreneurship (the lemonade stand) or self-discipline,
self-supervision and self-scheduling (the paper route), most teen
jobs these days are highly structured—what social scientists call
"highly routinized."

True, you still have to have the gumption to get yourself over   7
to the hamburger stand, but once you don the prescribed uniform,
your task is spelled out in minute detail. The franchise prescribes
the shape of the coffee cups; the weight, size, shape and color of
the patties; and the texture of the napkins (if any). Fresh coffee is
to be made every eight minutes. And so on. There is no room for
initiative, creativity or even elementary rearrangements. These are
breeding grounds for robots working for yesterday's assembly lines,
not tomorrow's high-tech posts.

There are very few studies of the matter. One is a 1984   8
study by Ivan Chamer and Bryna Shore Fraser. It relies mainly on
what teen-agers write in response to questionnaires rather than
actual observations of fast-food jobs. The authors argue that the

employees develop many skills, such as how to operate a food-preparation machine and a cash register. However, little attention is paid to how long it takes to acquire such a skill, or what its significance is. What does it matter if you spend 20 minutes learning to use a cash register and then "operate" it? What "skill" have you acquired? It is a long way from learning to work with a lathe or carpenter tools in the olden days or to program computers in the modern age.

A 1980 study by A. V. Harrell and P. W. Wirtz found that, among   9
those students who worked at least 25 hours per week while in school, their unemployment rate four years later was half of that of seniors who did not work. This is an impressive statistic. It must be seen, though, together with the finding that many who begin as part-time employees in fast-food chains drop out of high school and are gobbled up in the world of low-skill jobs.

Some say that while these jobs are rather unsuited for college-   10
bound, white, middle-class youngsters, they are "ideal" for lower-class, "non-academic," minority youngsters. Indeed, minorities are "over-represented" in these jobs (21 percent of fast-food employees). While it is true that these places provide income, work and even some training to such youngsters, they also tend to perpetuate their disadvantaged status. They provide no career ladders and few marketable skills, and they undermine school attendance and involvement.

The hours are often long. Among those 14 to 17, a third of   11
fast-food employees (including some school drop-outs) labor more than 30 hours per week, according to the Charner-Fraser study. Only 20 percent work 15 hours or less. The rest: between 15 and 30 hours. Often the restaurants close late, and after closing one must clean up and tally up. In affluent Montgomery County, where child labor would not seem to be a widespread economic necessity, 24 percent of the seniors at Walt Whitman High School in 1985 worked as much as five to seven days a week; 27 percent, three to five. There is just no way such amounts of work will not interfere with school work, especially homework. In an informal survey published in the most recent Walt Whitman yearbook, 58 percent of the seniors acknowledged that their jobs interfere with their school work.

The Charner-Fraser study sees merit in learning teamwork   12
and working under supervision. The authors have a point here. However, it must be noted that such learning is not automatically educational or wholesome. For example, much of the supervision

in fast-food places leans toward teaching one the worst kinds of compliance: blind obedience, or shared alienation with the "boss."

Supervision is often both tight and woefully inappropriate. Today, fast-food chains and other such places of work (record shops, bowling alleys) keep costs down by having teens supervise teens, often with no adult on the premises. There is no father or mother figure with which to identify, to emulate, to provide a role model and guidance. The work-culture varies from one place to another: Sometimes it is a tightly run shop (must keep the cash registers ringing); sometimes a rather loose pot party interrupted by customers. However, only rarely is there a master to learn from, or much worth learning. Indeed, far from being places where solid adult work values are being transmitted, these are places where all too often delinquent teen values dominate. Typically, when my son Oren was dishing out ice cream for Baskin-Robbins in upper Manhattan, his fellow teen-workers considered him a sucker for not helping himself to the till. Most youngsters felt they were entitled to $50 severance "pay" on their last day on the job.

The pay, oddly, is the part of the teen work-world which is most difficult to evaluate. The lemonade stand or paper route money was for your allowance. In the old days, apprentices learning a trade from a master contributed most, if not all, of their income to their parents' household. Today, the teen pay may be low by adult standards, but it is often, especially in the middle class, spent largely or wholly by the teens. That is, the youngsters live free at home ("after all, they are high school kids") and are left with very substantial sums of money.

Where this money goes is not quite clear. Some use it to support themselves, especially among the poor. More middle class kids set some money aside to help pay for college, or save it for a major purchase—often a car. But large amounts seem to flow to pay for an early introduction into the most trite aspects of American consumerism: Flimsy punk clothes, trinkets and whatever else is the last fast-moving teen craze.

One may say that this is only fair and square; they are being good American consumers, working and spending their money on what turns them on. At least, a cynic might add, these funds do not go into illicit drugs and booze. On the other hand, an educator might bemoan that these young, yet unformed individuals, so early in life are driven to buy objects of no intrinsic educational, cultural or social merit, learn so quickly the dubious merit of keeping up with the Jones' in ever-changing fads promoted by mass merchandising.

Many teens find the instant reward of money, and the youth   17
status symbols it buys, much more alluring than credits in calculus
courses, European history, or foreign languages. No wonder quite
a few would rather skip school—and certainly homework—and
instead work longer at a Burger King. Thus, most teen work these
days is not providing early lessons in work ethic; it fosters escape
from school and responsibilities, quick gratification and a short cut
to the consumeristic aspects of adult life.

Thus, ironically, we must add youth employment, not merely   18
unemployment, to our list of social problems. And, like many
other social ills, the unfortunate aspects of teen work resist easy
correction. Sure, it would be much better if corporations that
employ teens would do so in conjunction with high schools and
school districts. Educators could help define what is the proper
amount of gainful work (not more than "X" hours per school
week), how late kids may be employed on school nights (not
later than 9 p.m.), encourage employer understanding during
exam periods, and insist on proper supervision. However, corporations are extremely unlikely to accept such an approach which,
in effect, would curb their ability to draw on a major source of
cheap labor. And, in these laissez-faire days, Congress is quite
disinclined to pass new social legislation forcing corporations to
be more attentive to the education needs of the minors they so
readily employ.

Schools might extend their own work-study programs (start-   19
ing their own franchises?!) but, without corporate help, these are
unlikely to amount to much. Luckily, few school[s] (less than 10
percent) provide any credit for such work experience. But schools
that do should insist that they will provide credit for work only if
it meets their educational standards; only if they are consulted on
matters such as supervision and on-the-job training; and only if
their representatives are allowed to inspect the places of employment. School counselors should guide the youngsters only to
those places of work that are willing to pay attention to educational elements of these jobs.

Parents who are still willing to take their role seriously may   20
encourage their youngsters to seek jobs at places that are proper
work settings and insist that fast-food chains and other franchises
shape up or not employ their kids. Also an agreement should be
reached with the youngsters that a significant share of teen
earnings should be dedicated to the family, or saved for agreed-
upon items.

Above all, parents should look at teen employment not   21
as automatically educational. It is an activity—like sports—
that can be turned into an educational opportunity. But it
can also easily be abused. Youngsters must learn to balance
the quest for income with the needs to keep growing and
pursue other endeavors which do not pay off instantly—above
all education.

Go back to school.

The Dead-End Kids   MICHELE MANGES

In the following reading selection, Michele Manges, a writer for the Wall Street
Journal, *suggests that part-time jobs today are not teaching teenagers any worthwhile skills or attitudes. Instead, as she says, "… youngsters hustle at monotonous,
dead-end jobs that prepare them for nothing." As you read the selection, consider
her points in light of your own knowledge or experience.*

If just showing up accounts for 90 percent of success in life, as   1
Woody Allen claims, then today's teenagers ought to make great
recruits for tomorrow's permanent work force.

Well over half of them are already showing up in the part-time   2
work force doing after-school and summer jobs. In times past,
this kind of youthful zeal was universally applauded; the kids, we
thought, were getting invaluable preliminary training for the world
of work. But now a lot of people are *worried* about the surge in
youth employment. Why?

Because a lot of today's eight million working teens—55 percent   3
of all 16- to 19-year-olds—aren't learning anything much more
useful than just showing up.

Taste of Adulthood

Not that long ago many youngsters could get part-time or sum-   4
mer jobs that taught them the rudiments of a trade they could
pursue later. If this wasn't the case, they at least got a taste of the
adult world, working closely with adults and being supervised by
them. Also, in whatever they did they usually had to apply in a
practical way at least some of the skills they'd learned in school,
thus reinforcing them.

Today, however, a growing majority of working youngsters   5
hustle at monotonous, dead-end jobs that prepare them for nothing. They certainly make up one of the largest groups of underem-
ployed people in the country.

Many work in adolescent ghettos overseen by "supervisors" 6
barely older than they are, and they don't need to apply much of
anything they've learned in school, not even the simplest math;
technology has turned them into near-automatons. Checkout
scanners and sophisticated cash registers tot up bills and figure
the change for them. At fast-food joints, automatic cooking timers
remove the last possibility that a teen might pick up a smidgen of
culinary skill.

Laurence Steinberg, a Temple University professor and co- 7
author of a book on teenage employment, estimates that at least
three out of every four working teenagers are in jobs that don't
give them any meaningful training. "Why we think that wrapping
burgers all day prepares kids for the future is beyond me," he says.

In a study of 550 teens, Prof. Steinberg and his colleagues 8
found that those working long hours at unchallenging jobs tended
to grow cynical about work in general. They did only their own
defined tasks and weren't inclined to help out others, their sense
of self-respect declined, and they began to feel that companies
don't care about their employees. In effect, they were burning out
before they even joined the permanent work force.

A lot of teenaged workers are just bone-tired, too. Shelley 9
Wurst, a cook at an Ohio franchise steakhouse, got so worn out
she stopped working on school nights. "I kept sleeping through my
first-period class," she says. "If it wasn't for the crew I'm working
with, I wouldn't want to work there at all."

This sort of thing is all too common. "Some kids are work- 10
ing past 2 a.m. and have trouble waking up for morning classes,"
says Larry Morrison, principal of Sylvania (Ohio) Northview High
School. Educators like him are beginning to wonder whether teenage work today is not only irrelevant to future careers but even
damaging to them; the schoolwork of students who pour so much
time and energy into dead-end jobs often suffers—thus dimming
their eventual prospects in a permanent job market that now
stresses education.

As for the teens themselves, a great number would much 11
rather be working elsewhere, in more challenging or relevant jobs.
Some, like Tanya Paris, have sacrificed to do so.

A senior at Saratoga (Calif.) High School, she works six hours 12
a week with a scientist at the National Aeronautics and Space
Administration, studying marine algae, for no pay and no school
credit. The future biologist hopes that her NASA work will help
her decide which area of biology to pursue.

But most others either are lured by the money they can   13
make or can't find what they're looking for. Jay Jackson, a senior at
Northview High, says he'd take a pay cut from his $3.40-an-hour
job as a stock boy if he could find something allied to psychology,
his prospective career field. He hasn't been able to. Schoolmate
Bridget Ellenwood, a junior, yearned for a job that had something
to do with dentistry but had to settle for slicing up chickens at a
local Chick-fil-A franchise—a job, she says, "where you don't learn
much at all."

And More to Come

Expect more teen jobs where you don't learn much at all. The   14
sweeping change in the economy from making things to service,
together with the growth of computerized service-industry technology that leaves almost nothing to individual skill and initiative, is
expected to accelerate.

So the mindless and irrelevant part-time jobs open to teens in   15
the near future will probably increase, while the better jobs continue to decline. On top of that, a growing labor shortage, which
would drive up pay, figures to draw more kids into those jobs—
against their interests. "Teen-agers would be much better off doing
a clerical-type job or studying," says Prof. John Bishop of Cornell
University's Industrial and Labor Relations Center.

Efforts have been under way to cut back the number of hours   16
teens can work, but the worsening labor shortage is undercut-
ting them. Many educators are instead urging the states to start or
expand more high-school cooperative education programs. These
plans tie school and outside work to future career goals and provide
more structure and adult supervision than ordinary outside work.

Employers also prefer students with this kind of experience.   17
A recent study by the Cooperative Work Experience Education
Association found that 136 of 141 businesses in Arkansas would
hire a young applicant who had been in such a program over one
who had worked independently. "The goal is not to get kids to
stop working," says Prof. Bishop of Cornell. "It's to get them to
learn more."

Part-Time Work Ethic: Should Teens Go for It?
DENNIS McLELLAN

Dennis McLellan is a staff writer for the Los Angeles Times. *As you read the following article, note his attempt to consider the issue of teenage employment from an*

objective point of view, considering all sides of the issue. How well do you think he succeeds?

John Fovos landed his first part-time job—as a box boy at Alpha Beta on West Olympic—the summer after his sophomore year at Fairfax High School in Los Angeles. "I wanted to be independent," he said, "and I felt it was time for me to see what the world was really like." 1

Now an 18-year-old senior, Fovos works the late shift at the supermarket stocking shelves four nights a week. He saves about $50 a week, but most of his paycheck goes to his car payment and membership at a health spa. "The rest is for food—what I don't eat at home—and clothes." 2

Shelley Staats went to work part-time as a secretary for a Century 21 office when she was 15. Since then, she has worked as a cashier for a marine products company, scooped ice cream at a Baskin-Robbins, cashiered at a Video Depot and worked as a "floater" at May Co. 3

The Newport Harbor High School senior currently works about 25 hours a week in the lingerie department at the new Broadway in Costa Mesa. Although she saves about $200 a month for college, she said she works "to support myself: my car and clothes and just stuff I do, like going out." 4

Working also has helped her to learn to manage both her time and money, Staats said, and her work in the department store is providing experience for a future career in fashion merchandising. 5

But, she acknowledged, there are times when working while going to school has taken its toll. 6

"Last year I was sleeping in my first-period class half the time," admitted Staats, who occasionally has forgone football games and school dances because of work. "After a while, it just wears you out." 7

Nathan Keethe, a Newport Harbor High School senior who works more than 20 hours a week for an exterminating service, admits to sometimes feeling like the odd man out when he sees that fellow students "are out having a good time after school and I'm working. But then I think there's a lot of other kids out there working, too, and it doesn't seem so unusual." 8

Indeed, what clearly was the exception 40 years ago is now the rule. 9

Fovos, Staats and Keethe are riding the crest of a wave of part-time student employees that began building at the end of World War II and has steadily increased to the present. In 1981, according 10 to a study by the National Center for Education Statistics, 80% of high school students have held part-time jobs by the time they graduate.

Part-time work during the school years traditionally has been   11
viewed as an invaluable experience for adolescents, one that builds character, teaches responsibility and prepares them for entering the adult world.

But the authors of a provocative new book challenge conven-   12
tional wisdom, contending that an over-commitment to work during the school years "may make teenagers economically wealthy but psychologically poor..."

The book, *When Teenagers Work: The Psychological and*   13
Social Costs of Adolescent Employment, is by Ellen Greenberger, a developmental psychologist and professor of social ecology at the University of California, Irvine, and Laurence Steinberg, a professor of child and family studies at the University of Wisconsin.

Based on national research data and on the authors' own   14
study of more than 500 working and non-working students at four Orange County [California] high schools, the book reports that:

Extensive part-time employment during the school year may   15
undermine youngsters' education. Students who work long hours are more likely to cut back on courses at school, taking easier classes and avoiding tougher ones. And, say the authors, long hours of work begun early in the school years increase the likelihood of dropping out.

Working leads less often to the accumulation of savings or   16
financial contributions to the family than to a higher level of spending on cars, clothes, stereos, concerts and other luxury items.

Working appears to promote, rather than deter, some forms   17
of delinquent behavior. About 30% of the youngsters in their first part-time job have given away goods or services; 18% have taken things other than money from work; 5½% have taken money from work; and 17% have worked under the influence of drugs or alcohol, according to the Orange County study.

Working long hours under stressful conditions leads to   18
increased alcohol and marijuana use.

Teen-age employment—typically in dull or monotonous jobs   19
for which the sole motivation is the paycheck—often leads to increased cynicism about working.

Moreover, the authors contend that adolescents who work   20
long hours may develop the superficial social skills of an adult, but

by devoting too much time to a job they severely curtail the time needed for reflection, introspection and identity experimentation that is required to develop true maturity.

Such findings lead Greenberger and Steinberg to conclude "that the benefits of working to the development of adolescents have been overestimated, while the costs have been underestimated." 21

"We don't want to be read as saying that kids shouldn't work during the school year," Greenberger said in an interview. "Our argument is with over-commitment to work: That working long hours may interfere with other very important goals of the growing years." 22

The authors place the blame partly on the types of jobs available to young people today. By working in unchallenging, monotonous jobs in fast-food restaurants or retail shops, they contend, teen-agers learn few new skills, have little opportunity for meaningful contact with adults and seldom gain work experience that will lead to future careers. 23

"Parents and schools," Greenberger said, "should wake up from the dream that having a kid who works 30 hours a week is promoting his or her transition to adulthood." 24

Greenberger and Steinberg's findings, not surprisingly, do not sit well with the fast-food industry. 25

"The fast-food industry is probably the largest employer of young people in the United States," said Paul Mitchell, spokesperson for Carl Karcher Enterprises, which employs thousands of teen-agers in its Carl's Jr. restaurants. 26

"For most of those young people," Mitchell said, "it's their first job, the first time they are told that you make a product a certain way, the first time they work with money, the first time they are made aware to be there on time and do it right … and it's just a tremendous working experience." 27

Terry Capatosto, a spokeswoman for McDonald's, calls Greenberger and Steinberg's findings "absurd, to say the least." 28

"Working at McDonald's contributes tremendously to [young people's] personal development and work ethic," said Capatosto, noting that countless McDonald's alumnae have gone on to professional careers and that about half of the people at all levels of McDonald's management, including the company's president and chairman of the board, started out as crew people. 29

"The whole idea of getting students out in the community during the time they're also a student is a very productive thing 30 to do," said Jackie Oakes, college and career guidance specialist at Santa Ana High School.

Although she feels most students work "for the extras kids   31
want," Oakes said they worked for a variety of reasons, including
earning money to go on a trip with the school band and saving for
college.

As for work taking time away from studying, Oakes said, "I think   32
if a kid isn't interested in studying, having a job doesn't impact that."

Newport Harbor High School's Nathan Keethe, who usually   33
earns Bs, doesn't think he'd devote more time to schoolwork if he
weren't working. "Not really, because even when I wasn't working
I wasn't too devoted to school," he said, adding that "for somebody who is, I wouldn't recommend working too much. I do think
it would interfere."

Fairfax High's John Fovos, who works about 27 hours a week,   34
however, said his grade-point average actually has risen since he
began working part time. The motivation? "My parents told me if
my job hindered my grades, they'd ask me to quit," he said.

Although she acknowledges that some teen-age workers   35
may experience growth in such areas as self-reliance and
improved work habits, Greenberger said, "It's not evident that
those things couldn't be realized in other settings as well. There's
no evidence that you have to be a teen-age drone in order to
grow in those areas."

As for the notion that "it would be great to get kids out into   36
the workplace because they'll learn," Greenberger said that "the
news is not so good. On the one hand we find that relatively little
time on the job is spent using anything resembling higher-order
cognitive skills," she said. "Computation nowadays is often done
automatically by the cash register; so much for practicing arithme-
tic. Kids do extremely little writing and reading [on the job]. There's
also very little job training. In fact, most of the youngsters in our
survey reported their job could be done by somebody with a
grade-school education or less."

Balancing Act: High School Students
Making the Grade at Part-Time Jobs   MAUREEN BROWN

In this selection from the Los Angeles Times, *Maureen Brown interviews several
teenagers who work at part-time jobs. Keep the points from the previous two articles
in mind as you read these interviews. Do these students confirm or contradict the
ideas in the previous articles?*

First jobs have a way of permanently etching themselves in our   1
memories. Often, more than a paycheck was gained from that initial working experience.

Many of today's teens, like teens a generation ago, cut their   2
working teeth at fast-food restaurants. I always find it of interest
to learn that a successful executive, attorney, physician or teacher
was once a member of this business sector—and in a position well
below management.

A teen-ager's first job is one of many rites of passage children   3
and parents must go through. A dialogue of limits is appropriate
when the subject of taking a job arises.

It's important to determine what are acceptable hours of   4
employment and how many hours a week are permitted so that
the student can maintain studies and other school-related activities.
What about transportation? Job safety? How will the earnings
be spent?

For some families, the discussion of employment is frequently   5
not initiated by the child but rather by the parent. "I think it's time
we discuss the possibility of a job," has been uttered in numerous
households after a weekend of distributing funds to teen-agers for
entertainment and clothing.

While not feigning to have the answers to the question of   6
employment and teen-agers, a recent discussion with a group of
Mira Mesa teen-agers proved that more than money is gained
from a job.

Charlotte Iradjpanah, 17, a senior at Mira Mesa High, has been   7
working 10 to 20 hours a week at a Mira Mesa Burger King since
September.

"The job is close to my house and I needed the money for   8
senior activities," says Charlotte. "I'm also saving for college and
working keeps me out of trouble. A job is an opportunity to know
what it's like to hold responsibility. Sometimes I have to face the
fact that I have to go to work today and put aside my personal
preferences."

Working at Burger King does not exclude Charlotte from   9
participating in extracurricular activities at school. She is a
member of the speech and debate team and president of the
photography club.

"The job has actually strengthened my GPA since I've taken on   10
additional responsibilities," said Charlotte.

Jenni Hada, 18, a senior at Mira Mesa Summit High has been   11
at Burger King for 3 months. "I owe my parents some money and

want to buy a car, but working actually gives me something con-
structive to do with my free time," she says.

Mike Vo, 17, a junior at Mira Mesa High, who has been at   12
Burger King for the past month, has held a part-time job since he
turned 16. "I didn't like living off of my parents," he says.

Mike's parents were skeptical when their son first brought   13
up the subject of having a part-time job in addition to school.
"Once they saw that I could still bring home good grades and
have a job, they felt differently," says Mike.

As well as school and a part-time job, Mike is a participant in   14
the junior tennis circuit.

Charlotte, Jenni and Mike work with a manager who perceives   15
the commitment and organization it demands to have a part-time
job while in high school. Manager Wade Palmer, 28, started work at
Burger King at age 17 while in high school and senses the importance of allowing for flexibility in scheduling.

"We can work around your schedule," Palmer assures the   16
students.

Palmer views "listening to these teen-agers" as an important   17
facet of his role as a manager. Believing that "there are many valuable qualities one can develop on the job," Palmer delights in seeing former student-workers from his decade of work in North
County who have gone on into other fields.

"One is a banker in Mira Mesa, another is a paralegal, and   18
another is an assistant manager with Dixie line," proudly claims
Palmer.

Before In-N-Out Burger in Mira Mesa opened its doors in   19
August last year, the company sent out employment flyers and
solicited workers in the local high schools and colleges.

"We had over 800 applications for employment," says Bill   20
Mayes, 31, the manager of the store on Mira Mesa Boulevard. "Of
those 800 applicants, we selected 50."

Like Wade Palmer, Mayes started working with In-N-Out   21
Burger at age 17 while still in high school. He continued part-time
in college, and eventually went into management.

"I think students, with their great amount of energy, work out   22
very well in our restaurant," Mayes says. "At In-N-Out, we're looking for bright, friendly, outgoing people to meet our customers."

Ba Hog, 17, a Mira Mesa High student, is one of the 50 appli-   23
cants who met Mayes' criteria.

"At first, my parents doubted I could get a job here—lots of   24
people were applying," recalls Ba. "After I passed the first interview,

they cautioned me to not get my hopes up. When I passed the second interview, I could not wait to go home and tell them!"

"Since I've had this job, my parents have been giving me a little   25
more freedom—like staying out later," says Ba, who is trilingual—speaking Chinese, Vietnamese and English. "Now they feel I can better decide between what is right and wrong. Plus, my grades have not been affected since I started this job."

One other advantage of working, according to Ba, is that he   26
has been able to delegate some of his previous home responsibilities to his older brother, Nghia, 18, who now carries out the trash and rakes leaves for the employed Ba.

Michelle Gust, 17, a senior at Mt. Carmel High, has been work-   27
ing 10 to 15 hours a week at In-N-Out since its opening. Balancing school and a part-time job with senior class council, peer counseling groups, cross-country running and the Girl Scouts, which recently awarded her the "Silver Award," has made Michelle aware of meticulous time scheduling. In addition to these activities, Michelle also spent her fall learning about deadlines as she filled out college applications.

"Working has taught me the importance of communicating with   28
people," says Michelle. "The management wants you to communicate well with them and the customer. I've learned to be flexible."

When the lead part of Corie in the school play "Barefoot in   29
the Park" was won by Kimberley Belnap, 17, of Mt. Carmel High, her work schedule at In-N-Out required adjustment.

"My mom also talked to Bill, the manager, and we were able to   30
work out a schedule where I could still continue to work, be in the play and maintain my grades," she said.

"I've learned to budget my time. I'm the type of person who,   31
when I have more to do, I find more time," she said.

In addition to organizing her schedule, Kimberley notes that   32
since starting work at In-N-Out, she is painfully conscious of the service she receives in other restaurants. "I take a critical look at how others serve the public."

AFTER YOU READ

1. Work with other students to develop responses to these questions or to compare responses that you have already prepared. As you can see, there are conflicting ideas about whether or not part-time work benefits teenagers who are attending school. To come to terms with the issues involved, list the advantages or disadvantages that are discussed in each article.

2. Look for different ways in which these writers say part-time work affects school performance. Do they discuss positive as well as negative points?

3. Not all of the ideas in these articles are related to school performance. Make a list of the ideas that are not necessarily related to school but that are important to the thesis of each article.

WRITING ASSIGNMENT

Note

Working with several sources can be substantially more difficult than working with only one source. As you respond to one of these assignments, consider working with other students to clarify and organize your ideas.

1. What is your position regarding the benefits or drawbacks of the Internet? Do you see more benefits than dangers? More dangers than benefits? Write an essay in which you argue for your opinion. To support your thesis, use arguments and evidence from the articles you have read and from whatever relevant experiences you or people you know may have had.

2. What is your position regarding the benefits or drawbacks of high school students working while attending school? Write an essay in which you argue for or against such a practice. To support your thesis, use arguments and evidence from the articles you have read and from whatever relevant experiences you or people you know may have had.

3. Develop an argument based on reading selections in Chapter 7 or those in Part Four. Use arguments and evidence from those articles as well as from your own experiences or observations to support your position.

EVALUATING SAMPLE PAPERS

ARGUMENT ESSAY

Use the following criteria to evaluate the student essays below.

1. Introduction

Does the first paragraph employ an effective lead-in to introduce the topic? Does the thesis take a definite stand and make it clear that the author intends to support a debatable point?

1   2   3   4   5   6

2. Unity

Does each paragraph have a clear and specific topic sentence that introduces an argument in support of the thesis? Does the material in each paragraph clearly relate to its topic sentence?

1   2   3   4   5   6

3. Support

   Is the argument within each paragraph supported with facts, examples, statistics, and/or references to authority?

   1   2   3   4   5   6

4. Coherence

   Are transitions used between paragraphs? Are they used within paragraphs, especially when the writer is moving from one type of support to another?

   1   2   3   4   5   6

5. References to the Text

   Are direct quotations and paraphrases correctly introduced and smoothly incorporated into the text? Do they reflect the articles' points accurately?

   1   2   3   4   5   6

6. Tone and Attitude

   Has the writer recognized that other responses to this topic are possible? Has he or she raised and responded to obvious objections?

   1   2   3   4   5   6

7. Sentence Structure

   Do the sentences combine ideas that are related, using coordination, subordination, verbal phrases, or parallelism when appropriate? Are there too many brief, choppy main clauses?

   1   2   3   4   5   6

8. Mechanics, Grammar, and Spelling

   Does the paper contain a distracting number of errors of these kinds?

   1   2   3   4   5   6

9. Overall Ranking of the Essay

   1   2   3   4   5   6

Student Essay 1

This student essay contains references to two articles not included in this text.

Drugs, alcohol, and tobacco are all substances that can manipulate the body and mind. Out of those three substances, most people feel that one out of the three substances should be illegal even though they all have similar effects to the body. That one substance is drugs. Drugs today are seen as a big threat to society, even though it only kills 4,000 people per year compared to alcohol's 100,000 per year and tobacco's 300,000 per year rate. Knowing the death rates of all three substances, which one do you feel should be illegal? I feel that drugs should be legalized because the war on drugs will never be won, it will destroy the black market, and the value of drugs will decrease.

By legalizing drugs, we would be able to control the quality of drugs. William J. Bennett states that if the government does not stock crack in government drugstores, the crack junkies would go elsewhere to get it (294). Where else would they go? None other than the dealers that sell crack cocaine that has been "laced with insecticides and animal tranquilizers to heighten its effect" (Bennett 294). Would you be able to sleep at night knowing that if we do not legalize drugs to control its quality, we will allow these types of drugs to infest our cities, suburbs, and homes? If we legalize drugs, we can control its quality and produce drugs that are weaker. By making weaker drugs, we would help drug addicts gradually kick the habit.

In order to destroy the black market of drug sales, we need to legalize drugs. In "Should Drugs Be Legalized?" William J. Bennett states that if we legalize drugs, the black market will remain (291–297). The black market remaining may be true, but the value of drugs will decrease causing the profits that the drug cartels make to be not worth selling through the black market. For example, back in the prohibition days of the late 1920s, alcohol was the moneymaker for the Mafia and other organized crime groups. For years the Mafia profited off of alcohol which most Americans felt was illegal and immoral during that time period. But as soon as prohibition was repealed in 1933, the black market of alcohol was destroyed. Hodding Carter III states in "We're Losing the Drug War Because Prohibition Never Works," "Prohibition can't work, won't work, and never worked" (289). Today these words still hold some truth. The prohibition of drugs is only resulting in a rapidly growing black market. Unless we finally come to realize that prohibition is not the answer, the black market will remain.

Finally, the war on drugs is a complete waste of time. Why fight a war that will never be won? In fact, Van Deerlin states in "Police and Jails Have Failed" that "Mounting evidence that the campaign against drugs has proved no more successful than the ill-remembered Prohibition law aimed at alcohol in an earlier day" (198). For example, waiting in their car from a distance, two undercover police officers tape a drug sale that is about to go down between a junkie and a dealer. The junkie approaches the dealer, checks the merchandise, pays the dealer, and in an instant wrestles the dealer to the ground. While this is happening, the two police officers taping the sale, rush to the junkie's side, who is also another undercover police officer. They handcuff the dealer, book him, and lock him up. Twenty-four hours later, the dealer is released because the court system is booked for the next year or so. Within hours, the dealer restocks his supply and goes back to the same corner to sell the same drugs. This is the type of war that our justice department has been fighting for years. So how can we win the war? In "Best Remedy: Crack Down on User," Joseph Perkins states that the only way to bring down the drug cartels is to deprive them of their customers and, thus, their tremendous profits" (310). Do you really want to pay more taxes to build more jails, train more police officers, and train more judges? Statistics have shown that housing an inmate for one-year can cost as much as $50,000. I feel that the only way to win this war, is to stop treating users as criminals by giving them jail time, and start treating them as addicts by giving them therapy, a more effective and cheaper treatment.

A lot of time and money has been put into war on drugs and the education on how to say no to the use of them. But neither has been proven successful. We are wasting time trying to eliminate drugs from our world; therefore, we should open our eyes and legalize them.

Student Essay 2

Is it really meaningful for a person to work while attending school? Many students have a part time job while going to high school or college. Some enjoy the experience while others completely hate it. The pros and cons of working while going to school were discussed in Michele Manges' "The Dead End Kids," Dennis McLellan's "Part-Time Work Ethic: Should Teens Go for It?" and Maureen Brown's "Balancing Act: High School Students Making the Grade at Part-Time Jobs." After reading all three articles I came to the conclusion that working while going to school is not just okay, but better than not having a job.

Although I feel working is a plus while going to school, I do feel there are some disadvantages. One point against working is that while working nights one may not get home until late and he may still have homework to complete. Michele Manges says, "A lot of teenage workers are just bone-tired" (303), and one of the teenage workers that she interviewed explained that to do her job so late at night "I kept sleeping through my first period class" (303). Another negative effect that working may have on students is the stress that both the job and school bring to the student. Based on national research data and her own study of more than 500 students in Orange County, Ellen Greenberger found that working appears to promote forms of delinquent behavior and has also led students to increased alcohol and marijuana use (McLellan 306). All of these effects are being blamed on the jobs students are working while attending school. However, I feel there are many more positive effects from working than these few negative results.

One of the positive results from working a part-time job is the fact that a person learns how to manage his or her time and money. Shelley Staats, a senior at Newport Harbor High School, said that working has helped her to manage both her time and money, while her work in the department store is providing experience for a future career in fashion merchandising. Not only does she learn new responsibilities, she is gaining important information by working in the department store that will help her to decide what she likes and dislikes about her future careers (McLellan 305). Personally, I have run into a similar situation as Shelley's. As for my job, working at Eastview Community Center, I get to see all of the financial documents go through the office. Because I want to be an accountant after graduating from college, I enjoy seeing and observing the financial statements and balance sheets every month. After observing all the paperwork I have become aware of a few of the things my future job holds for me.

Not only do I not believe working causes a students grades to suffer, but I believe that in many instances getting a job has resulted in the student receiving better grades. John Fovos, a student at Fairfax High School, said as a result of getting a job his grade point average has actually risen due to the fact his parents told him if his grades dropped he would have to quit his job (McLellan 308). Following the same pattern, Charlotte Iradjpanah works 10 to 20 hours a week at a Mira Mesa Burger King. She states, "The job has actually strengthened my GPA since I have taken on additional responsibilities" (Brown 310). I believe in these situations the students were aware that if their grades slipped the parents would place the blame on their new jobs. This fear of losing their jobs caused the students to work harder than they had before.

The biggest plus to working is that it puts one out into the real world. Michelle Gust, a senior at Mt. Carmel High, explained "Working has taught me the importance of communicating with people. The management wants you to communicate with them and the customer. I have learned to be flexible" (Brown 311). I believe these are very important skills young people need to learn and a job for many young people is usually the first experience they receive in the real world. Personally, I have also gained many essential traits while working. One of these experiences also came across the lines of communication. My job consists of enforcing the rules throughout the community center. One day about a month ago I let some teenage kids onto the tennis courts even though they were not wearing the appropriate shoes. As a result, I ended up cleaning all of their black marks off of the court as well as getting docked some points on my evaluation.

Don't get me wrong, for when it comes to school, I believe that school should come first. However, having a job while going to school brings many plus's along with the job. A young person learns how to manage his money as well as managing his time between school, homework, and work. Many times the job will also result in the student bringing home better grades for he wants his parents to let him keep his job. Most importantly, receiving a job while still young lets one know and understand how the real world operates.

Student Essay 3

This student essay contains references to three articles not included in this text.

> *... a burglar ... broke into a home and killed the father of three children, aged nine, eleven, and twelve. The crime went unnoticed until ten hours later, when police entered the apartment after being called by neighbors and found the three children watching television just a few feet away from the bloody corpse of their father. (Cross 443)*

Doesn't this scene read like an unbelievable script for a bad movie? Unfortunately, according to Donna Woolfolk Cross in "Shadows on the Wall," it is a real-life situation, reported by United Press International. It illustrates the powerful hold that television has over young minds, and it points out how television can draw attention away from the real world, replacing reality with its own distorted fantasy world. I have to admit that I am one of the 1980's generation that grew up glued to the television, but I still think that in many ways the TV is one of the most dangerous devices invented in the last century.

One reason it's so dangerous is that it does exactly what the above quotation suggests—it replaces reality with illusion. Ms. Cross gives several studies to prove this point. One of them involved a group of children in a room where two people started to yell at each other and fight. The fight was projected on video screens, and rather than reacting to what was happening, the kids all sat and watched the screens. It was as if the video were more important than the people themselves (443). I've seen other situations that make me believe that television causes children to confuse reality and illusion. For instance, when I started high school, shows like *Beverly Hills 90210* had me thinking that all the kids there would look cool and be going to bed with each other. I was so worried that I would never fit in that for the first month I didn't even talk to anybody. Luckily, I finally figured out that real life was different from what I'd seen on TV, but I sure went through a lot of misery for nothing.

I think that TV is also dangerous because it pretends to be educational when it's really not. According to Paul Robinson in "TV Can't Educate," television cannot provide the time that is needed for a person to really think about an issue. Instead, all it can do is present bits and pieces of facts that ignore all sorts of more involved questions (439). I think this is really true. I remember watching *Sesame Street* as I grew up, and I can't remember ever really learning anything from it. I just liked Big Bird and Cookie Monster. I thought they were funny, but mostly I ignored or already knew all the things they did with the alphabet and numbers. Also, I practically never watch the news or shows like *Nightline* because I like to relax when I watch television, so for the most part the television is not really very educational for me.

The worst part about television is the violence and sex that are becoming so common, even during early evening hours. It seems to me that there is no way children can avoid being affected by all of the negative things they see every day and evening on television. Even the writers who argue in favor of TV admit how damaging this part of it can be. In "Don't Touch That Dial," Madeline Drexler refers to the "violence of primetime shows ... the sexism of MTV ... [and] the materialism of commercials" (428). Also, in "The Meaning of TV," William Henry III admits that without TV we might have a less violent society and a more restrained world where "premarital pregnancy and divorce were still treated with distaste rather than with sympathy" (429).

Some people think that TV doesn't cause as many problems as I have listed, but I don't see how they can really think that. Television is entertaining, and I have to admit that I watch it for that reason, but it's not educational, and it really does cause people to make bad judgments about what reality is like. When I have children, I don't think I'll want them to sit and stare at the TV all day, but I will let them watch shows that are entertaining and amusing.

SENTENCE COMBINING: A REVIEW

In the first seven chapters of this text, you have practiced using a variety of techniques to combine related ideas. In the paragraphs that follow, combine the related sentences using whichever techniques seem most appropriate. Here is a brief summary of the sentence-combining ideas you have studied.

Chapter 1: Embed adjectives, adverbs, and prepositional phrases in related sentences.

Chapter 2: Use coordination to combine sentences or parts of sentences that are grammatically alike.

Chapter 3: Use subordinate clauses to indicate the relative importance of related ideas.

Chapter 4: Use present participial phrases, past participial phrases, and infinitive phrases to combine related ideas.

Chapter 5: Use appositives when nouns or pronouns are used to rename other nouns and pronouns.

Chapter 6: Use parallel sentence structure to join items in a series or with correlative conjunctions.

Chapter 7: Vary the length and structure of your sentences to achieve sentence variety.

EXERCISE 8.1

1 The Salem witch trials are an example of why it is important to separate church and state. 2 These trials were held in 1692. 3 During the trials twenty people were executed. 4 The daughter of the minister of Salem Village began to act strangely. 5 Two of her friends also began to act strangely. 6 Salem Village is not far from the larger town of Salem. 7 A doctor diagnosed the girls as bewitched. 8 Tituba was the minister's West Indian slave. 9 She had been teaching the girls sorcery and fortune-telling games. 10 She was accused of witchcraft. 11 Two other women were also accused. 12 The trial that followed triggered a wave of other accusations. 13 The three girls basked in their notoriety. 14 They ignited a storm of witchcraft hysteria. 15 The frenzy spread to the rest of Massachusetts. 16 Eventually, the governor convened a special court. 17 That court formally charged more than 150 people. 18 By the end of it all, twenty-eight suspected witches had been convicted. 19 Nineteen of them were hanged. 20 In addition, the husband of one of them was crushed under a pile of stones. 21 He was crushed because he had refused to enter a plea.

1 Whether technology creates more jobs than it destroys has been debated for a long time. 2 Unemployment and economic crises have often been blamed on machines. 3 Steam-powered engines were able to produce cloth at much faster rates than handlooms and weavers in 19th-century England. 4 Weavers in 19th-century England destroyed the machines that destroyed their jobs. 5 Textile workers who destroyed steam-power driven looms were called Luddites. 6 Luddites could not stop steam-powered machines. 7 Machines did make the occupation of weavers obsolete. 8 Steam-powered machines made many other jobs that used to be done by hand obsolete as well. 9 Steam power created many new jobs in the thousands of factories that came into being due to steam power. 10. That pattern has repeated itself often in history. 11 A new technology destroys many jobs. 12 That new technology creates even more jobs. 13. That pattern is changing. 14 A number of economists and historians of technology are arguing that software and computers are destroying jobs. 15. Software and computers might be destroying jobs at rates never seen before. 16 They are destroying jobs without creating many new jobs. 17 Even surgeons might be replaced by robots. 18 Societies have to address this looming problem soon. 19 Few people are discussing this new problem. 20 Societies might have to reinvent what work means. 21 Societies might have to reinvent what role work plays in our lives.

1 Rabindranath Tagore was the first Asian writer to win the Nobel Prize in literature. 2 Rabindranath Tagore was born in India. 3 He was born in 1861. 4 In 1861, India was still colonized by Great Britain. 5 Tagore deplored colonialism. 6 He deplored it because it demoralized the Indian people. 7 The British education system implemented in India tried to alienate Indians from their own cultural heritage. 8 The British education system taught that British culture was superior to Indian culture. 9 Tagore

did not believe British culture was superior to Indian culture. 10 Tagore did want to learn about British and European cultures. 11 Tagore went to school in England. 12 He returned and worked on his family's estate in the Ganges river valley. 13 Among the farmers on the estate, he learned about Indian folklore, songs, and the concerns of average people. 14 Tagore's wish was to combine what he saw as best in both Western and Eastern traditions. 15 He attempted to combine Western and Eastern traditions in his novels and short stories. 16 His work criticizes British colonialism and shows the beauty and depth of Indian traditions. 17 His novels and short stories embrace some aspects of European culture. 18 Tagore founded a school at which Bengali was taught rather than English. 19 By 1921, the school had become a university teaching, as Tagore put it, the "different cultures and religions of the world and [creating] that mutual sympathy, understanding, and tolerance on which alone can the unity of mankind rest. 20 Tagore died in 1941 in Calcutta.

Part Three

Editing Skills

Effective writing requires care and precision, much more so than speaking. When speaking, we always have the opportunity to stop and explain ourselves further. When we write in college, business, and the professions, we make hundreds, even thousands, of separate choices, even in relatively brief pieces of writing. Some of the choices are large, such as those concerning the overall organization of our writing, and some of the choices are small, such as those concerning the placement of an apostrophe or comma. Other choices involve sentence patterns, words, and punctuation.

Skillful editing can enhance the quality of your writing and allow you to express yourself in the way that you desire. Not only does it allow you to write effectively, but it also gains you the confidence of your readers. Poor grammar and usage can cause your readers to feel that you have not thought carefully about either the form or the content of your writing. In this section, we will present the basic editing skills of a good writer. We begin with a few important definitions.

Some Basic Editing Terms 9

CLAUSE

A **clause** is a group of words that contains at least one subject and one verb. Here are some clauses:

     S   V

Angelina called Brad about the soccer game.

       S   V

The school was on lockdown.

       S   V

Nearly everyone applauded.

Here are some groups of words that are not clauses:

To find out the cause of the problem.

Trying out for the team.

To find out the cause of the problem is not a clause because it does not contain a subject and a verb. It does contain a form known as an infinitive ("to find"), but the infinitive is a **verbal**, and verbals cannot be used as the verb of a sentence.

Trying out for the team also lacks a subject and verb. This phrase contains another verbal—the *-ing* form of the verb. However, the *-ing* form cannot be used as the verb of a clause unless it is accompanied by a helping verb, as in the following clause:

 S   V

I <u>was trying</u> out for the team.

Clauses come in two types—main and subordinate.

MAIN CLAUSE

A **main clause** expresses a complete idea. Here are some main clauses:

>   Selma is a town in Alabama.

>   Have some red beans and rice. (Here, the understood subject is <u>you</u>.)

>   Where will you go?

SUBORDINATE CLAUSE

A **subordinate clause** begins with a word that prevents it from expressing a complete idea. Here are some subordinate clauses:

>   S V
>   <u>After</u> I eat my sushi …

>   S   V
>   … <u>which</u> Joe kept for himself.

>   S   V
>   <u>When</u> you inspect the kitchen …

The words that begin the above subordinate clauses are called **subordinators**. They come in two types— **subordinating conjunctions** and **relative pronouns**.

Subordinating Conjunctions		Relative Pronouns	
after	so that	that	who(ever)
although	than	which	whom(ever)
as if	unless	(and sometimes *when* or *where*)	
as long as	until		
because	when		
before	whenever		
even though	where		
if	wherever		
since	while		

Subordinate clauses may appear at the start, at the end, or in the middle of a sentence:

>   <u>After he had passed the bar exam,</u> Eduardo was ready to join a law firm.

>   Michelle was pleased <u>because Tyler brought her roses.</u>

>   The film <u>that we saw</u> was really boring.

(See pages 109–110 for a further discussion of subordinate clauses.)

SENTENCE

A **sentence** is a group of words that contains at least **one main clause**.

NOT A SENTENCE	Almost breaking his leg.
NOT A SENTENCE	After he hunted for a snipe.
SENTENCE	He almost broke his leg.
SENTENCE	After he hunted for a snipe, he felt foolish.

EXERCISE 9.1

Indicate whether the following are main clauses (MC), subordinate clauses (SC), or neither (N):

1. *American Sniper* was a big hit. _____
2. Shifting into warp speed. _____
3. People are excited about the iWatch. _____
4. When Cindy says that one more time. _____
5. What made you delete my term paper? _____
6. To praise the soloist in the orchestra. _____
7. He remembered the battle on the island of Pelileu. _____
8. Whether he will go to Harvard or Yale. _____
9. Looking at the parade through the periscope. _____
10. He ordered a Spam-and-okra pizza. _____
11. He went gaga over Beyoncé. _____
12. While Steve was reading one of his poems. _____
13. Haiti and Chile desperately seeking help. _____
14. Look up *triskaidekaphobia*. _____
15. Whining about what was said about him on CNN. _____
16. To watch Charles and Louis comparing hatchets. _____
17. Before Steve and Deborah discuss a poem. _____
18. They do not want to be interrupted. _____
19. Although I haven't finished my bacon cheeseburger. _____
20. It is a double pleasure to deceive the deceiver. _____

COORDINATING CONJUNCTION

The **coordinating conjunctions** are *and, but, or, nor, for, so,* and *yet.* An easy way to learn the coordinating conjunctions is to remember that their first letters can spell **BOYSFAN** (*But Or Yet So For And Nor*). These words join parts of a sentence that are grammatically equal. For example, they may join two subjects, two verbs, or two adjectives. They may also join two similar phrases, two subordinate clauses, or two main clauses.

TWO SUBJECTS	<u>Marlene</u> **and** her <u>partner</u> were looking for the stash of drugs.
TWO VERBS	Marshall Raylon <u>pulled</u> his pistol **and** <u>aimed</u> it at the moonshiners.
TWO ADJECTIVES	Tony Bennett felt <u>young</u> **and** <u>special</u> with Lady Gaga.
TWO SIMILAR PHRASES	Jamie wanted <u>to win the marathon</u> **or** <u>to place in the top three finishers.</u>
TWO SUBORDINATE CLAUSES	<u>When they saw the damage</u> **but** <u>before they saw the piercings,</u> Frank and Roberta yelled at the kids.
TWO MAIN CLAUSES	<u>I have mockingbirds in my backyard,</u> **and** <u>they mimic the sounds of the neighborhood's car alarms.</u>

(See pages 67–70 for a further discussion of coordinating conjunctions.)

CONJUNCTIVE ADVERB

A **conjunctive adverb** is a word or phrase that serves as a transition, usually between two main clauses. When a conjunctive adverb joins two main clauses, it is preceded by a semicolon and followed by a comma.

Percival enjoyed artichoke hearts; **however**, Consuela could not stand them.

Here is a list of the most commonly used conjunctive adverbs:

accordingly	however	next
as a result	indeed	otherwise
consequently	in fact	second
first	instead	still
for example	likewise	therefore
for instance	meanwhile	thus
furthermore	moreover	unfortunately
hence	nevertheless	

Do not use a semicolon before a conjunctive adverb that does not begin a main clause. For example, in the following sentences, the conjunctive adverbs are not immediately preceded by semicolons.

The man on the left, **meanwhile**, studied his bus schedule.

The cat yowled all night long; none of the neighbors, **however**, seemed to mind.

(See pages 71–72 for a further discussion of conjunctive adverbs.)

EXERCISE **9.2**

In the following sentences, identify all main clauses by underlining them once and all subordinate clauses by underlining them twice. Identify all coordinating conjunctions by labeling them CC, all subordinating conjunctions by labeling them SC, all relative pronouns by labeling them RP, and all conjunctive adverbs by labeling them CA.

   1. Mr. Harker bought a black cape because vampires are so popular these days.
   2. I lost the Apple Watch that I had bought just last week.
   3. An alpha female wolf was shot when she wandered outside of Yellowstone Park.
   4. The snow was two feet high in Boston; consequently, no one was allowed to drive.
   5. Messaging in your car can be hazardous to your health, and eating a snow cone can be dangerous too.
   6. Katie Perry is a popular singer, but some people prefer Diana Krall.
   7. Some people think that the myth of Icarus and Daedalus is a cautionary tale; however, others have found it to be an example of youthful exuberance.
   8. A doting grandfather can be a great asset, so I communicate with my Granddaddy Joe quite often.
   9. Hans adopted a dachshund even though he dislikes wieners.
  10. If I could stop eating peanut-butter-and-Spam ice cream, I might lose some weight.
  11. General Sherman devastated the South at the end of the Civil War; in fact, he almost completely destroyed Atlanta, Georgia.
  12. Joseph Campbell taught us much about myth, but Louis 1Armstrong taught us to swing.
  13. Although St. Francis is often depicted with birds, he had a special relationship with wolves also.
  14. Homer is a heroic eater because he eats sushi; moreover, he eats snails.
  15. Hera allowed Zeus to go to earth; however, she was suspicious of his swan costume.

EXERCISE **9.3**

In the following sentences, identify all main clauses by underlining them once and all subordinate clauses by underlining them twice. Identify all coordinating conjunctions by labeling them CC, all subordinating conjunctions by labeling them SC, all relative pronouns by labeling them RP, and all conjunctive adverbs by labeling them CA.

1 In April 2005, people in Hamburg, Germany, reported that toads had begun to explode in a local pond. 2 The toads' intestines were being propelled up to three feet away, but no one knew why. 3 Because so many toads had begun to swell and burst apart, the residents started calling the place "The Pond of Death." 4 Soon toads began to explode in a nearby lake across the border in Denmark. 5 Scientists who investigated the phenomenon wondered if the pond water contained a virus or fungus that was infecting the toads; however, tests revealed no evidence of disease in the toads or water. 6 Finally, a German scientist discovered the cause. 7 Hungry crows had developed a taste for toad livers. 8 They would attack a toad between its chest and abdominal cavity in order to peck out the liver; in addition, they were teaching other crows the trick. 9 When the toads would inflate their bodies in defense, the hole and missing liver led to a rupture of their blood vessels and lungs. 10 According to one veterinarian, such behavior is not unusual, although its occurrence in a populated area is not common.

Sentence Fragments

10

The easiest way to identify a *sentence fragment* is to remember that *every sentence must contain a main clause*. If you do not have a main clause, you do *not* have a sentence. You can define a fragment, then, as follows: A **sentence fragment** occurs when a group of words that lacks a main clause is punctuated as a sentence.

Using this definition, you can identify almost any sentence fragment. However, you will find it easier to locate fragments in your own writing if you know that fragments can be divided into three basic types.

THE THREE TYPES OF SENTENCE FRAGMENTS

1. *Some Fragments Contain No Clause at All.* This type of fragment is simple to spot. It usually does not even sound like a sentence because it lacks a subject or a verb or both.

    The band on the stage.

2. *Some Fragments Contain a Verbal but Still No Clause.* This fragment is a bit less obvious because a verbal can be mistaken for a verb. But remember, neither a participle nor an infinitive is a verb. (See Chapter 9 if you need to review this point.)

PARTICIPLE   The band <u>playing</u> on the stage.

INFINITIVE   <u>To play</u> a new song on the stage.

3. *Some Fragments Contain a Subordinate Clause but No Main Clause.* This type of fragment is perhaps the most common because it does contain a subject and a verb. But remember, *a group of words without a main clause is* not *a sentence.*

    <u>As</u> the band played on the stage.

    <u>Because</u> the swings in the park were wet.

REPAIRING SENTENCE FRAGMENTS

Once you have identified a fragment, you can repair it in one of two ways:

1. Add words to give it a main clause:

FRAGMENT   The band on the stage.

SENTENCE   The band <u>played</u> on the stage.

SENTENCE   The band on the stage <u>started to play.</u>

FRAGMENT   The band playing on the stage.

SENTENCE   The band <u>was</u> playing on the stage.

SENTENCE   The band playing on the stage <u>began its first song.</u>

FRAGMENT   Because the lights on the stage went out.

SENTENCE   <u>The band stopped playing</u> because the lights on the stage went out.

2. Join the fragment to a main clause written before or after it:

INCORRECT   The witch noticed Hansel in the woods. And Gretel walking with him.

CORRECT   The witch noticed Hansel in the woods and Gretel walking with him.

INCORRECT   The witch showed the children her fantastic house. While the children looked amazed.

CORRECT   The witch showed the children her fantastic house while the children looked amazed.

Of the two possible ways to correct fragments shown above, try to use the second method of joining fragments to nearby main clauses as often as possible. Doing so will help you avoid writing a string of short, choppy sentences, and it will help clarify the relationship between the ideas you are joining.

One final point might help you identify and correct sentence fragments. Remember that we all speak in fragments every day. (If a friend asks you how you are, you might respond with the fragment "Fine.") Because we speak in fragments, you may find that your writing seems acceptable to you even though it contains fragments. When you work on the exercises in this chapter, do not "rely on your ear" alone. Look at the sentences. **If they do not contain main clauses, they are fragments, no matter how correct they may sound.**

EXERCISE 10.1

Underline any fragment you find. Then correct it either by adding new words to give it a main clause or by joining it to a main clause next to it.

1. Daedalus was gathering feathers and wax. While trying to find Icarus.
2. Francis Ford Coppola, who made the *Godfather* series of films.
3. Before choosing the most beautiful goddess. Paris called his life insurance agent.
4. When Captain Kirk unexpectedly reappeared beside Spock. Spock showed no reaction at all.
5. Impressed by his latest workout. The Hulk decided to ask Arnold Schwarzenegger over for a healthy drink.
6. To keep people from discovering him. Spiderman hid in the attic among the webs.
7. Cole asked his mother for a Popsicle. Counted all of his Lego pieces. And then sorted them by color.
8. During elk hunting season, the wolves wandered past the boundaries of Yellowstone Park. The elk hunters killed many of them.
9. The class studied the novel *Moby Dick*. And wondered where the names Ahab and Ishmael came from.
10. Knowing the boat would sink before crossing the Potomac with the General. The colonial soldier acted quickly. To get some tar to patch the boat.
11. Even though Huck had never painted a fence before. Tom assured him that he could do a good job.
12. Alice thought that the Mad Hatter looked a lot like Edward Scissorhands and that the Queen looked very strange. It occurred to her that the mushroom had tasted odd.
13. Tomorrow we will experience a full solar eclipse. For the last time in this decade. It should be rather exciting.

14. Whenever Henry visited his father's pencil factory. He longed for the simple life back at the pond.

15. The deep blue skies. The rich green grass. The gentle afternoon breezes. The smell of the ocean. Karen missed them all.

EXERCISE 10.2

Underline any fragment you find. Then correct it either by adding words to create a main clause or by joining it to a main clause before or after it.

1 Many schools have banned *The Adventures of Huckleberry Finn* by Mark Twain. 2 Because they consider its vocabulary racist. 3 As most people know, this great novel concerns the travels of Huck Finn and Jim. 4 Who is a slave. 5 They experience many adventures and meet many types of people. 6 As they are rafting down the Mississippi. 7 Disturbed by many American attitudes and practices. 8 Particularly slavery. 9 Twain uses his novel to criticize them. 10 Huckleberry Finn believes that he has "stolen" Jim. 11 Because Jim is "owned" by a local widow. 12 During the course of their travels together. 13 Huck becomes friends with Jim. 14 And notices that Jim demonstrates all the characteristics of every compassionate human being. 15 When it becomes time for Huck to "return" Jim to his owner. 16 Huck decides not to. 17 The reader realizes that the main point of the novel is that human beings, no matter what color, cannot be owned and sold. 18 Ironically, Huck feels guilty. 19 About not returning Jim. 20 *The Adventures of Huckleberry Finn* is one of America's first anti-racist works of literature.

Fused Sentences and Comma Splices

11

The *fused sentence* and the *comma splice* are serious writing errors that you can correct with little effort. Either error can occur when you write a sentence that contains two or more main clauses.

FUSED SENTENCES

The **fused sentence** occurs when two or more main clauses are joined without a coordinating conjunction and without punctuation.

fused   Chelsea jumped into the pool she waved at her father.

As you can see, the two main clauses in the above fused sentence (*Chelsea jumped into the pool* and *she waved at her father*) have been joined without a coordinating conjunction and without punctuation of any kind.

COMMA SPLICES

The **comma splice** is a similar error. The comma splice occurs when two or more main clauses are joined with a comma but without a coordinating conjunction.

comma splice   The rain soaked all of the campers, they wondered when it would finally stop.

In this comma splice, the two main clauses (*The rain soaked all of the campers* and *they wondered when it would finally stop*) are joined by a comma, but a comma alone is not enough to join main clauses.

One of the most frequent comma splices occurs when a writer joins two main clauses with a comma and a conjunctive adverb rather than with a semicolon and a conjunctive adverb.

comma splice   President Obama had planned to spend Easter with his family, however, he was unable to because of problems in Iran.

REPAIRING FUSED SENTENCES AND COMMA SPLICES

Because both fused sentences and comma splices occur when two main clauses are joined incorrectly, you can correct either error using one of five methods. Consider these two errors:

fused   Karlene received a scholarship to Stanford she immediately called her family.

comma splice   Karlene received a scholarship to Stanford, she immediately called her family.

Both of these errors can be corrected in one of five ways:

1. **Use a comma and a coordinating conjunction**. (See page 68–69 for a list of coordinating conjunctions.)

   Karlene received a scholarship to Stanford, so she immediately called her family.

2. **Use a semicolon**.

   Karlene won a scholarship to Stanford; she immediately called her family.

3. **Use a semicolon and a conjunctive adverb**. (See page 71 for a list of conjunctive adverbs.)

   Karlene won a scholarship to Stanford; therefore, she immediately called her family.

Do not use a semicolon before a conjunctive adverb that does not join two main clauses. For example, in the following sentence, *however* does not need a semicolon.

   The person in the blue raincoat, **however**, has not seen this movie.

4. **Change one of the clauses to a subordinate clause by beginning it with a subordinating conjunction or relative pronoun.** (See page 109 for a list of subordinating conjunctions and relative pronouns.)

> **When** Karlene received a scholarship to Stanford, she immediately called her family.

5. **Punctuate the clauses as two separate sentences.**

> Karlene won a scholarship to Stanford. She immediately called her family.

Sometimes the two main clauses in a fused sentence or comma splice are interrupted by a subordinate clause. When this sentence pattern occurs, the two main clauses must still be connected in one of the five ways.

fused	Roberta sold her house even though she had thought she would always live there she could not afford the payments.
comma splice	Roberta sold her house even though she had thought she would always live there, she could not afford the payments.
possible correction	Roberta sold her house even though she had thought she would always live there; unfortunately, she could not afford the payments.

EXERCISE 11.1

Identify the following sentences as fused (F), comma splice (CS), or correct (C). Then correct each incorrect sentence using one of the five methods just discussed.

_____ 1. The marriage broker was afraid of the Duke of Ferrara he knew what was going to happen to the next duchess.

_____ 2. The *Winged Victory* statue at the Louvre Museum lacks a head, nevertheless, it is considered one of the world's most beautiful sculptures.

_____ 3. The newscaster made it to the top of Mount Kilimanjaro she was tired but elated.

_____ 4. As Ophelia talked to Hamlet, he became upset.

_____ 5. Willy Loman wanted only what was best for his sons, he was just mistaken about what that was.

_____ 6. Don Quixote stared at the windmill he raised his lance and attacked it.

_____ 7. Bill looked at he okra on his plate in despair and secretly forked it onto his napkin.

_____ 8. Zeus had the charger on for twenty-four hours, however, his lightning gun would still not fire.

_____ 9. After visiting Earth, the extraterrestrials headed for home, disappointed by their failure to discover any intelligent life.

_____ **10.** The frame of the painting of the horse nostrils, however, was beautiful.

_____ **11.** The rebels were excited as the Yankees retreated before their charge, then the rebels ran out of bullets.

_____ **12.** Little Miss Muffet sat on the log a spider decided to join her.

_____ **13.** Leonardo's knock-knock jokes were rather dumb, consequently, all Mona Lisa would do was smile politely.

_____ **14.** The sun had reached its zenith Doc Holliday and the Earp brothers entered the O.K. Corral.

_____ **15.** After fifteen years of hard labor, Jackson wondered if he would ever again see his home and family, but his brother Seymour had decided to rescue him and was about to make his move.

EXERCISE 11.2

Identify the following sentences as fused (F), comma splice (CS), or correct (C). Then correct each error using one of the five methods discussed in this chapter.

1 The Anasazi are also known as the ancient Puebloans they lived from about 600 to 1200 C.E. in the area of the Southwest U.S. known as The Four Corners. 2 The Navajos consider them to be their ancestors, other peoples make the same claim. 3 The sites where these ancient people lived are amazing they indicate that these "old ones," as the Navajos refer to them, were much ahead of their contemporaries 4 The most interesting feature of these sites is the dwellings, which are several stories high in many places. 5 Many were built within large caves on cliff sides these locations provided protection from weather and also from enemies. 6 Their pottery and other artifacts show a high degree of sophistication, in addition, they show that these people traded with other cultures hundreds of miles distant. 7 When explorers first came upon these unoccupied dwellings, they were mystified, it seemed that these people had abandoned their homes in great haste, perhaps even in a single day or week. 8 They found fireplaces with the ashes still in them baskets, pottery, and other tools were lying nearby completely intact. 9 Some have even speculated that aliens from other planets had captured them; others wonder if some cataclysmic weather event drove them away. 10 The most popular theory is that a bad drought caused them to move, however, no single reason for their fate has ever been proven. 11 Many people report feeling a strange aura surrounding these cliff houses when they visit them. 12 They are at the place where Colorado, Utah, New Mexico, and Arizona come together that setting is another reason that people find them mysterious.

Consistency in Verb Tense and Verb Voice

12

SHIFTS IN VERB TENSE

Like almost all English speakers and writers, you use verb tenses quite unconsciously. If you are discussing something that happened in the past, you use the past tense without giving it a second thought (I *ate* that entire turkey!). If you are writing about future events, you very naturally shift to future tense (I **will eat** that entire turkey!). Sometimes, however, writers accidentally shift from one tense to another when there is no reason to do so. Such unnecessary shifts occur most commonly between the past and present tenses:

past   *present*   *present*

My brother <u>felt</u> hungry, so he <u>goes</u> to a mini-mart and <u>buys</u> junk food.

Would you agree that there is no reason for the writer to shift to the present tense in the above example? All three actions occurred in the past, so all three should be written in the past tense. Of course, you *should* shift tenses if the meaning requires such a shift, as in the following example:

present   *future*

Alex <u>hopes</u> that he <u>will win</u> tonight's lottery because last weekend he
past
<u>lost</u> all of his rent money in Las Vegas.

PAST-TENSE VERBS ENDING IN -*D* AND -*ED*

Sometimes you might mistakenly write a past-tense verb in its present-tense form by leaving off a -*d* or -*ed* ending. This problem is particularly common for students who do not pronounce those endings when they speak. If such is the case in your writing, you need to look closely at each of your verbs as you proofread your papers. If you are discussing an event that occurred in the past, add -*d* or -*ed* where such endings are needed.

INCORRECT   After the party last night, Mark <u>thank</u> Diane for giving him a ride home.

CORRECT   After the party last night, Mark <u>thanked</u> Diane for giving him a ride home.

SUPPOSED TO, USED TO

Two verbs that are often incorrectly written without the -*d* ending are *suppose* and *use* when they are followed by the word *to*. Don't leave the -*d* off the ending just because you don't hear it. (It tends to be combined with the *t* in *to*.)

INCORRECT   Calvin is <u>suppose to</u> be on a diet, but he can't get <u>use to</u> skipping his usual dessert of chocolate chip ice cream.

CORRECT   Calvin is <u>supposed to</u> be on a diet, but he can't get <u>used to</u> skipping his usual dessert of chocolate chip ice cream.

VERB TENSE WHEN DISCUSSING SOMEONE ELSE'S WRITING

Throughout this text, you are asked to respond to what other writers have written. You should use the present tense when you write about someone else's writing—whether it be nonfiction, fiction, or poetry—or when you write about film. Be careful not to inadvertently shift to the past tense.

INCORRECT   In "Why I Won't Buy My Sons Toy Guns," Robert Shaffer <u>claims</u> toys are teachers. He <u>said</u> that toy guns will teach children to solve problems with violence.

CORRECT   In "Why I Won't Buy My Sons Toy Guns," Robert Shaffer <u>claims</u> toys are teachers. He <u>says</u> that toy guns will teach children to solve problems with violence.

EXERCISE 12.1

Revise the following paragraphs to correct any unnecessary shifts in verb tense:

1 In "The Thin Grey Line," Marya Mannes says that the difference between right and wrong is becoming blurred. 2 She wrote that today's society was losing its moral fiber. 3 I agreed with many of the points that Mannes makes.

4 One point I agree with was that the parents of today's children cross the "thin grey line" many times a day. 5 When I was a child, my parents use to hide my brother and me on the floor of our Pinto so they would not have to pay for us when we go to drive-in movies. 6 And when I am too old for a Kids' Meal at McDonald's, they would lie and get me one anyway. 7 As I grew older, these things do not seem wrong to me. 8 I thought that as long as I didn't get caught there is nothing wrong.

9 Mannes also wrote, "Your son's friend admitted cheating at exams because 'everybody does it.'" 10 I have to admit that I also have cheat on an exam or two and that many people I know have done the same. 11 In the eleventh grade a student I know manage to get a copy of the exam we were suppose to take the next day. 12 He then proceeds to distribute it to his friends, and no one ever was caught. 13 Did we all learn a lesson? 14 We sure did. 15 We learn how easy it is to cheat.

16 All in all, the morality of the nation was headed in the wrong direction. 17 And if this generation is bad, what will the next generation be like? 18 Mannes's solution was a good one. 19 We use to be a moral nation, and we can be one again if we educate people. 20 We should start with the children before they became corrupt in their thinking.

SHIFTS IN VERB VOICE

Verb voice refers to the relationship between the subject and the verb of a sentence. If the subject is *performing* ("doing") the action of the verb, the sentence is in the **active voice**. If the subject is *receiving* the action of the verb, the sentence is in the **passive voice**. Note that the subject is the "doer" in the following active-voice sentence:

active voice

                             S   V

A red-tailed hawk seized the unsuspecting rabbit.

(The subject—the hawk—*performs* the action.)

Now compare the above active-voice sentence with its passive-voice counterpart:

passive voice

                             S   V

The unsuspecting rabbit was seized by a red-tailed hawk.

(The subject—the rabbit—*receives* the action.)

IDENTIFYING VERB VOICE

To distinguish between active and passive voice, first identify the verb itself, and then ask the following questions:

1. Does the subject perform the action of the verb, or does it receive the action? If the subject performs the action, the sentence is in the active voice; if the subject receives the action, the sentence is in the passive voice.

2. Does the verb consist of a form of *to be* and a past participle? The forms of *to be* are *am, are, is, was, were, be, being,* and *been*. **Any** verb consisting of one of these verb forms **and** a past participle is in the passive voice. All of the following verbs, therefore, are automatically passive: *has been eaten, is passed, was purchased, might be seen, were stolen.*

CHOOSING THE ACTIVE VOICE

Most writers prefer the active voice, so they try not to shift to the passive voice unless there is a good reason to do so. One reason writers prefer the active voice is that it requires fewer words than the passive. In the above examples about the hawk and the rabbit, for instance, the active voice requires only seven words while the passive voice requires nine. Two extra words don't seem excessive, do they? But over the course of an entire essay, those needless words begin to add up, creating a sense of looseness and wordiness that can detract from the effectiveness of your writing.

Another reason writers choose the active voice is that passive-voice verbs, as the word *passive* implies, lack the forcefulness of active-voice verbs. Because the subject in the passive voice *receives* the action rather than *performs* it, there is a sense that the sentence is not moving forward. In fact, too many passive-voice verbs can make your writing dull and lifeless.

Finally, the passive voice often obscures the real performer of the action, either by placing that performer in a prepositional phrase following the verb or by omitting the performer altogether. Who, for example, is the person who denies the building permit in the following sentence?

> After serious consideration, your request for a building permit has been denied.

Not all verbs must be either active or passive. For example, when a form of *to be (am, are, is, was, were, be, being, been)* is the main verb of a sentence, no action is shown at all, so the verb is neither active nor passive. Verbs of this type are called linking verbs. Although these verbs are not passive, you can often improve your writing by replacing them with active-voice verbs.

                                  S   V

linking verb   Mrs. Mallard's driving <u>is</u> quite reckless.

                                S   V

active voice   Mrs. Mallard <u>drives</u> quite recklessly.

CHOOSING THE PASSIVE VOICE

If the above discussion has left you with the impression that you should write in the active voice, it has achieved its purpose. But don't be misled—the passive voice does have a place in good writing, particularly in the following situations:

1. Use the passive voice when the performer of an action is unimportant or when the receiver of the action needs to be emphasized.

    S   V

<u>All</u> of the buildings <u>had been inspected</u> by noon yesterday.

(Who did the inspecting is not important.)

2. Use passive voice when the performer of the action is unknown.

                    S   V

Last night my <u>car</u> <u>was stolen</u> from the Walmart parking lot.

(Who stole the car is not known.)

3. Use the passive voice when the receiver of the action needs to be emphasized.

                               S   V

During the Holocaust <u>Jewish people</u> <u>were murdered</u> by the hundreds of thousands.

(The receiver of the action—Jewish people—is being emphasized.)

CHANGING THE PASSIVE VOICE TO THE ACTIVE VOICE

Some people write too many sentences in the passive voice merely because they cannot figure out how to change them to the active voice. Use these suggestions to help you revise your passive sentences to active ones:

1. If the performer of the action is an object (usually following the verb), reverse the subject and the object.

                      S   O

passive voice   The new iPhone was purchased by John for $500.

                      S   O

active voice   John purchased the new iPhone for $500.

2. If the performer of the action has been left out of the sentence, write it in as the subject.

                      S   V

passive voice   Every official transcript was destroyed last night.

                      S   V

active voice   Last night's fire destroyed every official transcript.

3. Change the verb.

                                  V

passive voice   The marine sergeant was given the Medal of Honor for his heroism in Afghanistan.

                                V

active voice   The marine sergeant received the Medal of Honor for his heroism in Afghanistan.

EXERCISE 12.2

Rewrite the following sentences so that they use the active voice. When necessary, supply the missing performer of the action. Some of the sentences may already use the active voice.

1. Hester was forced to wear a scarlet letter "A" on her dress by the citizens of her town.

2. "California Dreamin'" is sung by Diana Krall on her album *Wallflower*.

3. I was told by someone that the film *Birdman* is about schizophrenia.

4. In 2004 Barack Obama was elected as the first African American president by the people of the United States.

5. The mail finally arrived at 2:30 A.M.

6. Yesterday a bag with $50,000 in it was returned by a citizen who wished to remain anonymous.

7. In the nineteenth century, thousands of American birds were illustrated and cataloged by John James Audubon.

8. The understanding of mythology was dramatically changed by the book *Hero with a Thousand Faces* by Joseph Campbell.

9. A collection of songs has been recorded by Lady Gaga and Tony Bennett.

10. When the word *input* was first used by writers to mean "advice," it was rejected as inappropriate jargon.

11. Agoraphobia bedeviled Emily for many years.

12. The leading role in the film *Gone Girl* was played by Ben Affleck.

13. A demonstration for a thirty-two-hour workweek was organized by the people of Chicago.

14. Cole was praised by his teacher for receiving a score of 100 on his spelling test.

15. A beautiful solo was played by Joshua Bell during the Beethoven violin concerto.

EXERCISE 12.3

Rewrite the following sentences so that they use the active voice. When necessary, supply the missing performer of the action. Some of the sentences may already use the active voice.

1 The apple, one of the most common fruits, has been referred to by people in many interesting ways. 2 It has been described by some readers of Genesis as the fruit that was eaten by Adam and Eve. 3 However, the apple is never alluded to anywhere in the Bible. 4 The "fruit of the tree" is referred to, but no specific fruits are ever named. 5 In addition, the proverb "The apple never falls far from the tree" has been used to account for similarities between parents and children. 6 "The apple of one's eye" has been employed to describe a person someone cherishes. 7 At one time the pupil of the eye was considered by many people to be a solid globe. 8 Also, the phrase "apples and oranges" will be used by people who are arguing to describe irreconcilable or fundamental differences. 9 Sometimes the term "rotten apple" might be applied by a member of a group to another member who is causing trouble or making poor decisions. 10 This latter meaning refers to the idea that a whole barrel of apples can be spoiled by one rotten one. 11 Finally, because the apple is a beautiful, delicious, healthy fruit and because it originated from the rose group of plants, the phrase "mom's apple pie" will be appreciated by anyone who loves apples.

Subject-Verb Agreement

13

Subject-verb agreement refers to the need for the form of the verb you have used in a sentence to match the form of its subject. If the subject of your sentence is singular, your verb must be singular. If the subject is plural, your verb must be plural.

You need to pay special attention to subject-verb agreement when you use present-tense verbs. **Most present-tense verbs that have singular subjects end in -*s*. Most present-tense verbs that have plural subjects do not end in -*s*.** Here are some examples:

Singular	Plural
The bird flie**s**	The birds fly
He sing**s**	They sing
It i**s**	They are
The child ha**s**	The children have
She doe**s**	They do

Notice that in each case the verb ends in -*s* when the subject is singular. This rule can be confusing because an -*s* at the end of a *noun* almost always means that the noun is plural, but an -*s* at the end of a *verb* almost always means it is singular.

PROBLEM AREAS

Almost all subject-verb agreement errors occur for one of two reasons: Either the writer has identified the wrong word as the subject of the verb or the writer has mistaken a singular subject for a plural one (or vice versa). The following points address these two problems:

1. **Subjects are never part of a prepositional phrase**. Prepositional phrases often occur between the subject and the verb. Do not confuse the object of the prepositional phrase with the subject of the verb.

   <pre>
    S   V
   </pre>
   <u>One</u> of our neighbor's dogs <u>barks</u> every night.

   The subject is *One*, not *dogs*, because *dogs* is part of the prepositional phrase *of our neighbor's dogs*. Here is a list of common prepositions to help you identify prepositional phrases:

about	because of	except	of	toward
across	behind	from	onto	until
after	below	in	over	up
among	beside	in spite of	past	upon
around	between	into	through	with
as	by	like	till	without
at	during	near	to	

2. **The order of the subject and verb is reversed in sentences that begin with *there* or *here* and in questions**.

   <pre>
           V   S
   </pre>
   There were several people in the park this morning.

   <pre>
         V   S
   </pre>
   Here is the person with the keys.

   <pre>
   V   S
   </pre>
   Is the plane on time?

   <pre>
    V   S
   </pre>
   Was the photo album in the box in the attic?

3. **Only the subject affects the form of the verb**.

   <pre>
              S   V
   </pre>
   Our least concern is the people next door.

   The singular verb form is correct here because the subject is the singular noun *concern*. The plural noun *people* does not affect the form of the verb.

4. **Two subjects joined by *and* are plural**.

   <pre>
        S   S   V
   </pre>
   The puppet and the grasshopper were an unusual pair.

   <pre>
    S   S   V
   </pre>
   Steak and eggs sound good to me.

5. If a subject is modified by *each* or *every*, it is singular.

S   S   V
Every can and bottle on the beach was picked up.

S   S   V
Each driver and bicyclist is eligible to enter the contest.

6. Indefinite pronouns are usually singular. See page 355 for a list of indefinite pronouns.

S   V
Each of the contestants is on the stage.

S   V
Everyone in the stadium has a white flag.

7. A few nouns and indefinite pronouns, such as *none, some, all, most, more, part,* and *half* (and other fractions) may sometimes be considered plural and sometimes singular, depending on the prepositional phrase that follows them.

singular

S   V
Some of the food is missing.

plural

S   V
Some of the cars were stolen.

8. When the subjects are joined by *either/or, neither/nor, not only/but also,* or *just or,* the verb agrees with the subject closer to it.

S   S   V
Neither Maria **nor** her sisters want to leave the house.

Of course, if you reverse the order of the subjects above, you must change the verb form.

S   S   V
Neither her sisters **nor** Maria wants to leave the house.

This rule also applies to questions.

V   S   S   V
Does Maria **or** her sisters want to leave the house?

V   S   S   V
Do her sisters **or** Maria want to leave the house?

Note

When you have helping verbs in a sentence, as in the example above, the helping verb—not the main verb—changes form.

9. Collective nouns usually take the singular form of the verb. Collective nouns represent groups of people or things, but they are considered singular. Some common collective nouns are *audience, band, class, committee, crowd, family, flock, group, herd, jury, society,* and *team*.

S   V
The jury was told to reach its verdict as quickly as possible.

S   V
My family goes to Yellowstone National Park every summer.

10. **The relative pronouns** *that, which,* **and** *who* **may be either singular or plural.** When one of these pronouns is the subject of a verb, you will need to know which word it refers to before you decide whether it is singular or plural.

                                               S   V

singular   I bought the peach that was ripe.

                                               S   V

plural   I bought the peaches that were ripe.

                                                   S   V

plural   Colleen is one of the students who are taking flying lessons.

                                                       S   V

singular   Colleen is the only one of the students who is taking flying lessons.

11. **A few nouns end in *-s* but are considered singular; they take the singular form of the verb.** These nouns include *economics, gymnastics, mathematics, measles, mumps, physics,* and *politics.*

                               S   V

International politics is not my favorite field of study.

                     S   V

Mathematics has been difficult for me.

12. **When units of measurement for distance, time, volume, height, weight, money, and so on are used as subjects, they usually take the singular verb form.**

                     S   V

Two teaspoons of sugar was all that the cake recipe called for.

                     S   V

Five dollars is too much to pay for a hot dog.

EXERCISE 13.1

Circle the subjects, and underline the correct verb form (in parentheses) for each one.

1. Almost anyone who has seen that director's films (has) (have) praised them.
2. The university's president and dean of business (worry) (worries) about the current level of enrollment.
3. The team using a Native American mascot (is) (are) refusing to change.
4. A man walking five dogs (passes) (pass) this corner every morning at about 8:00.
5. Two hundred miles (was) (were) more than Natasha was willing to walk.
6. There in your front yard (is) (are) the putting green and the koi pond that you ordered.
7. Each passenger boarding that airline's flights (receive) (receives) an iPad to enjoy during the trip.

8. Either your shirt or your pants in you current outfit (is) (are) the wrong color.

9. One of the detectives who (was) (were) seeking the escapee described him as psychotic.

10. A flock of all black pigeons (has) (have) been scaring people after dark in my neighborhood.

EXERCISE 13.2

Correct any subject-verb agreement errors in the following sentences. If a sentence is correct, do nothing to it. To check your answers, circle the subjects.

1. Neither my cat nor my two dogs likes to visit the veterinarian.
2. Each of the contestants in our local triathlon have undergone drug testing.
3. Here in my suitcase is the small rock and the lever that you requested, Sisyphus.
4. For no apparent reason, a group of elk hunters were shooting at the wolves that had wandered beyond the boundaries of Yellowstone Park.
5. Has the president or the Speaker of the House agreed to the compromise?
6. My son-in-law is one of the many graduates in California who is considering bankruptcy.
7. Between the two goalposts stands a cheerleader and a college student waving an American flag.
8. Each of the fifteen applicants from the three different cities were presented with a bowl of fruit.
9. The main problem with my okra extract diet are the chocolate bars that my roommate keeps bringing home.
10. Fifty gallons of gasoline were required for me to drive from San Francisco to Dallas.

EXERCISE 13.3

Correct all subject-verb agreement errors. Not all sentences will contain errors.

1 The custom of offering a blessing or word of goodwill when someone sneezes derive from a number of historical causes. 2 First, there was the ancient beliefs that a person's life force reside in the head and that a sneeze can dislodge that vital force. 3 Each of these beliefs were reinforced whenever a person died after an illness involving bouts of sneezing. 4 Someone who heard a person sneeze would perform a short ritual which were meant to protect that person's life force. 5 Later, in the fourth century B.C., Greek thinkers explained that

sneezing is caused when the body tries to expel irritating material that have come in through the nostrils. 6 However, they also recognized that bouts of sneezing precedes many illnesses, so they gave a blessing to people who sneezed, such as "May you enjoy good health!" 7 Then Roman physicians added to the custom by claiming that a series of strong sneezes actually help rid the body of spirits that causes illnesses. 8 They encouraged people to sneeze by saying "Congratulations!"
9 Finally, the common "God bless you" of today derive from the sixth century, when a deadly plague ravaged Italy. 10 One of its most telling symptoms were severe sneezes. 11 Pope Gregory the Great ordered people to ask for God's help in the form of "God bless you." 12 As the plague spread throughout Europe, killing hundreds of thousands of people, the response of "God bless you" to any sudden sneezes were widespread.

Pronoun Agreement and Reference

14

PRONOUN-ANTECEDENT AGREEMENT

Because pronouns stand for or take the place of nouns, it is important that you make clear in your writing which pronouns stand for which nouns. The noun that the pronoun takes the place of is called the **antecedent**. The term **pronoun-antecedent agreement** refers to the idea that a pronoun must match, or "agree with," the noun that it stands for in *person* and *number*.

PERSON

Person, in describing pronouns, refers to the relationship of the speaker (or writer) to the pronoun. There are three persons: *first person, second person*, and *third person*.

1. **First-person pronouns** refer to the person speaking or writing:

Singular	Plural
I	we
me	us
my, mine	our, ours

2. **Second-person pronouns** refer to the person spoken or written to:

Singular	Plural
you	you
you	you
your, yours	your, yours

3. **Third-person pronouns** refer to the person or thing spoken or written about:

Singular	Plural
he, she, it	they
him, her, it	them
his, her, hers, its	their, theirs

Because nouns are almost always in the third person, pronouns that refer to nouns should also be in the third person. Usually this rule poses no problem, but sometimes writers mistakenly shift from third to second person when they are referring to a noun.

> When a <u>person</u> first enters the Department of Motor Vehicles, <u>you</u> might feel overwhelmed by the crowd of people.

In this sentence, *you* has mistakenly been used to refer to *person*. The mistake occurs because the noun *person* is in the third person, but the pronoun *you* is in the second person. There are two ways to correct the sentence:

1. You can change the second-person pronoun *you* to a third-person pronoun.

   > When a <u>person</u> first enters the Department of Motor Vehicles, <u>he or she</u> might feel overwhelmed by the crowd of people.

2. You can change the noun *person* to the second-person pronoun *you*.

   > When <u>you</u> first enter the Department of Motor Vehicles, <u>you</u> might feel overwhelmed by the crowd of people.

Here is another incorrect sentence:

> Most <u>visitors</u> to the Safari Park will have a good time if <u>you</u> follow the signs and do not stray off the marked path.

One way to correct this sentence is to change *you* to *they* so that it agrees with *visitors:*

> Most <u>visitors</u> to the Safari Park will have a good time if <u>they</u> follow the signs and do not stray off the marked path.

NUMBER

Errors in number are the most common pronoun-antecedent errors. To make pronouns agree with their antecedents in **number**, use singular pronouns to refer to singular nouns and plural pronouns to refer to plural nouns. The following guidelines will help you avoid errors in number:

1. **When you use a pronoun to refer to words joined by *and*, you should use a plural pronoun unless the words are modified by *each* or *every*.**

   <u>Benjamin Franklin</u> and <u>Thomas Edison</u> were both known for <u>their</u> work with electricity.

   Every <u>dog</u> and <u>cat</u> in the kennel had lost <u>its</u> appetite.

2. Because the following indefinite pronouns are singular, you should use singular pronouns to refer to them.

anybody	either	neither	one
anyone	everybody	nobody	somebody
anything	everyone	no one	someone
each	everything	nothing	something

<u>Everything</u> that he said seemed to have <u>its</u> own secret meaning.

<u>Neither</u> of the contestants wanted to trade <u>her</u> prize for an unmarked door.

<u>One</u> of the children was staring sadly at <u>his</u> broken toy.

Note

In spoken English, the plural pronouns *they, them,* and *their* are often used to refer to the antecedents *everyone* or *everybody*. However, in written English the singular pronoun is still more commonly used.

> *Everybody* on the men's hockey team was determined to do <u>his</u> best.

3. You should use singular pronouns to refer to collective nouns. Some common collective nouns are *audience, band, class, committee, crowd, family, flock, group, herd, jury, society,* and *team*.

The <u>*class*</u> decided to skip <u>*its*</u> scheduled break in order to review for the test.

The <u>*family*</u> next door spent <u>*its*</u> summer at the Grand Canyon last year.

4. When antecedents are joined by the following words, you should use a pronoun that agrees with the closer antecedent.

either/or	neither/nor	nor
or	not only/but also	

Neither <u>Mr. Snead</u> nor the <u>golfers</u> remembered to bring <u>their</u> golf shoes.

The plural pronoun *their* agrees with the plural noun *golfers* because *golfers* is the closer noun.

SEXIST LANGUAGE

In the past it has been traditional to use masculine pronouns when referring to singular nouns whose gender could be either masculine or feminine. A good example is the sentence ***A driver*** *should slow down whenever* ***he*** *approaches a blind intersection*. Although the noun *driver* could be either masculine or feminine, traditionally only masculine pronouns like *he* or *his* have been used in a case like this one.

Because females make up over 50 percent of the English-speaking population, many of them have been justifiably dissatisfied with this tradition. The problem is that the English language does not contain a singular personal pronoun that can refer to either sex at the same time in the way that the forms of *they* can.

The solutions to this problem can prove awkward. One of the solutions is to use feminine pronouns as freely as masculine ones to refer to singular nouns whose gender could be masculine or feminine. Either of the following sentences using this solution is acceptable:

> A <u>driver</u> should slow down whenever <u>she</u> approaches a blind intersection.

> A <u>driver</u> should slow down whenever <u>he</u> approaches a blind intersection.

Another solution is to change the *he* to *he or she*. Then the sentence would look like this:

> A <u>driver</u> should slow down whenever <u>he or she</u> approaches a blind intersection.

As you can see, this solution does not result in a very graceful sentence. Still another alternative is to use *she/he*, but the result would be about the same as the one above. Sometimes a better solution is to change a singular antecedent to a plural one and use the forms of *they*, which can refer to either gender. Doing so would result in a sentence like this:

> <u>Drivers</u> should slow down whenever <u>they</u> approach a blind intersection.

This sentence is less awkward and just as fair. Finally, in some situations, the masculine pronoun alone will be appropriate, and in others the feminine pronoun alone will be. Here are two such sentences:

> <u>Each</u> of the football players threw <u>his</u> helmet into the air after the victory.

> (The football team is all male.)

> <u>One member</u> of the Saudi Arabian swim team passed <u>her</u> opponent ten yards before the finish line.

> (The swim team is all female.)

Whatever your solutions to this problem, it is important that you be logical and correct in your pronoun-antecedent agreement in addition to being fair.

EXERCISE 14.1

Choose the pronoun (in parentheses) that agrees with the antecedent. When you choose a pronoun, you may also need to change the verb.

1. There must be a lot of anxiety for a player entering the arena where (he or she) (they) (you) will play in the final game of the national basketball championship.

2. No one was allowed to take (his or her) (your) (their) cell phone on the corkscrew ride at Silicon Valley Land amusement park.

3. Whether a player can remain in the game depends on what (he or she) (you) (they) might say to the referee after the foul call.

4. The subcommittee of the president's financial advisors issued (its) (their) report on Tuesday.

5. Neither Soledad nor Erika was willing to reveal the subject of (her) (their) doctoral dissertation.

6. When a traveler arrives at the fork in the road, (you) (he or she) (they) will need to decide which one to take.

7. The members of the rowdy group in the line for the concert were asked to empty (his or her) (their) pockets.

8. All of the student senators agreed to read aloud from (his or her) (their) textbooks as a way to protest the tuition increase.

9. After winning three blue ribbons at the state fair, the team from Bacon, Missouri, loaded (its) (their) truck and headed for home.

10. Skinner could tell that either the pigeon or the mouse would soon learn to signal for (its) (their) food.

UNCLEAR PRONOUN REFERENCE

Sometimes, even though a pronoun appears to agree with an antecedent, it is not clear exactly which noun in the sentence is the antecedent. And sometimes a writer will use a pronoun that does not clearly refer to any antecedent at all. The following two points will help you use pronouns correctly.

1. A pronoun should refer to a specific antecedent.

After <u>James</u> gave his brother the present, <u>he</u> began to cry.

In this sentence, *he* could refer to James or his brother. To correct this problem, you can eliminate the unclear pronoun.

After <u>James</u> gave <u>his brother</u> the present, <u>his brother</u> began to cry.

Or you can revise the sentence so the pronoun refers to one specific antecedent.

<u>James</u> began to cry after <u>he</u> gave his brother the present.

2. Pronouns should not refer to implied or unstated antecedents. Be especially careful with the pronouns *this, that, which,* and *it*.

The game was canceled even though we had driven five hundred miles to see it; <u>this</u> was unfair.

In Paul Goodman's "A Proposal to Abolish Grading," <u>it</u> says that grades do more harm than good.

In the first example, there is no antecedent to which *this* can refer. In the second example, *it* seems to refer to something inside the article, but there is no antecedent given. The following sentences clarify the pronoun references:

> The game was canceled even though we had driven five hundred miles to see it; <u>to have a game canceled after we had driven so far</u> was unfair. In "A Proposal to Abolish Grading," <u>Paul Goodman says</u> that grades do more harm than good.

Sometimes a pronoun refers to a noun that is only implied in the first part of the sentence.

> Mr. Brouillard is a fisherman, <u>which</u> he does every weekend.

In this sentence, the *which* apparently refers to *fishing*, which is implied in the noun *fisherman;* however, there is no specific noun for the pronoun *which* to refer to. The faulty pronoun reference can be cleared up in several ways:

> Mr. Brouillard is a fisherman, <u>and he goes fishing</u> every weekend.

> Mr. Brouillard is a fisherman <u>who fishes</u> every weekend.

EXERCISE 14.2

Correct all errors in pronoun-antecedent agreement as well as in pronoun reference in the following sentences. If a sentence is correct, do nothing to it.

1. Juan watered Sal's plants while he was on vacation because he was a good brother.
2. Moses told the Israelites to cross the Red Sea ahead of the Egyptians because he knew what their lot would be.
3. When an applicant has his first job interview, you will probably be nervous.
4. As each diplomat argued the fate of their country, they consulted advisors.
5. The door attendant at the nightclub let the group from Mississippi go to the head of the line and then locked us out. This was not fair.
6. When someone sees the size of the roller coaster, you might be surprised and afraid.
7. When the precinct worker told the candidate about the results of the polls, he grinned.
8. Emily Dickinson wrapped her poems in a blue ribbon and gave it to her sister.
9. On the CNN evening news, it said that a peace treaty was probable.
10. Hansel and Gretel knew that you were not supposed to go into the woods after dark.

EXERCISE 14.3

Correct any errors in pronoun-antecedent agreement as well as in pronoun reference. Not all sentences contain errors.

1 Many everyday clothing fashions that appear to have no real purpose actually have a very practical cause for its existence. 2 For example, miners complained because the pockets of their blue jeans would split when you carried heavy tools in them. 3 This complaint bothered Levi Strauss because miners were his best customers, so they added rivets. 4 As time passed, everyone had to own their own pair of "Levi's," complete with rivets. 5 Another curious clothing custom is that of a man buttoning their clothing from right to left and a woman from left to right. 6 This started in the fifteenth century. 7 At that time, men generally dressed themselves, and, since most people are right-handed, you preferred to button clothing from right to left. 8 However, a woman who could afford the expensive buttoned clothing of the day generally had a maid who helped them dress. 9 When a maid faced her mistress, the maid's right hand was on their mistress's left; hence, buttons on women's clothing were sewn on the left side. 10 These are just a few of the many reasons a man or a woman dresses the way they do today.

Pronoun Case

15

Pronouns, like verbs, can appear in a variety of forms, depending on how they function in a sentence. For example, the pronoun that refers to the speaker in a sentence may be written as *I, me, my,* or *mine*. These different spellings are the result of what is called **pronoun case**.

The three pronoun cases for English are the *subjective*, the *objective*, and the *possessive*.

Subjective Case

Singular	**Plural**
I	we
you	you
he, she, it	they
who	who

Objective Case

Singular	**Plural**
me	us
you	you
him, her, it	them
whom	whom

Possessive Case

Singular	**Plural**
my, mine	our, ours
your, yours	your, yours
his, her, hers, its	their, theirs
whose	whose

SUBJECTIVE PRONOUNS

The **subjective pronouns** are *I, we, you, he, she, it, they,* and *who*. They are used in two situations:

   1. Subjective pronouns are used as subjects of sentences.

     S
     <u>I</u> will take the test next week.

       S
     <u>They</u> have stolen my car.

   2. Subjective pronouns are used when they follow linking verbs. Because the linking verb *identifies* the pronoun with the subject, the pronoun must be in the same case as the subject.

     S
     <u>It</u> was <u>he</u> who found the missing link.
        The subjective pronoun *he* is identified with the subject *it* by the linking verb *was*.

       S
     <u>That</u> was <u>I</u> you heard speaking on the phone.

     S
     <u>It</u> was <u>they</u> who won the final game of the series.

OBJECTIVE PRONOUNS

The **objective pronouns** are *me, us, you, him, her, it, them,* and *whom*. They are used in three situations:

   1. Objective pronouns are used as objects of prepositions.

     Oliver stared at the birthday card that Stanley had given <u>to him.</u>

     The disagreement <u>between Shayla and me</u> was not really very serious.

   2. Objective pronouns are used as direct objects of action verbs. The noun or pronoun that receives the action of the action verb is called the **direct object**. For example, in the sentence *Tuan visited Serena yesterday*, the verb is *visited*, an action verb. The direct object of *visited* is *Serena* because *Serena* receives the action of the verb *visited*. If you substitute a pronoun for *Serena*, it must be the objective pronoun *her: Tuan visited **her** yesterday*.

     Tyrone insulted <u>her</u> at the party last night.

     After we ate dinner, Juanita took <u>me</u> to the mall.

     Mr. Kong picked up all of the banana peels and threw <u>them</u> out the window.

   3. Objective pronouns are used as indirect objects. The indirect object indicates to whom or for whom (or to what or for

what) an action is directed, but the prepositions *to* and *for* are left out.

prepositional phrase	He gave the flowers <u>to her.</u>
indirect object	He gave <u>her</u> the flowers.

In the first sentence, *her* is the object of the preposition *to*. In the second sentence, the *to* is omitted and the pronoun is moved, making *her* the indirect object. In both sentences, the direct object is *flowers*. Here are other examples:

She had already told <u>him</u> the secret password.

My sister showed <u>them</u> a baseball that had been autographed by Babe Ruth.

POSSESSIVE PRONOUNS

The **possessive pronouns** are *my, mine, our, ours, your, yours, his, her, hers, its, their, theirs,* and *whose*. They are used in two situations:

1. Possessive pronouns are used as adjectives to indicate possession.

Penny could not believe what <u>her</u> ears had just heard.

Sheldon and Leonard looked sheepishly at <u>their</u> feet.

Rajesh looked at the car and wondered who had stolen <u>its</u> tires.

Note

The contraction *it's* means "it is." The word *its* is the only possessive form for *it*. (In fact, you do not use apostrophes with any of the possessive pronouns.)

2. Some possessive pronouns indicate possession without being used as adjectives. In this case, they may be used as subjects or objects.

I used my father's watch because <u>mine</u> was broken.
  Here the possessive pronoun **mine** is the subject of its clause.

Maria's room is neat, but <u>yours</u> is a mess.
  In this example, **yours** is the subject of its clause.

Arlo rented a car because he had sold <u>his.</u>
  Here the possessive pronoun **his** is a direct object.

COMMON SOURCES OF ERRORS IN PRONOUN CASE

COMPOUND CONSTRUCTIONS

Compound subjects and objects often cause problems when they include pronouns. If your sentence includes a compound construction, be sure you use the correct pronoun case.

compound subject	<u>Melissa and she</u> own a fifty-acre ranch.
compound after linking verb	That was <u>Leslie and I</u> whom you spoke to last night.
compound object of a preposition	After the fire, the police took statements from <u>my brother and me.</u>
compound direct object	Julio saw <u>Mark and him</u> at the racetrack.
compound indirect object	She gave <u>him and me</u> a reward when we found her lost dog.

In most cases, you can use a simple test to check whether you have chosen the right pronoun case when you have a compound construction. Simply remove one of the subjects or objects so that only one pronoun is left. For example, is this sentence correct? *Our host gave **Erin and I** a drink.* Test it by dropping **Erin and:** *Our host gave **I** a drink.* Now you can see that the *I* should be *me* because it is an object (an indirect object). The correct sentence should read: *Our host gave **Erin and me** a drink.*

WHO AND WHOM

When to use *who* or *whom* is a mystery to many writers, but you should have no problem with these pronouns if you remember two simple rules:

1. Use the subjective pronoun *who* or *whoever* if it is used as the subject of a verb.
2. Use the objective pronoun *whom* or *whomever* if it is not used as the subject of a verb.

   While standing in line at the bus depot, I saw someone <u>who</u> looked like my long-lost brother.
      Who is the subject of *looked*.

   The position will be given to the person <u>whom</u> the committee finds most qualified.
      Whom is not the subject of a verb.

   This wallet should be returned to <u>whoever</u> lost it.
      Whoever is the subject of *lost*.

COMPARISONS

When a pronoun is used in a comparison, you often need to supply the implied words to know what pronoun case to use. For example, in the sentence *My brother cannot skate as well as I*, the implied words are the verb *can skate: My brother cannot skate as well as I [can skate].*

   When we visited the petting zoo, the animals seemed to like my brother more than <u>me.</u>

You can tell that *me* is the correct case in this sentence when you supply the implied words:

> When we visited the petting zoo, the animals seemed to like my brother more than [they liked] <u>me.</u>

APPOSITIVES

An appositive is a word group containing a noun or pronoun that renames another noun or pronoun. When the appositive contains a **pronoun** that does the renaming, be sure that the pronoun is in the same case as the word it renames. (For more discussion of appositives, see pages 195–199.)

> Three employees—Miguel, Pierre, and I—were fired for insubordination.

Here *I* is in the subjective case because the appositive *Miguel, Pierre, and I* renames the word *employees*, the subject of the sentence.

> This report is the responsibility of only two people, Mark and <u>her.</u>

Here *her* is in the objective case because the appositive *Mark and her* renames *people*, the object of the preposition *of*.

EXERCISE 15.1

In each sentence, underline the correct pronoun form (in parentheses).

1. To Tommy and (I) (me), our teacher gave the opportunity of decorating our classroom for next term.
2. The candidate's dog kept biting at (its) (it's) master's ankles.
3. The senator's daughter and (she) (her) forgot to pack scarves before they left for the Middle East.
4. The neighbors in our cul-de-sac seem to enjoy slow-pitch softball more than (we) (us).
5. From (who) (whom) did you receive that leftover candy?
6. Has Lavera and (he) (him) told you whether they liked the new *Alice in Wonderland* better than the animated version?
7. This year's valedictorian honors went to two brilliant students, Clarise and (he) (him).
8. A two-week suspension will go to (whoever) (whomever) toilet-papered the principal's house.
9. Shelby wondered if her friends would give her twin brother and (she) (her) a surprise birthday party.
10. As Vera and (he)(him) faced the grizzly bear, they wondered what (its) (it's) intentions were.

EXERCISE 15.2

Correct any errors in pronoun case in the following sentences. Some sentences may not contain errors.

1. Diane Sawyer likes to watch Anderson Cooper on CNN, but her brother enjoys him less than her.
2. Where have Orville and he put the parachute?
3. He did not understand why Russell Crowe, who he had always admired, was unhappy with his performance in *Noah*.
4. While boating on the Thames, Dickens told Shakespeare and I that he had never ridden that huge Ferris wheel.
5. Its a shame he has not ridden the Ferris wheel because its height provides wonderful views of London at night.
6. Yvonne and Eunice, whom were passengers on the *Titanic*, feel uncomfortable whenever they take a bath.
7. Although Frank and Joe spoke to all of the neighbors, the cast members from *The Walking Dead* still sold more tickets than them.
8. Between Ramona and he stood a huge marble column covered with mysterious inscriptions.
9. Both Julianne and Dennis are great actors, but the Oscar judges gave Julianne more points than him.
10. For our two neighbors, Henri and her, watching the Canadians win the gold medal was the thrill of a lifetime.

EXERCISE 15.3

Correct any errors in pronoun case in the following sentences. Some sentences may not contain errors.

1 My daughter and me like to visit June Lake for a week during the summer. 2 June Lake is a ski resort in the winter, but in the summer, other visitors and us can rent the skiers' condos cheaply. 3 Its a good deal for both the condo owners and we summer visitors. 4 The people we rent from provide cooking utensils and bedding for my daughter and I. 5 Visitors find a wide variety of attractions for their families and they to enjoy. 6 Frank and Irma, whom own the bait shop on the lake, give us useful fishing tips. 7 We also rent boats from Irma and he. 8 One year Irma and my daughter drove to Yosemite, which is less than an hour away, while Frank and me fished at the lake. 9 Another regular visitor who we've become friends with over the years is a well-known sports celebrity. 10 Also near June Lake is the Mammoth Lakes area, where many restaurants are available for we and our friends. 11 My daughter and her boyfriend enjoy many activities in the village, but I usually stay on the lake most of the day because I enjoy fishing more than them. 12 June Lake is perfect for my dog and I because we can fish during the day and go to bed early, hoping that my daughter and him don't make too much noise when they come home late.

Misplaced and Dangling Modifiers

16

MISPLACED MODIFIERS

Misplaced modifiers are exactly what their name says they are—modifiers that have been "misplaced" within a sentence. But how is a modifier "misplaced"? The answer is simple. If you remember that a modifier is nearly always placed just before or just after the word it modifies, then a misplaced modifier must be one that has been mistakenly placed so that it causes a reader to be confused about what it modifies. Consider the following sentence, for example:

A police officer told us <u>slowly</u> to raise our hands.

Does the modifier *slowly* state how the officer told us, or does it state how we were supposed to raise our hands? Changing the placement of the modifier will clarify the meaning.

A police officer <u>slowly</u> told us to raise our hands.
   Here the word modifies the verb *told*.

A police officer told us to raise our hands <u>slowly</u>.
   Here the word modifies the infinitive *to raise*.

MISPLACED WORDS

Any modifier can be misplaced, but one particular group of modifiers causes quite a bit of trouble for many people. These words are *only, almost, just, merely,* and *nearly.* Consider, for example, the following sentences:

> By buying her new waterbed on sale, Maureen <u>almost</u> saved $100.

> By buying her new waterbed on sale, Maureen saved <u>almost</u> $100.

As you can see, these sentences actually make two different statements. In the first sentence, *almost* modifies *saved.* If you *almost* saved something, you did *not* save it. In the second sentence, *almost* modifies *$100.* If you saved *almost* $100, you saved $85, $90, $95, or some other amount close to $100.

Which statement does the writer want to make—that Maureen did *not* save any money or that she *did* save an amount close to $100? Because the point was that she bought her waterbed on sale, the second sentence makes more sense.

To avoid confusion, be sure that you place all of your modifiers carefully.

INCORRECT	Her coach told her <u>often</u> to work out with weights.
CORRECT	Her coach <u>often</u> told her to work out with weights.
INCORRECT	Kara <u>nearly</u> ate a gallon of ice cream yesterday.
CORRECT	Kara ate <u>nearly</u> a gallon of ice cream yesterday.

MISPLACED PHRASES AND CLAUSES

Phrases and clauses are as easily misplaced as individual words. Generally, phrases and clauses should appear immediately before or after the words they modify. Notice how misplaced phrases and clauses confuse the meaning of the following sentences:

> A bird flew over the house <u>with blue wings.</u>

> The irritated secretary slapped at the fly <u>typing the report.</u>

> They gave the food to the dog <u>left over from dinner.</u>

> Lucia smashed the car into a telephone pole <u>that she had borrowed from her sister.</u>

Obviously, misplaced phrases and clauses can cause rather confusing (and sometimes even humorous) situations. However, when such clauses are placed close to the words they modify, their meaning is clear:

> A bird <u>with blue wings</u> flew over the house.

> The irritated secretary <u>typing the report</u> slapped at the fly.

> <u>Typing the report,</u> the irritated secretary slapped at the fly.

> They gave the food <u>left over from dinner</u> to the dog.

> Lucia smashed the car that <u>she had borrowed from her sister</u> into a telephone pole.

Whether the modifier appears before or after the word it modifies, the point is that you should place a modifier so that it clearly refers to the correct word in the sentence.

DANGLING MODIFIERS

A **dangling modifier** is usually an introductory phrase (usually a verbal phrase) that lacks an appropriate subject to modify. Since these modifiers usually represent some sort of action, they need a **doer** or **agent** of the action represented.

For example, in the following sentence, the introductory phrase "dangles" because it is not followed by a subject that could be the "doer" of the action represented by the phrase:

> Singing at the top of his voice, the song was irritating everybody at the party.

The phrase *Singing at the top of his voice* should be followed by a subject that could logically perform the action of the phrase. Instead, it is followed by the subject *song*. Was the song *singing*? Probably not. Therefore, the modifying phrase "dangles" because it has no subject to which it can logically refer. Here are some more sentences with dangling modifiers:

> Completely satisfied, the painting was admired.
> **Was the *painting* satisfied?**

> After reviewing all of the facts, a decision was reached.
> **Did the *decision* review the facts?**

> To impress the judges, Cecil's mustache was waxed.
> **Did the *mustache* want to impress the judges?**

As you can see, you should check for dangling modifiers when you use introductory phrases.

CORRECTING DANGLING MODIFIERS

You can correct a dangling modifier in one of two ways:

1. **Rewrite the sentence so that its subject can be logically modified by the introductory modifier.**

> Completely satisfied, Charise admired the painting.
> **Charise was completely satisfied.**

> After reviewing all of the facts, I reached a decision.
> ***I* reviewed all of the facts.**

> To impress the judges, Cecil waxed his mustache.
> ***Cecil* wanted to impress the judges.**

2. Change the introductory phrase to a clause.

<u>When Charise was completely satisfied,</u> she admired the painting.

<u>After I reviewed all of the facts,</u> I reached a decision.

<u>Because Cecil wanted to impress the judges,</u> he waxed his mustache.

Note

Do not correct a dangling modifier by moving it to the end of the sentence. In either case, it will still "dangle" because it lacks a "doer," or agent, that could perform the action of the modifier.

INCORRECT

<u>After missing three meetings,</u> the request was denied.

There is no "doer" for *missing*.

STILL INCORRECT

The request was denied <u>after missing three meetings.</u>

There is no "doer" for *missing*.

STILL INCORRECT

<u>After missing three meetings,</u> Alfredo's request was denied.

Adding the possessive form *Alfredo's* does not add a "doer" of the action.

CORRECT

<u>After Alfredo had missed three meetings,</u> his request was denied.

Here the "doer" of the action is clear.

CORRECT

After missing three meetings, Alfredo found that his request had been denied.

Here *Alfredo* is clearly the person who missed the meetings.

EXERCISE 16.1

Identify and correct any misplaced or dangling modifiers in the following sentences. Some of the sentences may be correct.

1. Raiding the refrigerator, sodas, ice cream, chocolate candy bars, and Popsicles were acquired.
2. The bicycle made it to the finish line that he had borrowed from the French team.
3. Because she was nauseated, Anna only watched two episodes of *Survival*.
4. Bursting with enthusiasm, Belinda told her grandparents about the results of the soccer match.
5. After watching *Furious 7* six times, Marilyn's Fiat 500 awaited her in the parking lot.

6. Brandon sent some roses to his ailing grandmother with aphids.

7. After almost jogging to the top of the hill, Carol stopped for some Crocodile-Ade.

8. Arriving in a convoy of armored vehicles, the besieged town was supported by the marines.

9. After parking in the driveway, Alicia petted the family dog drinking a martini.

10. Having sung many of his most famous songs, Tony Bennett's legs felt like jelly, so he sat down at the edge of the stage.

11. The group of hounds annoyed the band that had been howling all night.

12. The master of ceremonies walked on stage reluctantly praising the winning act.

13. Betting a month's salary, the horse chosen by Ken finished last.

14. Because he wanted to impress his date, Gilroy almost ate seven pizzas in one hour.

15. Returning from her trip up the Nile River, Loretta found an asp inside her boxed lunch, which was deadly poisonous.

EXERCISE 16.2

Correct any misplaced or dangling modifiers in the following paragraph. Some sentences may be correct.

1 To put up with Howard, my college roommate, a good deal of tolerance was necessary. 2 Howard was racist, violent, and selfish. 3 Hanging on the wall next to his bed, Howard proudly displayed a Nazi flag. 4 He almost belonged to every racist organization on or off campus. 5 He even had a swastika tattooed to advertise his beliefs on his neck. 6 Once, when he was angry at someone, he grabbed a baseball bat and took a swing at him, which he kept under his bed. 7 Refusing to calm down or apologize, the police were finally called. 8 And then, one day he took my car and nearly drove it all the way to San Francisco, two hundred miles away. 9 Asking him to pay for the mileage and gas, he just laughed at me. 10 Howard was finally asked to leave the school, who was failing all his classes, when he threw a garbage can at one of his professors.

Comma Usage

17

The comma is probably more troublesome to writers than any other punctuation mark. Long ago commas were used to tell readers where to put in a slight pause. Although the placement of the comma does affect the rhythm of a sentence, today it also conveys many more messages than when to pause. Comma use can be broken down into four general rules:

1. **Use commas before coordinating conjunctions that join main clauses.**
2. **Use commas between elements in a series.**
3. **Use commas after introductory elements.**
4. **Use commas before and after interrupting elements.**

COMMAS BEFORE COORDINATING CONJUNCTIONS THAT JOIN MAIN CLAUSES

1. **Place a comma before a coordinating conjunction that joins two main clauses.**

   Richard Pryor was a hilarious comedian, **and** Robin Williams was also great in his own unique way.

   Hercules had to shovel a huge amount of horse manure, **or** he would never complete his task.

2. **Do not put a comma before a conjunction that joins other parts of a sentence, such as two words, two phrases, or two subordinate clauses.**

   Every morning Charlie shaves with his favorite cleaver **and** then goes down to breakfast with his family.

   (No comma is needed before *and* because it does not join two main clauses. It joins the verbs *shaves* and *goes*.)

   You can find good coffee **and** conversation at Kafana Coffee House **or** at Spill the Beans.

   (No comma is required before *and* because it joins the nouns *coffee* and *conversation*. No comma is required before *or* because it just joins the names of the coffee shops.)

COMMAS WITH ELEMENTS IN A SERIES

1. **Separate with commas three or more elements (words, phrases, clauses) listed in a series.** When the last two elements are joined by a coordinating conjunction, a comma before the conjunction is optional.

   WORDS
   The film *Vanilla Sky* was **intriguing, puzzling, and controversial.**

   PHRASES
   Omar enjoyed **cooking okra and Spam for his friends, competing in the Spam cooking contest at the fair, and betting on horses with strange names at the racetrack.**

   CLAUSES
   While shopping at the mall, **Quinlan bought pants that were much too big, his brother bought him a hat that he could wear backward, and his girlfriend bought some Doc Marten black boots.**

2. **Separate with commas two or more adjectives used to modify the same noun if you can put *and* between the adjectives without changing the meaning or if you can easily reverse the order of the adjectives.**

The bear waded into the **shallow, swift** river after the salmon.

The **witty, gregarious** comedian kept us laughing for hours with her stories.

Note You could use *and* between the adjectives. (The river is *shallow* and *swift;* the comedian is *witty* and *gregarious.*) You could also reverse the adjectives (the *swift, shallow* river or the *gregarious, witty* comedian).

3. **On the other hand, no commas are necessary if the adjectives cannot be joined by *and* or are not easily reversed.**

The computer technician wore **white cotton** gloves as she worked.

Notice how awkward the sentence would sound if you placed *and* between the adjectives (the *white and cotton* gloves) or if you reversed them (the *cotton white* gloves).

COMMAS WITH INTRODUCTORY ELEMENTS

1. **Use a comma after introductory words and phrases.**

Introductory Words

next	third	similarly	indeed
first	nevertheless	moreover	yes
second	therefore	however	no

Introductory Phrases

on the other hand	for example	in addition
in a similar manner	for instance	as a result
in other words	in fact	

Next, Persephone made the mistake of eating a pomegranate.

In addition, Charles purchased a remote electronic noise device to embarrass his colleagues.

2. **Use a comma after introductory prepositional phrases of five words or more.** However, you may need to use a comma after a shorter introductory prepositional phrase if not doing so would cause confusion.

Before the famous main attraction, a very good harmonica band entertained the audience.

In the film, actors kept changing into androids.

(Without the comma, this sentence might be read as *in the film actors.*)

3. **Use a comma after all introductory infinitive and participial phrases.**

infinitive phrase   **To eat a hot dog,** Ambrose had to forget his diet.

present participial phrase   **Running in the marathon,** Sam finally achieved his goal.

past participial phrase   **Congregated in the student union,** the students planned their protest.

(See pages 147–151 for a further discussion of infinitive and participial phrases.)

4. **Use a comma after a subordinate clause that precedes a main clause.**

Because Ulysses was bored, he wanted to go fishing again.

Although I am an English major, I sometimes say "ain't."

(See page 111 for a further discussion of punctuating subordinate clauses.)

COMMAS WITH INTERRUPTING ELEMENTS

Sometimes certain words, phrases, or clauses will interrupt the flow of thought in a sentence to add emphasis or additional information. These **interrupting elements** are enclosed by commas.

1. **Use commas to set off parenthetical expressions.** Common parenthetical expressions are *however, indeed, consequently, as a result, moreover, of course, for example, for instance, that is, in fact, after all, I think,* and *therefore*.

A new baseball glove was, **after all**, a luxury.

Her old one, **therefore**, would have to do for another season.

Note   Whenever a parenthetical expression introduces a second main clause after a semicolon, the semicolon takes the place of the comma in front of it.

Colin was looking forward to his vacation; **moreover**, he was eager to visit his family in England.

2. **Use commas to set off nonrestrictive elements. Nonrestrictive** elements are modifying words, phrases, or clauses that are *not* necessary to identify the words they modify. On the other hand, **restrictive** elements are those that *are* necessary to identify the words they modify. Restrictive elements are not set off with commas. Adjective subordinate clauses, participial phrases, and appositives require that you decide whether they are nonrestrictive or restrictive.

Adjective subordinate clauses begin with one of the relative pronouns: *who, whom, whose, which, that,* and sometimes *when* or *where.* They follow the nouns or pronouns that they modify. An adjective clause is **nonrestrictive** when it *is not necessary to identify the word it modifies.* It is enclosed in commas.

nonrestrictive

Dizzy Gillespie, **who helped develop the form of jazz known as bebop,** played an unusual trumpet.

> Because Dizzy Gillespie is named, the adjective clause *who helped develop the form of jazz known as bebop* is nonrestrictive. It is not needed to identify Dizzy Gillespie.

restrictive

One of the people **who helped develop the form of jazz known as bebop** was Dizzy Gillespie.

> Because *who helped develop the form of jazz* is needed to identify the "people" you are referring to, it is restrictive and is not set off with commas.

Here is another example of a nonrestrictive clause:

nonrestrictive

My youngest sister, **who is a paleontologist,** showed me her collection of skulls.

> Because a person can have only one youngest sister, the adjective clause *is not needed to identify her*, making it nonrestrictive.

(See page 111 for a further discussion of punctuating adjective clauses.)

Participial phrases that *do not contain information necessary to identify the word they modify* are nonrestrictive and are therefore set off by commas. Restrictive participial phrases do not require commas.

nonrestrictive

Van Gogh, **seeking something to paint,** looked up into the night sky.

> Because van Gogh is named, the participial phrase *seeking something to paint* is nonrestrictive. It is not needed to identify van Gogh.

restrictive

The man **painting in the middle of the night** called the work *Starry Night.*

> Because the man is not named, the participial phrase *painting in the middle of the night* is restrictive.

(See pages 147–151 for a further discussion of participial phrases.)

An **appositive** is a noun or pronoun, along with any modifiers, that **renames** another noun or pronoun. The appositive almost always follows the word it refers to, and it is usually set off by commas.

The computer, **an extremely useful tool,** has advanced a long way in just a few years.

> The noun *tool* renames the noun *computer.*

On the street, the Yugo, **the one with the rusty doors,** is an eyesore.

> The pronoun *one* renames the noun *Yugo.*

(See pages 195–199 for a further discussion of appositives.)

3. **Use commas to set off words of direct address.** If a writer addresses someone directly in a sentence, the words that stand for that person or persons are set off by commas. If the words in direct address begin a sentence, they are followed by a comma. If they end a sentence, they are preceded by a comma.

What if, **Charlie,** you were to hurt someone with one of your weapons?

Brent, you are hogging the ball.

I am sorry if I hurt your feelings, **Aaron.**

4. **Use commas to set off dates and addresses.** If your sentence contains two or more elements of a date or an address, use commas to set off these elements. The following sentences contain two or more elements:

We went to Magic Mountain on **Thursday, November 18, 2014,** because children were admitted free that day.

Concepcion had lived at 4590 **Portello Street, San Francisco, California,** for twelve years.

In 1992 she moved to 1754 **Pacific Court, Vista, California 92083,** to be near her mother.

Note   The state is not separated from the zip code by a comma.

EXERCISE 17.1

Add commas to the following sentences where necessary.

1. Although *Game of Thrones* seems to be the most popular TV series Evan prefers *Justified*.
2. The term *Trojan Horse* comes from the *Iliad* a Greek epic poem and it is also used by the computer industry.
3. The rap star in fact secretly listened to John Coltrane.
4. Agamemnon gladly left Troy burning picked up Cassandra and went to look for his wife.
5. The rosy dark dawn greeted the soldiers as they prepared for battle.
6. Dr. Grey knew that giving birth had changed her anatomy somewhat but she loved being a mother.
7. On April 6 2015 Duke beat Wisconsin in the final game of the NCAA playoffs.
8. Ludwig Beethoven who is one of the most famous classical composers was deaf when he composed most of his best works.
9. Marvin Jones first baseman for the London Lions committed his worst error in the first inning.

10. Batman called for the Batmobile rushed to the ballpark put on his bat uniform and got there in time to hit a homerun in the second inning.

11. The boy who stole the slave and then hid on Jackson's Island was Huckleberry Finn.

12. Send the feathers and wax to 8965 Maze Way Minotaur Ohio 09999 and make it quick Otto.

13. In an attempt to invade the Whitehouse a man flew a very small helicopter over the fence.

14. Stanley why do you keep screaming out Stella's name?

15. After the Civil War battle at Franklin Tennessee on November 30 1864 a Confederate widow named Carrie McGavock helped identify and bury over 2500 dead soldiers.

EXERCISE 17.2

Add commas to the following sentences where necessary.

1. Yes Icarus flew like a bird but he lived to regret it.

2. Caesar you should have worn your Kevlar vest.

3. I like to visit June Lake California to fish and I have already made my reservations for this July.

4. As of April 1 2015 the schools in Martin Luther King County would not allow students to read *Huckleberry Finn* the famous novel by Mark Twain because of certain words.

5. After the shooting in the town near St. Louis Missouri people were outraged; as a result thousands marched in protest.

6. Spiral Comet a local knucklehead searches daily for the black hole in Central Park.

7. My useful endurable iPad is never far from me.

8. Laying down his baton after conducting his *Ninth Symphony* Ludwig could not hear the loud applause because he was deaf.

9. Few customers ever gather at The Small Half Pint a large pub near my house.

10. While composing his famous novel *The Once and Future King* T. H. White was also training a goshawk.

11. Tom Wolfe who wrote the *Electric Kool-Aid Acid Test* said that it was P. T. Barnum who originally said "There is a fool born every day."

12. The New England Patriots won as a matter of fact as a result of the tight end's loose-fitting uniform a problem with the losing team's quarterback and a certain lightning bug in a jar sitting by Tom Brady's bedside.

13. June 24 1981 was a special day for Michelle for on that day she saw sunshine clouds and sky for the first time.

14. Named for Ceres the goddess of agriculture cereal is eaten at breakfasts all over the world.

15. For some strange reason that I don't understand some depressed people prefer "The Blue Period" a time during which Pablo Picasso painted
in shades of blue.

EXERCISE **17.3**

Add commas to the following sentences where necessary.

1 Mistletoe which is also known by the Latin name of *Vicsum album*
has long been considered to have unusual characteristics. 2 Today
it is known as the plant that provides an excuse to kiss someone but
its reputation as a plant with special powers goes back to the Bronze
Age. 3 Because it seems to appear out of nowhere the ancient Druids
thought the plant was sent from heaven. 4 In fact it is a parasite that
sinks its rootlike feelers into the top of a tree and then it literally sucks
the life juices out of it. 5 Growing slowly ruthlessly and patiently it
does not die until the tree that it is attached to dies. 6 Druid priests
would climb the tree and harvest the mistletoe which was believed to
cure toothache epilepsy and even infertility. 7 Although researchers
have recently found that mistletoe leaf extract might inhibit the growth
of cancer cells we also know that mistletoe is poisonous. 8 During the
days of the Roman Empire mistletoe was regarded as a symbol of peace.
9 Standing under a sprig of the plant enemies would throw away their
weapons declare a truce and embrace. 10 The origin of today's custom
of kissing under the mistletoe is not clear; however it may derive from
the Norwegian story of Frigga who kissed everyone who walked under
the mistletoe when her son came back to life.

Semicolons and Colons

18

THE SEMICOLON

1. **A semicolon is used to join two main clauses that are not joined by a comma and a coordinating conjunction.** Sometimes a conjunctive adverb follows the semicolon. (See page 71 for a list of conjunctive adverbs.)

   The generals checked Hitler's horoscope; it told them when to attack.

   Nancy wanted to check her horoscope; however, Ron advised against it.

2. **A semicolon can be used to join elements in a series when the elements require further internal punctuation.**

   By the time Guillermo reached home, he had worked for eighteen hours, which tired him out; he had had a car accident, which depressed him; he had drunk too much coffee, which made him jittery; and he had yelled at his partner, which made him remorseful.

3. **Do not use a semicolon to separate two phrases or two subordinate clauses.**

   INCORRECT

   Sonia is going to Little Vietnam because she likes the spring rolls; and because she likes the atmosphere.

   CORRECT

   Sonia is going to Little Vietnam because she likes the spring rolls and because she likes the atmosphere.

   (See pages 70–71 for further discussion of semicolon usage.)

THE COLON

1. **A colon is used to join two main clauses when the second clause is an example, an illustration, or a restatement of the first clause.**

   The party had been a great success: everyone had had fun and had gotten safely home.

   This incident is the same as all of the others: Wolfgang never agrees with any of our ideas.

2. **A colon is used when a complete sentence introduces an example, a quotation, a series, or a list.**

   The magazine covered a number of subjects related to biking: racing bicycles, touring bicycles, mountain bicycles, and safety equipment.

   In "The Cautious and Obedient Life," Susan Walton made the following statement: "Some people are born to follow instructions."

   The list on the refrigerator included the following requests: clean the kitchen, wash the car, make reservations at Jake's, and take a shower.

3. **A colon is generally not used after a verb.**

   INCORRECT

   My favorite foods are: red beans and rice, catfish, and pasta carbonara.

   CORRECT

   My favorite foods are red beans and rice, catfish, and pasta carbonara.

EXERCISE 18.1

Add semicolons or colons where necessary. (Some commas may need to be replaced with semicolons or colons.)

1. Dizzy picked up his trumpet then he blew a scorching version of "Salt Peanuts."
2. *Iago* means "James" in Italian, therefore, it is an appropriate name for the villain in *Othello* because St. James was said to have driven the Moors from Spain.
3. Adam washed his children's clothes in the new detergent Disappear amazingly, his children vanished.
4. When Helen began collecting ancient coins, she purchased the following items a jeweler's loupe, a telescope, a book on ancient Roman and Greek coins, and a catalog giving the prices of ancient coins.
5. My grandmother always followed the same recipe for lemon icebox pie combine Eagle Brand concentrated milk, frozen lemonade, and a graham cracker crust and place the mixture into the refrigerator.
6. The word *raptor* comes from the Latin word which means "to seize" raptors are birds that seize small animals to eat.

7. In "Why I Won't Buy My Sons Toy Guns," Robert Shaffer makes an interesting point "Any toy is teacher."

8. The painting of St. Francis contained the following animals a wolf, a finch, a rabbit, and an oriole.

9. On the aircraft carrier a huge banner contained the following words "Mission Accomplished."

10. Last summer we visited my cousin Alice, who lives in Monroe, South Dakota, my brother John, who lives in San Luis Obispo, California, and my friend Jim, who lives in Atlanta, Georgia.

EXERCISE 18.2

Add semicolons or colons where necessary. (Some commas may need to be replaced with semicolons or colons.)

1 Coffee is one of the most popular beverages in the United States, therefore, it is natural for people to wonder how the caffeine in coffee affects them. 2 To understand how caffeine works, one needs to understand the relationship between three chemicals adenosine, caffeine, and adrenaline. 3 Adenosine is one of the many chemicals in the brain it is the one that makes a person sleepy. 4 Caffeine's molecular structure is similar to adenosine's, as a result, caffeine binds to adenosine receptors when it enters the brain, but it doesn't activate the "sleepy" adenosine response. 5 Instead, caffeine works the opposite of adenosine it increases the neuron firing in the brain. 6 The nerve cells also speed up because caffeine has blocked the adenosine. 7 The pituitary gland senses an emergency situation, therefore, it tells the adrenal glands to release adrenaline. 8 The following reactions result the pupils dilate, the breathing tubes open up, the heart beats faster, the blood vessels on the surface constrict, the blood pressure rises, the blood flow to the stomach slows, and the muscles tighten. 9 In addition to all of these reactions, the liver releases sugar into the bloodstream the added sugar causes extra energy. 10 These complex bodily responses are what make coffee the popular drink it is today.

The Apostrophe 19

1. **Apostrophes are used to form contractions.**

   The apostrophe replaces the omitted letter or letters.

it is	it's
cannot	can't
I am	I'm
were not	weren't
they are	they're
is not	isn't
would have	would've
does not	doesn't

2. **Apostrophes are used to form the possessives of nouns and indefinite pronouns.**
   - Add *'s* to form the possessive of all singular nouns and indefinite pronouns.

singular nouns	The <u>boy's</u> bicycle was new.
	<u>Louis's</u> courage was never questioned.
indefinite pronouns	<u>Someone's</u> horn was honking
compound words	My <u>father-in-law's</u> car had a flat.
joint possession	<u>Julio and Maria's</u> mountain cabin is for rent.

- Add only an apostrophe to form the possessive of plural nouns that end in *-s*. However, add *-'s* to form the possessive of plural nouns that do not end in *-s*.

    Both <u>teams'</u> shoes were lined up on the field.

    The <u>Smiths'</u> house was on fire.

    The <u>women's</u> cars were parked in front of the house.

- Expressions referring to time or money often require an apostrophe.

    Sheila asked for a dollar's worth of candy.

    The player was given three days' suspension.

3. **Do not use apostrophes with the possessive forms of personal pronouns.**

Incorrect	Correct
her's	hers
our's	ours
their's	theirs

Note   *It's* means "it is." The possessive form of *it* is *its*.

EXERCISE 19.1

Correct apostrophe errors by adding apostrophes (or *-s*) or by removing apostrophes where necessary.

1. Bob Dylans next tour will include San Diego; Milt wont be able to get ticket's.
2. Troys walls fell not long after the Trojan Horse was wheeled into the city.
3. Its true that Tennessee Williams play *Streetcar Named Desire* was a hit, but he was afraid it wouldnt be.
4. Your new Lexus paint job is gorgeous, so Im going to get my old pickup repainted.
5. The childrens soccer uniforms were the same color as our's.
6. The grocerys selection of new detergent's wasnt enough for Mr. Jones.
7. A weeks vacation is not enough time to enjoy my father-in-laws cabin in Aspen.
8. Just as the universitys band began to play the national anthem, my sons trombone slide stuck.
9. Didnt Marlon Brandos acting in *Streetcar Named Desire* win an award?
10. The Salazars house was damaged by the flood, but her's wasnt.

EXERCISE **19.2**

Correct apostrophe errors by adding apostrophes (or -*s*) or by removing apostrophes where necessary.

1 One of my mothers favorite stories is about the time she organized all of the quilting club's in town to protest the Vietnam War. 2 The clubs members had always been politically active, so few people objected. 3 After just a few months work, they had made hundreds of quilts with slogan's on them objecting to the war. 4 My aunts quilt had pictures and names of people killed in the war. 5 Knowing my family, I wasnt surprised to hear that both of my grandmothers also participated in the quilting. 6 On the day designated for the protest, my uncle Charles leased twelve buses to take the quilters to the mayors office. 7 Uncle Charles younger brother had died in the war several year's earlier. 8 Once they were downtown, the women held up their quilts and chanted, "Its time to end the war!" 9 Newspapers from miles away covered the protest, and the local television stations daily schedule was interrupted to televise it. 10 My mother say's, "We werent a big group of thousands of people, but even small protests like ours can make a difference."

Quotation Marks 20

1. **Quotation marks are used to enclose direct quotations and dialogue.**

   As Oscar Wilde once said, "Fashion is a form of ugliness so intolerable that we have to alter it every six months."

   Will Rogers said, "Liberty doesn't work as well in practice as it does in speeches."

2. **Quotation marks are not used with indirect quotations.**

direct quotation	Tony said, "I'll play trumpet in the band."
indirect quotation	Tony said that he would play trumpet in the band.

3. **Place periods and commas inside quotation marks.**

   Eudora Welty wrote the short story "A Worn Path."

   "I am a man more sinned against than sinning," cried Lear.

4. **Place colons and semicolons outside quotation marks.**

   The class did not like the poem "Thoughts on Capital Punishment": it was silly, sentimental, and insipid, and the rhythm was awkward and inappropriate.

   The local newspaper ran a story titled "Mayor Caught Nude on the Beach"; it was just a joke for April Fools' Day.

5. **Place the question mark inside the quotation marks if the quotation is a question. Place the question mark outside the quotation marks if the quotation is not a question but the whole sentence is.**

   Homer asked, "What is for dinner, my dear Hortense?"

   Did Hortense really reply, "Hominy, okra, and barbecued Spam"?

6. **Place the exclamation point inside the quotation marks if the quotation is an exclamation. Place it outside the quotation marks if the quotation is not an exclamation but the whole sentence is.**

"I have a dream!" yelled Martin Luther King, Jr.

I insist that you stop calling me "dude"!

(See pages 162–165 for a further discussion of quotation marks.)

EXERCISE 20.1

Add quotation marks to the following sentences where necessary.

1. The professor used the poem Stopping by Woods on a Snowy Evening to begin his class.
2. Did Bottom say, I feel like an ass?
3. Chris played Bob Dylan's song A Hard Rain's A-Gonna Fall over and over.
4. Rachel Maddow often murmured that she was tired of Senator Hotwind.
5. Fairy Godmother, may I wash my feet first? asked Cinderella.
6. At the beginning of the hike, did John Muir say, Life is too short to waste?
7. Emily Dickinson said, I am going to write a poem about a humming-bird; however, she did not mention the word *hummingbird* in the poem.
8. The umpire yelled, You're out and then the players started complaining.
9. Woz used to say, I think; therefore, I'm probably not.
10. No one tips me anymore, sighed the door attendant.

EXERCISE 20.2

Add quotation marks to the following sentences where necessary.

1 When Sophia spent the evening with her friend Alicia at Alicia's house, she was surprised at the family's conversation during dinner. 2 Alicia's brother Paulo, who was taking a literature course at his college, said that he had been reading a short story by Eudora Welty titled Petrified Man. 3 I'd never read any short stories at all before I took this class, he said. 4 Sophia responded that she had never read Eudora Welty but that she enjoyed Flannery O'Connor. 5 Alicia's mother then asked Sophia, Have you ever read a poem called My Last Duchess? 6 Sophia nodded and said, I read it just last semester; Alicia's mother looked pleased. 7 Doesn't the Duchess die at the end? asked Alicia's father. 8 Later, the discussion turned to newspaper articles they had read. 9 Paulo asked, Did anyone see yesterday's article entitled We Need to Do More about Global Warming? 10 After a long discussion of the need for ecological awareness, Sophia thanked the family for its hospitality, and, when asked if she would like to come back the following week, she replied, Definitely!

Titles, Capitalization, and Numbers

21

TITLES

1. **Place in italics the titles of longer works, such as books, periodicals, plays, CDs, and television programs.**

   - Books: *Moby Dick, When the Rainbow Goddess Wept*
   - Plays: *The Glass Menagerie, A Doll's House, A Raisin in the Sun*
   - Pamphlets: *Grooming Your Labrador, Charleston's Ten Best Restaurants*
   - Long musical works: Mozart's *String Quartet in C Major*, Miles Davis's *Sketches of Spain*
   - Long poems: *Howl, The Faerie Queene*
   - Periodicals: *The Washington Post, Time*
   - Films: *Furious7, Gone Girl, Waiting for "Superman"*
   - Television and radio programs: *American Idol, Masterpiece Theater*
   - Works of art: El Greco's *Saint Matthew, Nike of Samothrace*

2. **Use quotation marks to enclose the titles of all shorter works, such as songs, poems, and short stories, as well as parts of larger works, such as articles in magazines and chapters in books.**

   - Songs: "The Sweetest Days," "Friends"
   - Poems: "My Last Duchess," "Dover Beach"
   - Articles in periodicals: "Three-Headed Snake Born as Two-Headed Brother Looks On," "The Last Stand"
   - Short stories: "A Jury of Her Peers," "Resurrection"
   - Essays: "Male Fixations," "A Custody Fight for an Egg"
   - Episodes of radio and television shows: "What's in a Name?"
   - Subdivisions of books: "The Cassock" (Chapter 29 of *Moby Dick*)

CAPITALIZATION

1. **Capitalize the personal pronoun *I*.**
2. **Capitalize the first letter of every sentence.**
3. **Capitalize the first letter of each word in a title except for *a*, *an*, and *the*, coordinating conjunctions, and prepositions.**

Note   The first letter of the first and last words of a title are always capitalized.

> *Dictionary of Philosophy and Religion*
>
> "A Good Man Is Hard to Find"

4. **Capitalize the first letter of all proper nouns and adjectives derived from proper nouns.**

- Names and titles of people: President Obama, William Shakespeare, Uncle Christopher, Ms. Hohman
- Names of specific places: Chicago, Smoky Mountains, Tennessee, The Armenian Cafe, Saturn, the South

Note   Do not capitalize the first letter of words that refer to a direction, such as *north, south, east,* or *west*. Do capitalize such words when they refer to a specific region.

> Alabama and Mississippi are among the states in the <u>South.</u>
>
> Turn <u>south</u> on Hill Street and go four blocks to the end of the street.

- Names of ethnic, national, or racial groups: Native American, British, French, Canadian, Hispanic, Russian
- Names of groups or organizations: National Organization for Women, Girl Scouts of America, Methodists
- Names of companies: General Motors, Nordstrom, PepsiCo, R. J. Reynolds
- Names of the days of the week and the months of the year but not the seasons: Saturday, April, winter, spring
- Names of holidays and historical events: the Gulf War, Christmas, the Battle of Concord
- Names of *specific* gods and religious writings: God, Zeus, Buddha, Koran, Yahweh, Bible

Note   The names of academic subjects are not capitalized unless they refer to an ethnic or national origin or are the names of specific courses. Examples include *mathematics, history, Spanish,* and *Physics 100*.

NUMBERS

The following rules about numbers apply to general writing rather than to technical or scientific writing.

1. **Spell out numbers that require no more than two words. Use numerals for numbers that require more than two words.**

   <u>Ninety-three</u> people attended the dean's retirement party.

   We have now gone <u>125</u> days without rain.

2. **Spell out numbers at the beginning of sentences.**

   <u>Two hundred thirty-five</u> miles is a long distance to rollerblade.

3. **Use numerals in the following situations:**

   - Dates: June 24, 2016; 55 B.C.E.
   - Sections of books or plays: Chapter 26, page 390; Act 5, scene 2, lines 78–90
   - Addresses: 3245 Sisyphus Street
   - Stonewall, Nebraska 90345
   - Decimals, percentages, and fractions: 7.5; 75%, 75 percent; 1/8
   - Exact amounts of money: $10.86; $6,723,001
   - Scores and statistics: Padres 10, Reds 0; a ratio of 4 to 1
   - Time of day: 5:23; 12:45

Note   Round amounts of money that can be expressed in a few words can be written out: *thirty cents, twelve dollars, three hundred dollars*. Also when the word *o'clock* is used with the time of day, the time of day should be written out: *eight o'clock*.

4. **When numbers are compared, are joined by conjunctions, or occur in a series, either consistently use numerals or consistently spell them out.**

   For the birthday party we needed <u>one hundred fifteen</u> paper hats, <u>two hundred twenty</u> napkins, <u>one hundred fifteen</u> paper plates and forks, <u>eight</u> gallons of ice cream, <u>three</u> cakes, <u>forty</u> candles, and <u>eight</u> cases of soda.

   or

   For the birthday party we needed <u>115</u> paper hats, <u>220</u> napkins, <u>115</u> paper plates and forks, <u>8</u> gallons of ice cream, <u>3</u> cakes, <u>40</u> candles, and <u>8</u> cases of soda.

EXERCISE 21.1

The following sentences contain errors in the use of titles, capitalization, and numbers. Correct any errors you find.

1. In arthur miller's play death of a salesman, willy loman is the main character; other characters are his Wife, linda, and his Sons, happy and biff.

2. 6,000 or more people are estimated to have died in the earthquake that occurred in nepal in april two thousand and fifteen.

3. The chief of the baltimore police department deployed over two thousand and fifty officers when riots broke out in Northern parts of the City.

4. roosevelt middle school enrolled exactly 300 students this year, and mr. robert's seventh grade class had twenty-five students, including cole vandervort.

5. On the first day of the two thousand fifteen season, the st. louis cardinals defeated the chicago cubs by a score of three to zero.

6. As a reward for keeping to his diet, mike's Wife gave him 10 butterfinger candy bars, two gallons of Chocolate and Peanut Butter ice cream, and 3 stouffer's pecan pies.

7. The hbo television series justified stars timothy oliphant as a u.s. marshall who goes after drug dealers in harlan county, kentucky.

8. My favorite bob dylan song is forever young, which is on the album planet waves; dylan often played this song with the band called the band.

9. The Faculty of the university of arizona gave its Basketball Team a dinner for making it to the ncaa basketball finals in two thousand fifteen.

10. During his women's studies 25 class, professor dietrich searched the magazine consumer reports for an analysis of the new mercedes automobile he planned to buy for his Wife.

EXERCISE 21.2

In the following sentences, correct any errors in the use of titles, capitalization, and numbers.

1 When brad awoke that wednesday morning, he was one happy fellow. 2 The first thing he saw was a thick copy of leo tolstoy's novel war and peace. 3 The night before he had read the first 100 pages of it, and he was pleased to find he really enjoyed it. 4 Today he was going to meet his girlfriend grace after he went to the Dentist's office. 5 Later in the day they were going to join his art class as it toured the chicago museum of art. 6 He was looking forward to seeing the famous painting by grant wood, american gothic. 7 He had heard that over Three Million Five Hundred Thousand people had traveled to chicago just to see this painting. 8 Grace met him at their favorite coffee shop, caffeinemania, where they listened to enya's popular song orinoco flow. 9 As they left the coffee shop, they saw a copy of time magazine with an article entitled prospects for end of war not good. 10 Wanting to stay in a good mood, brad and grace went for a slow 20-minute walk in the Winter air, and then they headed for the Museum to meet brad's Art Professor and the other members of his class.

Clear and Concise Sentences

22

If you are like most writers, your first drafts will have their share of confusing, murky sentences. Sometimes the point of a sentence can be completely lost in a maze of words that seems to lead nowhere. One sure way to improve such sentences is to learn to cut and rewrite and then to cut and rewrite again. Here are some areas to consider as you work toward clear, concise sentences.

REDUNDANCIES

Redundant wording consists of saying the same thing twice (or more than twice), using different words each time. Cut and rewrite redundancies.

redundant	We left for Los Angeles at 10:00 P.M. **at night.**
concise	We left for Los Angeles at 10:00 P.M.
redundant	My **brother is a man** who always pays his bills.
concise	My brother always pays his bills.
redundant	Good baseball players know the **basic fundamentals** of the game.
concise	Good baseball players know the fundamentals of the game.

NEEDLESS REPETITION

Repeating a word or phrase can weaken a sentence unless you are intentionally trying to emphasize the idea. Cut and rewrite needless repetition.

repetitive	My favorite **picture** is the **picture** of our house in Newport Beach.
concise	My favorite picture is the one of our house in Newport Beach.
repetitive	When my sister called me on the **telephone** at **two o'clock this morning**, I told her that **two o'clock in the morning** was too early **in the morning** for her to call on **the telephone.**
concise	When my sister phoned me at two o'clock this morning, I told her that she should not be calling so early.

ROUNDABOUT PHRASES

Replace phrases that say in four or five words what can be said in one or two.

Roundabout	Concise
at all times	always
at the present time	now
at this point in time	now
on many occasions	often
in this modern day and age	today
because of the fact that	because
due to the fact that	because
for the purpose of	for
until such time as	until
in spite of the fact that	although, even though
make reference to	refer to
be of the opinion that	think, believe
in the event that	if

EXERCISE 22.1

Revise the following sentences to eliminate redundancies, needless repetition, and roundabout phrases.

1. The wolverine broke into our mountain cabin that we have in the mountains and went down into the basement to find our garbage cans where we keep our garbage.

2. Due to the fact that our garbage cans are closed and sealed, the wolverine was unable to find any good tasting food that it thought would be delicious.

3. Many people of the medical and dietetic fields are of the opinion that the eating and consuming of wild catfish that are caught in the rivers and lakes are dangerous and not healthy to eat.

4. At the present time, the people of Nepal who have been harmed by the Nepal earthquake need help for the purpose of feeding them and providing food for them.

5. In the event of a band of singers and players providing a good and excellent performance, they should be given an ovation and applauded for their efforts.

6. Sarah was very glad and happy that her new wooden oak table for the purpose of dining would be arriving as soon as tomorrow.

7. Until such time as people are not permitted to join together, gather, and meet, they will continue to use and employ that right to make their points or express their opinions.

8. Even in this modern day and age my mother believes in her head that the earth is flat and not round.

9. Some people and persons in this country of ours are of the opinion that Shakespeare did not write and create his own plays.

10. When I was young, I thought in my mind that my father was a tall giant man, but when I grew and was taller, I could see he was not.

WEAK SUBJECTS AND VERBS

You can improve most writing by treating each sentence as if it told a story. Find the action of the story and make it the verb. Find the actor or "doer" of the action and make it the subject. Watch for the following situations in particular.

NEEDLESS *TO BE* VERBS

Replace *to be* verbs *(am, are, is, was, were, been, being, be)* with verbs that express an action.

weak	She **is** the one who **is** responsible for your damaged car.
improved	She **damaged** your car.
weak	His behavior **was** a demonstration of my point
improved	His behavior **demonstrated** my point.
weak	Sergio and Rene **were** the winners of the $10,000 raffle.
improved	Sergio and Rene **won** the $10,000 raffle.

NOMINALIZATIONS

Nominalizations are nouns formed from verbs. From *realize* we have *realization*. From *argue* we have *argument*. From *criticize* we have *criticism*. Nominalizations can hide both the action of the sentence as well as the performer of the action. When possible, change nominalizations to verb forms to clarify the actor and the action of the sentence.

weak
: Mario's **realization** of his **betrayal** by his business partner occurred when he saw the bank statement.

improved
: Mario **realized** that his business partner **had betrayed** him when he saw the bank statement.

weak
: Shelley's **request** was that we conduct an **examination** of the finances of the city council members.

improved
: Shelley **requested** that we **examine** the finances of the city council members.

UNNECESSARY INITIAL *IT* AND *THERE*

Sentences beginning with *it* and *there* often contain needless extra words. When possible, revise such sentences to focus on the actor and the action of the sentence.

wordy
: There is a belief held by many people that we should lower taxes.

improved
: Many people believe that we should lower taxes.

wordy
: It is imperative that we leave in five minutes if we want to arrive on time.

improved
: We must leave in five minutes if we want to arrive on time.

UNNECESSARY PASSIVE VOICE

See Chapter 12 for a discussion of active and passive voice. In general, use active voice verbs to emphasize the actor and the action of your sentences.

passive
: The car **was driven** two hundred miles by Mr. Ogilvey before he **was found** by the police.

active
: Mr. Ogilvey **drove** the car two hundred miles before the police **found** him.

EXERCISE 22.2

Revise the following sentences to strengthen weak subjects and verbs.

1. The students in his class have been inspired by their algebra instructor's encouragement.
2. There were a dozen doughnuts eaten by the members of the committee.
3. It is important that the dog owned by our neighbors be vaccinated for the protection of everyone on our street.

4. The source of her distress was that her performance in the soccer match was below her expectations of herself.

5. It was my friend's gerbil that has caused him to worry because it keeps escaping from its cage.

6. Because Jack and Harold's marriage was not approved of by Harold's mother, she was not in attendance at the wedding.

7. The abandonment of the animals in the zoo by the zookeepers was caused by the severity of the earthquake.

8. Music is used by many people as an experience in meditation and relaxation.

9. It is with deep sorrow that we have reached the realization that it is necessary to ask you to live somewhere else because of your drug use.

10. In addition to providing an examination of global warming, there was also a discussion of California's drought by the Berkeley professor.

EXERCISE **22.3**

Revise the following sentences to make them clearer and more concise.

1 Each and every one of us in this great country of the United States of America should all pay attention to the air and water and plants and other people and creatures around us. 2 It is a fact the some of these things are being abused and harmed by too many of us. 3 As a result, there are many people in this country who are worried and concerned about a thing called global warming. 4 The layers of air above us that protect us from solar radiation are in the process of becoming thinner because of all the things that come out of our cars and factories and manufacturing places. 5 It is reported by scientists that this thinning causes the polar caps, which are all the ice and snow at the top and bottom of the world, to melt. 6 This melting can be the causative factor in all sorts of weather changes that cause damage and destruction. 7 It is former Vice President Al Gore who has been warning us lately, and his words should be listened to by all of us about this problem. 8 But in addition all of us should each also try to do our own part. 9 If we all just drove our vehicles and cars fewer miles, that stuff that comes from our autos, called exhaust, would not thin or harm the atmosphere as much. 10 In conclusion of all this, it is necessary in this modern day and age that we pay attention to and think about how we treat our world and environment.

ESL Issues

23

If English is your second language, you know the confusion and frustration that can sometimes result when you try to apply the grammar rules and usage patterns of English. Of course, you are not alone. Anyone who has ever tried to learn a second language has encountered similar problems. This chapter reviews some of the more common issues faced by ESL writers.

COUNT AND NONCOUNT NOUNS

1. **Count nouns refer to nouns that exist as separate items that can be counted. They usually have singular and plural forms:** *one bottle, two bottles; one thought, two thoughts: one teacher, two teachers.*

2. **Noncount nouns refer to nouns that cannot be counted and usually do not take plural forms.** Here are some common noncount nouns:

   - Food and drink: *meat, bacon, spinach, celery, water, milk, wine*
   - Nonfood material: *equipment, furniture, luggage, rain, silver, gasoline*
   - Abstractions: *anger, beauty, happiness, honesty, courage*

   Note   **Noncount nouns** stay in their singular form. It would be incorrect to say *bacons, furnitures,* or *courages.*

3. **Some nouns can be either count or noncount, depending on whether you use them as specific, countable items or as a substance or general concept.**

NONCOUNT	The *fruit* in the bowl looks moldy.
COUNT	Eat all the *fruits* and vegetables that you want.
NONCOUNT	Time slows as you approach the speed of *light*.
COUNT	The *lights* in the stadium all went out.

ARTICLES WITH COUNT AND NONCOUNT NOUNS

INDEFINITE ARTICLES

1. **The indefinite articles are *a* and *an*. They are used with *singular count nouns* that are *general* or *nonspecific*. Usually, the noun is being introduced for the first time.**

Yesterday I saw **a dog** chase **a car** down the street.

An apple fell from the tree and rolled into the pool.

In these sentences, *dog, car,* and *apple* are general count nouns that could refer to any dog, car, or apple at all, so the articles *a* and *an* are used with them.

2. **Do not use indefinite articles with noncount nouns.**

INCORRECT	He has had a diabetes since he was young.
CORRECT	He has had diabetes since he was young.

DEFINITE ARTICLES

1. **The word *the* is a definite article. It is used with *specific nouns*, both *count* and *noncount*.**

2. **You can usually tell if a noun is specific by its context.** In some cases, other words in a sentence make it clear that the noun refers to a specific thing or things. In other instances, the noun has been mentioned in a previous sentence, so the second reference to it is specific.

I bought **the dog** that licked my hand. (This singular count noun refers to a *specific* dog, the one that licked my hand.)

A car and a motorcycle roared down the street. **The car** sounded as if it had no muffler. (This singular count noun refers to a *specific* car, the one in the previous sentence.)

The courage that he demonstrated impressed me. (This noncount noun refers to the *specific* courage of one man.)

ARTICLES WITH PROPER NOUNS

1. Use *the* with plural proper nouns (*the United States, the Smiths*).
2. Do not use *the* with most singular proper nouns (*John, San Diego, Germany*).
3. Use *the* with some singular proper nouns, including names of oceans, seas, and rivers (*the Mississippi River, the Atlantic Ocean*), names using *of* (*the Republic of China, the University of Colorado*), and names of large regions, deserts, and peninsulas (*the Mideast, the Sahara Desert, the Iberian Peninsula*).

NO ARTICLES

1. Articles are generally not used with noncount nouns or plural nouns that are making general statements.

   Racism and *prejudice* should worry *parents* and *teachers*.

   In this sentence, the noncount nouns *racism* and *prejudice* as well as the plural count nouns *parents* and *teachers* do not use articles because they are general, referring to *any* racism or prejudice and *any* parent or teacher.

2. Remember that all singular count nouns require an article, whether they are specific or general.

SPECIFIC	The *chicken* will look for some seed.
GENERAL	A *chicken* will look for some seed.

EXERCISE 23.1

In the spaces provided, write the appropriate article (*a, an,* or *the*) whenever one is needed. If no article is needed, leave the space blank.

1. Sonia read _____ poem to her friend who had just arrived in _____ San Diego.
2. We congratulated _____ winner of the award for _____ most unusual painting.
3. Whenever _____ bird lands on our fence, my daughter offers it _____ bird seed.
4. If you are in _____ accident, be sure to notify _____ police.
5. We drove to _____ Georgia in the middle of the hottest summer of _____ year.

HELPING VERBS AND MAIN VERBS

1. If a verb consists of one word, it is a main verb (MV).

   MV
   My father **stared** at the server.

2. **If a verb consists of two or more words, the last word of the verb is the main verb (MV). The earlier words are helping verbs (HV).**

          HV   MV

My father **is staring** at the server.

HELPING VERBS

1. **There are twenty-three helping verbs in English. Nine of them are called** *modals*. **They are always helping verbs.**

Modals	can	will	shall	may
	could	would	should	might
				must

2. **The other fourteen sometimes function as helping verbs and sometimes as main verbs.**

Forms of *do: do, does, did*

Forms of *have: have, has, had*

Forms of *be: am, is, are, was, were, be, being, been*

MAIN VERBS

1. **All main verbs use five forms (except for** *be*, **which uses eight).**

Base Form	**-s Form**	**Past Tense**	**Past Participle**	**Present Participle**
walk	walks	walked	walked	walking
call	calls	called	called	calling
eat	eats	ate	eaten	eating
ring	rings	rang	rung	ringing

2. **Regular verbs.** A regular verb forms its past tense and past participle by adding *-d* or *-ed* to the base form of the verb. In the above list, *call* and *walk* are regular verbs.

3. **Irregular verbs.** An irregular verb does not form its past tense and past participle by adding *-d* or *-ed*. Instead, it changes its spelling in a variety of ways. In the above list, *eat* and *ring* are irregular verbs.

COMBINING HELPING VERBS AND MAIN VERBS

When combining helping verbs and main verbs, pay careful attention to the verb forms that you use.

1. **Modal + base form.** After one of the nine modals (*can, could, will, would, shall, should, may, might, must*), use the base form of a verb.

INCORRECT   He **will leaving** soon.

CORRECT   He **will leave** soon.

2. *Do, does,* or *did* + **base form.** When forms of *do* are used as helping verbs, use the base form after them.

INCORRECT   **Did** your daughter **asked** you for a present?

CORRECT   **Did** your daughter **ask** you for a present?

3. *Have, has,* or *had* + **past participle.** Use the past participle form after *have, has,* or *had*. Check a dictionary if you are not sure how to spell the past participle.

INCORRECT   The monkey **has eating** all of the fruit.

CORRECT   The monkey **has eaten** all of the fruit.

4. **Forms of** *be* + **present participle.** To show continuous action, use the present participle (the -*ing* form) after a form of *be* (*am, is, are, was, were, be, been*).

INCORRECT   I **reading** the book.

CORRECT   I **am reading** the book.

5. **Forms of** *be* + **past participle.** To express passive voice (the subject receives the action rather than performs it), use a form of *be* followed by the past participle form.

INCORRECT   The football **was threw** by the quarterback.

CORRECT   The football **was thrown** by the quarterback.

EXERCISE 23.2

Correct any errors in the use of helping verbs and main verbs.

1. She will visiting her mother in Los Angeles after the drought is over.
2. Many of the almond trees in central California had dying from lack of water.
3. Did the governor made a statement about the lack of rain?
4. Herschel is wasting water, so his neighbor has call the city manager.
5. Herschel says he does not worries about the drought at all.

ADJECTIVES IN THE CORRECT ORDER

1. **In a series of adjectives, place determiners first.** (Determiners consist of articles, possessives, limiting and quantity words, and numerals.) Examples of determiners: *the old car, Jim's empty wallet, her sad face, this heavy box, some scattered coins, three dead trees.*

2. **If one of the modifiers is usually a noun, place it directly before the word it modifies:** *the boring <u>basketball</u> game, the rusty <u>trash</u> can.*

3. **Evaluative adjectives (***beautiful, interesting, courageous***) usually come before descriptive adjectives (***small, round, red, wooden***):** *the <u>beautiful red</u> rose, an <u>interesting wooden</u> cabinet.*

4. **Descriptive adjectives indicating size usually appear before other descriptive adjectives: but after evaluative adjectives:** *my <u>huge</u> leather sofa, a strange <u>little</u> old man.*

Note   In general, avoid long strings of adjectives. More than two or three adjectives in a row will usually sound awkward to the native English speaker.

EXERCISE 23.3

Arrange the following groups of adjectives in the correct order.

1. (dark, his, blue) vest
2. (dry, the, storm) drain
3. (basketball, a, thrilling) game
4. (tiny, alfalfa, many, new) sprouts
5. (worst, brother's, personal, his) habit

EXERCISE 23.4

Correct any errors in the use of articles, helping and main verbs, and adjective order in the following sentences.

1 Visitors who step through front door of Oscar's house are surprising at what they see. 2 On his wooden old coffee table is aquarium full of sawdust and the orange peels. 3 In the corner of the aquarium two miniature rats are play with dog biscuit. 4 Rats are name Vanilla Wafer and Marshmallow. 5 Vanilla Wafer is a black and white fat rat that is very friendly. 6 The Marshmallow is usually hide in the sawdust. 7 Once Marshmallow became very sick because he had eating the spoiled orange. 8 Oscar took him to the veterinarian who had open an office near grocery store on the corner. 9 Luckily, Marshmallow recovered, and he soon was play with Vanilla Wafer again. 10 Many people think that rats are disgusted, but Oscar has always love his happy two rats.

Part Four

Additional Readings for Writing

The reading selections on the following pages offer groups of related articles that can be used as multiple sources for synthesis or argument papers or that can be read and responded to individually. As you read these selections, consider the "Steps in Evaluating a Text" from Chapter 6:

1. Read the text actively.
   a. Determine its intended audience and purpose.
   b. Identify its thesis.
   c. Identify its main points.

2. Determine how well the main points are supported.
   a. Distinguish between facts and opinions.
   b. Distinguish between specific support and generalizations.
   c. Identify statistics, examples, and references to authority.

3. Test the article's points against your own knowledge and experience.
4. Consider any obvious objections that have been ignored.

SHOULD DRUGS BE LEGALIZED?

The Case for Drug Legalization   Gary E. Johnson

Gary E. Johnson was the first governor in the history of New Mexico to be elected to two four-year consecutive terms. He is a conservative Republican, a businessman, and a triathlete. He also is a leading advocate in the movement to legalize drugs (starting with marijuana), regulating and taxing them like alcohol. Drug abuse, he says, should be treated as a health issue—not left to the police and the courts.

I am a "cost-benefit" analysis person. What's the cost and what's   1
the benefit? A couple of things scream out as failing cost-benefit criteria. One is education. The other is the war on drugs. We are presently spending $50 billion a year to combat drugs. I'm talking about police, courts, and jails. For the amount of money that we're putting into it, I want to suggest, the war on drugs is an absolute failure. My "outrageous" hypothesis is that under a legalized scenario, we could actually hold drug use level or see it decline.

Sometimes people say to me, "Governor, I am absolutely   2
opposed to your stand on drugs." I respond by asking them, "You're for drugs, you want to see kids use drugs?" Let me make something clear. I'm not pro-drug. I'm against drugs. Don't do drugs. Drugs are a real handicap. Don't do alcohol or tobacco, either. They are real handicaps.

There's another issue beyond cost-benefit criteria. Should you   3
go to jail for using drugs? And I'm not talking about doing drugs and committing a crime or driving a car. Should you go to jail for simply doing drugs? I say no, you shouldn't. People ask me, "What do you tell kids?" Well, you tell the truth: that by legalizing drugs, we can control them, regulate and tax them. If we legalize drugs, we might have a healthier society. And you explain how that might take place. But you emphasize that drugs are a bad choice. Don't do drugs. But if you do, we're not going to throw you in jail for it.

New Laws and Problems

If drugs are legalized, there will be a whole new set of laws. Let   4
me mention a few of them. Let's say you can't do drugs if you're under 21. You can't sell drugs to kids. I say employers should be able to discriminate against drug users. Employers should be able to conduct drug tests, and they should not have to comply with the Americans with Disabilities Act. Do drugs and commit a crime?

Make it like a gun. Enhance the penalty for the crime in the same way we do today with guns. Do drugs and drive? There should be a law similar to one we have now for driving under the influence of alcohol.

I propose that we redirect the $50 billion that we're presently spending (state and federal) on the old laws to enforce a new set of laws. Society would be transformed if law enforcement could focus on crimes other than drug use. Police could crack down on speeding violations, burglaries, and other offenses that law enforcement now lacks the opportunity to enforce.

If drugs are legalized, there will be a new set of problems, but they will have only about half the negative consequence of those we have today. A legalization model will be a dynamic process that will be fine-tuned as we go along.

Does anybody want to press a button that would retroactively punish the 80 million Americans who have done illegal drugs over the years? I might point out that I'm one of those individuals. In running for my first term in office, I offered the fact that I had smoked marijuana. And the media were very quick to say, "Oh, so you experimented with marijuana?" "No," I said, "I smoked marijuana!" This is something I did, along with a lot of other people. I look back on it now, and I view drugs as a handicap. I stopped because it was a handicap. The same with drinking and tobacco. But did my friends and I belong in jail? I don't think that we should continue to lock up Americans because of bad choices.

And what about the bad choices regarding alcohol and tobacco? I've heard people say, "Governor, you're not comparing alcohol to drugs? You're not comparing tobacco to drugs?" I say, "Hell no! Alcohol killed 150,000 people last year. And I'm not talking about drinking and driving. I'm just talking about the health effects. The health effects of tobacco killed 450,000 people last year." I don't mean to be flippant, but I don't know of anybody ever dying from a marijuana overdose.

Less Lethal Than Alcohol

I understand that 2,000 to 3,000 people died in 1998 from abusing cocaine and heroin. If drugs were legalized, those deaths would go away, theoretically speaking, because they would no longer be counted as accidental. Instead, they'd be suicides, because in a legalized scenario drugs are controlled, taxed, and properly understood. I want to be so bold as to say that marijuana is never going to have the devastating effects on society that alcohol has had.

My own informal poll among doctors reveals that 75–80 percent 10
of the patients they examine have health-related problems due
to alcohol and tobacco. My brother is a cardiothoracic surgeon
who performs heart transplants. He says that 80 percent of the
problems he sees are alcohol and tobacco related. He sees about
six people a year who have infected heart valves because of intra-
venous drug use, but the infection isn't from the drugs themselves.
It's the dirty needles that cause the health problems.

Marijuana is said to be a gateway drug. We all know that, right? 11
You're 85 times more likely to do cocaine if you do marijuana.
I don't mean to be flippant, but 100 percent of all substance abuse
starts with milk. You've heard it, but that bears repeating. My new
mantra here is "Just Say Know." Just know that there are two sides
to all these arguments. I think the facts boil down to drugs being
a bad choice. But should someone go to jail for just doing drugs?
That is the reality of what is happening today. I believe the time has
come for that to end.

I've been talking about legalization and not decriminalization. 12
Legalization means we educate, regulate, tax, and control the
estimated $400 billion a year drug industry. That's larger than the
automobile industry. Decriminalization is a muddy term. It turns its
back to half the problems involved in getting the entire drug economy above the line. So that's why I talk about legalization, meaning
control, the ability to tax, regulate, and educate.

We need to make drugs controlled substances just like alcohol. 13
Perhaps we ought to let the government regulate them; let the
government grow or manufacture, distribute and market them. If
that doesn't lead to decreased drug use, I don't know what would!

Kids today will tell you that legal prescription drugs are harder 14
to come by than illegal drugs. Well, of course. To get legal drugs,
you must walk into a pharmacy and show identification. It's the difference between a controlled substance and an illegal substance. A
teenager today will tell you that a bottle of beer is harder to come
by than a joint. That's where we've come to today. It's where we've
come to with regard to controlling alcohol, but it shows how out
of control drugs have become.

Not Driving You Crazy

Drug Czar Barry McCaffrey has made me his poster child for drug 15
legalization. He claims that drug use has been cut in half and that
we are winning the drug war. Well, let's assume that we have cut it
in half. I don't buy that for a minute, but let's assume that it's true.

Consider these facts: In the late 1970s the federal government spent a billion dollars annually on the drug war. Today, the feds are spending $19 billion a year on it. In the late 1970s, we were arresting a few hundred thousand people. Today, we're arresting 1.6 million. Does that mean if drug use declines by half from today's levels, we'll spend $38 billion federally and arrest 3.2 million people annually? I mean, to follow that logic, when we're left with a few hundred users nationwide, the entire gross national product will be devoted to drug-law enforcement!

16   Most people don't understand, as we New Mexicans do, that the mules are carrying the drugs in. I'm talking about Mexican citizens who are paid a couple hundred dollars to bring drugs across the border, and they don't even know who has given them the money. They just know that it's a king's ransom and that there are more than enough Mexican citizens willing to do it. The federal government is catching many of the mules and some of the king-pins. Let's not deny that. But those who are caught, those links out of the chain, don't make any difference in the overall war on drugs.

17   I want to tell you a little bit about the response to what I've been saying. Politically, this is a zero. For anybody holding office, for anybody who aspires to hold office, has held office, or has a job associated with politics, this is verboten. I am in the ground, and the dirt is being thrown on top of my coffin. But among the public, the response is overwhelming. In New Mexico, I am being approached rapid-fire by people saying "right on" to my statements regarding the war on drugs. To give an example, two elderly ladies came up to my table during dinner the other night. They said, "We're teachers, and we think your school voucher idea sucks. But your position on the war on drugs is right on!"

18   What I have discovered, and it's been said before, is that the war on drugs is thousands of miles long, but it's only about a quarter-inch deep. I'm trying to communicate what I believe in this issue. Drugs are bad, but we need to stop arresting and locking up the entire country.

Why Drug Legalization Should Be Opposed   Charles B. Rangel

Congressman Charles B. Rangel is the second-longest currently serving member of the House of Representatives, serving continuously since 1971. He was the first African American to head the influential House Ways and Means Committee. In 2010 he was found guilty of ethics violations and stepped aside as Ways and Means chair. He has said his current term in the House will be his last.

In my view, the very idea of legalizing drugs in this country is   1
counterproductive. Many well-meaning drug legalization advocates
disagree with me, but their arguments are not convincing. The
questions that I asked them twenty years ago remain unanswered.
Would all drugs be legalized? If not, why?

Would consumers be allowed to purchase an unlimited sup-   2
ply? Are we prepared to pay the medical costs for illnesses that
are spawned by excessive drug use? Who would be allowed to
sell drugs? Would an illegal market still exist? Would surgeons, bus
drivers, teachers, military personnel, engineers, and airline pilots be
allowed to use drugs?

Drug legalization threatens to undermine our society. The argu-   3
ment about the economic costs associated with the drug war is a
selfish argument that coincides with the short-sighted planning that
we have been using with other social policies. With any legalization
of drugs, related problems would not go away; they would only
intensify. If we legalize, we will be paying much more than the $30
billion per year we now spend on direct health care costs associated with illegal drug use.

Drug legalization is not as simple as opening a chain of friendly   4
neighborhood "drug" stores. While I agree that some drugs might
be beneficial for medicinal purposes, this value should not be
exploited to suggest that drugs should be legalized. Great Britain's
experience with prescription heroin should provide a warning.
Until 1968, British doctors were freely allowed to prescribe drugs
to addicts for medicinal purposes. Due to the lack of rigorous con-
trols, some serious problems became associated with this policy.
Doctors supplied drugs to non-addicts, and addicts supplied legally
obtained drugs to the general population resulting in an increased
rate of addiction. There is plenty of evidence to show that drug
legalization has not worked in other countries that have tried it.
The United States cannot afford such experiments when the data
shows that drug legalization policies are failing in other countries.

In minority communities, legalization of drugs would be a   5
nightmare. It would be a clear signal that America has no interest
in removing the root causes of drug abuse: a sense of hopelessness that stems from poverty, unemployment, inadequate training
and blight. Legalization of drugs would officially sanction the total
annihilation of communities already at risk. Instead of advocating
drug legalization, we should focus our efforts on rebuilding schools,
strengthening our teachers, improving housing, and providing job
skills to young people.

The issue should not be whether or not drugs should be
legalized. Rather, we need to focus on changing the way the war
on drugs is being fought. The real problems are our emphasis on
incarceration, including mandatory minimum sentences, the unfair
application of drug laws, the disparity in sentencing between crack
cocaine and powder cocaine, and the failure to concentrate on the
root causes of drug abuse. These shortcomings in our drug policy
should not become a license for legalization. Many critics of the
drug war have the knowledge and skills to improve our national
drug control policy. Instead of supporting the Drug Czar, they use
their resources to blast all efforts to eradicate drugs in this country.
It is a shame that many educated and prominent people suggest
that the only dangerous thing about drugs is that they are illegal.

If we are truly honest, we must confess that we have never
fought that war on drugs as we have fought other adversaries. The
promotion of drug legalization further complicates the issue. We
must continue our efforts to stop the flow of illegal drugs into our
country. Most importantly, we need to remove the root causes of
drug abuse and increase our focus in the areas of prevention and
treatment through education. Rather than holding up the white
flag and allowing drugs to take over our country, we must continue
to focus on drug demand as well as supply if we are to remain a
free and productive society.

We're Losing the Drug War
Because Prohibition Never Works   Hodding Carter III

*An award-winning journalist and commentator, Hodding Carter III has won four
national Emmy Awards and the Edward R. Murrow Award for his public-television
documentaries. He served in the presidential campaigns of Lyndon Johnson in 1960
and Jimmy Carter in 1976. He has been an opinion columnist for* The Wall Street
Journal *and a frequent contributor to* The New York Times, The Washington
Post, *and many other newspapers and magazines.*

There is clearly no point in beating a dead horse, whether you are
a politician or a columnist, but sometimes you have to do it just
the same, if only for the record. So, for the record, here's another
attempt to argue that a majority of the American people and their
elected representatives can be and are wrong about the way they
have chosen to wage the "war against drugs." Prohibition can't
work, won't work, and has never worked, but it can and does have

monumentally costly effects on the criminal justice system and on the integrity of government at every level.

Experience should be the best teacher, and my experience with prohibition is a little more recent than most Americans for whom the "noble experiment" ended with repeal in 1933. In my home state of Mississippi, it lasted for an additional thirty-three years, and for all those years it was a truism that the drinkers had their liquor, the preachers had their prohibition, and the sheriffs made the money. Al Capone would have been proud of the latitude that bootleggers were able to buy with their payoffs of constables, deputies, police chiefs, and sheriffs across the state.

But as a first-rate series in *The New York Times* made clear early last year, Mississippi's Prohibition-era corruption (and Chicago's before that) was penny ante stuff compared with what is happening in the United States today. From Brooklyn police precincts to Miami's police stations to rural Georgia courthouses, big drug money is purchasing major breakdowns in law enforcement. Sheriffs, other policemen, and now judges are being bought up by the gross. But that money, with the net profits for the drug traffickers estimated at anywhere from $40 billion to $100 billion a year, is also buying up banks, legitimate businesses and, to the south of us, entire governments. The latter becomes an increasingly likely outcome in a number of cities and states in this country as well. Cicero, Illinois, during Prohibition is an instructive case in point.

The money to be made from an illegal product that has about 23 million current users in this country also explains why its sale is so attractive on the mean streets of America's big cities. A street salesman can gross about $2,500 a day in Washington, which puts him in the pay category of a local television anchor, and this in a neighborhood of dead-end job chances.

Since the courts and jails are already swamped beyond capacity by the arrests that are routinely made (44,000 drug dealers and users over a two-year period in Washington alone, for instance), and since those arrests barely skim the top of the pond, arguing that stricter enforcement is the answer begs a larger question: Who is going to pay the billions of dollars required to build the prisons, hire the judges, train the policemen, and employ the prosecutors needed for the load already on hand, let alone the huge one yet to come if we ever get serious about arresting dealers and users?

Much is made of the costs of drug addiction, and it should be, but the current breakdown in the criminal justice system is not one of them. That breakdown is the result of prohibition, not addiction. Drug addiction, after all, does not come close to the far vaster problems of alcohol and tobacco addiction (as former Surgeon General Koop correctly noted, tobacco is at least as addictive as heroin). Hard drugs are estimated to kill 4,000 people a year directly and several tens of thousands a year indirectly. Alcohol kills at least 100,000 a year, addicts millions more and costs the marketplace billions of dollars. Tobacco kills over 300,000 a year, addicts tens of millions, and fouls the atmosphere as well. But neither alcohol nor tobacco threatens to subvert our system of law and order, because they are treated as personal and societal problems rather than as criminal ones.

Indeed, every argument that is made for prohibiting the use   7
of currently illegal drugs can be made even more convincingly about tobacco and alcohol. The effects on the unborn? Staggeringly direct. The effects on adolescents? Alcoholism is the addiction of choice for young Americans on a ratio of about one hundred to one. Lethal effect? Tobacco's murderous results are not a matter of debate anywhere outside the Tobacco Institute.

Which leaves the lingering and legitimate fear that legaliza-   8
tion might produce a surge in use. It probably would, although not nearly as dramatic a one as opponents usually estimate. The fact is that personal use of marijuana, whatever the local laws may say, has been virtually decriminalized for some time now, but there has been a stabilization or slight decline in use, rather than an increase, for several years. Heroin addiction has held steady at about 500,000 people for some time, though the street price of heroin is far lower now than it used to be. Use of cocaine in its old form also seems to have stopped climbing and begun to drop off among young and old alike, though there is an abundantly available supply.

That leaves crack cocaine, stalker of the inner city and terror   9
of the suburbs. Instant and addictive in effect, easy to use and relatively cheap to buy, it is a personality-destroying substance that is a clear menace to its users. But it is hard to imagine it being any more accessible under legalization than it is in most cities today under prohibition, while the financial incentives for promoting its use would virtually disappear with legalization.

Proponents of legalization should not try to fuzz the issue,   10
nonetheless. Addiction levels might increase, at least temporarily, if legal sanctions were removed. That happened after the repeal of Prohibition, or so at least some studies have suggested. But while that would be a personal disaster for the addicts and their

families, and would involve larger costs to society as a whole, those costs would be minuscule compared with the costs of continued prohibition.

The young Capones of today own the inner cities, and the   11
wholesalers behind these young retailers are rapidly buying up the larger system which is supposed to control them. Prohibition gave us the Mafia and organized crime on a scale that has been with us ever since. The new prohibition is writing a new chapter on that old text. Hell-bent on learning nothing from history, we are witnessing its repetition, predictably enough, as tragedy.

Should Drugs Be Legalized?   William J. Bennett

William J. Bennett served as secretary of education and chair of the National Endowment for the Humanities under President Ronald Reagan, and as director of the Office of National Drug Control Policy under President George H. W. Bush. In 2000 he cofounded K12, a publicly traded online education company. The following article was written while he served as the national drug "czar" under former President George H. W. Bush.

Since I took command of the war on drugs [as director of   1
National Drug Control Policy in Washington, D.C.], I have learned from former secretary of state George Shultz that our concept of fighting drugs is "flawed." The only thing to do, he says, is to "make it possible for addicts to buy drugs at some regulated place." Conservative commentator William F. Buckley, Jr., suggests I should be "fatalistic" about the flood of cocaine from South America and simply "let it in." Syndicated columnist Mike Royko contends it would be easier to sweep junkies out of the gutters "than to fight a hopeless war" against the narcotics that send them there. Labeling our efforts "bankrupt," federal judge Robert W. Sweet opts for legalization, saying, "If our society can learn to stop using butter, it should be able to cut down on cocaine."

Flawed, fatalistic, hopeless, bankrupt! I never realized surrender   2
was so fashionable until I assumed this post.

Though most Americans are overwhelmingly determined to go   3
toe-to-toe with the foreign drug lords and neighborhood pushers, a small minority believe that enforcing drug laws imposes greater costs on society than do drugs themselves. Like addicts seeking immediate euphoria, the legalizers want peace at any price, even though it means the inevitable proliferation of a practice that degrades, impoverishes, and kills.

I am acutely aware of the burdens drug enforcement places   4
upon us. It consumes economic resources we would like to use
elsewhere. It is sometimes frustrating, thankless, and often dangerous. But the consequences of *not* enforcing drug laws would be far
more costly. Those consequences involve the intrinsically destruc-
tive nature of drugs and the toll they exact from our society in
hundreds of thousands of lost and broken lives … human potential
never realized … time stolen from families and jobs … precious
spiritual and economic resources squandered.

That is precisely why virtually every civilized society has found   5
it necessary to exert some form of control over mind-altering
substances and why this war is so important. Americans feel up
to their hips in drugs now. They would be up to their necks under
legalization.

Even limited experiments in drug legalization have shown that   6
when drugs are more widely available, addiction skyrockets. In
1975 Italy liberalized its drug law and now has one of the highest
heroin-related death rates in Western Europe. In Alaska, where
marijuana was decriminalized in 1975, the easy atmosphere has
increased usage of the drug, particularly among children. Nor does
it stop there. Some Alaskan schoolchildren now tout "coco puffs,"
marijuana cigarettes laced with cocaine.

Many legalizers concede that drug legalization might increase   7
use, but they shrug off the matter. "It may well be that there would
be more addicts, and I would regret that result," says Nobel laure-
ate economist Milton Friedman. The late Harvard Medical School
psychiatry professor Norman Zinberg, a longtime proponent of
"responsible" drug use, admitted that "use of now-illicit drugs
would certainly increase. Also casualties probably would increase."

In fact, Dr. Herbert D. Kleber of Yale University, my deputy in   8
charge of demand reduction, predicts legalization might cause a
"five-to-sixfold increase" in cocaine use. But legalizers regard this as
a necessary price for the "benefits" of legalization. What benefits?

1. Legalization Will Take the Profit out of Drugs

The result supposedly will be the end of criminal drug pushers and   9
the big foreign drug wholesalers, who will turn to other enterprises because nobody will need to make furtive and dangerous
trips to his local pusher.

But what, exactly, would the brave new world of legal-   10
ized drugs look like? Buckley stresses that "adults get to buy the
stuff at carefully regulated stores." (Would you want one in *your*

neighborhood?) Others, like Friedman, suggest we sell the drugs at "ordinary retail outlets."

Former City University of New York sociologist Georgette   11
Bennett assures us that "brand-name competition will be prohibited" and that strict quality control and proper labeling will be
overseen by the Food and Drug Administration. In a touching
egalitarian note, she adds that "free drugs will be provided to government clinics" for addicts too poor to buy them.

Almost all legalizers point out that the price of drugs will fall,   12
even though the drugs will be heavily taxed. Buckley, for example,
argues that somehow federal drugstores will keep the price "low
enough to discourage a black market but high enough to accumu-
late a surplus to be used for drug education."

Supposedly, drug sales will generate huge amounts of revenue,   13
which will then be used to tell the public not to use drugs and to
treat those who don't listen.

In reality, this tax would only allow government to share the   14
drug profits now garnered by criminals. Legalizers would have to
tax drugs heavily in order to pay for drug education and treatment
programs. Criminals could undercut the official price and still make
huge profits. What alternative would the government have? Cut
the price until it was within the lunch-money budget of the average sixth-grade student?

2. Legalization Will Eliminate the Black Market

Wrong. And not just because the regulated prices could be under-   15
cut. Many legalizers admit that drugs such as crack or PCP are
simply too dangerous to allow the shelter of the law. Thus criminals
will provide what the government will not. "As long as drugs that
people very much want remain illegal, a black market will exist,"
says legalization advocate David Boaz of the libertarian Cato
Institute.

Look at crack. In powdered form, cocaine was an expensive   16
indulgence. But street chemists found that a better and far less
expensive—and far more dangerous—high could be achieved by
mixing cocaine with baking soda and heating it. Crack was born,
and "cheap" coke invaded low-income communities with furious
speed.

An ounce of powdered cocaine might sell on the street for   17
$1200. That same ounce can produce 370 vials of crack at $10
each. Ten bucks seems like a cheap hit, but crack's intense ten- to
fifteen-minute high is followed by an unbearable depression. The

user wants more crack, thus starting a rapid and costly descent into addiction.

If government drugstores do not stock crack, addicts will find it 18
in the clandestine market or simply bake it themselves from their legally purchased cocaine.

Currently crack is being laced with insecticides and animal 19
tranquilizers to heighten its effect. Emergency rooms are now warned to expect victims of "sandwiches" and "moon rocks," life-threatening smokable mixtures of heroin and crack. Unless the government is prepared to sell these deadly variations of dangerous drugs, it will perpetuate a criminal black market by default.

And what about children and teenagers? They would obviously 20
be barred from drug purchases, just as they are prohibited from buying beer and liquor. But pushers will continue to cater to these young customers with the old, favorite come-ons—a couple of free fixes to get them hooked. And what good will antidrug education be when these youngsters observe their older brothers and sisters, parents, and friends lighting up and shooting up with government permission?

Legalization will give us the worst of both worlds: millions of 21
new drug users and a thriving criminal black market.

3. Legalization Will Dramatically Reduce Crime

"It is the high price of drugs that leads addicts to robbery, mur- 22
der, and other crimes," says Ira Glasser, executive director of the American Civil Liberties Union. A study by the Cato Institute concludes: "Most, if not all 'drug-related murders' are the result of drug prohibition."

But researchers tell us that many drug-related felonies are 23
committed by people involved in crime *before* they started taking drugs. The drugs, so routinely available in criminal circles, make the criminals more violent and unpredictable.

Certainly there are some kill-for-a-fix crimes, but does any 24
rational person believe that a cut-rate price for drugs at a government outlet will stop such psychopathic behavior? The fact is that under the influence of drugs, normal people do not act normally, and abnormal people behave in chilling and horrible ways. DEA agents told me about a teenage addict in Manhattan who was smoking crack when he sexually abused and caused permanent internal injuries to his one-month-old daughter.

Children are among the most frequent victims of violent, drug- 25
related crimes that have nothing to do with the cost of acquiring

the drugs. In Philadelphia in 1987 more than half the child-abuse fatalities involved at least one parent who was a heavy drug user. Seventy-three percent of the child-abuse deaths in New York City in 1987 involved parental drug use.

In my travels to the ramparts of the drug war, I have seen   26
nothing to support the legalizers' argument that lower drug prices would reduce crime. Virtually everywhere I have gone, police and DEA agents have told me that crime rates are highest where crack is cheapest.

4. Drug Use Should Be Legal since Users Only Harm Themselves

Those who believe this should stand beside the medical examiner   27
as he counts the thirty-six bullet wounds in the shattered corpse of a three-year-old who happened to get in the way of his mother's drug-crazed boyfriend. They should visit the babies abandoned by cocaine-addicted mothers—infants who already carry the ravages of addiction in their own tiny bodies. They should console the devastated relatives of the nun who worked in a homeless shelter and was stabbed to death by a crack addict enraged that she would not stake him to a fix.

Do drug addicts only harm themselves? Here is a former   28
cocaine addict describing the compulsion that quickly draws even the most "responsible" user into irresponsible behavior: "Everything is about getting high, and any means necessary to get there becomes rational. If it means stealing something from somebody close to you, lying to your family, borrowing money from people you know you can't pay back, writing checks you know you can't cover, you do all those things—things that are totally against everything you have ever believed in."

Society pays for this behavior, and not just in bigger insur-   29
ance premiums, losses from accidents, and poor job performance. We pay in the loss of a priceless social currency as families are destroyed, trust between friends is betrayed, and promising careers are never fulfilled. I cannot imagine sanctioning behavior that would increase that toll.

I find no merit in the legalizers' case. The simple fact is that   30
drug use is wrong. And the moral argument, in the end, is the most compelling argument. A citizen in a drug-induced haze, whether on his backyard deck or on a mattress in a ghetto crack house, is not what the founding fathers meant by the "pursuit of happiness." Despite the legalizers' argument that drug use is a matter of "personal freedom," our nation's notion of liberty is rooted in the ideal

of a self-reliant citizenry. Helpless wrecks in treatment centers, men chained by their noses to cocaine—these people are slaves.

Imagine if, in the darkest days of 1940, Winston Churchill had   31 rallied the West by saying, "This war looks hopeless, and besides, it will cost too much. Hitler can't be *that* bad. Let's surrender and see what happens." That is essentially what we hear from the legalizers.

This war *can* be won. I am heartened by indications that edu-   32 cation and public revulsion are having an effect on drug use. The National Institute on Drug Abuse's latest survey of current users shows a 37 percent *decrease* in drug consumption since 1985. Cocaine is down 50 percent; marijuana use among young people is at its lowest rate since 1972. In my travels I've been encouraged by signs that Americans are fighting back.

I am under no illusion that such developments, however hope-   33 ful, mean the war is over. We need to involve more citizens in the fight, increase pressure on drug criminals, and build on antidrug programs that have proved to work. This will not be easy. But the moral and social costs of surrender are simply too great to contemplate.

SHOULD THE MINIMUM LEGAL DRINKING AGE BE LOWERED?

The Minimum Legal Drinking Age: Facts and Fallacies

Traci L. Toomey, Carolyn Rosenfeld, and Alexander Wagenaar

The following selection, which originally appeared on the Web site of the American Medical Association, is adapted from an article that appeared in Alcohol Health & Research World *(now called* Alcohol Research & Health*). In it, the authors summarize the scientific research related to the minimum legal drinking age.*

Brief History of the MLDA

After Prohibition, nearly all states restricting youth access to alco-   1 hol designated 21 as the minimum legal drinking age (MLDA). Between 1970 and 1975, however, 29 states lowered the MLDA to 18, 19, or 20. These changes occurred when the minimum age for other activities, such as voting, also were being lowered (Wechsler & Sands, 1980). Scientists began studying the effects of the lowered MLDA, focusing particularly on the incidence of motor vehicle crashes, the leading cause of death among teenagers. Several studies in the 1970s found that motor vehicle crashes increased significantly among teens when the MLDA was lowered (Cucchiaro et al., 1974; Douglas et al., 1974; Wagenaar, 1983, 1993; Whitehead, 1977; Whitehead et al., 1975; Williams et al., 1974).

With evidence that a lower drinking age resulted in more traf- 2
fic injuries and fatalities among youth, citizen advocacy groups pressured states to restore the MLDA to 21. Because of such advocacy campaigns, 16 states increased their MLDAs between September 1976 and January 1983. Resistance from other states, and concern that minors would travel across state lines to purchase and consume alcohol, prompted the federal government in 1984 to enact the Uniform Drinking Age Act, which mandated reduced federal transportation funds to those states that did not raise the MLDA to 21. Among alcohol control policies, the MLDA has been the most studied: since the 1970s, at least 70 studies have examined the effects of either increasing or decreasing the MLDA.

Research Findings

A higher minimum legal drinking age is effective in preventing 3
alcohol-related deaths and injuries among youth. When the MLDA has been lowered, injury and death rates increase, and when the MLDA is increased, death and injury rates decline (Wagenaar, 1993).

A higher MLDA results in fewer alcohol-related problems 4
among youth, and the 21-year-old MLDA saves the lives of well over 1,000 youth each year (Jones et al., 1992; NHTSA, 1989). Conversely, when the MLDA is lowered, motor vehicle crashes and deaths among youth increase. At least 50 studies have evaluated this correlation (Wagenaar, 1993).

A common argument among opponents of a higher MLDA 5
is that because many minors still drink and purchase alcohol, the policy doesn't work. The evidence shows, however, that although many youth still consume alcohol, they drink less and experience fewer alcohol-related injuries and deaths (Wagenaar, 1993).

Research shows that when the MLDA is 21, people under age 6
21 drink less overall and continue to do so through their early twenties (O'Malley & Wagenaar, 1991).

The effect of the higher MLDA occurs with little or no enforce- 7
ment. Historically, enforcement has focused primarily on penalizing underage drinkers for illegal alcohol possession and/or consumption. For every 1,000 minors arrested for alcohol possession, only

130 merchants have actions taken against them, and only 88 adults who supply alcohol to minors face criminal penalties (Wagenaar & Wolfson, 1995).

Researchers conducted an in-depth review of enforcement actions in 295 counties in Kentucky, Michigan, Montana, and Oregon. The review showed that in a three-year period, 27 percent of the counties took no action against licensed establishments that sold alcohol to minors, and 41 percent of those counties made no arrests of adults who supplied alcohol to minors. Although the majority of the counties took at least one action against alcohol establishments and/or adults who provided alcohol to minors, many did not take such actions frequently (Wagenaar & Wolfson, 1995). 8

Regarding Europeans and alcohol use among youth, research confirms that Europeans have rates of alcohol-related diseases (such as cirrhosis of the liver) similar to or higher than those in the U.S. population (Single, 1984). However, drinking and driving among youth may not be as great a problem in Europe as in the U.S. Compared to their American counterparts, European youth must be older to obtain their drivers' licenses, are less likely to have a car, and are more inclined to use public transportation (Wagenaar, 1993). 9

De-Demonizing Rum: What's Wrong with "Underage" Drinking?
Andrew Stuttaford

Andrew Stuttaford is a contributing editor to National Review. *He has written on subjects ranging from post–Soviet Russia to* Xena, Warrior Princess. *Based in New York since 1991, Andrew's day job is in the financial sector.*

It was a day of shame for the Bushes, an incident made all the more embarrassing by the family's previous well-publicized difficulties with alcohol. I refer, of course, to the regrettable 1997 decision by then-governor George W. Bush to approve legislation further toughening the penalties for underage drinking. In Texas, the legal drinking age is 21. A typical Texan of 19—let's call her "Jenna"—is judged to be responsible enough to vote, drive, marry, serve in the military, and (this is Texas) be executed, but she is not, apparently, sufficiently mature to decide for herself whether to buy a margarita. The 1997 legislation made things worse: Miller Time could now mean hard time, a possible six months in jail for a third offense. 1

It is a ludicrous and demeaning law, but it has been policed   2
with all the gung-ho enthusiasm that we have come to expect in a
land where the prohibitionist impulse has never quite died. In Aus-
tin, there is now a special squad of undercover cops dedicated to
fighting the scourge of teenage tippling. In other words, they hang
around in bars.

The crusade does not stop there. The Texas Commission on   3
Alcohol and Drug Abuse boasts a campaign called "2young2drink,"
which features billboards, a hotline (Denounce your friends!), and
a program enticingly known as "Shattered Dreams." Other efforts
include the Texas Alcoholic Beverage Commission's sting operations (Make your kid a snoop!) and, for those parents 2stupid-
2think, a helpful series of danger signs compiled by the Texas Safety
Network. One early indicator that your child is drinking may be
the "smell of alcohol on [his] breath." Who knew?

But it's unfair to single out Texas. The legal drinking age has   4
been raised to 21 in every state, a dreary legacy of Elizabeth
Dole's otherwise unremarkable tenure as President Reagan's transportation secretary. She is not apologizing; her only regret is that
the age of barroom consent was not increased to 24. In her Jihad
against gin, Mrs. Dole forgot that the guiding principle of the Reagan administration was supposed to be a reduction in the role of
the state.

And, as usual, government is not going to do any good. The   5
only circumstances in which the approach taken by the zero-
tolerance zealots could have the faintest chance of success would
be in a society where alcohol was a rarity. Zero tolerance has
been a disastrous failure in the case of young people and illegal
drugs; how can it be expected to work with a product that is available in every mall or corner store? Sooner or later, your child will
be confronted with that seductive bottle. The only question is how
he is going to deal with it.

Not well, if the Dole approach continues to hold sway.   6
Demonizing alcohol—and thus elevating it to the status of forbidden fruit—is counterproductive. Adult disapproval magically
transforms that margarita from a simple pleasure into an especially
thrilling act of rebellion.

My parents avoided this error. Growing up in more tolerant   7
England, I could always ask them for a drink, and, fairly frequently,
I would even be given one. At least partly as a result, I went
through adolescence without feeling any need to drink a pint
to make a point. My drinks were for the right reasons. The only

recollection I have of any real parental anxiety in this area was when, at the age of about 13, I accepted a brandy from a friend of the family (an alleged murderer, as it happens, but that's another story). The worry was not the drink, but the uninsured glass containing it: antique, priceless, and, as our host explained to my trembling mother, quite irreplaceable. In the event, the glass survived me, and I survived the drink.

8 Parents, not bureaucrats, are the best judges of how and when their offspring should be permitted to drink. Intelligent parents don't let alcohol become a big deal, a mystery or a battleground. They teach its perils, but its pleasures, too. Have a bottle of wine on the table, and let the kids take a gulp; it will not, I promise, turn them into Frenchmen. Treat a drink as a part of growing up, as something to be savored within a family, rather than guzzled down in some rite to mark passage from that family.

9 Furthermore, too much of the discussion about alcohol in this country reflects prohibitionist fervor rather than scientific fact. We act as if alcohol were a vice, a degenerate habit that can—at best—be tolerated. In reality, it does not need to be apologized for. Alcohol has been a valuable part of Western culture for thousands of years. It can be abused, sure, but it can inspire as well as intoxicate, illuminate as well as irritate. In excess, the demon drink merits its nickname; in moderation, it can be good for you.

10 Ah yes, some will say, but what about drunk driving? They have a point. While it is possible to debate the numbers, there can be little doubt that the higher drinking age has coincided with a reduction in the number of highway deaths. But has the price been worth paying? The question sounds callous, particularly given the horrors of the individual tragedies that make up the statistics, but all legislation is, in the end, a matter of finding a balance between competing rights, interests, and responsibilities. We could, for example, save lives by denying drivers' licenses to those over 65, but we do not. We understand the trade-off: There is an interest in safer roads, but there is also an interest in allowing older people to retain their independence.

11 In the case of the drinking age, the balance has shifted too far in one direction, away from individual responsibility and towards government control. Raising the limit may have reduced drunken driving, but the cost in lost freedom has been too high, and, quite possibly, unnecessary: Alcohol-related auto accidents seem to be falling in most age categories. The problem of teen DWI is best dealt with directly, by strengthening the deterrents, rather

than obliquely, in the context of a wider attack on "underage" drinking—an attack that might, in fact, ultimately backfire on those whose interest lies in combating the drunk at the wheel.

For the most striking thing of all about the minimum drinking   12
age of 21 is how unsuccessful it has been. A 19-year-old in search of a drink will not have to hunt for long; just ask "Jenna." Almost impossible to police effectively, our current policy sends a signal to the young that our legal system is capricious, weak, occasionally vindictive, and not to be respected. In the interest of enforcing important laws—such as those against drunk driving—we should do what we can to make sure our young people see the police not as interfering busybodies, but as representatives of a mature, broadly respected moral order, who are prepared to treat them as adults. Those who believe government should be in the message-sending business should pay a little more attention to the message they are really sending, when they ask the police to enforce unenforceable—and frankly indefensible—taboos.

BEHAVIOR

Why Competition?   Alfie Kohn

Alfie Kohn writes and speaks widely on human behavior, education, and social theory. His criticisms of competition and rewards have helped shape the thinking of educators—as well as parents and managers—across the country and abroad. In the following reading selection, Kohn argues that "competition by its very nature is always unhealthy."

"W-H-I-T-E! White Team is the team for me!" The cheer is   1
repeated, becoming increasingly frenzied as scores of campers, bedecked in the appropriate color, try to outshout their Blue opponents. The rope stretched over the lake is taut now, as determined tuggers give it their all. It looks as if a few will be yanked into the cold water, but a whistle pierces the air. "All right, we'll call this a draw." Sighs of disappointment follow, but children are soon scrambling off to the Marathon. Here, competitors will try to win for their side by completing such tasks as standing upside-down in a bucket of shampoo or forcing down great quantities of food in a few seconds before tagging a teammate.

As a counselor in this camp over a period of several years,   2
I witnessed a number of Color Wars, and what constantly amazed

me was the abrupt and total transformation that took place each time one began. As campers are read their assignments, children who not ten minutes before were known as "David" or "Margie" suddenly have a new identity; they have been arbitrarily designated as members of a team. The unspoken command is understood by even the youngest among them: Do everything possible to win for your side. Strain every muscle to prove how superior *we* are to the hostile Blues.

And so they will. Children who had wandered aimlessly about the camp are suddenly driven with a Purpose. Children who had tired of the regular routine are instantly provided with Adventure. Children who had trouble making friends are unexpectedly part of a new Crowd. In the dining hall, every camper sits with his or her team. Strategy is planned for the next battle; troops are taught the next cheer. There is a coldness bordering on suspicion when passing someone with a blue T-shirt—irrespective of any friendship B.C. (Before Colors). If anyone has reservations about participating in an activity, he needs only to be reminded that the other team is just a few points behind.

"Why Sport?" asks Ed Cowan (*The Humanist*, November/December 1979). When the sports are competitive ones, I cannot find a single reason to answer his rhetorical query. Mr. Cowan's discussion of the pure—almost mystical—aesthetic pleasure that is derived from athletics only directs attention away from what is, in actuality, the primary impetus of any competitive activity: winning.

I would not make such a fuss over Color War, or even complain about the absurd spectacle of grown men shrieking and cursing on Sunday afternoons, were it not for the significance of the role played by competition in our culture. It is bad enough that Americans actually regard fighting as a sport: it is worse that the outcome of even the gentlest of competitions—baseball—can induce fans to hysteria and outright violence. But sports is only the tip of the proverbial iceberg. Our entire society is affected by—even structured upon—the need to be "better than."

My thesis is admittedly extreme; it is, simply put, that competition by its very nature is always unhealthy. This is true, to begin with, because competition and cooperation are mutually exclusive orientations. I say this fully aware of the famed camaraderie that is supposed to develop among players—or soldiers—on the same side. First, I have doubts, based on personal experience, concerning the depth and fullness of relationships that result from the need to become more effective against a common enemy.

Second, the "realm of the interhuman," to use Martin Buber's   7
phrase, is severely curtailed when those on the other side are
excluded from any possible community. Worse, they are generally
regarded with suspicion and contempt in any competitive enterprise. (This is not to say that we cannot remain on good terms
with, say, tennis opponents, but that whatever cooperation and
meaningful relationship is in evidence exists in spite of the competitiveness.) Finally, the sweaty fellowship of the locker room (or,
to draw the inescapable parallel again, the trenches) simply does
not compensate for the inherent evils of competition.

The desire to win has a not very surprising (but too rarely   8
remarked upon) characteristic: it tends to edge out other goals
and values in the context of any given competitive activity. When
I was in high school, I was a very successful debater for a school
that boasted one of the country's better teams. After hundreds
and hundreds of rounds of competition over three years, I can
assert in no uncertain terms that the purpose of debate is not to
seek the truth or resolve an issue. No argument, however compelling, is ever conceded; veracity is never attributed to the other side.
The only reason debaters sacrifice their free time collecting thousands of pieces of evidence, analyzing arguments, and practicing
speeches, is to win. Truth thereby suffers in at least two ways.

In any debate, neither team is concerned with arriving at a   9
fuller understanding of the topic. The debaters concentrate on
"covering" arguments, tying logical knots, and, above all, sounding
convincing. Beyond this, though, there exists a tremendous temptation to fabricate and distort evidence. Words are left out, phrases
added, sources modified in order to lend credibility to the position. One extremely successful debater on my team used to invent
names of magazines which ostensibly printed substantiation for
crucial arguments he wanted to use.

With respect to this last phenomenon, it is fruitless—and a   10
kind of self-deception, ultimately—to shake our heads and deplore
this sort of thing. Similarly, we have no business condemning
"overly rough" football players or the excesses of "overzealous"
campaign aides or even, perhaps, violations of the Geneva Con-
vention in time of war (which is essentially a treatise on How to
Kill Human Beings Without Doing Anything *Really* Unethical). We
are engaging in a massive (albeit implicit) exercise of hypocrisy
to decry these activities while continuing to condone, and even
encourage, the competitive orientation of which they are only the
logical conclusion.

The cost of any kind of competition in human terms is incal-   11
culable. When my success depends on other people's failure, the
prospects for a real human community are considerably diminished. This consequence speaks to the profoundly antihumanis-
tic quality of competitive activity, and it is abundantly evident in
American society. Moreover, when my success depends on my
being *better than*, I am caught on a treadmill, destined never to
enjoy real satisfaction. Someone is always one step higher, and
even the summit is a precarious position in light of the hordes
waiting to occupy it in my stead. I am thus perpetually insecure
and, as psychologist Rollo May points out, perpetually anxious.

… individual competitive success is both the dominant goal in   12
our culture and the most pervasive occasion for anxiety. … [This]
anxiety arises out of the interpersonal isolation and alienation from
others that inheres in a pattern in which self-validation depends on
triumphing over others (*The Meaning of Anxiety*, rev. ed.).

I begin to see my self-worth as conditional—that is to say, my   13
goodness or value become contingent on how much better I am
than so many others in so many activities. If you believe, as I do,
that unconditional self-esteem is a singularly important requirement for (and indicator of) mental health, then the destructiveness
of competition will clearly outweigh any putative benefit, whether
it be a greater effort at tug-of-war or a higher gross national
product.

From the time we are quite small, the ethic of competitiveness   14
is drummed into us. The goal in school is not to grow as a human
being or even, in practice, to reach a satisfactory level of intellectual competence. We are pushed instead to become brighter than,
quicker than, better achievers than our classmates, and the endless
array of scores and grades lets us know at any given instant how
we stand on that ladder of academic success.

If our schools are failing at their explicit tasks, we may rest   15
assured of their overwhelming success regarding this hidden
agenda. We are well trained to enter the marketplace and compete frantically for more money, more prestige, more of all the
"good things" in life. An economy such as ours, understand, does
not merely permit competition: *it demands it*. Ever greater profits
becomes the watchword of private enterprise, and an inequitable
distribution of wealth (a polite codeword for human suffering) follows naturally from such an arrangement.

Moreover, one must be constantly vigilant lest one's competi-   16
tors attract more customers or conceive some innovation that

gives them the edge. To become outraged at deceptive and unethical business practices is folly; it is the competitiveness of the system that promotes these phenomena. Whenever people are defined as opponents, doing everything possible to triumph must be seen not as an aberration from the structure but as its very consummation. (I recognize, of course, that I have raised a plethora of difficult issues across many disciplines that cry out for a more detailed consideration. I hope, however, to at least have opened up some provocative, and largely neglected, lines of inquiry.)

This orientation finds its way into our personal relationships as well. We bring our yardstick along to judge potential candidates for lover, trying to determine who is most attractive, most intelligent, and … the best lover. At the same time, of course, we are being similarly reduced to the status of competitor. The human costs are immense.   17

"Why Sport?," then, is a good question to begin with. It leads us to inquire, "Why Miss Universe contests?" "Why the arms race?" and—dare we say it?—"Why capitalism?" Whether a competition-free society can actually be constructed is another issue altogether, and I readily concede that this mentality has so permeated our lives that we find it difficult even to imagine alternatives in many settings. The first step, though, consists in understanding that rivalry of any kind is both psychologically disastrous and philosophically unjustifiable, that the phrase "healthy competition" is a contradiction in terms. Only then can we begin to develop saner, richer lifestyles for ourselves as individuals, and explore more humanistic possibilities for our society.   18

Are You Living Mindlessly?   Michael Ryan

In the following selection from Parade *magazine, Michael Ryan interviews Ellen Langer, a professor at Harvard University who has written many books and articles on mindfulness, including* Mindfulness, The Power of Mindful Learning, *and* Counterclockwise: Mindful Health and the Power of Possibility. *As you read the article, consider how you live your own life. Do you live mindfully or mindlessly?*

Have you ever been mindless? That's not thoughtless, it's mindless—and we all have been.   1

You've been mindless if you've ever "zoned out" and missed a highway exit; if you've put the cereal in the refrigerator and the milk in the cupboard; or if you've mumbled "you too" when the airport cab driver wishes you a good flight—even though you   2 knew you were catching a plane and he wasn't. Psychologists call this "automaticity"—putting your brain on autopilot and giving the usual responses, even if you aren't in the appropriate situation.

"Being mindless means you're not there," said Ellen Langer, a   3
professor of psychology at Harvard who is the author of *Mindfulness* and *The Power of Mindful Learning*. "You're not in the moment and aware of everything going on around you." I had gone to Cambridge, Massachusetts, to talk with Langer about mindlessness and its opposite, mindfulness, and how switching from one to the other can enrich our lives.

The penalty for mindlessness—letting ourselves operate with-   4
out thinking in a situation we think we're familiar with—can be as minor as missing our highway exit or finding warm milk in the cupboard. But mindlessness also can lead to failure, frustration—even tragedy.

Many of us learn to live mindlessly in our earliest school days   5
"Too often, we teach people things like, 'There's a right way and a wrong way to do everything, regardless of the circumstances,'" Langer explained. "What we should be teaching them is how to think flexibly, to be mindful of all the different possibilities of every situation and not close themselves off from information that could help them."

"I love tennis," Langer continued. "When I was younger, I went   6
to a tennis camp, and they taught me how to hold a racket when I served. Years later, I was watching the U.S. Open, and I realized that not one of the players held the racket that way." Langer saw that the world's best players had put thought and energy into developing a grip and a serve best suited to their individual talents.

"The problem comes in the way we learn," Langer said. "We are   7
rarely taught conditionally: 'This might be a good grip for you.' Usually, we're taught: 'This is the right grip.'" Being mindful—using imagination and creativity to learn what works best for you—is what makes the difference between an average player and a champ.

Langer served up other examples, like the woman who always   8
cut one end off her holiday roasts before putting them into the oven. The woman explained that her mother had always done it that way. The mother, in turn, said it was what her own mother did. When they approached the matriarch, the old woman told them that, as a young bride, she had a very small oven and had been forced to cook her meat in two parts. Mindlessly, the habit had been passed down for generations, long after the need for it had disappeared.

"If you ask most people, 'Is there more than one way to look at   9
anything?' they'll say, 'Of course,'" Langer said. "But it's remarkable
that so many go through life with a single-minded lens. It's not that
they wouldn't agree with other perspectives. It just doesn't occur
to them to look."

In one experiment, psychologists provided a group of sub-   10
jects with simple objects and asked them to explain their use.
The answers were straightforward: a screwdriver turned screws, a
sheet covered a bed, etc. But when they were asked what else the
items could be used for, people's creativity burst forth: the sheet
could be used as a tent for someone shipwrecked; the screwdriver
could be a tent peg, and so on. "When people see that there's
more than one way of looking at things, they become mindful,"
Langer said.

Langer and her colleagues have conducted a wide range of   11
experiments, which she documents in her two books. In one
experiment, students were given a reading assignment: Half were
told simply to learn the material, while the other half were told to
think about what they were reading in ways that made it meaningful to their own lives. When they were tested later, the second
group—the ones who thought about what they had read instead
of just "learning" it the old-fashioned way—scored far higher.

"The way you cultivate mindfulness," Langer said, "is to realize   12
that information about the world around you is endlessly interesting, and it looks different from different perspectives." But many
people operate mindlessly, pursuing routines rather than looking
for new details around them. The results can be disastrous.

Investigations of both the Three Mile Island and Chernobyl   13
nuclear accidents found evidence that technicians—numbed into
mindlessness by years of routine—had failed to respond in time
to changes in instrument readings that would have told them accidents were about to happen. The most widely accepted theory of
how Korean Air Lines Flight 007 went astray—it flew into Soviet
airspace and was shot down by an air-to-air missile—holds that
the pilots entered incorrect coordinates into their compass. Then,
literally on autopilot, they ignored cues from the 747's computers to reconsider their course. Like a driver who has traveled the
same highway a hundred times, they expected no problems and
saw none.

At its worst, mindlessness can help to destroy people's lives, as   14
Langer found in 1974, when she was studying patients and workers in nursing homes. "I argued that we should go around nursing

homes making life more complex, not easier," she said. "It's important for people to be in control of their lives, and the way to be in control is to be in the active process of mastering something. It's in the mastering that mindfulness comes in." Langer found that patients who lived in the wards where they were required to take charge of much of their daily routine—dressing themselves or choosing food—had lower mortality rates than people in comparable health who lived in the wards where attendants and nurses saw to all their needs. Langer also found that nursing-home workers who were taught to think mindfully about their work were less likely to quit. "If the workers realize that much of the burnout they experience is the result of mindless over-rhythmization, turnover goes down by a third," she reported.

Langer told me that mindlessness is also at the root of prejudice—but she said the way to solve it was with *more* discrimination, not less. "Prejudice comes from the mindless assumption that there are nonoverlapping categories," she explained. "You're either black or white, Jew or non-Jew. Most people, if they go far enough into their backgrounds, will find that they are not purebreds. The mistake we make in dealing with prejudice is trying to counter it by saying we're all one big human group, we're all the same." 15

Langer reasoned that, if we are mindful of each other's individual characteristics—not just race and religion but also height, weight, talent, even hair color—we will understand that each human being is unique. 16

We can be mindful in any situation, Langer said—even when faced with huge challenges. "If all you think about is how you're likely to fail at a challenge, you probably will," she said. "But if you ask yourself, 'What are 10 ways I could succeed at this?' your chances of success are much greater. Just noticing new things keeps you alive." 17

THE EFFECTS OF TELEVISION

TV Can't Educate   Paul Robinson

In the following selection, first published in the New Republic, *Paul Robinson argues that television and movies by their very nature cannot educate because they "are structurally unsuited to that process." Consider your own experiences with television—educational or otherwise—as you read this article.*

On July 20 [1978] NBC aired a documentary on life in Marin   1
County, a bedroom community just across the Golden Gate
Bridge from San Francisco. The program was called "I Want It All
Now" and its single theme was the predominance of narcissism
in Marin. The program's host, Edwin Newman, introduced viewers, in his studied casual manner, to a variety of "consciousness-
raising" groups ensconced in Marin and insinuated that this new
narcissistic manner was leading to a breakdown not only of the
family (a divorce rate of 75 percent was mentioned three times)
but also of traditional civic virtue. The following day the *San Francisco Chronicle* carried a long front-page article on the outraged
reaction of Marin's respectable citizenry to what it considered a
grossly distorted portrait of itself. Several residents argued, persuasively, that Marin was in fact a highly political suburb—that it
had been a hot spot of the anti–Vietnam War movement, and
that only last year it had responded dramatically to the water crisis in California, cutting back on water use much more than was
required by law. Television journalism appeared to be up to its old
tricks: producers saw what they wanted to see, and they were not
about to pass up the chance to show a woman being massaged
by two nude men and chirping about how delightful it was to
"receive" without having to "give."

I was reminded, however, improbably, of an experience in   2
Berlin, where I had spent the previous six months teaching. The
Germans are all exercised over a recent movie about Adolf
Hitler (*Hitler: Eine Karriere*), which is based on a biography by the
journalist Joachim Fest. The charge leveled against the film is that
it glorifies Hitler (though it uses nothing but documentary foot-
age; there are no actors), and it has been linked with a supposed
resurgence of Nazism in Germany, particularly among the young.
I saw only parts of the film and therefore can't speak to the justice of the charge. What I wish to report on—and what the Marin
program brought to mind—is a lecture I attended by a young
German historian from the Free University of Berlin, in which
he took issue with the film because it had failed to treat Hitler's
relations with the German industrialists, who were crucial in supporting the Nazi Party before it came to power and apparently
benefited from its success.

The critics of the Newman program and my young scholar   3
friend in Berlin were guilty of the same error. They both bought
the assumption that television and movies can be a source of

knowledge, that one can "learn" from them. By knowledge and learning I obviously don't mean an assortment of facts. Rather I have in mind the analytic process that locates pieces of information within a larger context of argument and meaning. Movies and TV are structurally unsuited to that process.

There is no great mystery here. It's a simple matter of time. 4 Learning requires one kind of time, visual media are bound to another. In learning one must be able to freeze the absorption of fact or proposition at any moment in order to make mental comparisons, to test the fact or proposition against known facts and propositions, to measure it against the formal rules of logic and evidence—in short, to carry on a mental debate. Television is a matter of seconds, minutes and hours, it moves inexorably forward, and thus even with the best will in the world (a utopian assumption), it can never teach. In the last analysis there is only one way to learn: by reading. That's how you'll find out about Hitler's relations with the German industrialists, if you can find out about them at all. Such a complex, many-layered phenomenon simply cannot be reduced to a scene (which would presumably meet my scholar-friend's objection) in which Hitler has dinner with Baron Krupp. Similarly, you will not find out about life in Marin county from an hour-long TV program or, for that matter, from a 24-hour-long one. What are the control populations? What statistical methods are being used? Is there more consciousness raising going on in Marin than in Cambridge? What is the correlation between narcissism and income level, educational background, employment, religious affiliation, marital status, sexual inclination and so forth? If these questions have answers, they are to be found in the books and articles of sociologists, not on TV.

I am prepared, indeed eager, to follow my argument to its logi- 5 cal conclusion: the worst thing on TV is educational TV (and not just on educational stations). By comparison, the gratuitous violence of most commercial shows is a mere peccadillo. Educational TV corrupts the very notion of education and renders its victims uneducable. I hear grown-ups launching conversations with, "Mike Wallace says that . . ." as if Mike Wallace actually knew something. Viewers hold forth authoritatively about South Africa, or DNA, or black holes, or whatever because they have watched a segment about them on *60 Minutes* or some such program. Complete ignorance really would be preferable, because ignorance at least preserves a mental space that might someday be filled with real knowledge, or some approximation of it.

There is a new form of slumming popular among intellectuals: watching "bad" (i.e., commercial) TV and even writing books about it (as Dan Wakefield has about the afternoon soap opera *All My Children*). I would like to think that the motive behind this development is revulsion against the intellectual pretensions of "good" TV. But, as often happens with academics, the reaction has been dressed up in phony theoretical garb. *All My Children*, we're supposed to believe, is the great American novel, heir to the tradition of Dickens and Trollope. Of course it's nothing of the sort. But it is very good entertainment. And that is precisely what TV is prepared to do: to entertain, to divert, above all to amuse. It is superbly amusing, ironically, for the same reason that it can't educate: it is tied to the clock, which has enormous comic potential. It is not accidental that one speaks of a comedian's "timing." Jack Benny would not be funny in print. He must wait just the right length of time after the robber threatens, "Your money or your life," before responding. (Imagine the situation in a novel: "The robber said, 'Your money or your life.' Jack took ten seconds trying to make up his mind.") Nor can you do a double-take in print, only on the screen. The brilliant manipulation of time made *The Honeymooners* so funny: Art Carney squandered it while Jackie Gleason, whose clock ran at double-time, burned. Audrey Meadows stood immobile, producing a magnificently sustained and silent obbligato to Gleason's frantic buffo patter.   6

Television, then, is superbly fit to amuse. And amusement is not to be despised. At the very least it provides an escape from the world and from ourselves. It is pleasurable (by definition, one might say), and it gives us a sense of union with humanity, if only in its foibles. Herbert Marcuse might even contend that it keeps alive the image of an unrepressed existence. Television can provide all this. But it can't educate.   7

Movies are faced with the same dilemma. The desire to educate accounts, I believe, for the increasingly deliberate pace of movies. It is as if the director were trying to provide room within his time-bound narrative for the kind of reflection associated with analysis. This was brought home to me recently when, during the same week, I saw the movie *Julia* in the theater and *Jezebel* on TV. The latter, made in 1938, portrays the tragedy of a strong-willed southern girl who refuses to conform to the rules of antebellum New Orleans society. The most striking difference between the two movies is their pace. *Jezebel* moves along swiftly (there is probably more dialogue in the first 15 minutes than in all of   8

Julia), treats its theme with appropriate superficiality and entertains effortlessly. *Julia*, on the other hand, is lugubrious and obviously beyond its depth. It succeeds only with the character of Julia herself, who, like Jezebel, is powerful, beautiful, virtuous and unburdened by intellectual or psychological complexity. By way of contrast, the narrative figure, Lilli, tries vainly to deal with issues that movies can't manage: the difficulty of writing, a relationship with an older man who is at once lover, mentor, and patient-to-be, the tension between literary success and political commitment. All of these are wonderfully captured in Lillian Hellman's memoir, but not even two fine actors like Jane Fonda and Jason Robards can bring such uncinematic matters to life on the screen. The "issue" of the memoir—despite all those meaningful silences—inevitably eluded the movie.

Let us, then, not ask more of movies and TV than they can deliver. In fact, let us discourage them from trying to "educate" us.   9

It's Good Enough for Me: The Renaissance in Children's Programming   Emily Nussbaum

Emily Nussbaum is the television critic for The New Yorker. *She has written about* The Good Wife, Girls, Mad Men, *and* Scandal, *among other shows. Previously, she worked at* The New Yorker *for seven years, editing the Culture Pages (and creating the Approval Matrix) and writing both features and criticism.*

When children's television comes up in conversation, everyone   1 knows the drill. Begin with the sinister idiom "screen time." To show you're no prig, make a warm remark about "Sesame Street." Name your favorite Muppet. (I suggest Beaker or the Swedish chef.) Then begin the lament, and lay it on thick, with comparisons to candy and drugs. Decry the trend of marketing to newborns, the co-branded toys, the childhood obesity, the dwindling attention spans, the fate of the picture book, the wasted hours the American child spends in front of the tube (three a day, on average!), and all those selfish, shower-taking parents who use TV as a babysitter.

For six decades, people have been wringing their hands with   2 worry, echoing panics about the corrupting influence of comic books and rock music. Not to mention radio: in 1936, the educator Azriel Eisenberg warned that parents "cannot lock out this intruder because it has gained an invincible hold of their children." Over the years, such rhetoric has shifted from the moral to the neural, with spiritual anxieties now expressed in the fear that young kids will grow addicted to dopamine squirts, their brains ruined rather than their souls.

I'm hardly immune to such concerns; like many parents, I limit   3
my children's Tivo time. (Except for weekend mornings. I'm not a saint.) But, as a critic, I'd argue that it's time to recognize what this exhausting, rancorous debate has obscured: a quiet renaissance among children's shows, many of them innovative in ways that parallel the simultaneous rise of great scripted television for adults. The best of these shows are as visually thrilling as they are well constructed. And, like the top dramas for adults, they harness to bold new ends the genre most deeply associated with episodic television's strengths—the formulaic procedural, familiar to viewers from series like "Law & Order."

Until 2005, I had no idea that such shows existed: if you don't   4
have young children, it's easy to condescend to the form. Then, as a new parent, I dutifully followed the American Academy of Pediatrics guidelines—no TV until two. I did so in the manner of other parents I knew, which is to say with my first child. By 2007, when I was juggling a two-year-old and a newborn, a little TV watching in the pre-early morning seemed pretty appealing. And it was then, rattled by sleep deprivation, that I discovered Miffy.

"Miffy and Friends" is a Claymation series based on the chil-   5
dren's books by the Dutch artist Dick Bruna, who created the character in 1955. The show presented a world so stunningly peaceful that I dreamed of entering it myself. It was drawn in the minimalist, mouthless style of "Hello Kitty." (The brand sued the owner of the popular Japanese character for ripping off Bruna's style; the two sides recently settled in court.) Its heroine lived with her animal friends in an idyllic Dutch town, but none of them spoke; their small dramas were narrated in voice-over. The pace was slow. The colors—red, blue, and yellow—were brilliant. It was like a shelter magazine for toddlers. The mood was so lulling that when, in one sequence, Miffy gave her broken toy a small, frustrated kick, my husband was startled. Yet, meditative as the show was, Miffy was a jolt to my expectations. This was children's TV? Why was it so beautiful?

Like most parents of my generation, I watched plenty of televi-   6
sion as a child, although my choices were comparatively narrow: there were just three networks, plus PBS. This was the seventies, the heyday of "Sesame Street" and "The Electric Company," shows created by Joan Ganz Cooney and her team of progressive researchers at the Children's Television Workshop, whose

goal, according to "Street Gang: The Complete History of Sesame Street," by Michael Davis, was to "master the addictive qualities of television and do something good with them." (Almost everyone behind breakthrough children's shows had a do-gooder's passion to redeem the dirty medium.) Set in a city, among a diverse cast of puppets and humans, the Children's Television Workshop productions gleamed with liberal sophistication, with fast-paced skits that satirized TV news and advertising—"This episode is brought to you by the letter P!" There was also the meltingly empathetic Mister Rogers, who had been around since the sixties; the junky vaudeville productions of Sid and Marty Krofft; the droll ultraviolence of the Looney Tunes cartoons; and reruns of sweet old classics like "Kukla, Fran and Ollie.

In the eighties, children's programming took a dive, with the rise of loud, aggressive series like "He-Man" and "She-Ra," half-hour toy commercials disguised as television shows. Cable had blown the market open, but there was little focus on quality, and the Saturday-morning lineup was dominated by cheap animation from Hanna-Barbera, the once proud institution behind "Tom and Jerry," which was now off-loading crass content like "The Smurfs" and "Challenge of the GoBots." This type of series began to wane after 1990, when Congress passed the Children's Television Act, and networks were required to demonstrate that their programming slates included educational material—although what was "good for children" was not necessarily the same as "good." In 1992, that big purple optimist "Barney" became a hit. In 2000, Nickelodeon débuted "Dora the Explorer," which featured a Latina heroine and a curriculum of puzzle-solving. Brassy and wholesome, and kryptonite to adults, "Dora" became such a powerful brand that it supercharged the market. I'd seen the show in passing. I was not a fan.

Yet in 2007 I was amazed to discover a sparkling universe of alternatives, some mainstream, some niche. To my theoretical alarm and pragmatic delight, many were aimed at children between two and five years old, with companies like Nickelodeon, PBS Kids, and Disney vying to find a new Dora. There were so many shows that subgenres emerged, from the realistic, like "Little Bill," to the psychedelic, like the hip "Yo Gabba Gabba!" Some had video-game aesthetics, like "The Backyardigans"; others featured whimsical collage-scapes, like the British "Charlie and Lola." And there were plenty of variety acts, including "Jack's Big Music Show." Owing to the burgeoning "kindie pop" phenomenon, my morning viewing

7

8

now featured regular guest appearances by stars like Mos Def and the Ting Tings.

Every one of these shows had the requisite educational bona   9
fides, including the behemoths "Dora the Explorer"; its spinoff "Go, Diego, Go!"; and the comparatively humane "Blue's Clues," which premièred in 1996. As Malcolm Gladwell suggested in "The Tipping Point," these Nickelodeon hits were constructed, as "Sesame Street" had been, by means of research and analysis. But the new scientific approach was aimed primarily at making a show "sticky"—that is, magnetizing the attention spans of little kids. The resulting episodes were rigorously formulaic and no fun for adults. On "Dora," 2-D characters stare out of the screen, yell a question, and then pause for a response, catering to a toddler's learning style. "Blue's Clues" is gentler, but just as repetitious. "An adult considers constant repetition boring, because it requires reliving the same experience over and over again," Gladwell writes. "But to preschoolers repetition isn't boring, because each time they watch something, they are experiencing it in a completely different way."

"Sesame Street" was still on PBS, but I couldn't get my kids   10
to watch it. To them, the series felt choppy and aggressive, full of parodies of things they'd never heard of. Like all revolutionary TV comedies, from "Monty Python" to "30 Rock," "Sesame Street" was at heart a satirical commentary on television. The series my sons favored were milder, more immersive, with stories that reflected child-size dramas: tantrums, sharing, and fantasies of adventure in the larger world.

Among the best of these shows was "Wonder Pets," which   11
was created in 2006 by Josh Selig, a show runner who grew up within the children's-television industry. Selig appeared on "Sesame Street" as a child, and then, as an adult, wrote for that show and several others. In 1999, he founded Little Airplane Productions, which created and produced "Oobi," "3rd & Bird," and the new series "Small Potatoes." Like everyone in his industry, Selig has been forced to navigate the many pressures of the modern production process, from the demands that shows be "toyetic" (an ugly neologism describing a show's capacity for selling products) to the trend described in Dade Hayes's illuminating book "Anytime Playdate" (2008) as KGOY, "marketing shorthand for 'kids getting older younger.'"

"Wonder Pets" demonstrates that a series can emerge from   12
this process with idiosyncratic, even auteurist sensibilities, despite the pressure to be at once "sticky," multi-platform, and educational.

Selig told me that he pitched "Wonder Pets" to the children's cable channel Nick Jr. with a simple cutout photograph of a guinea pig. But then he brought in the visual artist Jennifer Oxley, and their collaboration resulted in a sensually dazzling series, a revelation to anyone brought up on the schlock aesthetics of Hanna-Barbera. In Selig's innovation, the dialogue on "Wonder Pets" is sung operetta style, with a live orchestra used during the recording. Oxley invented a technique called "photo-puppetry," in which real photographs are manipulated, broken down, and rigged for animation, invoking a layered universe of textures. Like "Miffy," "Wonder Pets" is peaceful, yet also witty and emotional, with themes recognizable from modern notions of child development: the emphasis is on teamwork, empathy, and working through frustration, rather than on self-esteem.

Still, it's the show's narrative repetitions that are most striking. 13 Each episode begins with the sound of children laughing as they say goodbye to their class pets. (Sometimes we hear a scrap of dialogue, such as a child telling his mother he's losing a tooth.) In the empty classroom, we zoom in on Linny the guinea pig, Tuck the turtle, and a duckling named Ming-Ming. A pencil holder rattles, creating a telephone ring, and the pets get their mission: there's an animal in trouble! Singing as they prepare, the Wonder Pets build a "flyboat" from toys. The optics are so dense they're nearly kaleidoscopic. The pets pull on thematic costumes; the walls show children's drawings that are linked to the plot. (In an episode in which the pets rescue a hedgehog in London, there's a teacup, Big Ben, and a bowler hat.) As they sing the show's chorus ("What's gonna work? / Teamwork!"), the pets confront and solve a technical problem; later, they will use that solution to save the animal. In the hedgehog episode, they pry open a toy box; at the story's climax, they repeat this act by prying the hedgehog out of a topiary.

The Wonder Pets' rescues superficially resemble the plots of 14 "Dora," which also favor global veterinary emergencies. (Until I watched children's TV, I had no idea that there were so many animals in trouble.) But the series has none of "Dora" 's formulaic blandness; instead, it bursts with tiny, sophisticated jokes, both musical and visual. When the hedgehog pops out, he rolls through croquet wickets. In a Japanese episode, the characters enter a gorgeous brushstroke-style painting. The pets have toddler personalities, at times bratty and flawed: in one of the funniest episodes, the melodramatic MingMing sings a melancholy aria that ends with "The animal in trouble is . . . me!" Ollie, a bunny who refuses to collaborate, creates a rival team called the Thunder Pets, consisting of himself and two inanimate objects: a rock and a toy frog

Like "Dora," "Wonder Pets" teaches kids about other parts of   15
the globe. What's a plover? What's a fjord? Like "Blue's Clues," it traffics in problem solving. But what really unifies these shows is how strongly their satisfactions echo those of legal procedurals. As with a show like "Law & Order," there's enormous pleasure for a repeat viewer in knowing what comes next, then enjoying small variations. At the climax, Ming-Ming always sings, 'This! Is! Sew-wious!" At the finale, a grateful parent appears. "Thank you ever so much," the mother hedgehog says, and she invites the Wonder Pets for tea. As always, they have celebratory celery and fly home.

"Ni Hao, Kai-Lan" resembles "Dora" even more directly: it's   16
interactive, with pauses and drills, but it teaches kids social skills (plus a little Mandarin) instead of focussing on analytical think-ing. It's more alien to adult sensibilities, and according to Hayes's "Anytime Playdate," which traces the development of the show, it was hammered into shape by means of focus groups and cor-porate consultation. Even so, the series is in its way as intoxicat-ing as "Wonder Pets," owing to the lush symbolic universe of the illustrations, by Karen Chau, the show's creator. In each episode, the saucer-eyed heroine, Kai-Lan, coaches the viewer in techniques for handling envy, calming down, and continuing to try: it's like cognitive-behavioral therapy for the toddler soul. On this series and others, there's an emphasis on perseverance; so many shows have songs about trying hard that my sons began singing them during difficult tasks.

One typical "Ni Hao, Kai-Lan" episode dramatizes the notion   17
that good friends keep their promises. But the episode nests that lesson in dizzying, fractal imagery: Kai-Lan spins on a merry-go-round, then observes a mini-universe of snails with their own tiny merry-go-round. (It breaks, and she promises to fix it.) An ant races by on a scooter in the shape of a panda. (Kai-Lan's friend is tempted to break his promise in order to go race with him.) A pink rhino floats overhead, taking some dancing worms for a promised merry-go-round-like spin. When, finally, Kai-Lan gets back on her own merry-go-round—which is shaped like a ladybug, with ladybug-shaped seats—the structure rises from the ground and spins away. Kai-Lan makes the shape of a heart with her hands, sending a bright-red heart into the air like a balloon. Despite the pedagogy, the show feels as fizzy as a carbonated drink—it's a message of joy that doesn't match any particular curriculum.

Television for adults and television for children are usually dis-   18
cussed as entirely separate entities, with different aims. But the way
that shows like "Wonder Pets" and "Ni Hao, Kai-Lan" took a successful formula, then built something handsome on its blunt scaf-
folding, reflects the evolution of modern television. "Law & Order"
debuted in 1990. It was a sleek, pleasurable, and lucrative model,
and it spawned endless imitators and spinoffs. Then, as the century
turned, auteurist creators began to do something intriguing: they
produced dramas like "The Shield," "Dexter," "Dollhouse," and "Terriers," experimental series that didn't abandon the pleasures of
episodic TV but took its familiar DNA and twisted it hard. These
shows weren't always commercial hits: "Terriers" was cancelled
after one season. Similarly, the most interesting children's shows
don't always get the highest ratings. (If they aren't sufficiently
"toyetic," they will have a short run.) But, like their adult analogues,
they can find fresh audiences through reruns, DVDs, and online
streaming.

Now, I'm not suggesting that "Wonder Pets" is the kiddie ver-   19
sion of "The Wire." (Maybe it's more like "Monk.") But there's
something inspiring in the way that these shows find freedom, and
beauty, by respecting their medium's innate strengths and con-
straints, instead of viewing them with disdain.

Even at their most revolutionary, of course, such shows are   20
reflexively wholesome. And, in theory, I sympathize with another
modern prejudice common to parents of my cohort, the Bruno
Bettelheim–inflected notion that children's art should be not familiar but shocking, a way of purging fears and anxieties—the stuff of
Roald Dahl and Neil Gaiman. There are days when I get nostalgic
for the corrosive edge of the Bugs Bunny cartoons (that said,
when I actually re-watched them not long ago I was alarmed to
find the characters shooting one another in the face). It's perfectly
reasonable to be repelled by preachy shows, although I confess
that I dislike them primarily when they promote values that I find
odious; "Thomas and Friends," for example, a depressingly popular
British series, might as well be a blueprint for Victorian economics,
with its fetishistic emphasis on "usefulness" and docility.

Yet television is different from books or movies. The medium   21
is intimate, invited into our homes like a vampire. TV shows, with
their episodic iterations, create a trusting bond between viewers
and characters. Many children watch shows alone; even parents
averse to "using television as a babysitter" may pop in a DVD on
a tantrum-y afternoon. Selig told me that American shows rarely

touch on death or divorce, because networks are cautious about any subject that might require a parent's explanation. And the more I watched preschool shows the more open I became to their benign morality. When my kids began to grow out of them, I was thrilled to come across Disney's "Phineas and Ferb," an even more sophisticated procedural, and one whose values I could get behind, with its utopian, throwback vision of a childhood free of endless adult oversight.

"Phineas and Ferb" is an animated show that was created by 22 Dan Povenmire and Jeff (Swampy) Marsh, formerly of "The Simpsons," "Family Guy," and "Spongebob Squarepants." Povenmire and Marsh pitched the show for fifteen years before finally selling it. By that point, they both had young kids of their own. "It would probably have been a funny show if we'd written it back then," Povenmire told me. "But it would also have been harsher and edgier—less sweet."

"Phineas and Ferb" is almost sonnet-like in its precision. In 23 eleven minutes (each episode has two sections), the script links three plots. In the A plot, the nine-year-old half brothers Phineas and Ferb fill a summer day with some insanely ambitious project: making a building as high as the moon, a time machine, a rollercoaster. In the B plot, their tween sister Candace tries to get their mother to "bust" them for their dangerous plan. But she always fails, because in the C plot their pet platypus, Perry—who is actually a secret agent named Agent P—has a Rocky-and-Bullwinkle-like showdown with a hapless Germanic villain named Doofenshmirtz, who builds his own superpowered machines. This battle inevitably causes the boys' project to disappear just before their mother spots it.

But that formula doesn't account for the wit and narrative 24 daring of the series, which has a sprawling ensemble of minor characters, a catchy song or two in every episode, and a fusillade of repeated motifs, from Doofenshmirtz's evil-justifying backstories to the moment when someone says, "Hey, where's Perry?" Even better is the pedagogy sunk into each episode, and sometimes made explicit: the show's radical vision of childhood as a time of unsupervised independence. Povenmire and Marsh claim they had no philosophy when they started (they were just "curmudgeons about kids playing too many video games"), but the series could easily have been inspired by the book "Shopcraft as Soulcraft," which celebrates technical self-reliance and craftsmanship, or by the free-range-parenting movement. Phineas is a cheerful, intrepid engineer, so engaged by his inventive projects that he becomes an unwitting rebel against the zeitgeist of helicopter parenting and ultra-safety. In the one episode in which Candace does manage to bust her brothers (the excellent "Phineas and Ferb's Quantum Boogaloo"), her act triggers a bleak future in which parents child-proof their children and all creativity is crushed.

The series is hardly the first show designed to appeal to parents as well as to children: like "Sesame Street," it flatters the tastes of parents who like some clever with their sweet. But it may be the first children's series in which the moral instruction, rather than the jokes, is aimed as much at parents as at children. Once your kids have finished watching the episode, "Phineas and Ferb" suggests, you might think about releasing them into the back yard, with a pile of lumber and a tool belt. Who knows? They might build a tower as high as the moon.

25

Appendix

Writing the
Research Paper

Writing a research paper may at first seem like an overwhelming task to you, but it really is not. Although research papers do take more time than shorter, less-complicated essays, they certainly should not cause the worry and anxiety that so many students seem to feel when they think about research assignments. After all, a research paper is just an extended essay supported with material that you have found in outside sources. And if you have written one of the essay assignments in Chapters 7 or 8, you have already practiced paraphrasing, quoting, and documenting source material.

GETTING STARTED

CHOOSING AN APPROPRIATE TOPIC

- As you choose your topic, make sure you understand the assignment. How long is the paper supposed to be? How many sources are required? When is it due? Does the assignment require argument, such as taking a position on the legalization of gambling in your state? Or does it ask for explanation and discussion, such as an examination of the effects of gambling on different personality types?

- Don't choose a topic that is too broad. If you have never written a research paper before, you might think you need an extra-large topic, but you don't. Trying to tackle a broad topic like the problems that gambling has caused different cultures throughout history will result in a paper that covers many different points in a very superficial way. The length of a good research paper comes from fewer points discussed in depth, with many supporting ideas and facts drawn from research.

DEVELOPING A PRELIMINARY THESIS OR RESEARCH QUESTION

- As you know, the thesis states the central idea of your paper. Usually it is written as the last sentence of the introduction. If you are writing an argument, it is the statement your entire paper must prove: *The drawbacks of legalized gambling in California far outweigh any benefits.* If you are writing a factual report, it states the central point of the report: *One of the basic causes of homelessness is mental illness—either clinical depression or schizophrenia.*

- If you know what position you want to argue or what point you want to make, write a preliminary thesis statement and move on to your research. However, if you do not know where you stand on an issue, write a question that you want your research to answer: *Should gambling be legalized in California? What are the primary causes of homelessness?* Once you have completed your research, replace your question with a statement of the conclusion you have drawn. That statement will now serve as your thesis.

DOING THE RESEARCH

First, a warning about research: A research paper is not a paraphrase of an encyclopedia article, nor is it a patchwork of quotations from your sources. It is a presentation of *your ideas*, supported by research. In other words, *you* and *your ideas* are a major part of the paper, even if your ideas were not clearly formed before you began your research. That said, let's look at some of the best sources for your research.

REFERENCE BOOKS

Sometimes the best way to start your research is to read general articles on your topic in encyclopedias or specialized reference works. You'll find these books in the reference section of the library. Use **general encyclopedias**, such as *The New Encyclopedia Britannica* or *Encyclopedia Americana*. Both will give you articles written by experts on the subject and will provide lists of other works you should read. **Specialized encyclopedias**, such as *Encyclopedia of Psychology* or *Encyclopedia of Biological Sciences*, can also be very helpful. Ask your librarian what other specialized reference works might provide you with information about your topic.

BOOKS

Books are an important source for many research papers. You can locate books on your topic by using the library catalog, which most libraries now make available through **computer terminals**. Simply type in keywords related to your subject matter, as you would if you were searching for materials on the Internet. The keywords you choose, of course, will be critical to a successful search. Don't give up if the words you use do not produce results at first. If you need to, ask one of the librarians which keywords might be appropriate for your topic. Before you leave your terminal to find the book on the library's shelves (called **stacks**), record its entire **call number** (a series of letters and numbers, usually toward the top or bottom of each entry on the computer) as well as the title and the author's name.

PERIODICALS

Periodicals consist of magazines, newspapers, and scholarly journals. These sources will have the most current research on your topic. To find periodicals, consult one of the **indexes** your library subscribes to. You will find some of them in printed, bound volumes in the reference section, but most popular indexes are available through databases accessible through the same computer terminals as books. (Many school libraries now provide students with passwords to access these databases from home.)

SUBSCRIPTION DATABASES

Most college libraries now have subscription databases that allow you to use any computer to access full-text articles or article abstracts from newspapers, magazines, scholarly journals, and encyclopedias. **Full-text articles** reproduce articles exactly as they appeared in print, so you don't need to find the original sources. **Article abstracts** provide brief summaries of articles that appeared in periodicals. To find the complete article, you will need to find the original periodical. (Do not use article abstracts as sources. You must find the complete article to use the material in your paper.) Common subscription databases are *JSTOR, Academic Search Premiere* (from EBSCOhost), *Opposing Viewpoints* (from GaleNet), *ProQuest Newspapers* (from ProQuest), and *CQ Researcher* (a database that provides reports on a wide variety of current issues).

SOURCES FOR FACTS AND STATISTICS

To find facts and statistics, consult the library's volumes of *The Statistical Abstract of the United States, Information Please Almanac*, and *Facts on File*. You will find these and other volumes of statistics in the reference section. In addition, if your library subscribes to the *Opposing Viewpoints* computerized database, type in a keyword for your subject. When a list of sources appears, click on the "Statistics" tab at the top of the page to find articles that offer statistical information on your subject.

THE INTERNET

The Internet is a powerful source of information. Often a simple search using one keyword will produce thousands, even hundreds of thousands of **hits** (sites containing the keyword you entered). Typing the keyword *immigration* into a Google search, for example, will result in over 216 *million* hits. As you can see, using the Internet requires that you **focus** your search as well as carefully **evaluate** the information you find there. Here are some popular search engines and their Web site addresses:

GOOGLE	http://google.com
BING	http://www.bing.com
YAHOO	http://www.yahoo.com
DOGPILE	http://www.dogpile.com

To Focus Your Internet Search, Take the Following Steps:

- Use a more precise term. Using *illegal immigration* instead of *immigration*, for example, reduces the number of hits to 25 million (still an impossible number to work with).
- Put quotation marks around terms containing more than one word. Now the search engine will look only for documents that contain the two words in that specific order. "*Illegal immigration*" results in 5.7 million hits.
- Add another keyword or phrase, connecting it with AND. "*Illegal immigration*" AND "*border patrol*" results in 377,000 hits.
- Limit your search to sites that are not commercially oriented. The last part of a Web address, or URL (Uniform Resource Locater), identifies the nature of the Web site:

.COM	commercial (sites designed to sell something or make a profit)
.NET	commercial or personal
.ORG	a nonprofit organization (aims to promote a cause)
.GOV	government
.EDU	college or educational institution

Consider limiting your search to .gov, .edu, and .org sites, which are generally the most reliable. For example, you can limit your search results to government sites by adding *site:gov* (no space between *site:* and *gov*) at the end of your keywords. *"Illegal immigration" AND "border patrol" site:gov* now produces 7,000 hits—still a very large number, but far fewer than 216 million! Finally, another way to limit the number of results is to use Google Scholar (www.scholar.google.com), which restricts your search to sources that are likely to be scholarly. Remember, *any* material drawn directly from the Internet needs to be evaluated carefully.

To Evaluate Your Internet Sources, Consider the Following Questions:

- Is the source current? When was it created?
- Is the source reliable? (Restricting your search to .org, .gov, or .edu sites will help you avoid many unreliable sources.)
- Is the author qualified to write about your research topic? (Some .edu sites are written by students, not by experts on your topic.)
- Does the information seem fair and objective? (Even nonprofit .org sites are often promoting a specific cause. Does the presentation seem fair?)

TAKING NOTES

- Before you take notes from any source, write down, print, or save all the information that you might need later for your Works Cited page:

FOR A BOOK	author, title, edition (if not the first), place of publication, publisher, and date of publication
FOR AN ARTICLE FROM A PERIODICAL	author, title of an article, title of publication, date, volume and issue numbers, and page numbers
FOR MATERIAL FROM A LIBRARY DATABASE OR THE INTERNET	same material as above, but also the name of the database or Web site, date of electronic publication (if available), date you visited the site, and Internet address (URL)

- Make a copy of the article or portion of the book you intend to use. (Be sure to write all of the above publication information on the copy.) Now you can mark up this copy for all you want.
- Read the source, underlining and highlighting major ideas and any places that seem to express significant points. Don't take notes yet. Just read and underline.
- Now take notes from what you have underlined. Use a separate sheet of paper (or note cards, if you prefer). As much as possible, use your own words in your notes. Next to each notation, identify the source

and page number. If you write down *anything*, word for word, place quotation marks around it and identify the source and page number.

A warning: Some students skip taking notes and try to write their paper directly from the material they highlighted. Don't do it. The result is almost always a paper that reads like a string of loosely related quotations and summaries.

- When you have taken all of your notes, read them again. Mark those that seem particularly important. As best you can, identify notes that discuss similar ideas even though they come from different sources.

WRITING THE PAPER

ORGANIZING YOUR THOUGHTS AND WRITING THE FIRST DRAFT

- Once you have completed your research, set it aside for a moment and spend some time writing out your own thoughts. After all, your paper should present your views, as informed by the research you have done. What seem to be the most important issues in what you have read? Have your own ideas changed at all? Check the thesis that you started with. Does it still express the central idea that your research will support? If you need to revise it, do so now.
- The best way to organize your material is to think through your paper from first paragraph to last, *writing a rough outline as you do*. **Don't skip this step.** The temptation now will be to start writing the essay itself. However, you will find it *much easier* to write if you first think the paper through, writing down in brief phrases and sentences the basic ideas that you will include in each section. Write down your responses to questions like these:

INTRODUCTION	What material should I include here? Should I open with background information? Do I have a striking anecdote or case study from my research that might make an effective opening?
FIRST SECTION	What point should the first section of the body of my paper discuss? What material from my research should I include in this section? (Look through your notations from research to find materials that should be included in your first section.) How many paragraphs will this section include?
SECOND AND LATER SECTIONS	Ask the same questions for each section, and write brief notes in the form of a rough outline.

- If you have prepared a thorough rough outline, you will now find it much easier to write the first full draft of the paper. Don't worry about the perfect writing style. Just follow your rough outline and present your ideas as clearly as you can.

INTEGRATING SOURCES INTO YOUR PAPER

- As you write your paper, you will present your ideas from research in three ways: as *direct quotations, paraphrases,* and *summaries:*

DIRECT QUOTATIONS	Direct quotations are word-for-word repetitions of the original source. Always place quotation marks around them. (**Exception:** Long quotations set off from the text do not use quotation marks.) Use direct quotations sparingly to avoid the appearance of a paper that is merely a string of quotations. No more than 10 to 15 percent of your paper should be direct quotations.
PARAPHRASES	Paraphrases are ideas from the original source written in your own words and writing style. Usually paraphrases are about the same length as the ideas were in their original form.
SUMMARIES	Summaries are ideas from the original source written in your own words and writing style. They differ from paraphrases in that summaries usually condense several paragraphs or more from the original source into a few sentences.

- Each direct quotation, paraphrase, or summary should be *integrated* into your paper with a transition. Do not simply "dump" one into your paragraph. Compare the following examples:

"DUMPED" QUOTATION	Many people believe that the residents of homeless shelters are just lazy and unmotivated, but such a view is much too simplistic. "Most people who end up in homeless shelters are suffering from schizophrenia, clinical depression, or post-traumatic stress syndrome."
QUOTATION WITH TRANSITION	Many people believe that the residents of homeless shelters are just lazy and unmotivated, but such a view is much too simplistic. **According to a recent study by Daniel Moriarty, a Stanford psychologist,** "Most people who end up in homeless shelters are suffering from schizophrenia, clinical depression, or post-traumatic stress syndrome."
DUMPED PARAPHRASE	Many people believe that the residents of homeless shelters are just lazy and unmotivated, but such a view is much too simplistic. Many of them are suffering from serious mental and emotional disorders.

PARAPHRASE WITH TRANSITION

Many people believe that the residents of homeless shelters are just lazy and unmotivated, but such a view is much too simplistic. **According to a recent study by Daniel Moriarty, a Stanford psychologist,** many of them are suffering from serious mental and emotional disorders.

Note

For a further discussion of integrating paraphrases and quotations into your paper, see pages 162–165.

AVOIDING PLAGIARISM

- Plagiarism occurs when you present someone else's words or ideas as if they were your own. When you directly quote from another work, you *must* use quotation marks as well as identify the source of the quotation. When you paraphrase or summarize from another work, you also *must* identify the source. Not doing so is plagiarism.
- A more subtle type of plagiarism occurs when you change only a few words in a passage, keeping most of the style as in the original, and then present the passage as a paraphrase. When you paraphrase or summarize, use your own writing style. Try not to copy the style of the original.

DOCUMENTING YOUR SOURCES

If you use someone else's ideas, facts, examples, or statistics, you must *document* your source in two places:

- In *parenthetical references* within the body of the paper
- On the *Works Cited* page at the end of your paper

You must document sources even if you do not quote them directly and even if you only paraphrase or summarize the ideas of someone else. You do not need to document facts that are common knowledge, such as *Neil Armstrong was the first person to walk on the moon.*

PARENTHETICAL REFERENCES WITHIN THE BODY OF THE PAPER

Today's writers no longer use an elaborate footnote system together with Latin expressions at the bottom of the page. Instead, they use the method of the MLA (Modern Language Association) or the APA (American Psychological Association). Both methods use *parenthetical references*, although in slightly different ways. The following information is based on the MLA, the method used in English classes and the humanities.

Parenthetical references are placed within the paper directly after *all direct quotations, summaries,* or *paraphrases.* In them, you give readers just enough information so that they can find the full source on the Works Cited page at the end of your paper. The three most common parenthetical references are:

1. **Page number only.**   This is the most common parenthetical reference. Use only a page number if you have already identified the author within the transition:

   According to Royster, "Both groups could see the defeat of the Confederacy coming" (187).

Since you have given the last name of the author within the sentence, the reader can easily find the full source on your Works Cited page. The page number is all that you need in parentheses.

2. **Last name of author and page number.**   Include the last name of the author in the parentheses if you have not yet identified the author:

   Toward the spring of that year, the leaders of both armies knew that the days of the Confederacy were numbered (Royster 187).

3. **Title and page number.**   Use the title within the parentheses if your source does not have an author listed and if you haven't already mentioned the title in your text. You do not need to use the entire title. Include just enough of it to lead the reader to the right place on your Works Cited page.

   The bitterness has become "rancid in the veins of Southerners" ("Sherman's" 77).

The entire title is "Sherman's March and Southern Attitudes," but one word is all that is needed to lead the reader to the article on the Works Cited page.

Special Situations in Parenthetical References

- **Citing a statement by one author that is quoted in the work of another author.** If your source quotes some *other* source and you also want to quote that other source, use "qtd. in" (quoted in):

  According to Anigami, "The circumstances of one's life are often a mirror of one's inner dynamics" (qtd. in Rangel 142).

  In this example, you have an article by *Rangel,* not by *Anigami.* Rangel has quoted what Anigami said or wrote, and you want to use the same quotation.

- **Citing a work by two or three authors.** In such a situation, include all of the last names in the citation:

  A recent article in *USA Today* reports that Bush's attempts to change the nation's immigration laws have divided his political base (Jackson and Kiely A4).

- **Citing material from the Internet or electronic indexes.** As with other sources, use the author's last name and page number if available. If no author is given, use the first major word of the title. Material downloaded from the Internet or from the library's periodical indexes *often does not show page numbers*. In that case, include in the parentheses only the author's last name or a portion of the title if no author is given:

  According to a May, 2006, article in the *National Review,* "The latest Gallup poll, from early April, has 47% of the public thinking that immigration should be decreased, 35% who want it left as is and only 15% who want it increased" ("No Left Turn").

  This entry is downloaded from an online database that did not provide page numbers, so none is given here. In addition, no author was identified with the source, so part of the title is used instead.

Punctuation with Parenthetical References

Place the period that ends your sentence at the end of and outside the parentheses. Look at the examples above. Note that the period is placed after the parentheses, not before them.

(**Exception:** Quotations longer than four lines are set off by indenting them one inch from the left margin. If multiple paragraphs are quoted, indent them one-half inch from the left margin rather than one inch. No quotation marks are used, and the period is placed at the end of the last word, before the parentheses.)

THE WORKS CITED PAGE

The Works Cited page is the last page of a research paper. It is an alphabetical list of all the sources you have quoted, paraphrased, or summarized in your paper. There are precise conventions to be followed carefully when putting together this page:

- Begin the list on a new page after the last page of your text.
- Center the heading *Works Cited* at the top.
- Include only the sources that you have used in your paper.
- List the works alphabetically according to the last name of the author or, lacking that, using the first main word in the title.
- Begin typing the first line of each entry at the left-hand margin. Indent the second and subsequent lines five spaces (or one-half inch).
- Double-space all entries, and double-space between each entry.
- The main parts of each entry are the author, the title, the publishing information, and the medium of publication (i.e. "Print," "Web," "Film," "DVD"). Separate each main part with periods.
- Italicize the titles of books and magazines, and place quotation marks around the titles of articles.

(For a sample Works Cited page, refer to page 465.)

Examples of Entries

In the following examples, if no author is given for your source, begin your entry with the title of the source instead.

- **Book**

    Author. *Title*. City: Publisher, Date. Medium

    Royster, Charles. *The Destructive War*. New York: Random House, 1991. Print.

- **Article in a Magazine Published Every Week or Two Weeks**

    Author. "Title of Article." *Title of Magazine* Full Date: Page number(s) of entire article. (Write a plus sign after the page number if the article is not printed on consecutive pages.) Medium.

    Lyons, Daniel. "The Health Geeks: Microsoft's Bid to Fix Medical Care." *Newsweek* July 19, 2010: 26. Print.

- **Article in a Magazine Published Every Month or Two Months**

    Author. "Title of Article." *Title of Magazine* Month and Year: Page number(s) of entire article. (Write a plus sign after the page number if the article is not printed on consecutive pages.) Medium.

    Slessarev-Jamir, Helene. "Looking for Welcome." *Sojourners Magazine* April 2006: 26–30. Print.

- **Article in a Newspaper**

    Author. "Title of Article." *Title of Newspaper* Date, Section: Page number(s) of entire article. (Write a plus sign after the page number if the article is not printed on consecutive pages.) Medium.

    Gorman, Anna. "Arizona Law Is Just One of Many." *Los Angeles Times* 17 July 2010: A1+. Print.

- **Article in a Journal**

    Author. "Title of Article." *Title of Journal*. Volume Number. Issue Number (Year): Page number(s) of entire article. Medium.

    Tolson, David. "Sherman's Dastardly Deed." *Annals of the Confederacy*. 55.1 (1994): 367–80. Print.

- **Article in an Anthology**

    Author. "Title of Article." *Title of Anthology*. Editor. City: Publisher, Date. Page number(s) of entire story or article. Medium.

    Blackmur, R. P. "The Method of Marianne Moore." *Selected Essays of R. P. Blackmur*. Ed. Denis Donoghue. New York: Ecco, 1986. 119–44. Print.

- **Article from a Library's Online Database**

    Author. "Title of Article." [Using the format in the examples above, include the title of the periodical as well as the dates and page numbers.] *Name of Database*. Medium. Date of Access. (Include URL only if required by instructor.)

    Brush, Silla. "One Tough Border Collie." *U.S. News and World Report* April 17, 2006: 32. *Academic Search Premier*. Web. 23 May 2010.

- **Material from the Internet**

  Author (if available). "Title of Article" (if applicable). *Title of Web site*. Publisher (or n.p. if none given), Publishing Date (or n.d. if none given). Medium. Date of Access.

  Obama, Barack. "Statement by President Barack Obama on Bombings in Iran." *The White House*. United States Government, 16 July 2010. Web. 18 July 2010.

- **No Author Given**

  Use the first main word of the title. Alphabetize according to that word.

  "The South's Anger." *The Knoxville Sentinel*. 25 Jan. 1945: E2–3. Print.

- **More Than One Author**

  Use the last name for first author only. List subsequent authors by first and last names.

  Erianger, Steven and Alison Mitchell. "U.S. Officials Rethink Need to Deploy Troops." *The San Diego Union-Tribune*. 16 Nov. 1996: A1+. Print.

- **More Than One Work by the Same Author**

  For entries after the first one, use three hyphens and a period in place of the author's name. Alphabetize the works by the titles.

  Kooser, Ted. *Delights & Shadows*. Port Townsend, WA: Copper Canyon Press, 2004. Print.

  ———. *Sure Signs*. Pittsburgh: University of Pittsburgh Press, 1980. Print.

- **Radio or Television Program**

  "Title of Episode" (if there is one). *Name of Program*. Network. Local station. Broadcasting City. Date. Medium.

  A Prairie Home Companion. NPR. KPBS, St. Paul, Minnesota. 17 Nov. 2009. Radio.

- **Recorded Films or Movies**

  Title. Director. Performers (if relevant). Distributor. Release Year. Medium.

  The Civil War: A Film by Ken Burns. Dir. Ken Burns. Perf. David McCullough, Sam Waterston. PBS. 1990. DVD.

- **Personal Interview**

  Name of person. Medium. Date.

  Sanchez, Maria. Personal Interview. 25 May 2010.

SAMPLE STUDENT RESEARCH PAPER

Roleson 1

Ryan Roleson

Professor McDonald

English 50

May 5, 2015

A Story Still Being Written

The debate over legalization of euthanasia is a timeless battleground that has been fought upon for generations. Many years before our generations began arguing it, the ancient Greeks and Romans conflicted over the value of human life. Many thought that if life is unbearable, one has the right to commit suicide and viewed the use of euthanasia as a simple fact of life. However, others opposed euthanasia because they thought it was a violation of the commands of the gods, who valued human life regardless of its quality (Porter, Johnson, and Warren 90). Today, it is known as physician-assisted suicide, though it is also common to refer to it directly as euthanasia. Legalization of physician-assisted suicide is a complex and bitter debate that involves sharp and often bitter disagreement.

One reason for disagreement regards the ability of palliative care to stop or slow the physical pain of a hospitalized individual. Proponents of assisted death argue that in many cases, patients are not receiving appropriate pain relief, justifying euthanasia as a way to prevent further suffering: "In the United States alone, tens of millions of

Writer's name

Instructor

Course

Date

Title centered

Double-spacing
is used
throughout.

Parenthetical
reference is
used for a
paraphrase.

Thesis

Roleson 2

people—patients with cancer...and others—receive inadequate pain relief, causing unnecessary suffering and giving impetus to the euthanasia movement" (Porter, Johnson, and Warren 91). It is obvious that many people would prefer a quick, painless death to months of suffering in a cold, sterile hospital room. Paul Schotsmans, a professor of medical ethics in a major university in Belgium, writes about the painful death of his brother, a healthy, active man who was suddenly diagnosed with cancer: "The pain, the lack of air...regularly I had him in my arms during these days, as he was begging for air, begging for a nurse, reproaching me that I was not quick enough" (335). Though his brother finally dies in the hospital, Professor Schotsmans, who was once stalwart in his opposition to physician-assisted suicide, still experiences a dilemma. He opposes putting an end to another person's life, yet he asks, "Is it sometimes not better and more human to do this than let someone go through this process of suffering?" (335).

However, euthanasia can also be opposed for equally compelling reasons. According to Ersek, critics of euthanasia contend that suffering is no reason for killing. They say that helping someone die violates the sanctity of life, an idea that is basic to many religious beliefs (51). Furthermore, the American Nurses Association (ANA) has opposed euthanasia by the defining principle of nonmaleficence. Its position is that "nursing profession's covenant with society is to assist people in living the fullest lives possible, not to help them end their lives" (Ersek 51). Not only has the possibility of legalizing euthanasia been challenged as outright murder, but it could also lead to a higher likelihood of patients feeling compelled to request aid in dying for less justifiable reasons than physical pain. Critics of euthanasia contend that if it were made legal, palliative care would slide down the slippery slope to preferring euthanasia over other medical treatment. They fear that patients might be coerced into assisted suicide because pain-killing drugs are so expensive and caring for them takes so much time and effort (Ersek 51). To put it bluntly, should we have our grandparents killed simply because an intensive-care retirement home costs too much?

Proponents of euthanasia respond by pointing out the benefits of legalization. According to them, some nurses and physicians already practice assisted suicide, so legalization will provide accountability and oversight (Ersek 52). For example, in Oregon, the Department of Health and Human Services has supervised assisted suicide since its implementation in 1997. Each year, it publishes a report with details of who prescribes medication, alternatives discussed, and whether patients are impaired by psychological disorders (Ersek 51). It is obvious that euthanasia is a dangerous tool, but, to proponents, its potential to relieve the suffering of terminal hospital patients far outweighs the possibility of its abuse.

Proponents also claim that "sanctity of life," which critics try to position against euthanasia,

> Paraphrase is identified by author and page number.

Roleson 4

should not be defined by mere existence. They point
out, for example, that patients with paralyzing
disabilities should not be kept suffering in hospital
beds. The British House of Lords' decision in
Airedale NHS Trust v. Bland concerned a seventeen-
year-old comatose survivor kept alive for approximately
three years. The young man's parents went to court
to get permission to remove his life support. The
court eventually ruled that "existence in a
persistent vegetative state" does not benefit the
patient (Godlovitch, Mitchell, and Doig). A Canadian
court in Alberta also adopted this position for a
Canadian case and further defined it to include the
"sanctity of life." The court said that "life is
sacred, not in the sense of bare existence, but in a
personal sense: how that patient construes a
meaningful life—their life as they see it and how
they wish to live" (Godlovitch, Mitchell, and Doig).

Opponents of legalization dispute the point by
further arguing that euthanasia, once legalized, is
bound to be abused. They hold that life is inherently
sacred, regardless of a person's disabilities. For
opponents of euthanasia, "life is of such intrinsic
value and the "slippery slope" dangers are so evident
that euthanasia cannot be tolerated" (Huxtable and
Campbell). As an example of such abuse, critics point
out how far down the "slippery slope" palliative care
has gone in countries such as the Netherlands, where
euthanasia is legal:

> Nearly a third of all Dutch doctors
> hold physician-assisted suicide to be
> legitimate in very old people who are

Page numbers
are not given
when the
printout from an
online database
does not
provide them.

Roleson 5

>tired of living. Congruent with this
>view, when the new Dutch law was debated
>and enacted in Parliament, the (now
>former) Health Minister stated that
>suicide pills should be distributed
>among the elderly. (Materstvedt)

Opponents contend that this kind of ethical abuse begins with its legalization. Simply because euthanasia is legal and being supervised by a government agency, that does not mean that it will not be abused.

Proponents respond that the right to life includes the right to death as well. Though the two may sound contradictory, it seems comical to suggest that the government has control over who enters the pearly gates of heaven. Proponents argue that a right to traditional types of palliative care includes the right to euthanasia: "People should have the right to make decisions about ending their own life in the same way they can choose or refuse other types of medical therapies" (Ersek 49–50). Proponents believe that not only does the necessity of autonomy include taking one's own life, but it also relieves unwanted feelings of separation on the part of a patient. As mentioned previously, Professor Schotsmans faced a similar situation while his brother was in the hospital. He comments on how lonely and isolated his brother was: "[M]edical and paramedical staff and family members have the chance to go away, to 'breathe' in normal life, but the dying patient remains left finally at his own" (336). Patients are left alone to waste away in a

Quotations longer than four lines are set off from the left margin by 10 spaces (one inch). No quotation marks are used.

Roleson 6

hospital bed, while their friends and family continue to live their lives. To respect a patient's autonomy is to recognize that it is not enough to simply wait for a suffering person to die.

A final response from opponents of euthanasia consists of a different meaning of autonomy. Critics believe that "euthanasia...will damage autonomy in the most fundamental sense by eradicating the very possibility of future autonomous acting as such" (Materstvedt). Living all of life's opportunities, they say, is what gives a person autonomy. Furthermore, assisting in death is no simple favor: "Opponents of assisted suicide argue that the right to choose [euthanasia] doesn't extend to the right to die by asking health care officials to assist in hastening death" (Ersek 51).

The debate regarding the legalization of euthanasia is an emotionally charged battle that must be settled. Though some states or countries have implemented euthanasia, the conflict is far from over. Liberal proponents of euthanasia are just as sure as their conservative opponents of their opinions, and no end to this argument is in sight. Euthanasia has a long, hard road ahead of it before it reaches its destination. But let the growth of this debate bear sweet fruits by its end so that the most people can be helped in the least amount of time.

Ellipses are used to indicate omitted words.

Roleson 7

Works Cited

Ersek, Mary. "Assisted Suicide: Unraveling a Complex
     Issue." *Nursing 2005* 35.4 (2005): 48–52. Print.

Godlovitch, Glenys, Ian Mitchell, and Christopher
     James Doig. "Discontinuing Life Support in
     Comatose Patients: An Example from Canadian Case
     Law." *Canadian Medical Association Journal* 179.2
     (2005): 1172–3. *Academic Search Premier*. Web.
     11 May 2005.

Huxtable, Richard, and Alastair V. Campbell.
     "Palliative Care and the Euthanasia Debate: Recent
     Developments." *Palliative Medicine* 17 (2003): 94–96.
     Academic Search Premier. Web. 11 May 2005.

Materstvedt, Lars Johan. "Palliative Care on the
     'Slippery Slope' towards Euthanasia?" *Palliative
     Medicine* 17 (2003): 387–92. *Academic Search
     Premier*. Web. 11 May 2005.

Porter, Theresa, Punporn Johnson, and Nancy A. Warren.
     "Bioethical Issues Concerning Death: Death, Dying,
     and End-of-Life Rights." *Critical Care Nursing
     Quarterly* 28.1 (2005): 85–92. Print.

Schotsmans, Paul T. "The Ethical Claim of a Dying
     Brother." *Christian Bioethics* 9 (2003): 331–36.
     Print.

New page is used for Works Cited page.

Double-spacing is used throughout.

Sources are listed alphabetically by last name.

Second and subsequent lines are indented 5 spaces.

Article from an online database includes database information.

Credits

Chapter 01

P. 7–9: Erma Bombeck, "Live Each Moment for What It's Worth," June 23, 1991. Copyright © 1991 by Erma Bombeck. All rights reserved. Reproduced by permission of Aaron M. Priest Literary Agency. **P. 9–11:** From WILL: THE AUTOBIOGRAPHY OF G. GORDON LIDDY, by G. Gordon Liddy, Copyright © 1980 by the author. **P. 11–15:** Dirmann, Tina. "Anonymous Sources." LA Times Magazine, March 8, 2009. http://www.latimes.com/la-mag-mar052009-cityofangels-story.html#page=1

Chapter 02

P. 45–46: Russell, Bertrand, Excerpt from The Autobiography of Bertrand Russell. Vol. I. pp. 3-4. Georg Allen & Unwin, 1967. Copyright © 1967 by the Bertrand Russell Peace Foundation Ltd. All rights reserved. Reproduced by permission of the Taylor & Francis Group. **P. 46–48:** From PASSAGES by Gail Sheehy, copyright © 1974, 1976 by Gail Sheehy. Used by permission of Dutton, a division of Penguin Group (USA) Inc. **P. 51–53:** From The Washington Post, Copyright © 1977, George Will, "I Will Not Buy a Fishamagig." The Washington Post. All rights reserved. Used by permission and protected by the Copyright Laws of the United States. The printing, copying, redistribution, or retransmission of the Material without express written permission is prohibited. **P. 53–56:** Specified selection from Soul of a Citizen: Living with Conviction by Paul Rogat Loeb, Copyright © 2010 by the author and reprinted by permission of St. Martin's Press, LLC and Writers House, LLC. All Rights Reserved. **P. 56–59:** © 2014 National Public Radio, Inc. News report entitled "Not-So-Social-Media: Why People Have Stopped Talking on Phones" by Alan Greenblatt originally published on NPR.org on May 9, 2015, and is used with the permission of NPR. Any unauthorized duplication is strictly prohibited.

Chapter 03

P. 90–92: Excerpt(s) from DAVE BARRY TALKS BACK by Dave Barry, copyright © 1991 by Dave Barry. Used by permission of Crown Books, an imprint of the Crown Publishing Group, a division of Penguin Random House LLC and Miami Herald on behalf of Dave Barry. All rights reserved. Any third party use of this material, outside of this publication, is prohibited. Interested parties must apply directly to Penguin Random House LLC and the Miami Herald for permission. **P. 92–95:** Bob Chase, "Fear of Heights: Teachers, Parents, and Students Are Wary of Achievement" in NEA Today, April 26, 1998. Copyright © 1998 National Education Association. Reprinted by permission. **P. 95–98:** Emily Greenhouse/The New Yorker; © Conde Nast. **P. 98–102:** Emily Greenhouse/The New Yorker; © Conde Nast.

Chapter 04

P. 126–131: Used with permission of The Chronicle of Higher Education Copyright© 2015. All rights reserved. **P. 131–135:** Used with permission of The Chronicle of Higher Education Copyright© 2015. All rights reserved. **P. 136–138:** Cooper, Brittney. "We Treat Racism Like It's Going Extinct: It's Not." PBS http://www.pbs.org/newshour/author/brittney-cooper/ **P. 138–141:** Used with permission of The Chronicle of Higher Education Copyright© 2015. All rights reserved. **P. 143–144:** Reprinted with permission of the author. **P. 145:** Reprinted with permission of the author. **P. 146:** Reprinted with permission of the author. **P. 150–151:** Adapted from Lawrence D. Gadd, The Second Book of the Strange (Amherst, NY: Prometheus Books).

Chapter 05

P. 158–161: George Packer/The New Yorker; © Conde Nast. **P. 169–173:** Mimi Avins, "The Bachelor: Silly, Sexist, and, to Many, Irresistible" in the Los Angeles Times, April 27, 2002. Copyright © 2002 by the Los Angeles Times. All rights reserved. Reproduced by permission. **P. 173–177:** Coontz, Stephanie. "For Better, For Worse: Marriage Means Something Different Now," Washington Post, May 1, 2005, p. B1. Reprinted with permission. **P. 177–181:** Republished with permission of The Wall Street Journal, from Jonathan Safran Foer, "Let Them Eat Dog", Wall Street Journal (http://www.wsj.com/articles/SB10001424052748703574604574499880131341174); permission conveyed through Copyright Clearance Center, Inc. **P. 181–185:** Hudson, Laura. "Why You Should Think Twice Before Shaming Anyone on Social Media." Wired Magazine. © Conde Nast. **P. 193:** Reprinted with permission of the author. **P. 194–195:** John Hamerlinck, "Killing Women: a Pop-Music Tradition" in the Humanist, July-August 1995. All rights reserved. Reproduced by permission of the author.

Chapter 06

P. 208–211: Arax, Mark. "Uncle Sam Doesn't Always Want You." LA Times. http://articles.latimes.com/2010/jun/13/entertainment/la-ca-peter-schrag-20100613. **P. 212–218:** Trachtenberg, Stephen Joel. "Education Is Not a Luxury." World and I, 19.3 (March 2004), p. 281. Reprinted with permission. **P. 218–221:** Elaine Minamide, "History 101: Pass the Popcorn, Please" in San Diego Union-Tribune. Copyright © 1998. All rights reserved. Reproduced by permission of the

467

author. **P. 221–225:** Bady, Aaron. "Public Universities Should Be Free." Aljazeera America. http://america.aljazeera.com/opinions/2013/11/public-universitieshighereducation.html

Chapter 07

P. 244–247: Sidney Hook, "In Defense of Voluntary Euthanasia" in the New York Times, March 1, 1987. Copyright © 1987 by the New York Times Co. All rights reserved. Reproduced by permission. **P. 247–249:** Teresa R. Wagner, "Promoting a Culture of Abandonment" in the San Diego Union Tribune, June 25, 1998. Copyright © 1998 by Teresa R. Wagner, Family Research council. All rights reserved. Reproduced by permission of the author. **P. 249–251:** Kenneth Swift, The Right to Choose Death in latimes.com, June 25, 2005. All rights reserved. Reproduced by permission of the author. **P. 251–253:** Lawrence Rudden and Gerard V. Bradley, "Death and the Law: Why the Government Has an Interest in Preserving Life" in World & I, May 2003. Copyright © 2003 World & I. All rights reserved. Reproduced by permission. **P. 254–258:** Ann Friedman/The New Yorker; © Conde Nast. **P. 259–260:** Used with permission of The Chronicle of Higher Education Copyright© 2015. All rights reserved. **P. 260–262:** Harvey, Katherine. "Online Dating Odds Getting Better." San Diego Union-Tribune. http://www.utsandiego.com/news/2015/jan/26/online-dating-success-wyldfire-neqtr-singldout/ **P. 262–270:** "Online Dating and Relationships" Pew Research Center, Washington, DC (October, 2013) http://www.pewinternet.org/2013/10/21/online-dating-relationships/.

Chapter 08

P. 287–291: Konnikova, Maria. "Is Internet Addition a Real Thing." The New Yorker. © Conde Nast. **P. 291–296:** Khazan, Olga. "Lost in an Online Fantasy World." The Washington Post, August 18, 2006. All rights reserved. Reproduced by permission. **P. 296–299:** Wright, Will. "Dream Machines." WIRED, April 2006. Reprinted by permission of the author. **P. 299–301:** © 2015 National Public Radio, Inc. News report entitled "Searching Online May Make You Think You're Smarter Than You Are" by Poncie Rutsch originally published on NPR.org on April 2, 2015, and is used with the permission of NPR. Any unauthorized duplication is strictly prohibited. **P. 301–306:** Amitai Etzioni, The Fast-Food Factories: McJobs Are Bad for Kids in the Washington Post, August 24, 1986. All rights reserved. Reproduced by permission. **P. 306–308:** Republished with permission of Dow Jones & Company, from Michele Manges, "The Dead-End Kids" in The Wall Street Journal, February 9, 1990; permission conveyed through Copyright Clearance Center, Inc. **P. 308–312:** Dennis McLellan, "Part-Time Work Ethic: Should Teens Go For It?" in the Lost Angeles Times, Nov. 7, 1986. All rights reserved. Reproduced by permission. **P. 312–315:** Maureen Brown, "Balancing Act: High School Students Making The Grade At Part-Time Jobs" in the Los Angeles Times, February 6, 1992. All rights reserved. Reproduced by permission. **P. 317–318:** Reprinted with permission of the author. **P. 319–320:** Reprinted with permission of the author.

Chapter 24 (Part 04)

P. 406–411: Gary E. Johnson, The Case for Drug Legalization in The World and I, Feb. 2000, vol. 15, no. 2, p. 34. **P. 411–413:** Charles B. Rangel "Why Drug Legalization Should be Opposed." As appeared in Criminal Justice Ethics, Volume 17, Number 2, [Summer/Fall 1998], pp. 2-20. Reprinted by permission of The Institute for Criminal Justice Ethics, 555 West 57th Street, Suite 607, New York, NY, 10019-1029. **P. 413–416:** Hodding Carter III, "We're Losing the Drug War Because Prohibition Never Works" in the Wall Street Journal, July 13, 1989, p. A15. Reprinted by permission of the author. **P. 416–421:** Reprinted with permission from Reader's Digest. Copyright © 1990 by The Reader's Digest Association, Inc. **P. 421–423:** The Minimum Legal Drinking Age, website http://www.ama-assn.org/ama/pub/category/13246.html. Adapted from Toomey, T. L" C. Rosenfeld, and A. C. Wagenaar, "The Minimum Legal Drinking Age: History, Effectiveness and Ongoing Debate," Alcohol, Health and Research World, vol. 20, no. 4, 1996, p. 214. **P. 423–426:** 2001 by National Review Inc., 215 Lexington Avenue, New York, NY 10016. Reprinted by permission. **P. 426–430:** Copyright © 1980 by Alfie Kohn. Reprinted from The Humanist with the author's permission. For more on this topic, please see www.alfiekohn.org or Kohn's book "No Contest: The Case Against Competition." **P. 430–433:** Michael Ryan, Are You Living Mindlessly? in Parade, Mardl I, 1998. Copyright © Michael Ryan. All rights reserved. Reproduced by permission of The Michael Ryan Estate. **P. 433–437:** Paul Robinson, "TV Can't Educate" in the New Republic, August 12, 1978. All rights reserved. Reproduced by permission of the author. **P. 437–445:** Emily Nussbaum/The New Yorker; © Conde Nast.

Appendix

P. 459–465: Reprinted with permission of the author.

Indexes

Subject Index

Boldface entries denote specific words discussed in the text